The Integration Debate

Racial integration, and policies intended to achieve greater integration, continue to generate controversy in the United States, with some of the most heated debates taking place among long-standing advocates of racial equality. Today, many nonwhites express what has been referred to as "integration exhaustion" as they question the value of integration in today's world. Many whites also exhibit what has been labeled "race fatigue," arguing that we have done enough to reconcile the races. Many policies have been implemented in efforts to open up traditionally restricted neighborhoods, while others have been designed to diversify traditionally poor, often nonwhite, neighborhoods. Still, racial segregation persists, along with the many social costs of such patterns of uneven development. This book explores both long-standing and emerging controversies over the nation's ongoing struggles with discrimination and segregation. More urgently, it offers guidance on how these barriers can be overcome to achieve truly balanced and integrated living patterns.

Chester Hartman is Director of Research for the Washington, DC-based Poverty & Race Research Action Council. He is also founder and former Chair of The Planners Network, a national organization of progressive urban planners. His most recent books include *City for Sale: The Transformation of San Francisco, Between Eminence and Notoriety: Four Decades of Radical Urban Planning,* and *A Right to Housing: Foundation for a New Social Agenda.*

Gregory D. Squires is a Professor of Sociology, and Public Policy and Public Administration at George Washington University. Previously, he worked for the U.S. Commission on Civil Rights and HUD and served as a member of the Federal Reserve Board's Consumer Advisory Council. He has published several books on civil rights issues and has written for many academic and general interest publications, including the *New York Times, Washington Post, Housing Policy Debate,* and *Urban Studies.*

The Integration Debate
Competing Futures for American Cities

Edited by
Chester Hartman and
Gregory D. Squires

Routledge
Taylor & Francis Group

NEW YORK AND LONDON

First published 2010
by Routledge
270 Madison Ave, New York, NY 10016

Simultaneously published in the UK
by Routledge
2 Park Square, Milton Park, Abingdon, Oxon OX14 4RN

Routledge is an imprint of the Taylor & Francis Group, an informa business

© 2010 Taylor & Francis

Typeset in Minion by EvS Communication Networx, Inc.
Printed and bound in the United States of America on acid-free paper by Edwards Brothers, Inc.

Library of Congress Cataloging in Publication Data
The integration debate : competing futures for American cities / edited by Chester Hartman and Gregory D. Squires. — 1st ed.
p. cm.
Includes index.
1. United States—Race relations. 2. United States—Ethnic relations. 3. City and town life—United States. 4. Cities and towns—United States. 5. Social change—United States. 6. United States—Social conditions—1960–1980. 7. United States—Social conditions—1980– I. Hartman, Chester W. II. Squires, Gregory D.
E184.A1I1725 2009
305.800973—dc22
2009003469

ISBN 10: 0-415-99459-4 (hbk)
ISBN 10: 0-415-99460-8 (pbk)
ISBN 10: 0-203-89046-9 (ebk)

ISBN 13: 978-0-415-99459-0 (hbk)
ISBN 13: 978-0-415-99460-6 (pbk)
ISBN 13: 978-0-203-89046-2 (ebk)

Contents

Acknowledgments   xi

Foreword   xiii
   HENRY CISNEROS

1   Integration Exhaustion, Race Fatigue, and the American Dream   1
   CHESTER HARTMAN AND GREGORY D. SQUIRES

Reviews current debates over the merits of racial integration and current policy initiatives to desegregate the nation's metropolitan areas. Acknowledges continuing and wide-ranging costs of segregation (exacerbated by rising economic segregation) for those victimized by discriminatory processes, and identifies issues that will have to be addressed if the nation is to truly move towards more balanced and integrated living patterns.

2   Welcome to the Neighborhood? The Persistence of Discrimination
   and Segregation   9
   SHANNA L. SMITH AND CATHY CLOUD

Outlines how the federal Fair Housing Act could be utilized as a valuable tool to promote integration but has not been properly enforced; explains how the creation of diverse communities has been inhibited by discriminatory actions on the part of the real estate community; and provides information about steps that have been and could be taken to achieve neighborhood integration.

3   From Segregation to Integration: How Do We Get There?   23
   NANCY A. DENTON

Outlines the increasing diversity of the U.S. population, including how it varies by age, metropolitan area, and region; argues that these demographic changes could foster integration if we have place-specific policies that can take advantage of them; and discusses how moving from segregation to integration is a process which must begin with examination of the types of neighborhoods that actually exist, not segregation indices.

4   Creating and Protecting Prointegration Programs Under the Fair
    Housing Act   39
    JOHN P. RELMAN, GLENN SCHLACTUS, AND SHALINI GOEL

    Examines judicial responses to different strategies that have been employed to
    promote and maintain integrated communities; identifies types of strategies
    and situations where prointegration programs are most likely to be upheld by
    the courts; illuminates the relevant legal considerations by closely examining
    how courts might respond to a creative prointegration program in Ohio that
    has not been challenged.

5   Achieving Integration Through Private Litigation   53
    MICHAEL P. SENG AND F. WILLIS CARUSO

    Traces how private litigation has been a primary vehicle for enforcement of
    the substantive provisions of the Fair Housing Act; reviews the limitations
    of lawsuits in removing the structural barriers to fair housing in our society;
    and recommends statutory and regulatory reforms that would make litigation
    a better tool to achieve integration.

6   Constitutional and Statutory Mandates for Residential Racial
    Integration and the Validity of Race-Conscious, Affirmative
    Action to Achieve It   67
    FLORENCE WAGMAN ROISMAN

    Reviews the inconsistent treatment of race-conscious government actions
    since the 1940s, focusing on affirmative, race-conscious conduct designed to
    promote housing integration. Discusses the 1866 and 1968/1988 federal fair
    housing acts and their authority in the Thirteenth Amendment, and considers
    ways in which the Thirteenth Amendment allows broader scope than might
    be warranted for statutes rooted only in the Fourteenth Amendment.

7   Housing Mobility: A Civil Right   85
    ELIZABETH K. JULIAN AND DEMETRIA L. MCCAIN

    Argues that housing mobility is a remedy for the Constitutional violation of
    racial segregation in federally-assisted housing programs; proposes statu-
    tory language giving individuals the power to assert that right on their own
    behalf; and describes how the Dallas housing mobility program operated by
    the authors' nonprofit organization works.

8   Desegregated Schools With Segregated Education   99
    WILLIAM A. DARITY, JR. AND ALICIA JOLLA

    Reviews how educational inequities are no longer solely shaped by residential
    segregation but are increasingly based on differential access to quality instruc-
    tion and curricula within schools, selectively determined by race. Effective
    alternatives include evidence from an urban elementary school that challenged
    this tendency by expanding access to its gifted and talented program and from
    Project Bright Idea, a K-2 critical thinking curriculum.

9   The Effects of Housing Market Discrimination on Earnings
    Inequality   119
    SAMUEL L. MYERS, JR., WILLIAM A. DARITY, JR.,
    AND KRIS MARSH

    Examines the empirical relationship between residential segregation in a met-
    ropolitan area and racial wage disparities in the same metropolitan area; details
    the correlation between loan denial rates and racial wage disparities in MSAs
    and accounts for competing factors explaining these patterns; concludes that
    eradicating residential segregation or diminishing racial gaps in loan denials
    will not have any immediate impact on narrowing earnings gaps.

10 Racial/Ethnic Integration and Child Health Disparities   131
    DOLORES ACEVEDO-GARCIA, THERESA L. OSYPUK,
    AND NANCY MCARDLE

    Discusses the effects of neighborhood environment on child health and de-
    velopment. Examines the extent of racial/ethnic disparities in neighborhood
    environment—a result of residential segregation—facing U.S. children, and
    their implications for racial/ethnic disparities in child health and development
    and along the life course.

11 Integration, Segregation, and the Racial Wealth Gap   153
    GEORGE LIPSITZ AND MELVIN L. OLIVER

    Examines how housing discrimination has allowed whites to "lock in" advan-
    tages of homeownership and its attendant subsidies while limiting the ability
    of African Americans to accumulate wealth. Explains how government and
    financial institutions have conspired to limit and even "strip" hard-gained
    home equity from Black and other minority communities, most recently evi-
    denced by the racial effects of the subprime mortgage crisis. Remedies should
    include asset-building strategies for individuals, but also adequate government
    investments in Black communities capable of addressing the cumulative, col-
    lective, and continuing costs of discrimination and segregation.

12 Two-Tiered Justice: Race, Class, and Crime Policy   169
    MARC MAUER

    Analyzes the forces in recent decades that have produced a "race to incarcer-
    ate" resulting in a world-record prison population in the U.S.; and assesses
    the intersection of policy changes in criminal justice with the dynamics of a
    segregated society, including racially biased law enforcement practices and
    disproportionate imprisonment for people of color that in turn results in
    declining life prospects and political influence.

13 Residential Mobility, Neighborhoods, and Poverty: Results
    from the Chicago Gautreaux Program and the Moving
    to Opportunity Experiment   185
    STEFANIE DELUCA AND JAMES E. ROSENBAUM

Examines how residential mobility may impact the experiences and outcomes of low-income black families. Reviews small and large studies of the Gautreaux program, showing its impact on education, jobs, integration, and long-term residential location. While MTO attempted to improve upon Gautreaux, analyses indicate that it provided a stronger research design, but a weaker mobility program. Discusses implications for the design of subsequent residential mobility programs.

14 The Ghetto Game: Apartheid and the Developer's Imperative
    in Postindustrial American Cities   199
    MINDY THOMPSON FULLILOVE, LOURDES
    HERNÁNDEZ-CORDERO, AND ROBERT E. FULLILOVE

Reviews the series of urban policies that have led to displacement: segregation, redlining, urban renewal, catastrophic disinvestment/planned shrinkage, HOPE VI, gentrification, and others. Proposes that tools of urban design have a repairng role to play. Reviews the work and ideas of renowned French urbanist Michel Cantal-Dupart.

15 The Myth of Concentrated Poverty   213
    STEPHEN STEINBERG

Challenges the validity and political uses of the concept of "concentrated poverty." Research has failed to prove the two core assumptions—that concentration per se exacerbates the negative effects of poverty, and that deconcentration of poverty is beneficial for the poor. This dubious theory, moreover, is deployed when poor minorities occupy urban space that is ripe for gentrification, and has provided moral and intellectual justification for the demolition of public housing under the HOPE VI program.

16 Integration: Solving the Wrong Problem   229
    JANET L. SMITH

Examines the limits to past and current integration strategies; offers a framework that builds on a human rights agenda and on the Right to the City movement in order to demonstrate how critical it is to look beyond trying to attain some end (integration) and instead focus on reducing racism and eliminating policies that privilege the white position.

17 The Legacy of Segregation: Smashing Through the Generations   247
    ROGER WILKINS

Delineates the self-replicating phenomenon of black urban poverty, which is older than the nation itself. Discusses the psychic, physical, and economic brutality employed to make slaves out of black human beings and how shunning (separating and segregating) removed most blacks from the richness of life and served to pump the pride in whiteness to grotesque proportions that led from denial of education to the campaign of lynchings in the late nineteenth and early twentieth centuries. Describes how this enduring American cultural trait (without the lynchings) has created toxic and impoverished black communities—even after all of the civil rights and uplift activity of mid-twentieth century America. The result is compacted poverty in urban areas that can be deadly to children born into it, whether death comes from early criminality, illiteracy, from a bullet or disease. The result is not simply an American dilemma, but an American disgrace.

Contributors	265
Index	277
Rights and Permissions	285

Acknowledgments

Many people have made this book possible and we want to thank those who have made particularly significant contributions. First we want to thank the National Fair Housing Alliance (NFHA) for the many ways it has supported this project. In addition to the chapter written by Shanna Smith and Cathy Cloud, NFHA, of course, has been a leading force in the nation's pursuit of fair housing and racial integration. We also want to thank Michael Seng and his colleagues at The John Marshall Law School who organized a conference that led to the publication of this book. The university's Fair Housing Legal Support Center has also been a critical advocate for fair housing and racial integration in the United States. Finally, we want to thank the contributors to this book, and not just for their chapters that appear here. All of them have devoted their careers to the realization of equal opportunity throughout American society. We all hope this book will advance the values and goals for which these individuals have labored.

An orthographic note: With regard to terminology on race and racial categories, we opt to let each author use whatever is her or his word, punctuation, capitalization preference; such usage embodies issues that, for many, have levels of meaning well beyond mere style, and we choose not to impose any arbitrary single format or rule.

Foreword

Racial and ethnic discrimination, along with the segregation that inevitably follows, constitutes one of the nation's saddest legacies. As Americans, we rightfully take pride in those advances which mark our history—the freedoms which resulted from the Civil War and Reconstruction, the Civil Rights Movement, the United Farm Workers' labor victories, and the Presidential election of 2008. But each victory also signals the distance we have yet to go. *The Integration Debate* illuminates the continuing costs of the legacy of discrimination and lays out the policy choices for overcoming it.

Progress has always flowed from the efforts of diverse constituencies. The civil rights legislation of the 1960s needed the clout of a savvy President, the leadership of a civil rights icon, and the organizing skills of a labor leader. If lawyers, economists, and other professionals are increasingly vital parts of the movement, millions of anonymous citizens are ever more vital. And perhaps we are finally learning about the important roles that community organizers have always played. These are among the lessons reinforced by this book.

Hartman and Squires have brought together some of the nation's leading scholars, activists, lawyers, and others who have continued the struggles led by Lincoln, Johnson, King, Chavez, and so many others. They do not always agree on specific tactics. Indeed, much remains to be learned about how we as a nation can go about the business of eliminating the stain of discrimination. But any differences among the contributors to this book pale in comparison to the light they shine on the unfinished work of eliminating segregation. Our task is nothing less than eradicating that aspect of American life which Roger Wilkins rightfully refers to not as an American dilemma but rather an American disgrace.

Henry Cisneros
Former Secretary of HUD
Former Mayor of San Antonio
Co-Chair, National Commission on Fair Housing
and Equal Opportunity

CHAPTER 1

Integration Exhaustion, Race Fatigue, and the American Dream

CHESTER HARTMAN AND GREGORY D. SQUIRES

I love Puerto Ricans and Negroes
As long as they don't move next
door. (Phil Ochs 1965, "Love Me, I'm a Liberal")

When the federal Fair Housing Act of 1968 was being debated, Senator Walter Mondale famously stated that "the reach of the proposed law was to replace the ghettos by truly integrated and balanced living patterns." But the nation has had a long, uneasy relationship with the concept of integration. Several legal mandates, social science research reports, and advocacy positions have endorsed the pursuit of integration, but segregation remains a dominant reality in virtually all U.S. cities and their surrounding areas. In recent years, the value of integration appears to be losing its hold. "Integration exhaustion" on the part of nonwhites and "race fatigue" on the part of whites have deflated some of the pressure for integration. Many suggest that today we live in a "post-civil rights world," and so perhaps the need for integration, like the Civil Rights Movement itself, has faded.

This would be an unfortunate vision on which to base public policy or private practice when it comes to issues of race, and particularly racial inequality, in the United States today. Certainly, there has been substantial progress in recent years. Racial minorities now occupy positions in business, entertainment, politics, and virtually all areas in larger numbers than ever before, with the election of Barack Obama being the most significant, but hardly the only, breakthrough of recent years. At the same time, racial inequality and racial

1

segregation stubbornly persist, and at great cost to both the victims and to society as a whole. If many barriers have been broken, significant gaps remain. If recent efforts to desegregate the nation's neighborhoods have disappointed, new and better approaches are required. If integration does not "work," as some critics claim, it may well be because it has never really been tried, as most fair housing advocates assert. Separate but equal has been tried and clearly found wanting to all but the most diehard racists. The challenge, for all, remains the dismantling of remaining vestiges of discrimination and the realization of "truly integrated and balanced living patterns."

Integration Exhaustion? Race Fatigue?

As Sheryll Cashin and many other scholars observe, for many nonwhite, particularly African-American families, integration is not the goal that it was a generation ago. In *The Failures of Integration*, Cashin quotes one black resident of a middle-class Atlanta neighborhood: "When I have to work around them all day, by the time I come home I don't want to have to deal with white people anymore" (Cashin 2004, 18). A young African-American journalist wrote on the editorial page of the *Washington Post*:

In the small act of choosing to buy our home where we did, I believe that we became part of a growing group of African Americans who are picking up where the civil rights movement left off. From our perspective, integration is overrated. It's time to reverse an earlier generation's hopeful migration into white communities and attend to some unfinished business in the hood. (Hopkinson 2001 quoted in Cashin 2004, 19)

And as Cashin herself recounted,

But in conversation after conversation with black friends, acquaintances, and strangers, integration is simply not a priority in the way that getting ahead is. What black people now seem most ardent about is equality of opportunity. As one black acquaintance once put it, rather than wanting to integrate with whites, black people now seem more interested in having what whites have. (Cashin 2004, 28)

Joe Feagin and Melvin Sikes interviewed middle-class blacks who expressed similar attitudes, many of whom report experiences of being a "pioneer" and question if it is worth it all, clearly expressing integration exhaustion. One corporate executive described the maltreatment he received because of his race and concluded: "The only place it probably doesn't affect me, I guess, is in my home…but outside one's home it always affects me" (Feagin and Sikes 1994, 224).

If many blacks are tired of the struggle for racial integration, many whites believe American society has done enough. Race fatigue has set in for many, according to Thomas and Mary Edsall (1991), who describe the antipathy many whites have to paying taxes they believe go to support programs that are no longer needed. A 2008 *New York Times* poll found that 48% of whites oppose programs to help minorities get ahead, with 26% believing that they themselves are now victims of racial discrimination (Blow 2008). Cashin (2004, xii) reported that approximately half of all whites believe blacks and whites have equal access to jobs, education, and health care, even though black family income persists at about two-thirds the white median, with similar gaps in health, education, and other areas of life.

In a more fundamental redefinition of the situation, some scholars, white and nonwhite, believe the key battles of the Civil Rights Movement were fought and won in the 1960s, and that any remaining racial gaps can be explained largely by cultural failures on the part of nonwhites, particularly blacks, themselves (McWhorter 2000, 2006; Sowell 1984; Steele 1990; Thernstrom and Thernstrom 1997). Pointing to the "cult of victimology" (how many blacks see themselves only as victims), "separatism" (the belief that they do not have to play by conventional rules because of their victimization), and "anti-intellectualism" (going to school means acting white and identifying with the oppressor), John McWhorter (2000, x) concludes: "The black community today is the main obstacle to achieving the full integration our Civil Rights leaders sought."

The Continuing Costs of Segregation

But racial segregation persists, and the social costs are compounded by increasing economic segregation. If nationwide statistical measures of segregation have declined somewhat for African Americans, segregation from whites for Hispanics and Asians has increased slightly. And in those major metropolitan areas where the black population is concentrated—cities like Chicago, Detroit, Milwaukee—black/white segregation persists at traditionally hypersegregated levels (Iceland, Weinberg, and Steinmetz 2002). And racial isolation has been exacerbated by a dramatically increased concentration of poverty.

If some middle-class, professional minorities are residing in neighborhoods previously closed to them, poor people—particularly poor people of color—are increasingly falling down and dropping out (Massey 2007). The number of high-poverty census tracts (those where 40% or more of the residents live on incomes below the official poverty line) surged from 1,177 in 1970 to 2,510 in 2000, with the number of residents in those neighborhoods growing from 4.1 million to 7.9 million (Jargowsky 1996, 2003). Preliminary research by Paul Jargowsky (2008) reveals that since 2000 these numbers have continued to shoot upwards. These patterns are not race-neutral. Whereas just 5% of poor whites lived in high-poverty areas in 1990, 30% of poor blacks did (Rusk 1999, 106). In perhaps a more revealing sign of the times, the share of middle-income census tracts declined from 58% to 41% between 1970 and 2000 while the share of poor people living in middle-income areas declined from just over half to 37%, and their share living in low-income areas grew from 36% to 48% (Booza, Cutsinger, and Galster 2006).

The combination of persistent racial segregation and rising concentration of poverty has had serious, often deadly, consequences for many who are in fact victims.

A wealth of social science research has documented that residents of predominantly nonwhite, segregated neighborhoods experience a wide range of disamenities. Such families are far more likely to:

- be victims of crime, while being underserviced and overpoliced by a criminal justice system in which incarceration rates have skyrocketed in recent years;
- attend inferior schools, which leads to inferior job opportunities and less opportunity to move into more stable (and more integrated) communities;
- receive fewer and inferior public services and private amenities (access to retail stores, entertainment, convenient transportation);
- be exposed to polluted air and water, toxic waste facilities, and other environmental hazards;
- have less access to health care;
- be victimized by predatory lenders and other fringe bankers (e.g., payday lenders, check-cashers, pawn shops) and have less access to conventional banking services; and
- have difficulty learning about job opportunities and getting to those jobs that are available. (Carr and Kutty 2008)

In sum, as Douglas Massey (2001, 424) concluded: "Any process that concentrates poverty within racially isolated neighborhoods will simultaneously increase the odds of socioeconomic failure within the segregated group."

Integration Initiatives and Emerging Controversies

Several public policy initiatives have been launched in recent years in efforts to replace at least some ghettos with more balanced living patterns. Gautreaux, Moving to Opportunity (MTO), and HOPE VI are just some of the better-known buzzwords in housing circles that have generated some new housing opportunities, a growing body of social science research, and intense controversy.

Many families who participated in these programs were able to move to safer, healthier communities, where their children are more likely to graduate from high school and go on to college, and to have fewer encounters with police. The benefits are clearest in the Gautreaux program, where many more poor black families made long-distance moves from predominantly poor black to predominantly white suburbs than in the MTO program, where most moves were from poor to nonpoor neighborhoods, but often in nearby communities, frequently within the same school district. And the HOPE VI findings are even more ambiguous and problematic because, unlike Gautreaux and MTO in which participants volunteered to move, HOPE VI families were involuntarily relocated (Buron 2004; Goering and Feins 2003; Rosenbaum, DeLuca, and Tuck 2005).

But these initiatives have not been universally hailed. Even among some long-standing civil rights advocates, they have come under harsh scrutiny. Some claim these mobility initiatives have met with less success than their proponents and some researchers suggest; that the primary objective and outcome is to displace poor people and provide unjustifiable subsidies to well-connected developers who profit by the gentrification that ensues; that they constitute another version of urban renewal which undervalues the social capital of even poor communities, destroying the lives of many vulnerable families in the process; and that the entire discussion of concentrated poverty unfairly stigmatizes poor people and particularly poor people of color (Fullilove 2004; Goetz 2003; Reed and Steinberg 2006).

These critiques also invoke related long-standing debates over strategies for replacing ghettos with balanced living patterns. For example: Is there a right to stay put (Hartman 1984), with the expectation that adequate public services and private amenities will be available? To what extent should public policy and private practice emphasize gilding the ghetto (community reinvestment and development) versus deconcentration (helping people move out)? Should we eliminate, expand, or modify current mobility programs? Clearly, there is a role for fair housing law enforcement, but should that authority remain at HUD or be moved to an independent agency (National Commission on Fair Housing and Equal Opportunity 2008), and to what extent can law enforcement lead to more integrated neighborhoods? These are some of the emerging controversies explored in the chapters that follow.

The cast of characters we assembled for this book is an extraordinary collection of researchers and activists (most playing both roles), all of whom have a deep commitment to racial justice (see their minibios in the Contributors Section, p. 265), but with a range of well-informed views on the best ways to achieve that goal.

Shanna Smith and Cathy Cloud are central figures in the nation's most important fair housing organization, and they lay out realistically the current scene with regard to residential patterns by race and the nation's efforts to change those patterns. Sociologist/demographer Nancy Denton offers an impressive picture of how current and future changes in the nation's population composition offer possibilities for progress toward integration.

Then there are those all-important actors, the lawyers, putting forward their views and plans regarding legal strategies to achieve integration. John Relman and his current and former lawfirm colleagues Glenn Schlactus and Shalini Goel have achieved remarkable success in winning cases and large awards after proving discriminatory behavior by a variety of malefactors. Michael Seng and Willis Caruso of the John Marshall Law School, where essential fair housing work is done via its Fair Housing Legal Support Center, detail the ways in which private litigation strategies can succeed. Florence Wagman Roisman, a long-time legal theoretician/tactician/activist, puts forward a set of specific proposals, the most innovative of which is use of the Constitution's Thirteenth Amendment, banning slavery. And Elizabeth Julian and Demetria McCain of the Inclusive Communities project describe their varied and effective assistance strategies in Dallas to bring about racially integrated neighborhoods.

The next set of chapters deals with the deleterious consequences of segregated housing patterns in key areas of residents' lives. William Darity, Jr. of Duke and Alicia Jolla, formerly of Charlotte, address the educational consequences. Samuel Myers, Jr. of the University of Minnesota, Prof. Darity again, and Kris Marsh of the University of Maryland explore the impact on earnings inequalities. Dolores Acevedo-Garcia and Nancy McArdle of the Harvard School of Public Health and Theresa Osypuk of Northeastern University's Bouvé College of Health Sciences examine the negative health consequences for children. George Lipsitz and Melvin Oliver of the University of California, Santa Barbara lay out what increasingly is recognized as a central racial issue: wealth disparities. And Marc Mauer of The Sentencing Project demonstrates the negative consequences of segregation for crime and criminal justice policy.

Lastly, we present a series of more sweeping chapters that focus on housing policies and the politics associated with them. Stefanie DeLuca of Johns Hopkins and James Rosenbaum of Northwestern University detail both positive and mixed/limited results from Chicago's Gautreaux Program and the subsequent multicity Moving to Opportunity Program. Mindy Thompson Fullilove, Lourdes Hernandez-Cordero, and Robert Fullilove of Columbia University's Mailman School of Public Health present a disturbing framework for looking at mobility strategies, drawing on urban renewal history, with emphasis on the destruction of positive social capital/networking/supportive functions that even neighborhoods in poor physical condition can provide for their residents, and the difficulties of renewing such positive features in a new and different area. Stephen Steinberg of the City University of New York offers a damning critique of the entire notion of concentrated poverty and its presumed impacts, blasting it in particular for its role in leading activists, researchers, and others to pay insufficient attention to the structural issues underlying poverty and racism in the United States. And Janet Smith of the University of Illinois at Chicago, in a critique somewhat similar to Steinberg's, says, as her chapter title puts it, that in attempting to deal with integration, we are trying to solve the wrong problem.

Finally, Roger Wilkins of George Mason University offers a fascinating and moving personal life history, weaving into it important elements of our nation's history. One message that comes through loud and clear is the imperative of moving toward the goal of integrated living.

This book provides a harsh reminder of the grave costs of segregation. But it also identifies some of the perhaps unintended consequences that have been encountered in at least preliminary efforts to realize more integrated living patterns. It offers all of us an opportunity to revisit and perhaps challenge long-standing assumptions and beliefs. It is to be hoped that such exploration will lead to more effective policies that will realize truly integrated living.

Despite the controversies that prevail, even among long-standing proponents of equality, few would dispute that racial segregation and concentrated poverty are ongoing challenges, if not life-and-death struggles, for a great many in the nation's metropolitan regions. Most observers would concur that more balanced, equitable development to replace the ghettos and patterns of uneven development is a desirable, if not essential, objective. This book explores many of the pitfalls of prior efforts and provides guidance on how public policy and private action can move in the direction Walter Mondale pointed to in 1968.

Phil Ochs is no longer with us. But the title of Stephen Grant Meyer's book—*As Long As They Don't Move Next Door* (2000)—is just one more reminder that discrimination and segregation remain severe nationwide problems. If the nation should choose to respond, the following pages can provide valuable guidance.

References

Blow, Charles M. 2008. "Racism and the Race." *New York Times* (August 8), A-19.

Booza, Jason C., Jackie Cutsinger, and George Galster. 2006. *Where Did They Go? The Decline of Middle-Income Neighborhoods in Metropolitan America*. Washington, D.C.: The Brookings Institution.

Buron, Larry. 2004. *An Improved Living Environment? Neighborhood Outcomes for HOPE VI Relocatees*. Washington, D.C.: Urban Institute, Metropolitan Housing and Communities Center.

Carr, James H., and Nandinee Kutty. 2008. *Segregation: The Rising Costs for America*. New York: Routledge.

Cashin, Sheryll. 2004. *The Failures of Integration*. New York: Public Affairs.

Edsall, Thomas Byrne, and Mary D. Edsall. 1991. *Chain Reaction: The Impact of Race, Rights, and Taxes on American Politics.* New York: W.W. Norton.

Feagin, Joe R., and Melvin P. Sikes. 1994. *Living With Racism: The Black Middle-Class Experience.* Boston: Beacon Press.

Fullilove, Mindy Thompson. 2004. *Root Shock: How Tearing Up City Neighborhoods Hurts America and What We Can Do About It.* New York: Ballantine Books.

Goering, John, and Judith D. Feins. 2003. *Choosing a Better Life: Evaluating the Moving to Opportunity Social Experiment.* Washington, D.C.: The Urban Institute Press.

Goetz, Edward G. 2003. *Clearing the Way: Deconcentrating the Poor in Urban America.* Washington, D.C.: The Urban Institute Press.

Hartman, Chester. 1984. "The Right to Stay Put." In *Land Reform, American Style,* eds. Charles Geisler and Frank Popper. Totowa, NJ: Rowman & Allanheld, 302–18.

Hopkinson, Natalie. 2001. "I Won't Let D.C. Lose Its Flavor." *Washington Post* (June 17)., B, 1.

Iceland, John, Daniel H. Weinberg, and Erika Steinmetz. 2002. *Racial and Ethnic Residential Segregation in the United States: 1980–2000.* U.S. Census Bureau, Series CENSR-3. Washington, D.C.: U.S. Government Printing Office.

Jargowsky, Paul. 1996. *Poverty and Place: Ghettos, Barrios, and the American City.* New York: Russell Sage Foundation.

———. 2003. *Stunning Progress, Hidden Problems: The Dramatic Decline of Concentrated Poverty in the 1990s.* Washington, D.C.: The Brookings Institution.

———. 2008. Comments at Roundtable Discussion. Presented at Racial and Ethnic Disparities among Low-Income Working Families. Urban Institute, Washington, D.C., December.

Massey, Douglas S. 2001. "Residential Segregation and Neighborhood Conditions in U.S. Metropolitan Areas." In *America Becoming: Racial Trends and Their Consequences,* eds. Neil J. Smelser, William Julius Wilson, and Faith Mitchell. Washington, D.C.: National Academy Press, 391–434.

———. 2007. *Categorically Unequal: The American Stratification System.* New York: Russell Sage Foundation.

McWhorter, John H. 2000. *Losing the Race: Self-Sabotage in Black America.* New York: Free Press.

———. 2006. *Winning the Race: Beyond the Crisis in Black America.* New York: Gotham Books.

Meyer, Stephen Grant. 2000. *As Long As They Don't Move Next Door: Segregation and Racial Conflict in American Neighborhoods.* Lanham, MD: Rowman & Littlefield.

National Commission on Fair Housing and Equal Opportunity. 2008. *The Future of Fair Housing: Report of the National Commission on Fair Housing and Equal Opportunity.* Executive Summary. December. Washington, D.C.: National Fair Housing Alliance.

Reed, Adolph, and Stephen Steinberg. 2006. "Liberal Bad Faith in the Wake of Hurricane Katrina." *The Black Commentator* 182: 1–9.

Rosenbaum, James, Stefanie DeLuca, and Tammy Tuck. 2005. "New Capabilities in New Places: Low-Income Black Families in Suburbia." In *The Geography of Opportunity: Race and Housing Choice in Metropolitan America,* ed. Xavier de Souza Briggs. Washington, D.C.: Brookings Institution Press, 150–75.

Rusk, David. 1999. *Inside Game Outside Game: Winning Strategies for Saving Urban America.* Washington, D.C.: The Brookings Institution Press.

Sowell, Thomas. 1984. *Civil Rights: Rhetoric or Reality?* New York: William Morrow.

Steele, Shelby. 1990. *The Content of Our Character: A New Vision of Race in America.* New York: St. Martin's Press.

Thernstrom, Stephan, and Abigail Thernstrom. 1997. *America in Black and White: One Nation, Indivisible.* New York: Simon and Schuster.

CHAPTER 2

Welcome to the Neighborhood?

The Persistence of Discrimination and Segregation

SHANNA L. SMITH AND CATHY CLOUD

As a premise, we do not accept as meaningful the term *integration exhaustion* because we believe there has been no significant residential integration in the United States. As an alternative, we believe people may be weary of the talk about America's commitment to integration without an accompanying set of actions with which to achieve it, or that people may be weary of the concept of integration that only involves moves by people of color to predominantly White neighborhoods. But to be exhausted by integration itself is impossible.

In this chapter, we focus on three concepts:

1. that the federal Fair Housing Act could be utilized as a valuable tool to promote integration but has not been properly enforced;
2. that the achievement of diverse communities has been inhibited by the actions of the real estate community; and
3. that viable, tangible actions have been and should be taken to achieve neighborhood integration.

The Fair Housing Act Prohibits Housing Discrimination and Promotes Residential Integration

The Civil Rights Act of 1968, commonly known as the Fair Housing Act, was passed by Congress and signed by President Lyndon Johnson just seven days after the assassination of Dr. Martin Luther King, Jr. on April 4, 1968. When President Johnson signed the law, he said, "I do not exaggerate when I say that the proudest moments of my Presidency have been times such as this when I have signed into law the promises of a century."[1] The "promises of a century" were embodied in the Civil Rights Act of 1866 passed by Congress in April of that year:

All citizens of the United States shall have the same right, in every State and Territory, as is enjoyed by white citizens thereof to inherit, purchase, lease, sell, hold and convey real and personal property. (42 U.S.C. § 1982)

The promises of equal housing opportunities made in 1866 had yet to be realized[2] by 1966, so Senators Walter Mondale (D-MN) and Edward Brooke (R-MA) introduced fair housing legislation. Mondale and Brooke drafted legislation that went beyond other civil rights laws to include provisions for residential racial integration, but it failed to pass until April of 1968, in response after King's assassination. The Fair Housing Act articulated two goals: to eliminate housing discrimination through enforcement of the law, and to intentionally promote residential integration. A strong enforcement provision was included, but was stripped from the bill by Senator Everett Dirksen (R-IL). Congress placed authority for enforcement of the Fair Housing Act in the newly created U.S. Department of Housing and Urban Development (HUD).

The first mandate of the law—to eliminate housing discrimination through effective enforcement—was never realized by the government. The law allowed HUD only to "determine to resolve" or "determine not to resolve" a complaint after an investigation. If HUD determined to resolve a complaint, all it could do was ask the respondent if she or he wanted to attempt conciliation. If the respondent refused to conciliate or conciliation failed, HUD had to close the case. For the complainant, the only option for enforcement was to file his or her own lawsuit in federal district court.

From 1968 to 1988, any effective enforcement of the Fair Housing Act was achieved primarily through individuals filing such lawsuits, private nonprofit fair housing agencies and testers filing as plaintiffs, or the Department of Justice bringing "pattern or practice" suits. Even though HUD's enforcement mechanism was impotent, the statute itself was carefully crafted and given broad interpretation by the courts across the country, including the U.S. Supreme Court. As a result, private, nonprofit fair housing agencies vigorously investigated and tested rental, sales, lending, and homeowners' insurance complaints, and fair housing groups and others filed federal and state lawsuits against individual landlords, apartment owners, real estate companies, banks and mortgage lenders, and homeowners' insurance companies.[3] During this period, many of the real estate sales lawsuits addressed the impact of racial steering[4] on perpetuating residential segregation and stigmatizing neighborhoods. Plaintiffs used both the Fair Housing Act and the Civil Rights Act of 1866 to sue because the 1968 Fair Housing Act set a limit of $1,000 in punitive damages, while the Civil Rights Act of 1866 had no such limitations. The availability of punitive damages plays a critical role in persuading rental, real estate sales companies, and other housing-related businesses to comply with the Fair Housing Act. Actual damages can be less than $2,000 for many plaintiffs involved in rental discrimination cases, and compensatory damages awarded for embarrassment, humiliation, pain, and suffering often do not reflect the real injury suffered. With the risk of being caught and severely punished for violating the Fair Housing Act so minimal,[5] a company could simply factor this "expense" into the cost of doing business. Apartment owners and real estate companies could engage in practices that kept an apartment building or neighborhood exclusively White. Mortgage lenders and insurance companies could continue to redline or provide inferior products, charge unfair prices, or limit or deny mortgage loans or homeowners' insurance in neighborhoods because of their racial composition.

The Fair Housing Amendments Act of 1988 (FHAA) overhauled the 1968 law in several ways: It removed the limitation on punitive damages; extended the time to file a complaint from six months to one year for an administrative complaint and two years to file in federal court; gave HUD authority to issue a charge of discrimination and pursue litigation through the administrative law judge (ALJ) process; and provided a complainant whose complaint was charged by HUD with the option of using the HUD ALJ process or electing to go into federal district court with the Department of Justice bringing the complaint. Among other changes, the FHAA also expanded fair housing protections to families with children and people with disabilities. The FHAA was designed to bring about effective enforcement by HUD and Justice. However, since 1988, enforcement by both HUD and Justice has been sporadic at best and was virtually nonexistent during the George W. Bush Administration.[6]

The second mandate of the Fair Housing Act—to promote residential integration—was supported by the U.S. Supreme Court in the landmark decision *Trafficante et al. v. Metropolitan Life Insurance Company et al.* (1972). In this case, both White and Black tenants of a large apartment complex alleged that they had been deprived of the benefits of multicultural, multiracial associations. The U.S. Supreme Court said that the plaintiffs had articulated an injury under the Fair Housing Act and had standing to sue. In *Trafficante*, the White plaintiffs claimed they had been injured because:

1. They had lost the social benefits of living in an integrated community;
2. they had missed business and professional advantages that would have accrued if they lived with members of minority groups; and
3. they suffered embarrassment and economic damage in social, business, and professional activities from being "stigmatized" for living in a "white ghetto."

Has *Trafficante* been Utilized to Promote Residential Integration?

With so few fair housing cases brought nationally, it is interesting to note that significant challenges to housing segregation actually have been brought. Private, nonprofit fair housing agencies, municipalities, and neighborhood organizations have been plaintiffs/complainants in federal and state fair housing lawsuits or administrative complaints alleging that Whites, Blacks, or Latinos are being steered by real estate companies to neighborhoods in which their race predominates, thereby perpetuating residential segregation.[7] Steering is also used effectively to gentrify neighborhoods. Once a neighborhood becomes (in real estate agent lingo) the "location, location, location," people of color are not afforded the same opportunities to compete for homes. Homes in gentrifying neighborhoods often sell quickly. For example, real estate agents and sellers will decide to accept offers on a home for just one day. Too often, only the agents at the listing company are fully aware of the offering. Minority-owned companies and other agents of color may never hear about the exclusive offering. This type of real estate practice can seriously limit or deny people of color and others protected by the Fair Housing Act the opportunity to compete for homes.

Cases have also been filed against mortgage lenders and homeowners insurance companies because they failed to do business or provided services and products at a higher cost in integrated or predominantly African-American and Latino neighborhoods in violation of the Fair Housing Act.[8] Plaintiffs/complainants alleged that these discriminatory practices or policies perpetuated residential segregation and injured not only Black or Latino residents, but White residents as well. Additionally, the ground-breaking and important cases of *Village of Bellwood v. Gladstone et al.* (1979) and *City of Evanston v. Baird & Warner* involved these cities working with local fair housing agencies to gather evidence and document racial steering. If it is left unchecked, steering results in rapid racial transition of neighborhoods. The collaborative efforts between cities and fair housing agencies resulted in landmark decisions and settlements.

Trafficante-type arguments for injury were also made in fair housing complaints about homeowners' insurance practices and policies. Investigations into homeowners' insurance practices were initiated in 1977–78 by community and fair housing groups in Chicago, Cleveland, and Toledo. A couple of fair housing complaints were filed with HUD, but investigations were never completed.[9] In the 1990s, large-scale testing and litigation was undertaken by private fair housing agencies to challenge underwriting policies and practices that limited or denied coverage based on the age or value of housing, or that provided inferior and more expensive policies to homeowners living in integrated or predominantly African-American or Latino neighborhoods.[10] These lawsuits alleged that *all* homeowners in the neighborhoods adversely affected by the discriminatory policies were injured and that these policies perpetuated residential segregation by artificially depressing home values, lowering the tax base, and consequently reducing city services, including reducing tax dollars available for education. Only one lawsuit went through trial—*HOME v. Nationwide Insurance Company*.[11] All of the other lawsuits were settled prior to trial.

Liberty Mutual was sued by three local fair housing agencies and the National Fair Housing Alliance (NFHA), alleging redlining and other discriminatory practices. The settlement included $13 million for community development and $1 million for a national media campaign to address racial steering practices by real estate companies. Each plaintiff organization used its portion of the community development monies to foster homeownership preservation or redevelopment. NFHA, for example, continues to provide grants of up to $5,000 to homeowners to make repairs in two predominantly African-American neighborhoods affected by discriminatory underwriting policies. Plaintiffs in homeowners' insurance cases make *Trafficante*-type claims, alleging that discriminatory underwriting standards limit or deny homebuyers from purchasing homes in integrated or predominantly Black communities, thus restricting their opportunity to have multicultural, multiracial associations.

Private Market Actions Inhibit Integration

With so many homes currently in foreclosure or pre-foreclosure across the country, it raises the question of how real estate agents are marketing the "best buys" to current home-seekers and investors. Does racial steering occur? Do real estate agents save the best buys for people they know? Do people of color have the same access to good deals on foreclosed homes? Today's financial crisis is but a current manifestation of decades of discrimination in housing markets.

Acts of discrimination by rental and real estate agents work to limit the housing choices of home shoppers, as well as perpetuate segregated patterns of living. Work by fair housing groups, research organizations, and other civil rights agencies around the country documents extensive levels of discrimination in marketplaces throughout the United States, and we highlight here our work in this area over the past decade or so. We begin, however, with a brief summary of national research that provides a baseline estimate of the extent of discrimination in rental and real estate transactions.

The U.S. Department of Housing and Urban Development has conducted three national surveys of housing market discrimination based on the use of paired testing: the first (Housing Market Practices Survey) in 1977, the second (Housing Discrimination Study) in 1989, and the most recent in 2000 (Housing Discrimination Study or HDS 2000). Unfortunately, these studies tend to grossly underestimate the true extent of discrimination, as they are limited by methodology and data-gathering restrictions. For example, HDS 2000 excluded from the analysis transactions in which a home-seeker was unable to obtain an appointment over the phone. Numerous studies have documented the practice of discrimination by "linguistic profiling" (Baugh, Idsardi, and Purnell 1999), a common phenomenon in which services are denied because of the perceived race, gender, or ethnicity of a caller. Since a large percentage of housing-related transactions begin with a phone call and since fair housing personnel who worked on HDS 2000 reported to NFHA that up to 30% of the paired tests involved discrimination over the telephone, the exclusion of these tests from the results unnecessarily lowers the percentage levels of discrimination.

HDS results were also compromised by the limited advertising pool from which testing targets were selected, as they were confined to major metropolitan daily newspapers and did not include neighborhood newspapers, posted signs, and other forms of advertising that we have learned are commonly used by housing providers who want to limit the potential pool of applicants. Houses selected and shown by real estate agents were not extensively mapped in order to determine patterns of racial/ethnic steering, and most tests did not contain complete narratives that would have provided evidence of discriminatory practices and racial steering. Tests were conducted in predominantly minority neighborhoods, which would clearly limit the levels of discrimination against minority home-seekers. The incidence of discrimination against White testers was subtracted from the incidence of discrimination against minority testers, the net result of which is an undercounting of the full extent of discrimination against minorities. Even with these and other limitations, however, the HDS 2000 documented the following levels of discrimination:

- In rental markets:
  - Whites received favored treatment over Blacks 22% of the time;
  - Whites received favored treatment over Hispanics 26% of the time;

- Whites received favored treatment over Asian Americans 21.5% of the time; and
- Whites received favored treatment over Native Americans 28.5% of the time.
- In real estate markets:
  - Whites received favored treatment over Blacks 17% of the time;
  - Whites received favored treatment over Hispanics 20% of the time; and
  - Whites received favored treatment over Asian Americans 20.4% of the time;
  - Racial geographic steering (based primarily just on comments by agents and not including geographic patterns of properties recommended/ shown) takes place in both rental and sales markets and actually increased in real estate markets since 1989 by 7.5%.

Even given the lower boundary estimates of discrimination in the HDS, NFHA estimates that more than 3.7 million instances of discrimination occur annually in the United States.[12] However, this estimate does not include discrimination on the basis of other protected characteristics, including disability and familial status, which represent two of the three categories of complaints filed most often with HUD (the other top category—race—is included in the estimate). It also does not include discrimination in mortgage lending and insurance markets, making an estimated 4 million annual instances of discrimination entirely probable.

Rental Discrimination: Audits Conducted by Private Fair Housing Organizations

The National Fair Housing Alliance and its member fair housing organizations routinely conduct audits of housing providers. NFHA has received several grants from HUD for the creation of new fair housing organizations in Montgomery, AL; Fresno, CA; San Antonio and Houston, TX; New Orleans, LA; Gulfport, MS; and Boston, MA. As part of their initial activities, each organization conducted a paired testing audit of rental housing providers in their service areas. Each found significant levels of discrimination against African-American and, in some cases, Latino home-seekers, as follows:

- Fresno, CA (1995): 74% discrimination against African Americans and 77% discrimination against Latinos (Fair Housing Council 1995);
- Montgomery, AL (1995-96): 69.6% discrimination against African Americans (Central Alabama Fair Housing 1996);
- New Orleans, LA (1995–96): 77% discrimination against African Americans (Greater New Orleans Fair Housing Action Center 1996);

- San Antonio, TX (1997): 68% discrimination against African Americans and 52% discrimination against Latinos (San Antonio Fair Housing Council 1997);
- Houston, TX (2000–2001): 80% discrimination against African Americans and 65% discrimination against Latinos (Greater Houston Fair Housing Center 2001);
- Boston, MA (2000–2001): 63% discrimination against African Americans (The Fair Housing Center of Greater Boston 2001); and
- Gulfport, MS (2004): 71% discrimination against African Americans (Gulf Coast Fair Housing Center 2004).

NFHA also conducted rental testing immediately following the Gulf Coast hurricanes in 2005. Given the high incidence of housing discrimination, we realized immediately after the hurricanes that many persons forced to flee the Gulf Coast were likely to be victims of discrimination when seeking rental housing in other communities. Therefore, we implemented a testing program in 17 cities located in five states: Alabama, Florida, Georgia, Tennessee, and Texas. Differential treatment was identified at rental housing complexes in all 17 cities. Out of 65 paired tests of rental housing providers, African Americans experienced discrimination in 43 of the transactions— a rate of 66% (National Fair Housing Alliance 2005). The testers identified themselves as couples with two children relocating from the Gulf Coast due to the hurricanes. The testers were matched on home-seeking characteristics and qualifications, including that they were being relocated by their employer, and the African-American testers were slightly better qualified than their White counterparts. Many types of differential treatment were detected in the tests, but most fell into the following categories:

- Failure to tell African Americans about available apartments or provide other meaningful information;
- Failure to return telephone messages left by African Americans, while calls to Whites were returned;
- Quoting higher rent prices or security deposits to African-American testers; and/or
- Offering special inducements or discounts to White renters.

So we see that continued practices of discrimination in rental markets, even in times of crisis, prohibit home-seekers from being provided with housing opportunities on an equal basis, perpetuating segregation based on race and national origin.

Real Estate Sales: NFHA's Enforcement Testing Program

Upon conclusion of the HDS 2000 (which cost more than $20 million) and only in response to strong urging by fair housing organizations,[13] HUD awarded $1 million in contract funds to conduct follow-up enforcement testing of housing providers identified as providing differential treatment during the HDS. NFHA was the contractor for about two-thirds of the money (supplementing its grant award with more than $500,000 of its own funds) and conducted testing in 12 metropolitan areas, mostly in the Eastern part of the country and in Texas. The testing was conducted in late 2003 through early 2005. In all 12 areas in which NFHA conducted testing, some real estate agents made blatant discriminatory comments, such as "I can't not take you to certain neighborhoods—that is against the law—but let's just say I wouldn't want to live there"; or "There are a lot of [Hasidic] Jews in the neighborhood, but you don't have to worry because they would not mix with your kids;" or "The law doesn't allow me to have a preference over races or anything; I just tell people what is there and they decide."

Several types of discriminatory treatment were documented in the tests, including many practices that perpetuate segregation. In 20% of the paired tests, African-American or Latino testers were denied service by real estate agents or were provided very minimal service, including refusal to make appointments to meet with Black or Latino testers; failure to show up for appointments with Black or Latino testers; and failure to show any homes to Black or Latino testers, even after meeting with the tester. White testers were sometimes offered incentives like contributions to closing costs or lower interest rates, but these incentives were not offered to the Black or Latino testers. In many tests, Black or Latino testers were required to provide a pre-approval letter or other financial documentation prior to viewing houses, but the White tester was not required to provide any documentation. While there were some tests in which the White, Black, and Latino testers were required to provide some type of documentation, there were no tests in which a White tester was required to provide documentation but the minority tester was not.

The most dramatic finding of the testing was the overall rate of steering based on race or ethnicity. For the tests in which a tester actually got to see homes for sale, the rate of racial steering was 87% (White testers were steered to White neighborhoods while African-American and Latino testers saw no houses at all; or White testers were steered to White neighborhoods while African-American and Latino testers were steered to predominantly minority neighborhoods). In one test, an agent told the White tester that he had prepared two sets of listings but wouldn't need one set of listings once he saw the tester was White. Another agent literally drew red lines around Brooklyn Heights, New York

City neighborhoods he identified as White, and told the White tester to limit his housing search to those areas. These types of practices occurred even in tests in which testers asked for housing in different types of neighborhoods than those they were shown. For example, an African-American tester in the Detroit area indicated he wanted to live in a suburban community and would not mind a commute to downtown Detroit, but he was only shown homes in African-American neighborhoods in Detroit.[14]

While not the exclusive cause of segregation, discriminatory real estate practices clearly contribute to continued patterns of racial and ethnic segregation in the United States. Many people believe in the concept that "birds of a feather flock together"—that personal preference accounts for segregated living patterns. But those people are out of touch with discriminatory real estate practices and the evidence of what *actually* happens to home-seekers who seek housing in diverse communities.

Actions to Achieve and Maintain Neighborhood Integration

The U.S. Supreme Court in *Trafficante* and other cases gave us the legal tools to fight racial steering, block-busting, and redlining. Research has clearly documented the nature and extent of housing discrimination in America, but little has been done to promote residential integration through effective communications, using all types of technologies to erase stereotypes and open minds. It is possible, but difficult, given discriminatory market forces, to foster and preserve integrated neighborhoods. Since 1920, the Cincinnatus Association (CA) has been conducting studies and making recommendations about the needs of the city of Cincinnati and surrounding communities. The Association completed a report, *Stable Integrated Neighborhoods*, for the Stephan H. Wilder Foundation in 2007 that looked at 14 integrated neighborhoods to determine if they remained so over a long period of time, and found that over 30 years these communities remained integrated. One neighborhood remained 75% Black over a period of 30 years. The report states that all 14 neighborhoods "either maintained or increased their level of integration." Finally, the report's Executive Summary concludes: "These results directly challenge and contradict the notion that integrated neighborhoods and communities are undesirable places in which to make a home. Rather, they are thriving communities presenting enrichment opportunities for all, resulting in much to celebrate and feel uniquely good about."

The report's evidence clearly challenges the notion of a racial tipping point. People have assumed that White flight invariably will occur when the Black population in a neighborhood reaches a certain percentage. However, many reports discussing tipping points fail to measure the impact of block-busting, panic peddling,[15] and racial steering by real estate agents.

Panic peddling still happens and is used to encourage a homeowner to list his or her home for sale or to discourage a White person from considering a neighborhood in which his or her race does not predominate.[16] The CA report found that the socioeconomic status remained "essentially constant over the period 1980–2000 and in seven communities actually increased." Finally, the report states:

> Residents of the three largest integrated communities said they placed high value on the following: (1) Learning about others who are different, (2) Being among and helping develop tolerant people, (3) Living in a purposefully diverse neighborhood, (4) Having multiple kinds of housing to choose from, (5) Having an abundance of small businesses and support services, (6) Having active faith communities, (7) Having safe communities, and (8) Getting more people engaged in community events and decision-making.

Without the efforts of active community leaders, progressive politicians, civil rights attorneys, academics, and fair housing organizations, however, it is difficult to both create and maintain diverse communities. America must make a commitment to achieve the dual purpose of the Fair Housing Act. Research and enforcement are critically important components for success, but these components must be fully supported by educational efforts about the benefits of residing in diverse communities. Communities of color and integrated neighborhoods are too often the victims of negative stereotypes promoted by real estate agents, appraisers, lenders, insurers, and media stories. If we are to actually reap the professional and social benefits of living in integrated neighborhoods, as the Supreme Court said we are entitled to, then it is essential to create and implement a national multimedia campaign promoting these benefits to Whites, Blacks, and other people of color.

This media campaign should be a public/private partnership with corporate America. Many corporations support workplace diversity, yet most employees leave their diverse work environment each night and go home to racially segregated neighborhoods. The National Fair Housing Alliance approached State Farm Insurance Company with this issue, and we jointly created the first fair housing media campaign to encourage Whites, in particular, to be open to residential integration and learn about the benefits of racially and culturally diverse neighborhoods. The initial goal of this media campaign is to encourage Whites to think about what they are missing by living in their segregated neighborhoods. This print, radio, and movie theater advertising campaign was released in June 2008 in Atlanta, Chicago, and metro Washington, DC. The website http://www.aricherlife.org has all of the print and radio public service spots and is a resource center for people to learn about the benefits of neighborhood diversity and ways to encourage residential integration.

With the first African-American President in the (ironically named) White House, what better time to use federal fair housing education funds to promote residential integration?

Viable actions to eliminate housing discrimination and achieve residential integration must reach beyond research and enforcement actions and create strong educational messages that teach us to say it and mean it: Welcome to the neighborhood.

Notes

1. Speech made at signing of bill on April 11, 1968.
2. *Jones v. Alfred H. Mayer Co.*, 392 U.S. 409 (1968).
3. Literally hundreds of complaints were filed in federal district courts against apartment companies and real estate brokers, and a dozen or so lending lawsuits were filed. Homeowners' insurance investigations were undertaken by a few fair housing groups in Dayton, Toledo, and Cleveland Heights, but these important lawsuits prior to 1988 were not brought by fair housing groups: *Dunn v. Midwestern Indemnity*, 472 F. Supp. 1106 (S.D. Ohio 1979); *Mackey v. Nationwide Insurance Cos.*, 724 F. 2d 419 (4th Cir. 1984); *McDiarmid v. Economy Fire & Casualty Co.*, 604 F. Supp. 105 (S.D. Ohio 1984).
4. The Supreme Court has defined racial steering as "directing prospective home buyers interested in equivalent properties to different areas according to their race." *Gladstone Realtors v. Village of Bellwood*, 441 U.S. 91, 94 (1979).
5. The first Housing Market Practices Study in 1979 estimated that more than 2 million instances of housing discrimination occurred annually against African Americans. There were approximately 35 private fair housing centers in 1979 handling about 15,000 complaints. These groups were located in New York City, Chicago metro area (4), Ohio (7), Milwaukee, Gary, Atlanta, California (12), Richmond, New Jersey, Pennsylvania (3), and Buffalo, New York. In 2006, there were an estimated more than 3.7 million instances of housing discrimination; however, less than 30,000 complaints were filed with HUD, state or local government agencies, and private fair housing agencies.
6. See the National Fair Housing Alliance, *Fair Housing Trends Reports* 2001–2008, available at http://www.nationalfairhousing.org. The Citizens' Commission on Civil Rights conducted several comprehensive studies of government enforcement of the Fair Housing Act during the 1980s and 1990s, available at http://www.cccr.org.
7. Key cases include *City of Evanston v. Baird & Warner*, 1990 WL 186575, N.D.Ill., November 15, 1990, 1989 WL 134310, N.D.Ill., October 24, 1989; *Gladstone v. City of Bellwood*, 441 U.S. 91 (1979); *Village of Bellwood v. Dwivedi*, 895 F.2d 1521 (7th Cir. 1990); *City of Chicago v. Matchmaker Realty*, 982 F.2d 1086 (7th Cir. 1992); *Brown v. Federle Realtors*, 73-9051 (S.D. Ohio 1973); and *Hannah v. Sibcy Cline*, 147 Ohio App.3d 198, 2001-Ohio-3912.
8. See *City of Baltimore v. Wells Fargo*, No. 1:08-CV-00062-BEL (D.Md. 2008); *NFHA et al. v. Travelers/Aetna*, No. 1:00-CV-01506 (D.D.C. 2000); *Toledo Fair Housing Center v. Nationwide*, 94 Ohio Misc. 2d 14 (1993), 17 (1996), 127 (1996), 145 (1996), 151 (1997), 185 (1997), 186 (1998), Lucas County (Ohio) Court of Common Pleas; *Toledo Fair Housing Center v. Farmers*, 61 F. Supp. 2d 681 (N.D. Ohio 1999); 64 F. Supp. 2d 703 (N.D. Ohio 1999). *HOME of Richmond v. Nationwide* (VA State Court, jury verdict, 1998); *Laufman v. Oakley Building and Loan Co.*, 408 F. Supp. 409 (S.D. Ohio 1976); *Harrison et al. v. Heinzeroth Mortgage Company*, 430 F. Supp. 893 (N.D. Ohio 1977); *Old West End Association v. Buckeye Federal Savings & Loan*, 675 F. Supp. 1100 (N.D. Ohio 1987); *McMillian v. Huntington National Bank*, No. 85-7530 (N.D. Ohio May 24, 1985); *National Fair Housing Alliance et al. v. Prudential Insurance Company*, 208 F.Supp.2d 46 (D.C. 2002); *National Fair Housing Alliance et al. v. Liberty Mutual Insurance Company*, No.1:98-CV-00928 (D.D.C. 1998); HUD complaints: *NFHA v. State Farm Insurance*, *NFHA v. Allstate Insurance*, *NFHA v. Nationwide Insurance*.

9. Toledo Fair Housing Center clients filed complaints against Allstate and Erie Insurance Companies, but no HUD investigations were completed.
10. In the late 1980s, the Toledo Fair housing Center pioneered homeowners' insurance testing, using test homes in Black and White neighborhoods. In 1992, the National Fair Housing Alliance received a grant from HUD to conduct testing of homeowners' insurance companies in ten cities. Administrative complaints were filed by the NFHA against State Farm, Allstate, and Nationwide. Between 1995 and 1999, NFHA coordinated homeowners' insurance testing with fair housing agencies in Cincinnati, Milwaukee, New Orleans, Richmond, and Toledo. These investigations resulted in lawsuits being filed and settled against Liberty Mutual, Nationwide, Travelers, Aetna, and Prudential insurance companies. Richmond and Toledo brought separate lawsuits against Nationwide Insurance.
11. HOME of Richmond won the largest jury verdict in fair housing history—$100 million in punitive damages. While the appeal was pending, the case was settled for $25.5 million plus significant affirmative relief, including opening offices in underserved neighborhoods, marketing products to minority consumers, revising underwriting guidelines—actions that might not have been ordered by a court.,
12. For the basis of this estimate, see NFHA's *2004 Trends Report* (available at http://www.nationalfairhousing.org), which reports findings from a study of Housing Discrimination Study 2000 data by John Simonson, University of Wisconsin—Platteville.
13. Fair housing groups, including NFHA, argued that it was unconscionable for HUD to sit on the extensive evidence of discrimination documented through HDS 2000. Ultimately, HUD awarded $1 million in post-HDS enforcement funds (compared to the more then $20 million spent on the research testing).
14. Extensive information about the real estate testing results can be found at http://www.nationalfairhousing.org.
15. Definition from *Encyclopedia of Real Estate and Mortgage* terms: "panic peddling—the practice by a real estate licensee of soliciting listings through the illegal use of written or oral statements, or any other behavior that tends to create fear or alarm concerning the presence or imminent presence in the neighborhood of members of a minority status (race, gender, religious affiliation, handicap, familial status, or national origin)." http://www/homesurfer.com/encyclopedia/p/panic_peddling.html
16. Between 2004 and 2007, NFHA's real estate sales investigations in several cities document agents telling potential White buyers the race or national origin of next-door neighbors or stating that a neighborhood is Black or Latino.

References

Baugh, John, William Idsardi, and Thomas Purnell. 1999. "Perceptual and Phonetic Experiments on American English Dialect Identification." *Journal of Language and Social Psychology,* 18: 10–30.

Central Alabama Fair Housing Center. 1996. "Discrimination in the Rental Market: A Study of Montgomery, Alabama." January. http://www.nationalfairhousing.org (accessed March 2009).

Fair Housing Center of Greater Boston, The. 2001 "We Don't Want *Your* Kind Living Here: A Report on Discrimination in the Greater Boston Rental Market." April, http://www.nationalfairhousing.org (accessed March 2009).

Fair Housing Council of Fresno County. 1995. "Rental Audit Study," http://www.nationalfairhousing.org (accessed March 2009).

Greater Houston Fair Housing Center. 2001. "Rental Audit," http://www.nationalfairhousing.org (accessed March 2009).

Greater New Orleans Fair Housing Action Center. 1996. "The Greater New Orleans Rental Audit," http://www.nationalfairhousing.org (accessed March 2009).

Gulf Coast Fair Housing Center. 2004. "Fair Housing Rental Study 2004: An Audit Report on Race and Family Status Discrimination in the Mississippi Gulf Coast Rental Housing Market." http://www.nationalfairhousing.org (accessed March 2009).

National Fair Housing Alliance. 2005. *No Home for the Holidays: Report on Housing Discrimination Against Hurricane Katrina Survivors,* http://www.nationalfairhousing.org (accessed November 2008).

San Antonio Fair Housing Council. 1997. "San Antonio Metropolitan Area Rental Audit," http://www.nationalfairhousing.org (accessed March 2009).

Trafficante v. Metropolitan Life Insurance Co., 409 U.S. 205 (1972).

Turner, Margery Austin, Stephen L. Ross, George C. Galster, and John Yinger. 2001. "Discrimination in Metropolitan Housing Markets, National Results from HDS 2000." Washington, DC: Urban Institute, http://www.huduser.org/publications.

CHAPTER 3

From Segregation to Integration

How Do We Get There?

NANCY A. DENTON

Segregation. Integration. These two terms evoke a host of images and feelings in the minds of many. For social scientists, lawyers, and policymakers, both terms raise issues of race. The earliest studies focused on two groups, African Americans and whites. That we are no longer in a two-group world has been often noted, and the segregation of Asians, Hispanics, and the various subgroups of each has been measured, analyzed, and generally found to be lower than that of African Americans. A broad brush summary of research conducted after the 2000 Census showed a familiar pattern: Segregation of African Americans from whites is substantially higher than that of Hispanics, which is higher than that of Asians. Between 1990 and 2000, segregation did not change much for Hispanics and Asians, due largely to continuing immigration, and it declined for African Americans. However, the declines were largest in places with relatively small black populations, newer places in the South and West, while older, industrial cities in the Northeast and Midwest showed small declines in black-white segregation (Iceland 2004; Logan 2003; Logan, Stults, and Farley 2004; Wilkes and Iceland 2004). So residential segregation remains an important fact of life in cities in the United States.

Less attention, however, has been paid to the implications of this greater diversity for the future of measuring segregation or documenting integration, as the most commonly used measures all compare only two groups at a time. While some have used multigroup indices (Fischer 2003; Reardon and Firebaugh 2002), and emphasized differences in multiethnic metropolitan

23

areas (Frey and Farley 1996; Iceland 2004), no one has really addressed the question of what the increasing diversity of the population implies for the future of segregation and integration in the United States. To do so requires that we examine the magnitude and location of the increasing population diversity, review definitions of segregation and integration, and explore segregation at the neighborhood rather than metropolitan area level.

Scholarly work on segregation almost always has integration as its explicit or implicit goal. Consider, for example, the studies of the harmful effects of residential and school segregation on African Americans: They imply—even if they do not directly state—that integration would be better because white neighborhoods are safer, have better schools, higher housing values, better amenities (Sampson, Morenoff, and Gannon-Rowley 2002). Studies of the benefits of segregation for new immigrant groups often emphasize initial benefits of immigrant neighborhoods, but then discuss the limitations of remaining in enclaves and the benefits of spatial assimilation into more integrated neighborhoods that follows longer residence (Alba et al. 1999; Logan, Alba, and Zhang 2002).

At the same time, there is evidence that many are tired of this entire topic. For whites, this is known as "race fatigue"—for blacks, "integration exhaustion." Some of those who do discuss integration are against it or argue that it has failed (Cashin 2004; Patterson 1998). The academic literature and popular media are replete with comments to the effect of "people like to live with their own" or other indicators of integration fatigue: It hasn't worked (Feagin and Sikes 1995). Of course, the reality is that integration has seldom really been tried, and where it has been tried it has been much more successful than people think (Ellen 2001; Nyden et al. 1998; Nyden, Maly, and Lukehart 1997).

While this chapter is not going to lay out a detailed road map of how to move from segregation to integration, the title directs attention to the *process* of getting from one to the other. Current research has abundantly demonstrated the causes and consequences of current levels of segregation (Massey and Denton 1993; Oliver and Shapiro 1995, among many others), but the specifics of a process of moving to integration are notably absent in these studies. Furthermore, it is segregation, not integration, that is commonly measured, and focusing on it may make the situation seem more hopeless than it is. If one focuses on process and change, other issues emerge.

This chapter will make three main points: First, that future demographic changes have the potential to lower segregation. Demography is definitely no guarantee, but it can be argued that demography could be used to foster integration. Second, since different demography prevails in different places— increasing diversity is not evenly distributed—then the process of moving from segregation to integration will have to be place-specific as well. Third, to move from segregation to integration requires thinking about process, rather than looking at how much or how little segregation indices change. In particular, it requires examining what types of neighborhoods actually exist, thinking about which of them are integrated now, and how best to move others toward integration.

The Role of Demography

Current and future demographic changes have important implications for segregation because segregation is almost always highest between non-Hispanic whites and blacks (Farley and Frey 1994; Logan, Stults, and Farley 2004; Massey and Denton 1987; Wilkes and Iceland 2004). Thus, the extent to which the black–white model no longer accurately describes the nation's population because there are other numerically significant population sub-groups has the potential to decrease segregation. If nothing else, the presence of other groups will change the terms of the debate. And the evidence for this demographic shift is overwhelming.

The first piece of evidence is the demographic process of immigration. Approximately 1.2 million immigrants arrive in our country each year, primarily from Latin America and Asia (U.S. Department of Homeland Security 2008). It is well known that immigration is increasing the diversity of the population. According to the most recent population projections[1] of the U.S. Bureau of the Census, shown in Figure 3.1, non-Hispanic whites will be a numerical minority, less than 50% of the U.S. population, beginning in 2042 (U.S. Census Bureau 2008). What is less often emphasized is that the

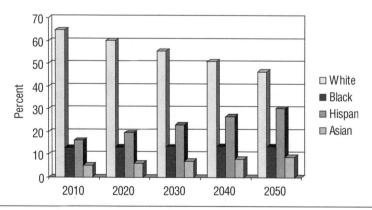

Figure 3.1 U.S. population by race/ethnicity projected 2010–2050. Source: U.S. Census Bureau, 2008, Table 6. Percent of the projected population by race and Hispanic origin release date: August 14, 2008. (NP2008-T6). Note: Whites are non-Hispanic Whites. Blacks and Asians are "alone or in combination."

effect of immigration on population diversity is felt in two ways: through the immigrants themselves, and through their native-born children. Put another way, the increasing diversity of the U.S. population will continue regardless of what happens to immigration. Changes in immigration will affect the *pace* of the increasing diversity, not the *fact* of increasing diversity.

A second way that demography is relevant to the discussion of segregation and integration is through the age structure. A comparison of the median ages among the major population subgroups shows that nearly 14 years separate the oldest from the youngest. Non-Hispanic whites are significantly older than the other groups and their median age is expected to be just over 41 years in 2010. Asians, the next oldest with a median age of 34.3 years, will be seven years younger than whites. Next are blacks, whose median age of 31.6 puts them about three years younger than Asians and four years older than Hispanics whose median age will be 27.5 years in 2010. All groups are projected to get older in future decades, but the patterns of age differences remain essentially the same (U.S. Census Bureau 2008).

As a result of these age differences, the race/ethnic compositions of different age groups of the population are quite different and they shift to being majority minority at different times, as shown in Figures 3.2. Children—those 17 and younger—will be majority minority in 2023, 19 years earlier than the total population and only just over a decade from now. That change will occur for the working-age population in 2039, three years before the total population, and later still for the population aged 65 and over (U.S. Census Bureau 2008). The different race/ethnic compositions of different age groups have profound implications for social institutions such as schools and the family. In schools, children will be in a majority minority world sooner than the adults who teach them. Non-Hispanic white elderly will be relying on minority workers for Social Security retirement support and personal care. Contacts across age groups that are routine in modern society, such as those between schoolchildren and their teachers, the elderly and their caregivers, grandparents and their grandchildren's playmates, and new hires and more senior employees, will increasingly have race/ethnic as well as age dimensions.

A third demographic change that will influence integration is changes in the relative sizes of the race/ethnic groups. As seen in Figure 3.1, the relative size of the white population will decrease over time as a result of immigration and the children of immigrants. Since there are fewer black immigrants, the relative size of the black population will grow ever so slightly, from about 14% now to 15% in 2050 (U.S. Census Bureau 2008). After decades of being the second largest group after non-Hispanic whites, blacks are now the third largest group. Thus, the black–white segregation model will no longer

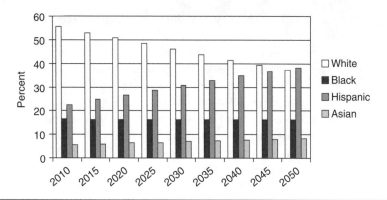

Figure 3.2a Persons aged 0–19.

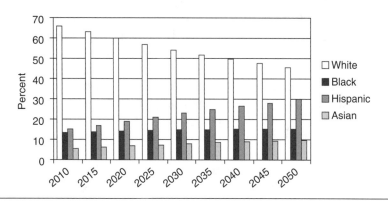

Figure 3.2b Persons aged 20–64.

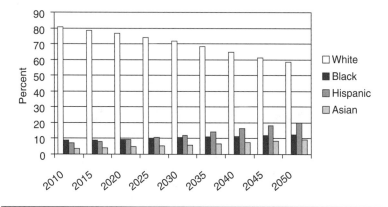

Figure 3.2c Persons aged 65 plus.

predominate, though the history of residential segregation remains based firmly in that model.

The relative race/ethnic distributions within the major age groups, when combined with the relative sizes of the groups, also points to a series of opportunities, because resources will open up. In jobs, the retirement of the baby boomers will free up good jobs for others, and likewise, as baby boomers age, their housing will also become available. To the extent that the baby boomers are overwhelmingly white compared to those following them, this represents opportunities for minorities (Alba 2009; Myers 2007). Of course, whether the nation makes use of these opportunities to increase social justice remains unknown, as does their effect on integration.

Implications of Regional Differences in Diversity for Moving from Segregation to Integration

So far, demographic change at the national level has been discussed. But these changes will not be felt equally across the United States. While the Census Bureau does not provide projections for specific regions or metropolitan areas, information from the 2000 Census and the 2007 American Community Survey gives a relatively clear overview of the current distribution. Figure 3.3 shows the U.S. population by region in 2000 and 2007. Clearly, the Western region is the most diverse and the Midwest the least. The black population is highest in the South. From 2000 to 2007, diversity increased in all regions.

Beyond regional variation, immigrants are not evenly spread across the states in the United States, but are concentrated in what are known as gateway states. Just six states—California, Florida, Illinois, New York, New Jersey, and Texas—are home to about two-thirds of the nation's foreign-born popula-

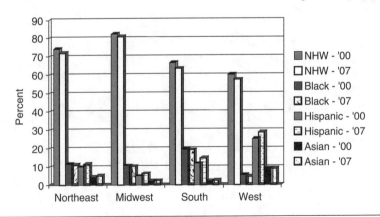

Figure 3.3 Race/ethnicity of U.S. population by region, 2000–2007. Source: U.S. Bureau of the Census, Census 2000 and 2007 American Community Survey.

tion. Between 2000 and 2007, the non-Hispanic white population declined and the Asian and Hispanic populations increased in these states. However, even among the gateway states there is considerable variation. For example, California was already a majority minority state by 2000 and became more so by 2007, while Illinois was 68% non-Hispanic white in 2000, and this percentage declined to 66 in 2007. Residents of other states do not experience the increasing population diversity to the same extent as do those who live in gateway states. However, even within gateway states, immigrants are concentrated in metropolitan areas such as Los Angeles, New York, Miami, and Chicago, so not all areas of the gateway states are equally diverse.

The increasing diversity of the population is felt differently, not only across states and metropolitan areas, but *within* metropolitan areas as well. Within metropolitan areas, immigrants have traditionally settled in the central city, but this is no longer the case. According to Frey (2006, 1), "Minority groups remain the demographic lifeblood of inner counties in older metropolitan areas, but they are increasingly fueling growth in fast-growing outer suburban and exurban counties as well."

Though immigrants are increasingly likely to go directly to the suburbs, and the suburbs are the location of immigrant assimilation (Alba et al. 1999), relative differences in diversity between central cities and suburbs remain enormous, as do the implications of the central city-suburban divide for discussions of segregation and integration. The development of the suburbs was financed by the federal government and enacted under racially discriminatory conditions (Jackson 1985; Massey and Denton 1993). Rather than being a mere historical artifact, the suburbs set up a level of segregation across their boundaries that keeps overall indices high even today. Minorities are much less likely to live in suburbs, and segregation indices tend to be much higher in the central city (Lewis Mumford Center 2001). Inner-ring suburbs often have poverty and disorder issues similar to the city (Berube and Tiffany 2004). Since suburbs are their own political entities, the center city boundary plus the suburban political jurisdictions give segregation an inertia that is very difficult to overcome. Living in the suburbs brings better amenities—better schools, higher housing values, greater access to jobs.

A final point about geographical differences in population diversity is that the patterns just described are beginning to break down. Immigrants are increasingly likely to go to nongateway places (Frey 2006; Singer, Hardwick, and Brettell 2008). Though their numbers there are still relatively small, their growth rates are enormous as result of their small population base. This settlement pattern is expected to continue, thus increasing the areas where the growing population diversity can be seen. One might argue that their presence in these newer areas is more noticeable than in the gateway areas because the new settlement areas have only had white and sometimes black populations for a couple of generations. In addition, these places often lack services to facilitate the adaptation of the immigrants (Waters and Jimenez 2005). The uneven settlement of immigrants. combined with the age differences discussed above, means that children in particular are more diverse. In one-third of metropolitan areas, less than half the population under age 15 is non-Hispanic white, including both gateway and new destinations such as Washington, DC, Chicago, Phoenix, and Atlanta (Frey 2006). These geographical differences in increasing population diversity suggest that policies for moving toward integration are likely to vary from place to place.

The Process of Moving from Segregation to Integration

While the demographic changes just discussed provide the potential to decrease segregation, actually moving from segregation to integration will require addressing some new questions compared to past analyses of segregation. The first question is what do we mean by integration? Integration implies that spatially located resources such as neighborhoods, jobs, or schools will be shared by members of different race/ethnic groups. This sharing has been very helpfully conceptualized by john powell (2008) and Xavier de Souza Briggs (2005) among others as *opportunity*, which moves the emphasis from "people who do or do not look like me" to the actual benefits some neighborhoods provide and others don't (Briggs 2005). However, the link between race and neighborhood amenities remains strong. From a fair housing point of view, integration means that all neighborhoods are open to everyone, without reference to race, according to preferences and ability to pay, what Ellen (2001) calls a focus on process. But she points out that a focus on "results" involves examining the racial distribution found in neighborhoods, regardless of how it came about (2001, 15).

In defining integration, we could possibly agree that it means not living where 99% or more of the people look like you. But what about 95% or more of one race/ethnic group? 90% or more? Is there a specific point when a neighborhood goes from being segregated to being integrated? By measuring segregation rather than integration, social scientists have effectively sidestepped the issue of defining integration in a meaningful way. For example, the Index of Dissimilarity[2] would be zero if every neighborhood had the same proportion of two groups as the overall metropolitan area, thus implying that an integrated neighborhood varies from place to place, as the distribution of the population varies. But when asked about the racial composition of neighborhoods they'd prefer, respondents in Boston, Detroit, Atlanta, and Los Angeles did not give the overall metropolitan area racial composition as their answer (Charles 2001).

Next, what is the relationship between measures of segregation and integration? The most often used measure of segregation, the Index of Dissimilarity, is easy to compute and interpret, and its long history of use facilitated examining changes over time. So how low must dissimilarity be for the place to be considered integrated? Traditional interpretations have held that indices below 30 were low, between 30 and 60 moderate, and above 60 high. This interpretation rests on the assumption that other things besides race influence neighborhood choice (e.g., housing type, cost, location relative to jobs, schools, and families). Would an Index of Dissimilarity of 30 or less then be considered integration? Or does integration mean that measures of segregation should be zero? But "perfect evenness" is an ideal, not a policy. As discussed above, race/ethnic groups are of radically different sizes. For small groups, evenness would presume a tiny number of a group per neighborhood. If a group is only 1% of the population, and the average tract size is 5,000, then there would be 50 people of that group in each neighborhood. But since people live in households, two-person households implies 25 households, four-person implies about 12, etc. If the tract is smaller in size than average, as many of them are in central cities, it is easy to see how using the ideal of evenness as measured by the Index of Dissimilarity quickly leads to unrealistic results.

Thinking about moving toward integration also necessitates looking at the distribution of actual neighborhoods where people currently live by race/ethnic composition rather than at a summary index for an entire metropolitan area. So a third issue concerns the number of groups needed for a neighborhood to be integrated. Segregation has traditionally been measured as "segregation from non-Hispanic whites" because the Index of Dissimilarity only considers two groups at a time, and because non-Hispanic whites control so much of the power and resource base in the United States. So it could be argued that integrated neighborhoods should contain whites. But specifying which particular groups should be present is more difficult. The different population group sizes, unevenness of population distribution by race/ethnicity and segregation patterns suggests that there will be many neighborhoods where members of a particular group do not live. Using less than 1% of the neighborhood population as the cut-off, among neighborhoods in the metropolitan United States in 2000, non-Hispanic whites do not live in only 2.5% of them while Asians do not live in 43.7% of them, no doubt reflecting the fact that these are the largest and smallest population groups respectively, as well as the concentration of Asians in the West. Differing levels of segregation are clearly seen for the other two groups: Blacks are not present in 28.4% of metropolitan neighborhoods, while Hispanics are not found in only 19.2%, indicating their greater access to more neighborhoods.

Given the large number of neighborhoods that blacks, Hispanics, and Asians do not live in, as well as their different distributions across the United

States, it is meaningful to look at how often a group lives with other members of that group. Figure 3.4 classifies neighborhoods with at least 1% of a group by the percentage of that group living in that type of neighborhood. So if the group is whites, the percent is of whites, if it is blacks, it is percent black. This allows the isolation of the groups to be compared to each other. In the top panel of Figure 3.4, the distribution is of *people*, showing the percent of that group's population who lives in each type of neighborhood, a measure of how segregated they are. In the bottom panels, the distribution is of *neighborhoods*, actual physical places to live. It is neighborhoods that will need to be integrated in order to promote integration, and we must decide at what level a

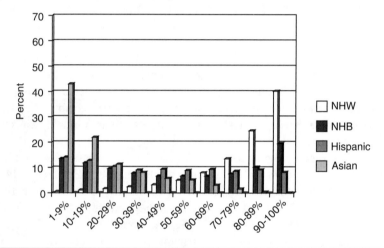

Figure 3.4a Percent of group population by percent of same group in neighborhood.

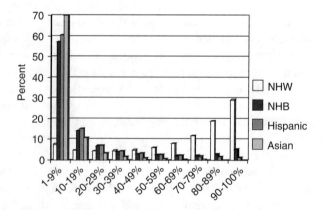

Figure 3.4b Percent of group neighborhoods by percent of same group in neighborhood. Source: Author's calculation from Census 2000 SF3 data. Note: NHW = Non-Hispanic White, NHB = Non-Hispanic Black.

neighborhood can be considered "integrated" in order to measure integration meaningfully. In addition, the extent that the distribution of neighborhoods differs from that of people informs us about the neighborhood-level process of moving from segregation to integration. The distributions in both panels are U-shaped, indicating more people or neighborhoods at either high or low concentrations of the group.

What is striking about the Figures is how *unevenly*, compared to the other groups, the white population and neighborhoods where whites live are distributed. The dramatic clustering of the white population in panel (a) and of white neighborhoods in panel (b) contrasts starkly with the pattern shown for other groups. About two-thirds of the white population lives in neighborhoods that are at least 80% white, with almost 40% living in neighborhoods that are 90 to 100% white (panel a). About half of the neighborhoods where whites live are at least 80% white, and very few neighborhoods where whites live are less than two-thirds white (panel b). Whites are clearly the least evenly distributed across neighborhoods of differing percentages white.

Looking at the black population, what is striking is how *evenly* they are distributed across neighborhoods with varying percentages of blacks. In contrast to whites, less than one-third of the black population live in neighborhoods that are 80% or more black. Over 10% of the black population lives in neighborhoods that are 1 to 9% black, and just under 20% lives in neighborhoods at the other extreme, 90 to 100% black (panel a). Neighborhoods where blacks live are heavily clustered at the low end, with almost two-thirds of them less than 20% black (panel b).

The pattern for the Hispanic population in Figure 3.4 is similar to that for the blacks, with Hispanics living in neighborhoods with varying percentages of other Hispanics, though most of the neighborhoods where they live have relatively few Hispanics. Asian neighborhoods and population patterns are a distinct contrast, as there are very few neighborhoods with high percentages of Asians, and Asians are very unlikely to live with other Asians. While these statistics may be surprising, given the high segregation of blacks, what they point out is that extremely high segregation is limited to a relatively small number of places and to only part of the population. So nationally, the percentage of the group living in highly segregated neighborhoods is higher than the percentage of the group's neighborhoods that are that segregated. Put another way, if we examined the data in Figure 3.4 for a highly segregated area like Chicago, the patterns change quite a bit, as blacks in particular are much more likely to live with other blacks and their neighborhoods are more likely to have mainly blacks in them.

The point of discussing the distributions of people and neighborhoods is to raise the question of at what point does one decide if a neighborhood is integrated? If we had public policy money to invest in promoting integration, in which neighborhoods would we start programs? Neighborhoods that have 1 to 9, 10 to 19, and 20 to 29% of a particular group could certainly be considered integrated, as over two-thirds of their populations are of a different group or groups. At the other extreme, neighborhoods where more than 90% of residents are of the same group could be considered segregated, and many would be willing to classify those that are occupied by 80 to 89% same-group members as segregated as well. It is clear from panel b of Figure 3.4 that the overwhelming majority of neighborhoods where 80 to 89 or 90 to 100% of the people are of the same race are occupied by whites. So in terms of moving neighborhoods toward integration, white neighborhoods are the place to start. If we could figure out how to get these neighborhoods to be less than 90 to 100 or 80 to 89% white, then we would be moving toward integration. The fact that most of the highly segregated neighborhoods are white does offer an interesting possibility, however. Severely segregated black, and, to a lesser extent, Hispanic neighborhoods tend to be places lacking in amenities and opportunities. Largely white neighborhoods on the other hand tend to be relatively rich in amenities, making it easier to convince people to live in them.

But what about the remaining neighborhoods, those whose residents are 30 to 79% members of the same group? The first point is that compared to neighborhoods at the extremes, there are relatively fewer neighborhoods where the population is between 30 and 79% of the same group. In panel b of Figure 3.4 the general pattern for all groups is U-shaped, with more neighborhoods at either low or high percentages of the group, or at the highly segregated extreme for whites and the least segregated extreme for Asians. Thus, there are relatively few neighborhoods in the middle range where people are living with about half members of their own race.

A second issue that arises is how many other groups have to be present with whites for integration to occur. Thus far diversity has been examined with four groups—non-Hispanic whites, non-Hispanic blacks, Hispanics, and Asians—so simplistically, a perfectly integrated neighborhood would be 25% of each group. However, the relative sizes of the populations and the unevenness of their distribution across larger-level geographic units makes this not feasible. Some might argue, based on the history of segregation, that blacks must be included in order for a neighborhood to be integrated. Such an approach may work in places where there is a large black population, but it is meaningless in metropolitan areas where the percentage of blacks is very low. Metropolitan areas as geographically dispersed as Albuquerque, NM; Boulder, CO; El Paso, TX; Eugene, OR; Olympia, WA; Salt Lake City, UT; Santa Barbara, CA, and Scranton, PA are less than 3% black. Some metro areas are mainly white, while others are majority Hispanic. Likewise, other metro areas have minuscule proportions of Asians or Hispanics. Despite the fact that people do not think of matching their metropolitan area population when they think of integration, it is clear that the presence of particular groups in particular areas will determine the limits of integration and make it vary somewhat from place to place, albeit not necessarily as precisely as limiting it to the overall proportion in the area.

The final issue that emerges from looking at integration from the point of view of neighborhoods rather than populations is that integration and segregation can coexist. Because of the different sizes of groups, and their differing dispersal across the urban landscape, it seems clear that integration will be defined differently in different locales. That leads to the very real possibility that people will live in neighborhoods that they see as diverse, while large numbers of minorities remain in neighborhoods that lack opportunities, with only other people like themselves as neighbors. In other words, depending on one's definition, people could come to see their own neighborhood as integrated before integration has proceeded very far in the metropolitan area or country as a whole.

Conclusion

This chapter examines the increasing diversity of the population in the United States and how that diversity is experienced in different states, across and within metropolitan areas. There is little doubt that the U.S. population is becoming more diverse, though this diversity is greater in some states and metropolitan areas than others. It will also be felt sooner among younger age groups and later among the elderly, though to the extent that the elderly rely on those younger for support, it will affect them as well.

It also examines issues related to the measurement and definition of segregation and integration, arguing that social scientists have sidestepped the issue of defining integration by only measuring segregation. It argues that the value of segregation indices is not an appropriate measure of integration, nor do segregation indices suggest concrete steps that could lead to integration. Focusing on the value of the Index of Dissimilarity gives continuity with past research. But while indices give the overall picture, they do not necessarily suggest action steps. In part, this is because they rely on averages for entire metropolitan areas. But it is actual neighborhoods that must be integrated. By examining the number of neighborhoods that would need to be integrated and the proportions of people living in them, it is possible to move away from the artificiality of "evenness" and gain a different perspective on moving from segregation to integration. A key finding is that from a neighborhood perspective, the vast majority of neighborhoods in need of integration efforts, because they are 80 to 89 or 90 to 100% occupied by persons of the same race, are all-white neighborhoods, not those that are predominantly black or Hispanic. Since those neighborhoods generally are amenity-rich, it is hoped that this focus on neighborhoods will move us closer to developing implementable policies.

If integration is the goal, then it must be able to be defined in such as way that progress toward it can be measured in a meaningful fashion. Merely tracking the changes in segregation indices, while important, is not enough. We must specify places where integration is likely to take place and encourage it in those places. Once a neighborhood is integrated, it should be celebrated for having achieved this goal, and helped to maintain it. Given regional differences in population diversity, the specific policies needed to achieve and maintain integration will not necessarily be the same everywhere. The demographic changes currently in progress do present a unique opportunity for integration. What remains to be seen is how much progress is made.

Notes

1. Population projections are made using a cohort component method. They require that assumptions be made about the birth rate, death rate, net international migration rate, and infant mortality rate, separately for each race/ethnic group.
2. The Index of Dissimilarity compares the segregation of two groups on a scale that ranges from 0 to 100. When it is zero, every neighborhood has the same proportion of each group as the city as a whole. More information can be found in Massey and Denton 1987.

References

Alba, Richard. 2009. *Blurring the Color Line: The New Chance for a More Integrated America.* Cambridge, MA: Harvard University Press.
———, John R. Logan, Brian Stults, Gilbert Marzan, and Wenquan Zhang. 1999. "Immigrant Groups in the Suburbs: A Reexamination of Suburbanization and Spatial Assimilation." *American Sociological Review* 64: 446–60.
Berube, Alan, and Thacher Tiffany. 2004. *The Shape of the Curve: Household Income Distributions in U.S. Cities, 1979–1999.* The Living Cities Series. Washington, DC: Brookings Institution.
Briggs, Xavier de Souza, ed. 2005. *The Geography of Opportunity: Race and Housing Choice in Metropolitan America.* Washington, DC: Brookings Institution.
Cashin, Sheryll. 2004. *The Failures of Integration: How Race and Class Are Undermining the American Dream.* New York: Public Affairs.
Charles, Camille Zubrinsky. 2001. "Processes of Racial Residential Segregation." In *Urban Inequality: Evidence from Four Cities,* ed. Alice O'Connor, Chris Tilly, and Lawrence D. Bobo. New York: Russell Sage Foundation, 217–71.
Ellen, Ingrid Gould. 2001. *Sharing America's Neighborhoods: The Prospects for Stable Racial Integration.* Cambridge, MA: Harvard University Press.
Farley, Reynolds, and William H. Frey. 1994. "Changes in the Segregation of Whites from Blacks during the 1980s: Small Steps Toward a Racially Integrated Society." *American Sociological Review* 59: 23–45.
Feagin, Joe R., and Melvin P. Sikes. 1995. *Living With Racism: The Black Middle-Class Experience.* Boston: Beacon Press.
Fischer, Mary J. 2003. "The Relative Importance of Class and Race in Determining Residential Outcomes in U.S. Urban Areas, 1970–2000" *Urban Affairs Review* 38(5): 669–696.
Frey, William H. 2006. *Diversity Spreads Out: Metropolitan Shifts in Hispanic, Asian, and Black Populations Since 2000.* The Living Cities Series. Washington, DC: Brookings Institution.
———, and Reynolds Farley. 1996. "Latino, Asian and Black Segregation in U.S. Metropolitan Areas: Are Multiethnic Metros Different?" *Demography* 33(1): 35–50.

Iceland, John. 2004. "Beyond Black and White: Metropolitan residential segregation in multi-ethnic America." *Social Science Research* 33: 248–271.

Jackson, Kenneth. 1985. *Crabgrass Frontier: The Suburbanization of the United States*. New York: Oxford University Press.

Lewis Mumford Center. 2001. "The New Ethnic Enclaves in America's Suburbs." http://mumford. albany.edu/census/suburban/SuburbanReport/page1.html (accessed August 26, 2008).

Logan, John. 2003. "Ethnic Diversity Grows, Neighborhood Integration Lags Behind." In *Redefining Urban and Suburban America: Evidence from Census 2000*, ed. Bruce Katz and Robert E. Lang. Washington, DC: The Brookings Institution Press, 235–256.

——, Richard Alba, and Wenquan Zhang. 2002. "Immigrant Enclaves and Ethnic Communities in New York and Los Angeles." *American Sociological Review* 67: 299–322.

——, Brian Stults, and Reynolds Farley. 2004. "Segregation of Minorities in the Metropolis: Two Decades of Change." *Demography* 41: 1–22.

Massey, Douglas S., and Nancy A. Denton. 1987. "Trends in the Residential Segregation of Blacks, Hispanics, and Asians: 1970–1980." *American Sociological Review* 52: 802–825.

——.1993. *American Apartheid: Segregation and the Making of the Underclass*. Cambridge, MA: Harvard University Press.

Myers, Dowell. 2007. *Immigrants and Boomers: Forging a New Social Contract for the Future of America*. New York: Russell Sage Foundation.

Nyden, Philip, John Lukehart, Michael T. Maly, and William Peterman. 1998. "Neighborhood Racial and Ethnic Diversity in U.S. Cities." *Cityscape* 4(2): 1–17.

——, Michael Maly, and John Lukehart. 1997. "The Emergence of Stable, Racial and Ethnically Diverse Urban Communities: A Case Study of Nine U.S. Cities." *Housing Policy Debate* 8(2): 491–534.

Oliver, Melvin L., and Thomas M. Shapiro. 1995. *Black Wealth/White Wealth: A New Perspective on Racial Inequality*. New York: Routledge.

Patterson, Orlando. 1998. *The Ordeal of Integration*. Washington, DC: Civitas.

powell, john. 2008. "Race, Place, and Opportunity." The American Prospect. http://www.prospect. org/cs/articles?article=race_place_and_opportunity (accessed September 30, 2008).

Reardon, Sean F., and Glenn Firebaugh. 2002. "Measures of Multigroup Segregation." *Sociological Methodology* 32: 33–67.

Sampson, Robert J., Jeffrey D. Morenoff, and Thomas Gannon-Rowley. 2002. "Assessing Neighborhood Effects: Social Processes and New Directions in Research." *Annual Review of Sociology* 28(1): 443–478.

Singer, Audrey, Susan W. Hardwick, and Caroline B. Brettell, eds. 2008. *Twenty-First-Century Gateways: Immigrant Incorporation in Suburban America*. Washington, DC: Brookings Institution Press.

U.S. Bureau of the Census. 2000. "Census 2000 Geographic Terms and Concepts." http://www.census. gov/geo/www/tiger/glossry2.pdf (accessed August 31, 2008).

——. 2008. "United States Population Projections by Age, Sex, Race, and Hispanic Origin: July 1, 2000–2050." http://www.census.gov/population/www/projections/methodstatement.html (accessed August 6, 2008).

U.S. Census Bureau. 2007. "American Community Survey. 2007. Hispanic or Latino by Race, Table B03002." http://www.census.gov/geo/www/tiger/glossry2.pdf (accessed August 6, 2008).

U.S. Department of Homeland Security. 2008. Yearbook of Immigration Statistics: 2007. Yearbook of Immigration Statistics: 2007. Available online at: http://www.dhs.gov/ximgtn/statistics/publications/yearbook.shtm (accessed August 16, 2008).

Waters, Mary C., and Tomas R. Jimenez. 2005. "Assessing Immigrant Assimilation: New Empirical and Theoretical Challenges." *Annual Review of Sociology* 31: 105–125.

Wilkes, Rima, and John Iceland. 2004. "Hypersegregation in the Twenty-First Century." *Demography* 41(1): 23–36.

CHAPTER 4

Creating and Protecting Prointegration Programs Under the Fair Housing Act

JOHN P. RELMAN, GLENN SCHLACTUS, AND SHALINI GOEL

Two broad remedial objectives underlie the Fair Housing Act: nondiscrimination and integration. Evidence of these twin goals can be found throughout the statute itself, in the legislative history of the 1968 Act, and in Supreme Court decisions interpreting the law.

The Act's preface declares in sweeping language that "[i]t is the policy of the United States to provide, within constitutional limitations, for fair housing throughout the United States" (42 U.S.C. § 3601). The Supreme Court has interpreted this language to make clear "the broad remedial intent of Congress embodied in the Act," which in turn reflects "a strong national commitment to promot[ing] integrated housing."[1]

The goals of nondiscrimination and integration were generally viewed by the Fair Housing Act's legislative sponsors as complementary. Congress adopted the Act in the wake of the highly publicized report by the National Advisory Commission on Civil Disorders, which had warned that the "Nation is moving toward two societies, one black, one white—separate and unequal."[2] Creating barriers to discrimination (the nondiscrimination goal), it was thought, would inevitably lead to the eradication of segregation (the integration goal). Thus, the Act's principal sponsor, Senator Walter Mondale, explained that blacks were unable to move to white suburbs because of the "refusal by suburbs and other communities to accept low-income housing.... An important factor contributing to exclusion of Negroes from such areas, moreover, has been the policies and practices of agencies of government at all levels."[3] Similarly, Senator Edward Brooke noted that blacks could not move to better neighborhoods because they were "surrounded by a pattern of discrimination based on individual prejudice, often institutionalized by business and industry, and Government practices."[4]

Four decades after passage of the Fair Housing Act, achieving the goal of integration has met with mixed results. There has undoubtedly been progress; some empirical evidence supports the conclusion that "more neighborhoods in metropolitan America are shared by blacks and whites [as of 2004] than [in prior decades]," and many racially integrated neighborhoods appear reasonably stable.[5] But for every study showing progress, there are others that describe a continuing pattern of entrenched, and in some cases, worsening segregation.[6]

The reasons for such limited progress are many and complicated. Some of the failure is attributable to continuing discrimination by landlords and other housing providers; some of it is likely due to facially neutral practices and policies of local governments that have the effect of reinforcing pre-existing residential segregation; and some of the failure is clearly due to a chronic insufficiency of resources (regardless of political administrations in Washington) available for government enforcement and prosecution of the fair housing and lending laws that both the Congress and state legislatures have worked hard over the last four decades to pass.

Another reason is that opponents of integration strategies have had success striking down certain types of integration plans in court challenges that focus on the potential conflict between the goals of nondiscrimination and integration. This has complicated advocates' ability to promote integration. The case of *United States v. Starrett City Associates*, 840 F.2d 1096 (2d Cir. 1988), demonstrates how a conflict can arise. *Starrett City* involved a New York City (Brooklyn) apartment complex with over 5,800 units that established a quota system—64% white, 22% black, and 8% Hispanic—to preserve integration and prevent "tipping" into an all-minority development because of "white flight."[7] The result was that it was harder for minorities to get an apartment than for whites; minorities effectively faced ceiling quotas.[8] The court held that the quota system violated the goal of nondiscrimination, and therefore the Fair Housing Act, even though it promoted integration.

The goal of this chapter is to assist fair housing advocates in locating the line between integration strategies that courts may reject, as in *Starrett City*, and those that are most likely to withstand scrutiny. In the analysis that follows, we survey a few of the various types of prointegration strategies that have been attempted, consider the case law assessing these strategies, and seek to identify the prointegration strategies that may be employed going forward. Advocates should not shy away from prointegration strategies, but in designing them must be cognizant of the lessons learned from judicial decisions.

Broadly speaking, the most important prointegration strategies fall into one of three categories: (1) court-ordered programs based on findings of prior discrimination; (2) voluntary programs adopted in the absence of a finding of prior discrimination; and (3) affirmative marketing programs that seek to publicize housing opportunities to those populations who might not otherwise know about them.

Court-Ordered Prointegration Programs Designed to Remedy Prior Discrimination

Of the three categories listed above, the most robust prointegration programs are available where a court has found that a public housing authority or other public entity has previously engaged in intentional discrimination. Although race-conscious prointegration programs by public entities must satisfy strict scrutiny under the Equal Protection Clause, courts have long recognized "the compelling interest of remedying the effects of past intentional discrimination."[9] Thus, where a public entity has engaged in prior discrimination, its prointegration program need only be narrowly tailored to pass constitutional muster. Accordingly, prointegration programs by public entities that have engaged in prior discrimination have largely been upheld.

For example, in *Schmidt v. Boston Housing Authority*, 505 F. Supp. 988 (D. Mass. 1981), a state court had earlier found that the Boston Housing Authority's developments were segregated and ordered the Authority to propose revisions to its tenant selection, assignment, and transfer programs in order to desegregate its buildings.[10] The state court then approved a consent decree which gave priority to applicants who wanted housing in one of the authority's developments in which members of their racial group were "substantially in the minority," determined by whether there were fewer individuals of that race than expected based on the number of individuals of that race eligible for public housing.[11] When a group of white residents of South Boston challenged the plan, a Massachusetts District Court held that the plan was constitutional, given that there was no evidence of intentional discrimination[12] and that it was lawful under the Fair Housing Act, because it did not have a racially discriminatory effect—both whites and racial minorities could benefit from minority preference status, based on the population of the building to which they wanted to move.[13]

Although the effect of the plan was that whites were not given minority preference status for low-income housing in the desirable South Boston area because the Housing Authority's developments there were already largely white, the court explained that this did not violate the Fair Housing Act:

[T]here is no federally protected right to housing in a particular community, an allegation which lies at the essence of plaintiffs' action. Nor may plaintiffs attempt to keep members of another racial group from entering the community.... And clearly there is no federally protected right to low income public housing. Discriminatory effect cannot be established with reference to a single community.[14]

Based on this analysis, and after noting HUD's affirmative duty to remedy the effects of past racial segregation under Section 3608 of the Fair Housing Act, the court granted summary judgment to the Housing Authority, concluding that its race-conscious tenant assignment program was lawful.[15]

Similarly, in *Jaimes v. Lucas Metropolitan Housing Authority*, 833 F.2d 1203 (6th Cir. 1987), a district court imposed an affirmative action plan on the Lucas Metropolitan Housing Authority (formerly named the Toledo [OH] Housing Authority) after finding that it, along with HUD, "were responsible for intentional discrimination and segregation."[16] The plan, modeled after the *Schmidt* program, provided for a 3:1 ratio of white to minority tenants in each public housing location, offering new applicants the first available unit in locations where their race was in the minority, and giving a slight preference to integrative transferees and applicants, after those with hardship needs.[17]

Applying strict scrutiny to the program, the Sixth Circuit concluded that remedying past discrimination was a compelling governmental interest and upheld the program as narrowly tailored, except for the strict 3:1 ratio, to the extent that it preferred whites or blacks. The court cautioned that "the concept of identifying a ratio representing the racial mix of both those currently residing in the Lucas Metropolitan Housing Authority's housing and those on the waiting list is both permissible and desirable as a goal for integration. But it should not be interpreted as a strict racial quota."[18] Although it emphasized that the plan should be temporary, the Sixth Circuit explained that the district court had broad equitable powers to remedy past wrongs and that in this circumstance "the imposition of racial goals is proper and necessary."[19]

The long-standing line of authority approving prointegration strategies designed to address past discrimination continued in *Raso v. Lago*, 135 F.3d 11 (1st Cir. 1998), which involved a private developer in an urban renewal area who had received a HUD grant to construct mixed-income housing in the West End of Boston. The developer adopted a tenant assignment plan that sought to increase opportunities for minority applicants to be placed in low-income housing units. Former residents of the West End seeking to occupy the new development invoked a requirement by the Boston Redevelopment Authority giving preference to former tenants who had been displaced by development of an urban renewal area.[20]

At the time, HUD was subject to a consent decree requiring it to make efforts to ensure that the racial composition of HUD-assisted public housing in largely white neighborhoods in Boston reflected the racial composition of the city of Boston as a whole.[21] Because former West End residents were overwhelmingly white, while the city population was 41% minority, giving former residents an automatic preference would have made the development virtually all-white. Instead, the developer adopted a plan whereby former tenants were preferred for 55% of the housing—including most of the market-rate units and some of the low-income units—while the rest of the units—including almost all of the low-income units—were open to all applicants.[22]

The court rejected an Equal Protection challenge brought by former white residents, concluding that "Benign intentions do not immunize government action, but they substantially narrow the inquiry."[23] The court explained that even though the plan had a racial motive—to increase minority opportunities for low-income housing in the area—it was not suspect and should not be subject to strict scrutiny, given that it functioned only to make a subset of apartments available to all applicants instead of reserving them for former residents.

In short, prointegration programs are particularly likely to be upheld when they are designed to remedy past intentional discrimination. Based on the case law to date, public entities seeking to use race-conscious strategies to address past intentional discrimination may further bolster the likelihood that a remedial program will be upheld in two ways: first, by devising facially neutral policies that promote racial integration in general and apply equally to minorities and nonminorities[24] and second, by avoiding strict quotas in favor of more flexible race-conscious policies.[25]

Voluntary Prointegration Programs in the Absence of Past Discrimination

Many publicly-funded entities have implemented race-conscious programs designed to enhance integration on their own initiative and in the absence of any finding of past intentional discrimination. The most important statutory authority for such programs is supplied by section 3608(d)(5) of the Fair Housing Act, which requires the HUD Secretary to administer HUD's programs "in a manner affirmatively to further the policies of this subchapter." Because integration is one of the main policies underlying the Act, courts have interpreted this provision to mean that HUD and local housing authorities that receive funds from HUD must both affirmatively promote integration and avoid taking action that sets back integration.

In *Shannon v. HUD*, 436 F.2d 809 (3d Cir. 1970), for example, the Third Circuit held that the obligation meant that a public housing authority could not site new low-income housing projects likely to be occupied by minorities in predominantly minority neighborhoods, as this would increase racial segregation:

Possibly before 1964 the administrators of the federal housing programs could...remain blind to the very real effect that racial concentration has had in the development of urban blight. Today such color-blindness is impermissible. Increase or maintenance of racial concentration is prima facie likely to lead to urban blight and is thus prima facie at variance with the national housing policy.[26]

Similarly, in *NAACP v. Secretary of HUD*, 817 F.2d 149, 154-55 (1st Cir. 1987), the First Circuit held that HUD must at least consider the effect of its programs on the racial and socioeconomic composition of an area, to ensure that its programs are not furthering segregation:

> [A]s a matter of language and of logic, a statute that instructs an agency "affirmatively to further" a national policy of nondiscrimination would seem to impose an obligation to do more than simply not discriminate itself.... [The Fair Housing Act's goal of opening the nation's housing stock to persons of every race and creed] suggests an intent that HUD do more than simply not discriminate itself; it reflects the desire to have HUD use its grant programs to assist in ending discrimination and segregation, to the point where the supply of genuinely open housing increases.[27]

In short, ample authority supports the proposition that public entities may and should take steps to affirmatively promote integration—even if they have not engaged in past intentional discrimination.

These authorities also support the proposition that private entities receiving no government assistance may likewise promote integrated housing, though they have no affirmative obligation to do so. It would be incongruous to attribute to Congress the view that it is in the national interest for public entities to promote integration, but that purely private entities are barred from trying to do the same.

In this area, however, proponents of integrative strategies must be careful to avoid structures that might be viewed as creating a ceiling on the amount of housing that is available to people because of their membership in a particular class. In such situations, some courts have given higher priority to the goal of nondiscrimination than to the goal of integration.

The first challenge to a prointegration program came in *Otero v. New York City Housing Authority*, 484 F.2d 1122 (2d Cir. 1973). The New York City Housing Authority was required by regulation to give first priority for newly constructed low-income housing to present and former occupants of the site, who were predominantly nonwhite. Because doing so would very likely have resulted in racially tipping the integrated neighborhood into an all-minority ghetto, in violation of the Authority's duty to integrate, it preferred white applicants over nonwhite applicants for the apartments. When the program was challenged by former minority residents, the Second Circuit concluded that "the Authority is under an obligation to act affirmatively to achieve integration in housing. The source of that duty is both constitutional and statutory,"[28] and that pursuant to that duty "[a]ction must be taken to fulfill, as much as possible, the goal of open, integrated residential housing patterns, and to prevent the increase of segregation, in ghettos, of racial groups whose lack of opportunities the Act was designed to combat."[29] Based on this duty, the court upheld the program, although it required a high burden of proof—"convincing evidence"—that adhering to the prior resident priority regulation would otherwise have thwarted integration.[30]

Certain other race-conscious prointegration programs adopted in the absence of a finding of past discrimination have not fared as well, demonstrating potential vulnerabilities of such programs. In these cases, courts have become ensnared in the potential conflict between the goals of integration and nondiscrimination. The problem in each came down to the same thing— ceilings were put in place that effectively limited the housing available to certain groups. *Otero* notwithstanding, the safest course in most situations is to avoid the use of such devices.

For example, in *Starrett City*, the Second Circuit severely limited the reach of *Otero* and invalidated racial quotas used to maintain a racially integrated community. The United States brought suit against the development's landlords for violating the Fair Housing Act by adopting the racially discriminatory quotas noted in the introduction to this chapter. Importing analysis from Title VII[31] cases, the court rejected these quotas because they were not temporary (unlike the one-time preference in *Otero*), as there was no history of prior discrimination or discriminatory imbalance, and because the quotas operated to bar minorities' access to the housing development.[32] Although the court assured that it "d[id] not intend to imply that race is always an inappropriate consideration under Title VIII in efforts to promote integrated housing,"[33] *Starrett City* shows that, in the absence of prior discrimination, programs that create ceilings on the amount of housing available to some people are susceptible to challenge.

Likewise, in *United States v. Charlottesville Redevelopment & Housing Authority*, 718 F. Supp. 461 (W.D. Va. 1989), a housing authority whose public housing project was occupied almost exclusively by African Americans imposed a 50-50 ratio for black and white tenants in order to integrate the project, invoking its obligation to affirmatively further integration.[34] Upon a legal challenge by the United States, the court struck down this tenant assignment program as a violation of the Fair Housing Act, concluding that the duty not to discriminate has priority over the duty to integrate. To that end, the court stated that it "d[id] not find that the duty to integrate will necessarily override the duty to avoid discrimination,"[35] and concluded that "the duty to avoid discrimination must circumscribe the specific particular ways in which a party under the duty to integrate can fulfill that second duty."[36] But it hastened to add that the duty to integrate was still valid under the statute:

> [M]erely because this particular policy is impermissible, [the housing authority] cannot discard its duty to pursue the goal of integration.... While the scope of this policy advancing integration must be circumscribed, that does not mean that the legal principle of integration goes away, that [the housing authority's] duty to seek integration fades away, or that the legal value of integration has no force.... [T]he value of integration is one of which [the housing authority] is obligated to take account in some fashion, for its "traces" still remain and have force over the defendant.[37]

The integration program in *Burney v. Housing Authority of Beaver County*, 551 F. Supp. 746 (W.D. Pa. 1982), suffered a similar fate. There, the court struck down an integration maintenance program developed by a housing authority to address racial imbalances in housing projects.[38] Under the program, at housing projects that were racially imbalanced (meaning that they had more tenants of one race than would be expected based on the percentage of tenants of that race in all of the authority's housing projects), applicants of underrepresented races would have priority for placement.[39] The court concluded that the program violated the Equal Protection Clause because it operated to limit housing opportunities for African Americans and that it violated the Fair Housing Act, because the authority had not shown that no less discriminatory alternative could have satisfied its affirmative furtherance obligation.[40]

Starrett City and its progeny present obstacles to the use of race-conscious strategies to promote integration in the absence of any finding of prior intentional discrimination, but they do not stand in the way of many useful approaches. Given the long-standing judicial recognition that integration is a major goal of the Fair Housing Act, public entities can and should devise strategies to affirmatively promote integrated communities.

Of course, the courts' recent tendency to subordinate integration to nondiscrimination where the two goals are most clearly in conflict means that integration policies are more likely to be upheld when they pursue racial goals in a way that is facially neutral. Moreover, while recent trends have not been favorable, the case law to date does not foreclose race-conscious policies where there are significant racial imbalances in a housing authority's projects, particularly where those policies do not have the effect of limiting housing opportunities for historically marginalized groups. Cases like

Starrett City underscore the need for vigorous litigation to obtain findings of past discrimination which will provide the foundations for the broadest prointegration remedies.

Affirmative Marketing Programs

The third category of cases, and the least controversial, involves public and private entities that have made efforts to publicize housing opportunities to those racial groups underrepresented in an area in order to integrate the community. Pursuant to the affirmative furthering obligation of Section 3608(d) (5), HUD issued Affirmative Fair Housing Marketing regulations, which require applicants to federal fair housing programs to "pursue affirmative fair housing marketing policies,"[41] such as "publicizing to minority persons the availability of housing opportunities,"[42] and to submit an Affirmative Fair Housing Marketing Plan to HUD.[43] HUD's Affirmative Fair Housing Marketing Requirements Handbook further explains that applicants should identify those racial groups least likely to apply for housing and detail proposed outreach efforts to make the availability of the housing known to those groups.[44] HUD's Fair Housing Planning Guide similarly calls on local governments to "examine a wide array of issues in order to identify and address impediments to fair housing choice."[45] With these regulations in the background, courts have generally upheld affirmative marketing efforts.

For example, in *Steptoe v. Beverly Area Planning Association*, 674 F. Supp. 1313 (N.D. Ill. 1987), a private nonprofit fair housing group seeking to promote integration instituted a program that provided information about housing only to individuals seeking to make "nontraditional moves"—i.e., whites moving into integrated areas and minorities moving into predominantly white areas.[46] Moreover, the group fully informed those using its services about its policies.[47] The court held that this practice did not constitute racial steering in violation of the Fair Housing Act because the group was not involved in any real estate transactions, since housing information was readily available to those seeking to make traditional moves and the group acted only to increase the existing supply of housing information, and because the group fully informed home-seekers of its policies.[48] The court concluded that the Fair Housing Act did not even apply to the fair housing group, since it did not engage in the provision of housing.[49]

The legality of affirmative marketing efforts was more squarely confronted in *South-Suburban Housing Center v. Greater South Suburban Board of Realtors*, 935 F.2d 868 (7th Cir. 1991). A nonprofit fair housing group purchased homes in a predominantly African-American census block in Park Forest, Illinois; listed the homes with a real estate company; and imposed an affirmative marketing plan requiring the company to advertise to both whites and minorities but to make special outreach efforts to attract white home-buyers, including advertising in newspapers with a largely white circulation and distributing information to apartments with largely white tenants and employers with largely white employees.[50] When the real estate company listed the homes, the local Board of Realtors filed a complaint against the company for racial steering in violation of the Fair Housing Act.

The Seventh Circuit explained that, unlike racial quotas, affirmative marketing programs do not "subordinat[e] the goal of equal housing opportunity to the goal of integration,"[51] but merely target particular groups, without excluding minorities from housing opportunities. "Thus, we are not dealing with conflicting goals, for the affirmative marketing plan furthers the goal of integration while providing equal opportunities to all."[52] The court concluded that the affirmative marketing plan directing information about housing in a largely black area to largely white audiences actually furthered both of the Fair Housing Act's goals—both integration and "making housing equally available to all by stimulating interest among a broader range of buyers."[53] Consequently, the court upheld the plan because it "merely provided additional information to white homebuyers concerning properties they might not otherwise consider, and involved no lessening of efforts to attract black homebuyers to these same properties."[54] Although the plan was lawful, the court also held that the Board of Realtors was not required by the Fair Housing Act to cooperate with the fair housing group's affirmative marketing plan or to list the group's homes.[55]

In sum, both public and private entities may engage in affirmative marketing. Unlike policies in which racial classifications inform particular decisions to grant or deny housing opportunities, race-conscious marketing programs have not been thought to implicate the tension between the prointegration and antidiscrimination provisions and goals of the Fair Housing Act.

Applying the Legal Rules

As the discussion above demonstrates, the rules that govern different types of prointegration strategies are complicated. As a result, it is not always easy to apply these rules to new situations. For advocates who are not versed in the technicalities of law, sometimes it is helpful to see how a real-life example would be analyzed if it were subjected to the type of legal scrutiny that would be applied by a court. This section explores how the rules discussed above would apply to a creative prointegration strategy implemented in Shaker Heights, Ohio.

Shaker Heights is a suburb of Cleveland with a population of 29,000. African Americans constitute 37% of Shaker Heights' population, but are concentrated close to the town's border with the city. Since 1985, a nonprofit organization called the Fund for the Future of Shaker Heights has worked with the town to develop a mortgage program that provides financial incentives to promote integrated living patterns. The program offers low-cost mortgages to whites buying homes in neighborhoods in Shaker Heights where whites are underrepresented relative to the county as a whole, and to African Americans buying homes in neighborhoods where African Americans are underrepresented. The loans may be as large as 10% of the purchase price or $18,000, whichever is higher.

The first step in analyzing the Fund's program is to identify the types of issues that might arise in a legal challenge. That is, what are reasons that an opponent might claim the program violates the Fair Housing Act or the Equal Protection Clause? One reason is that the program is not race-neutral. To the contrary, race is the key factor in determining whether an applicant will be permitted to participate. Relatedly, while whites and African Americans may both receive loans through the program, they may not do so with respect to the same homes.

The next step is to review the core rules of engagement for analyzing a prointegration program. The first rule is that a public entity that previously engaged in intentional discrimination has extra leeway to pursue prointegration strategies to remedy its past conduct. The next is that race-neutral programs are more likely to be upheld than race-conscious ones. A third rule tells us that, among race-conscious programs, the most questionable are those that employ strict quotas, particularly quotas that limit where someone can live because of race. Fourth, the goal of nondiscrimination may well prevail when it comes into direct conflict with the goal of integration and there is a limit on the housing available. And finally, affirmative marketing to promote integration is legal.

What do these rules mean for the Shaker Heights mortgage program? On the one hand, the program is race-conscious, was not created in direct response to a court finding of past intentional discrimination, and does not fall into the mold of a traditional affirmative marketing program.

On the other hand, the program does not employ any type of quota and nobody is prevented from purchasing a home in any part of town. Nor does the program conflict with the goal of nondiscrimination. This is because the Fund's low-cost loans are available to whites and African Americans alike on a generally equal basis, depending on the neighborhood in which they want to buy a home (and because provisions are made for members of all other races to participate). Of Shaker Heights' ten neighborhoods, whites are underrepresented in five, African Americans are underrepresented in four, and the program is unavailable in the tenth because it is already racially balanced.

On balance, these factors strongly suggest that the Shaker Heights program would survive judicial scrutiny. Some caveats must be kept in mind, however. If the Fund only offered loans to members of one race, as did a now-discontinued mortgage incentive program in another Ohio town, its legality would be more doubtful. And in areas that are extremely segregated (e.g., minorities make up 50% of the population but are highly concentrated in just 10% of the neighborhoods), it could be that one racial group has much greater access to the benefit than another.[56]

Those caveats notwithstanding, the Shaker Heights program shows that there is a strong legal case for creative strategies that occupy the middle ground between race neutrality and quotas, even without a judicial finding of past intentional discrimination. By structuring programs like the Fund's to offer benefits to everyone, advocates can avoid or at least minimize the potential tension between the Fair Housing Act's goals of nondiscrimination and integration. This will allow resources to be applied lawfully and successfully to the ongoing pursuit of racial integration in all communities across the country.

Conclusion

Promoting racial integration was one of the overarching purposes of the Fair Housing Act and continues to serve as a legally permissible basis for public and private housing policy. Cases addressing strategies employed to achieve and maintain integration demonstrate that housing providers have ample authority to pursue this goal.

An important theme that emerges from cases like *Jaimes v. Lucas Metropolitan Housing Authority* and *Raso v. Lago* is that this authority carries greatest weight where a public entity seeks to remedy past intentional discrimination. This points up the need for fair housing attorneys to continue to litigate cases involving systemic discrimination. Strong factual findings in such cases will provide the firmest foundation for the widest array of prointegration remedies.

A second important theme is that communities may take race into account in an effort to devise policies that will produce and maintain integrated communities. In fact, as *Shannon v. HUD* shows, local government agencies are actually susceptible to legal challenge if they do not consider the impact on racial integration of decisions such as where to locate a new public housing development.

A third theme is that programs that rely on strict racial quotas where the supply of housing is limited are the most suspect. This is the lesson of *United States v. Starrett City Associates* and *United States v. Charlottesville Redevelopment & Housing Authority*.

Fortunately, this is tempered by a fourth rule: As in *Schmidt v. Boston Housing Authority*, programs may rely extensively on race as long as they refrain from restricting the access that certain groups have to housing. Affirmative marketing programs are a prime example and provide an important opportunity to promote integration. These programs explicitly consider race on a regular basis, but as the court held in *South-Suburban Housing Center*, they do not discriminate against one race in favor of another. Mortgage incentive programs like the one in Shaker Heights are another example and should be upheld because their benefits are available to people of all races who want to participate in voluntary efforts to integrate their community.

Collectively, the tools available to advocates to promote the Fair Housing Act's goal of integrating neighborhoods, towns, and cities throughout the country are many and varied. Applied with a careful eye to the limits that some courts have imposed where integration and nondiscrimination could come into conflict, these tools hold great promise for helping to achieve both of these important goals.

Notes

1. *Havens Realty Corp. v. Coleman*, 455 U.S. 363, 380; *Linmark Assocs., Inc. v. Township of Willingboro*, 431 U.S. 85, 95 (1977).
2. Report of the National Advisory Commission on Civil Disorders 1, 13 (1968). Washington, DC: U.S. Government Printing Office.
3. 114 Cong. Rec. 2277 (1968).
4. Id. at 2526.
5. Lynette A. Rawlings, Laura E. Harris, and Margery A. Turner, *Race and Residence: Prospects for Stable Neighborhood Integration, Neighborhood Change in Urban America* (Urban Institute, 2004), p. 2, http://www.urban.org/UploadedPDF/310985_NCUA3.pdf (accessed March 25, 2009).
6. See Eric Schmitt, "Segregation Growing among U.S. Children," *New York Times*, May 6, 2001 (citing study performed by researchers at the State University of New York at Albany showing that segregated living patterns of children worsened significantly from 1990 to 2001 in many large Northeastern and Midwestern metropolitan areas).
7. *Starrett City Assocs.*, 840 F.2d at 1098-99. The decision does not discuss the remaining 6% of the development's population.
8. Id. at 1099, 1102.
9. *Parents Involved in Community Schools v. Seattle Sch. Dist. No. 1*, 127 S.Ct. 2738, 2752 (2007) ("PICS"); see also *Jaimes v. Lucas Metro. Hous. Auth.*, 833 F.2d 1203, 1207-08 (6th Cir. 1987) (citing *Hills v. Gautreaux*, 425 U.S. 284, 297 (1976); *Swann v. Charlotte-Mecklenburg Bd. of Educ.*, 402 U.S. 1, 16 (1971)). When a government program is challenged under the Constitution's Equal Protection Clause, the judicial test applied depends on the content of the program. The test is at its most difficult and known as "strict scrutiny" "when the government distributes burdens or benefits on the basis of individual racial classifications" (PICS, 127 S. Ct. 2751). In such cases, the program must be "narrowly tailored to achieve a compelling government interest." Id. at 2751 (internal citations omitted).
10. *Schmidt*, 505 F. Supp. at 991.
11. Id. at 991–92.
12. Id. at 993.
13. Id. at 995.
14. Id. (internal citations omitted).
15. Id. at 996–97.
16. *Jaimes*, 833 F.2d at 1205.
17. Id. at 1206.
18. Id. at 1207.
19. Id. at 1208.

20. *Raso,* 135 F.3d at 13.
21. Id. at 14.
22. Id.
23. Id. at 16.
24. See, e.g., *Schmidt,* 505 F. Supp. at 995; *Raso,* 135 F.3d at 16.
25. See *Jaimes,* 833 F.2d at 1207.
26. *Shannon,* 436 F.2d at 820-21.
27. *NAACP,* 817 F2d at 154-55l accord *Davis v. N.Y.C. Hous. Auth.,* 278 F.3d 64, 83-88 (2d Cir. 2002) (holding that working family preference that significantly slows integration violates the Fair Housing Act).
28. *Otero,* 484 F.2d at 1133.
29. Id. at 1134; see also *Daubner v. Harris,* 514 F. Supp. 856, 868 (S.D.N.Y. 1981) (upholding priority for performing artists in subsidized housing that would have resulted in white-minority ratio proportional to the population of the area, and concluding that race is a legitimate consideration in establishing integrated tenancy).
30. Id. at 1136.
31. Title VII prohibits employment discrimination, while Title VIII is the Fair Housing Act.
32. *Starrett City Assocs.,* 840 F.2d at 1101-02.
33. Id. at 1103.
34. *Charlottesville Redevelopment & Housing Auth.,* 718 F. Supp. at 462.
35. Id. at 467.
36. Id. at 468.
37. Id. at 468-69.
38. *Burney,* 551 F. Supp. at 749.
39. Id. at 750.
40. Id. at 770.
41. 24 C.F.R. § 200.610.
42. Id. § 200.620(a).
43. Id. § 108.20(b).
44. See generally *Almonte v. Pierce,* 666 F. Supp. 517, 520-22 (S.D.N.Y. 1987) (discussing HUD regulations and handbook regarding affirmative fair housing marketing plans).
45. *Fair Housing Planning Guide,* Vol. 1, at 2–16, http://www.hud.gov/offices/fheo/images/fhpg.pdf (accessed March 23, 2009).
46. *Steptoe,* 674 F. Supp. at 1315.
47. Id. at 1319.
48. Id. at 1319-20.
49. Id. at 1320.
50. *South-Suburban Housing Ctr.,* 935 F.2d at 873.
51. Id. at 883.
52. Id.
53. Id. at 884.
54. Id.
55. Id. at 886.
56. One way around this problem might be to expand the geographic scope of the program to include several towns or counties.

CHAPTER 5

Achieving Integration Through Private Litigation

MICHAEL P. SENG AND F. WILLIS CARUSO

Private litigation has always been an important enforcement mechanism under the Fair Housing Act. Under the original Fair Housing Act, Title VIII of the Civil Rights Act of 1968,[1] the Justice Department was authorized to bring "pattern and practice" cases,[2] and the Department of Housing and Urban Development (HUD) could correct discriminatory housing practices by "informal methods of conference, conciliation, and persuasion."[3] But the central enforcement mechanism was through private suits in the federal and state courts.[4] In *Trafficante v. Metropolitan Life Insurance Co.* (1972, 211), Justice Douglas commented that:

> Since HUD has no enforcement powers and since the enormity of the task of assuring fair housing makes the role of the Attorney General in the matter minimal, the main generating force must be private suits in which, the Solicitor General says, the complainants act not only on their own behalf but also "as private attorneys general in vindicating a policy that Congress considered to be of the highest priority."

Most of the private suits brought under the 1968 Fair Housing Act were for declarative or injunctive relief, and damage awards were low. Punitive damages were limited to $1,000.[5] The Act provided for attorney fees to successful plaintiffs, but only if the court found that the plaintiff was financially unable to assume the attorney fees.[6] A study by Professor Robert Schwemm

53

(1981) found that damage awards in fair housing cases ranged from $1 to $20,000, and most of the awards were at the low end of the spectrum. The Justice Department brought some successful "pattern and practice" actions under the 1968 Act, but most of these actions were against public housing authorities that discriminated in their admission policies or municipalities that tried to keep minorities out of their communities through restrictive land use regulations.[7]

Congress expanded the enforcement mechanisms in the Fair Housing Amendments Act of 1988[8] and provided what are perhaps the broadest remedies in any of the civil rights laws. In introducing the Amendments, Senator Edward Kennedy explained the need for vigorous enforcement:

> ...[T]he Fair Housing Act we passed in 1968 has proved to be an empty promise because the legislation lacked an effective enforcement mechanism. For two decades, fair housing has been a right, without a remedy.... Housing discrimination exists in America today, and it exists in epidemic proportions.... In some respects, housing discrimination is the most invidious form of bigotry. It isolates racial and ethnic minorities and perpetuates the ignorance that is the core of bigotry. And discrimination in housing hampers progress to achieve equality in other vital areas as well.... The existing fair housing law is a toothless tiger. It recognizes a fundamental right; but it fails to provide a meaningful remedy.[9]

The 1988 Act continued to encourage private litigation.[10] It removed the caps on punitive damages[11] and provided that attorney fees must be awarded to successful plaintiffs, regardless of their financial status.[12] But Congress went further. The Act was amended to provide a whole new administrative enforcement mechanism. Aggrieved parties can file complaints at HUD, which is required to investigate and attempt conciliation.[13] If HUD finds that the complaint is supported by "reasonable cause," HUD must file an enforcement action before an administrative law judge (ALJ).[14] In addition to awarding injunctive and declarative relief, the ALJ can award compensatory damages to the aggrieved party and civil penalties to the United States.[15] The only remedy an ALJ cannot award is punitive damages to the aggrieved party. HUD counsel prosecutes the case before the ALJ, but private attorneys are allowed to intervene on behalf of the aggrieved party.[16] If one of the parties elects to have the matter heard in federal court, the Department of Justice files and prosecutes the case.[17] The aggrieved party can recover full relief, including punitive damages, and a private attorney can intervene on the aggrieved party's behalf.[18]

In theory, the administrative process was designed to be faster and more efficient than the private litigation route and, because the government prosecutes the case instead of the aggrieved party, much less costly. Aggrieved parties still have the option of going directly into court if that is what they desire and, unlike in employment discrimination cases under Title VII of the Civil Rights Act of 1964,[19] they are not required to exhaust their administrative remedies.

No other federal civil rights statute provides such a comprehensive remedial scheme, and one could reasonably have expected that finally, under the 1988 Fair Housing Amendments Act, the original goal of the 1968 Act—"to replace the ghettos 'by truly integrated and balanced living patterns'"[20]—would be achieved. To date, this goal has not been achieved, and one would have to be an eternal optimist to believe that without a new commitment at all levels, the goal of the Act will be achieved any time in the immediate future.

America remains segregated (Carr and Kutty 2008). Indeed, today America may be even closer to what the Kerner Commission feared was a movement toward two separate societies where most Americans live in segregated and often unstable housing communities.[21]

Why hasn't there been more progress? We appear to have the remedies, but the situation on enforcement is much the same as Senator Kennedy described when he introduced the 1988 Fair Housing Amendments Act.[22]

The U.S. Department of Justice has brought many successful fair housing "pattern and practice" cases.[23] However, the resources of this moderately sized public law firm will never be sufficient to handle the volume of fair housing complaints nationwide.

Similarly, the HUD administrative process has never been truly successful despite the efforts of different Administrations to move the investigative process forward in a timely and effective manner. HUD ALJs have decided some truly landmark cases. But even in the good years, the number of cases decided by the HUD ALJs was small, and in the past several years, the number has almost completely dried up. This chapter will not dissect the administrative process to determine whether the problem rests with HUD, which continues to fail to charge a high volume of significant fair housing cases, with the ALJs themselves, or with the parties and their counsel, who more and more elect to go to court rather than take the more expedited route through an administrative hearing.[24]

In any event, these are not concerns that will be addressed in this chapter. The focal point of fair housing enforcement has always been private litigation. As the recent enforcement record demonstrates, private litigation continues to be the primary enforcement mechanism, the same as it was 40 years ago.

The Structural Lawsuit

An often unheralded contribution of *Brown v. Board of Education* (1954), *Baker v. Carr* (1962), and similar civil rights cases in the 1950s and 1960s was the introduction into American jurisprudence of the structural lawsuit and the civil rights injunction (Chayes 1976; Fiss 1978, 1979). The structural lawsuit utilized injunctions to reform institutions so that they would not discriminate or otherwise violate civil rights in the future. The focus was thus on prospective relief and not on retroactive relief in the nature of damages.

While sometimes debunked by critics of so-called judicial activism today, the structural lawsuit played a substantial role in demolishing the Jim Crow system of segregation that existed in the South into the 1970s. The structural lawsuit recognized broad standing by aggrieved persons, often acting as private attorneys general, to address basic malfunctions in our government and society. Courts retained jurisdiction during the period of transition in order to ensure flexibility in shaping the proper remedy. The focus was not on collecting large damage awards, as in the traditional personal injury action, but on implementing the public interest, as reflected by our Constitutional values (Fiss 1979, 9).

An excellent example of the use of structural lawsuits was Cairo, Illinois in the 1960s and 1970s. Nearly every public official in this town of approximately 6,000 residents was a defendant in at least one civil rights action. Lawsuits were brought against the police to protect the right to demonstrate; against the school district to integrate the schools; against the city and county to employ African-American workers; against City and County officials to appoint African Americans to boards and commissions; against election officials to dismantle the City's commission form of government; against the public housing authority to desegregate public housing; and against the County prosecutor and local judges to ensure equal justice in criminal proceedings.[25] Each of these lawsuits resulted in a successful judgment or consent decree, except the suit against the prosecutor and judges (*O'Shea v. Littleton* 1972).[26]

Not surprisingly, the Fair Housing Act has provided a solid statutory basis to bring structural lawsuits. The Act provides broad standing and remedies. That the Fair Housing Act could be enforced by private attorneys general was articulated in the very first U.S. Supreme Court decision interpreting the Fair Housing Act. In *Trafficante v. Metropolitan Life Insurance Co.* (1972), the Supreme Court held that a white resident of a racially segregated apartment building can sue on behalf of African-American applicants. Later, in *Gladstone Realtors v. Village of Bellwood* (1979), the Supreme Court upheld the standing of municipalities to sue real estate brokers who are engaged in steering activities that injure the municipality; and in *Havens Realty Corp. v. Coleman* (1979), the Supreme Court upheld the standing of private fair housing organizations and testers who are injured by the racial steering practices of a real estate agency.

The U.S. Courts of Appeal have further facilitated the use of the structural lawsuit by ruling, in accordance with the jurisprudence in employment cases under Title VII of the 1964 Civil Rights Act (*Griggs v. Duke Power Co.* 1971), that a violation of the Fair Housing Act can be established by showing that a housing provider's policy or practice has a disparate impact on a protected class (*Huntington Branch, NAACP v. Town of Huntington* 1988:935; *Metropolitan Housing Development Corp., v. Village of Arlington Heights* 1977, 1288–89). The disparate impact approach dispenses with the requirement that complainants meet the Constitutional standard of showing that the defendant's action was "purposeful" (*Washington v. Davis* 1976; *Village of Arlington Heights v. Metropolitan Housing Development Corp.* 1977).

Racial discrimination suits brought against the City of Black Jack, Missouri to enjoin its ordinance forbidding the construction of multifamily housing within the city (*United States v. City of Black Jack* 1974) and against Arlington Heights, Illinois to enjoin its denial of a variance to its zoning ordinance to permit the construction of multifamily dwellings (*Metropolitan Housing Development Corp., v. Village of Arlington Heights* 1977) are examples of successful structural lawsuits. Suits against the Chicago Housing Authority to prevent the construction of public housing in segregated neighborhoods and requiring the dispersal of public housing throughout that city (*Gautreaux v. Chicago Housing Authority* 1982) and against the City of Yonkers, New York to desegregate public housing as well as that city's public schools (*United States v. Yonkers Board of Education* 1986) are excellent examples of the structural lawsuit being used to dismantle segregated neighborhood patterns.[27]

Cases continue to be brought seeking prospective relief, but damages for past violations are often central to the litigation. Examples are the fair lending cases brought by the U.S. Department of Justice to force lending institutions to make loans equally in African-American as in white neighborhoods (*United States v. Chevy Chase* 1994; *United States v. Decatur Federal* 1992) and the suits brought against major property insurers that had redlined minority neighborhoods and refused to insure properties there, without any cost or risk justification (*NAACP v. American Family Insurance Co.* 1992; *Nationwide Mutual Insurance Co. v. Cisneros* 1995). Most recently, the City of Baltimore has filed a lawsuit against the Wells Fargo Banking Corporation, which is accused of redlining minority neighborhoods in the city and selling high-cost loans without any cost justification. The City alleges injury because of the many defaults and foreclosures and the loss of a solid tax base due to the defendant's discriminatory predatory lending practices (*Mayor and City Council of Baltimore v. Wells Fargo Bank, N.A.* 2008). In July 2008, a federal jury awarded $11 million to 67 African-American plaintiffs against a county and its water authority that for over 50 years refused to provide them with public water service because plaintiffs lived in a predominantly African-American neighborhood within a virtually all-white county (*Kennedy v. City of Zanesville, Ohio* 2008).

These and other structural lawsuits based on the Fair Housing Act have resulted in substantial integration initiatives. Why then hasn't the structural lawsuit been more successful in achieving integration nationwide? One reason may be that not enough fair housing actions have been filed nationwide. Also, most housing discrimination in the United States occurs by individual housing providers and "alternative governance" organizations such as condominium boards and homeowners' associations, and is thus difficult to remedy in a single structural lawsuit.

Another reason may be that a more conservative judiciary has made it difficult to prosecute a structural lawsuit. In *O'Shea v. Littleton* (1972), the Supreme Court warned that federal judges should not anticipate that a plaintiff will be injured and should not issue an injunction until it is shown that other remedies have been exhausted or are not available.

The Supreme Court has similarly emphasized in a number of school desegregation decisions that the plaintiff has the burden of showing that the injury has been caused by the defendant (*Allen v. Wright* 1984) and that the remedy is narrowly tailored to remedy that particular violation (*Millilken v. Bradley* 1974, 744; *Missouri v. Jenkins* 1995, 88). Thus, it becomes more and more difficult to convince a court that there is a nexus between individual acts of discrimination and discrimination in the broader housing market. An example is Judge Richard Posner's ruminations about whether neighborhood segregation is the result of steering by real estate brokers or of the independent choices of individual home-seekers (*Village of Bellwood v. Dwivedi* 1990, 1529–33).

Most telling of how a court today is likely to dispose of a complicated structural lawsuit is the approach taken by the Supreme Court in *City of Cuyahoga Falls, Ohio v. Buckeye Community Hope Foundation* (2003). Buckeye made a request for a variance to construct interracial multifamily housing in an all-white community. The City delayed approval by resorting to a referendum. The project was ultimately built when the Ohio Supreme Court held that the referendum process violated Ohio law. But the delay was costly to the developer, and the lawsuit that ended up in the U.S. Supreme Court was primarily about the resulting damages from the delaying tactics. The Supreme Court held that resort to a referendum that was authorized at the time by Ohio law when the result was never implemented did not state a claim under the Fair Housing Act. The Court analyzed the claim with blinders on and ignored the basic question of whether the entire process was designed to thwart the developer's efforts to build integrated housing in a segregated community. What the decision illustrates is that today the courts will not scratch below the surface to find a civil rights violation.

Individual Actions for Injunctive Relief

Because the courts are unlikely to find a nexus between individual acts of discrimination and the larger structural defects in the housing market, fair housing advocates are left with the alternative of suing the individual landlord, seller, or broker[28] who came into immediate contact with the victim of a discriminatory housing practice. Under the 1968 Fair Housing Act, most individual lawsuits sought to secure the housing unit. Thus, temporary restraining orders and preliminary injunctions were regularly requested and granted by the courts. Once granted, many of these actions quickly settled.

The 1988 Fair Housing Amendments Act aimed to further expedite the process by allowing the government to obtain "prompt judicial action" even when the victim filed an administrative complaint.[29] However, the remedy is rarely used today.

Why are so few requests for temporary restraining orders made today? In some cases, victims may fear retaliation or be reluctant to locate where it is evident that they are not wanted—something Sheryll Cashin calls "integration exhaustion" (Cashin 2004, 9–28).[30] Even though the Fair Housing Act makes retaliation illegal,[31] individual renters or buyers may not want the hassle they associate with filing a complaint (Abravanel 2002, 497). Clearly, HUD has not made the seeking of prompt judicial action a priority in its education and outreach efforts. Furthermore, fair housing advocates may conclude that most judges today will be reluctant to grant preliminary relief without the benefit of a fully developed record. They may also conclude that if they are turned down for preliminary relief, the chances of settling the case with a substantial damage award to the victim are diminished.

Thus, for whatever reasons, securing prompt preliminary relief in fair housing actions has become rare, and there is no sign that this situation is likely to change in the immediate future.

Individual Actions for Damages

One of the major initiatives by fair housing advocates in recent years has been to increase the amount of damages awarded in fair housing cases. In a classic article written in 1992, HUD Administrative Law Judges Alan Heifetz and Thomas Heinz (1992) outlined the theories that can be used to establish a claim for damages. Out-of-pocket expenses may, in individual cases, when documented, be substantial. This is especially true when the loss of housing affects the victim's access to work or other tangible benefits.

Mental suffering and humiliation in fair housing cases are often severe and, if properly established, can be analogized to defamation or intentional infliction of mental distress awards. As Judge Heinz observed in *Secretary v. Gruzdates* (1998):

> Actual damages in housing discrimination cases may include damages for intangible injuries such as embarrassment, humiliation, and emotional distress caused by the discrimination. Damages for emotional distress may be based on inferences drawn from circumstances of the case, as well as on testimonial proof. Because emotional injuries are by nature qualitative and difficult to quantify, courts have awarded damages for emotional harm without requiring proof of the actual dollar value of the injury. The amount awarded should make the victim whole.
>
> Racial discrimination strikes at the heart of a person's identity. Race and skin color are immutable characteristics irrelevant to whether someone is qualified to buy or rent housing. As racial discrimination has been unlawful in this country for many years, it is reasonable to expect that a person of color would suffer deep frustration, anger, and humiliation upon experiencing discrimination during a search for housing.

Judges Heifetz and Heinz also suggested in their article that damages can be awarded for "lost housing opportunity" when the housing is unique to the aggrieved individual—for instance, because of its location near needed medical facilities, nearness to family members, or proximity to schools or work.

There are some large damage awards. For example, in *Broome v. Biondi* (1997), a court awarded a total of $1.5 million to an African-American couple denied housing by the board of a housing cooperative because of the couple's race. In *Phillips v. Hunter Trails* (1982), a court awarded $320,000 because of racial discrimination by a homeowners' association. In a recent case involving lost housing opportunity—*Secretary v. Fung and Ho* (2008)—HUD Administrative Law Judge Constance O'Bryant awarded $74,629 and a civil penalty of $11,000 based on the emotional distress and humiliation, loss of housing opportunity, and tangible losses and inconvenience caused to the victims in a racial discrimination suit.

Unfortunately, large damage awards in fair housing cases are still not commonplace and until they are, it is unlikely that the threat of litigation will be a substantial factor in deterring those who consider it in their interest to discriminate. Individual victims are reluctant to file charges and, even when they do, they are reluctant to testify in detail about the humiliation and pain that they have endured (Seng, Einhorn, and Brown 1992). Establishing and being awarded substantial damages in a fair housing action is still a crapshoot that most victims are unwilling to endure. Thus, while individual damage actions are important, they alone will not achieve the fair housing goal of "truly integrated and balanced living patterns."[32]

Can Fair Housing Litigation Achieve the Goal of Integration?

At present, the prospect of achieving an integrated society through litigation looks remote. In 1993, Massey and Denton (1993, 225—emphasis in original) observed: "Although Chicago's fair housing groups have pushed private enforcement to the legal limit, they have produced *essentially no change* in the degree of racial segregation within that urban area."

Litigation is useless unless a victim of housing discrimination is willing to step forward to demand equal treatment. However, as noted above, many victims are unwilling to do this.[33] Standing to sue in the federal courts under the Federal Fair Housing Act is already pushed as far as Article III of the Constitution permits. Therefore, it is unlikely that the definition of an "aggrieved person" could be expanded to allow more persons to file fair housing actions in the federal courts. However, standing could be completely eliminated at the administrative level (Seng 2008; *Gettman v. Drug Enforcement Administration* 2002; *Ritchie v. Simpson* 1999).[34] This would facilitate more complaints to HUD by fair housing organizations because they would be relieved of explaining how they or their members have suffered an injury. Such complaints could prompt investigations that provide information that is useful in private litigation.

Success in litigation ultimately depends upon the facts. The plaintiff must prove the truth of the allegations made in the complaint. This is always a difficult task. Setting up burden-shifting devices in disparate treatment cases similar to those used in cases where a policy or practice is alleged to have a disparate impact might facilitate some actions. For instance, if the housing provider has a disproportionate number of nonminority occupants when the housing is located in an area with a large minority concentration, this statistical imbalance could be used to shift the burden to the housing provider to explain the absence of minorities in this particular project.[35]

Similarly, presumed damages for humiliation and mental suffering could make it more attractive for plaintiffs to file fair housing complaints. They could recover without subjecting themselves to extensive psychological questioning. The law could then allow the plaintiff to prove additional damage in cases involving exceptional injury. Damages are set in workman's compensation actions. Whether a court would uphold them in the civil rights context against a due process challenge is unknown.

Another encouragement to bring a lawsuit could come from allowing civil penalties awarded in fair housing actions to go to the complainant rather than to the public treasury. While civil penalties are not a large amount, they would provide an incentive to complainants to bring fair housing actions, especially when out-of-pocket damages are not extensive.

These legislative changes, while they might be helpful, would still probably not result in enough lawsuits to transition us to a truly integrated living environment. The causes of segregation are systemic and rooted in the relationship between housing and the other inequalities in American society. These are problems that are especially difficult to attack in the traditional private lawsuit.

The Fair Housing Act does have a unique provision that has only rarely figured into private litigation—the affirmative duty of federal officials to further fair housing.[36] However, the provision does not contain a private right of action (*NAACP v. Secretary of HUD* 1987).[37] Federal officials can be sued only under the Administrative Procedure Act[38] for administrative review (*NAACP v. Secretary of HUD* 1987). Such suits have been successful when federal funding decisions promote existing segregated neighborhood patterns (*Darst-Webb Tenant Ass'n Board v. St. Louis Housing Authority* 2003; *Dean v. Martinez* 2004; *King v. Harris* 1979; *Otero v. New York Housing Authority* 1972; *Thompson v. HUD* 2005).[39]

Congress could put more teeth into the affirmative duty to further fair housing by providing expressly for enforcement of the duty through a private right of action. Actions for administrative review provide only limited remedies, and these remedies could be expanded through a private right of action.

Congress could further rely on Section 5 of the Fourteenth Amendment to expand the "affirmative duty" provision to apply to all state action affecting housing. The Supreme Court has recognized that Congress' powers are at their zenith under Section 5 when it seeks to eliminate racial discrimination (*Board of Trustees of the University of Alabama v. Garrett* 2001, 373; *City of Boerne v. Flores* 1997, 526).

Congress could also require private housing providers and "alternative governance" organizations like condominium boards and homeowners' associations to affirmatively further fair housing.[40] In *Jones v. Alfred E. Mayer* (1968), the Supreme Court recognized that Congress can regulate racial discrimination by private housing providers because dismantling our nation's racial ghettoes is justified under Congress' power to eliminate the badges and incidents of slavery under section 2 of the Thirteenth Amendment. Congress could direct that HUD exercise its rule-making powers to promulgate guidelines for private housing providers on how to comply with this affirmative duty.

Imposing an affirmative duty to further fair housing is not in conflict with the United States Supreme Court's decisions on affirmative action (*Adarand Constructors, Inc. v. Pena* 1995; *City of Richmond v. J.A. Croson Company*

1989; *Grutter v. Bollinger* 2003). The affirmative action remedy that triggers strict scrutiny under the Fourteenth Amendment operates to exclude persons because of their race or color. Affirmative marketing efforts do not operate to exclude anyone and are fully consistent with Equal Protection requirements (*South Suburban Housing Center v. Greater South Suburban Board of Realtors* 1992). Furthermore, by emphasizing that the roots of housing discrimination go back to slavery, Congress will be returning to the core reason behind the adoption of the post-Civil War amendments and the majestic power that those amendments gave to Congress. The advantage of stressing an affirmative duty to further fair housing is that it takes a lot of the burden off the home-seeker and places it where it belongs—on the housing provider and on policymakers who have created the dual housing market we have today.

Conclusion

The dual housing market we have today did not just happen. It is the result of deliberate policy choices by government officials and those in the private market (Carr and Kutty 2008; Cashin 2004, 101–23; Hirsch 1998; Massey and Denton 1993). The problem with fair housing litigation as it has existed for the past four decades is that it places the burden to dismantle the dual market on the individual housing seeker. Thus, to end segregated housing patterns requires large numbers of victims who are willing to spend the time, shoulder the cost, and risk retaliation to file individual lawsuits. This makes little economic sense and is unrealistic.

Congress got it right when it placed an affirmative duty on government officials to further fair housing. But Congress should go further in allocating this duty and in providing a private right of action for victims of housing discrimination to enforce this duty. An affirmative duty without the threat of a civil lawsuit is worthless. Congress should also expand the right to administrative standing, adjust the concept of a prima facie case in disparate treatment claims, and provide presumed damages and civil penalties to successful litigants. Private litigation continues to be at the heart of fair housing enforcement. We will not move to a color-blind society with "truly integrated and balanced living patterns" without successful private enforcement initiatives.

Notes

1. Pub. L. No. 90-284, title VIII, April 11, 1968, §§ 801–819, 82 Stat. 81 codified at 42 U.S.C. §§ 3601–3619.
2. Section 813(a).
3. Section 810(a).
4. Section 812(a).
5. Section 812(c).

6. Section 812(c).
7. A good example is *United States v. City of Black Jack*, 508 F.2d 1179 (8th Cir. 1974, *cert. denied*, 422 U.S. 1042 (1975), where the court found that the City had engaged in racial discrimination by passing a zoning ordinance preventing multifamily dwellings in the municipality.
8. Pub. L. No. 100-430, Sept. 13, 1988, 102 Stat. 1619 (1988), codified at 42 U.S.C. §§ 3601–3619.
9. Cong. Rec., page 19711 (Aug. 1, 1988).
10. 42 U.S.C. § 3613(a).
11. 42 U.S.C. § 3613(c).
12. 42 U.S.C. § 3613(d).
13. 42 U.S.C. § 3610(a)(B) and (b).
14. 42 U.S.C. § 3612(b).
15. 42 U.S.C. § 3612(g)(3).
16. 42 U.S.C. § 3612(c).
17. 42 U.S.C. § 3612(o).
18. 42 U.S.C. § 3614(e).
19. 42 U.S.C. § 2000e.
20. Remarks of Senator Walter Mondale, 114 Cong. Rec. 3422, quoted in *Trafficante v. Metropolitan Life Insurance Co.*, 409 U.S. 205, 211 (1972).
21. The Fair Housing Act was passed shortly after the Kerner Commission declared that America was "moving toward two societies, one black, one white—separate and unequal." *Report of the National Advisory Commission on Civil Disorders* (1968, 1).
22. Cong. Rec., page 19711 (Aug. 1, 1988).
23. Most prominent in recent years have been the Department's equal lending suits in the 1990s, e.g., *United States v. Decatur Federal*, Fair Housing/Fair Lending Reporter ¶ 19,377 (N.D.Ga. 1992) (Consent Decree); *United States v. Chevy Chase*, Fair Housing/Fair Lending Reporter ¶ 19,385 (D.D.C. 1994) (Consent Decree), and the more recent suits to enforce the accessibility provisions of the Fair Housing Act, e.g., *United States v. Edward Rose & Sons*, Civil No. 02 CV 73518 (E.D.Mich. 2007), *United States v. Tanski*, Civil No. 04-CV-714 (N.D.N.Y. 2008) (Consent Decree), and against sexual harassment. E.g., *United States v. Calvert*, Civil No. 06-0655-CV-W-DW (W.D.Mo. 2008) (Consent Decree); *United States v. James*, Civil No. 5:06 CV 06044 DW (W.D. Mo. 2008) (Consent Decree).
24. Indeed, it is interesting to speculate why defendants continually risk the imposition of punitive damages by electing to go to court rather than electing to be heard by an ALJ.
25. These lawsuits are described in Michael P Seng, "The Cairo Experience: Civil Rights Litigation in a Racial Powder Keg," 61 *University of Oregon Law Review* 285 (1982); reprinted at http://www.jmls.edu/fairhousingcenter/commentary.shtml.
26. In dismissing the lawsuit, the Supreme Court relied on newly formulated principles of ripeness and principles of equity.
27. At the state level, the best example of the structural lawsuit are the Mount Laurel decisions in New Jersey—e.g., *South Burlington County NAACP v. Township of Mount Laurel*, 67 N.J. 151, 336 A.2d 713 (1975); 92 N.J.158, 456 A.2d 390 (1983).
28. See *Mayer v. Holley*, 537 U.S. 280 (2003), where the Supreme Court held that the general principles of agency law control whether employers or principals are liable in an action filed under the Fair Housing Act.
29. 42 U.S.C. § 3610(e).
30. Seniors especially fear retaliation if they complain about discrimination. *Findings and Conclusions: Senior Housing Research Project* (The John Marshall Law School Fair Housing Legal Support Center 2008), 178–81. Report is available at http://www.jmls.edu/fairhousingcenter/commentary.shtml.
31. 42 U.S.C. § 3617.
32. Remarks of Senator Walter Mondale, 114 Cong. Rec. 3422, quoted in *Trafficante v. Metropolitan Life Insurance Co.*, 409 U.S. 205, 211 (1972).
33. An exception is the case where a person with disabilities claims a denial of a reasonable accommodation. One reason why we are seeing more of these cases may be because this type of case turns not on proving unequal treatment but rather on whether the accommodation is necessary and not burdensome on the housing provider. *Wisconsin Community Services, Inc. v. City of Milwaukee*, 465 F.3d 737 (7th Cir. 2006). This resolution was largely based on a cost-benefit analysis.

34. Seng, "Standing to Complain in Fair Housing Administrative Investigations, Fair Housing Commentary" (2008) http://www.jmls.edu/fairhousingcenter/commentary.shtml.
35. Such an approach would, for instance, have changed the result in *Simms v. First Gibraltar Bank*, 83 F.3d 1546 (5th Cir.), *cert. denied*, 519 U.S. 1041 (1996).
36. 42 U.S.C. § 3608(d). In addition to applying to HUD, this provision applies to every other federal agency that administers housing programs, including the Department of Defense, the Department of Agriculture, the Department of the Interior, the Federal Reserve, the Federal Trade Commission, the Internal Revenue Service, and the Department of the Treasury. *Jorman v. Veterans Administration*, 579 F. Supp. 1407 (N.D.Ill. 1984).
37. But see *Young v. Pierce*, 544 F. Supp. 1010 (E.D. Tex. 1982).
38. 5 U.S.C. § 702.
39. And see *United States ex rel. Anti-Discrimination Center of Metro New York, Inc. v. Westchester County*, 495 F. Supp.2d 375 (S.D.N.Y. 2007). The cause of action is based on a violation of the False Claims Act. The suit alleges that the County falsely certified that it had complied with the affirmative duty to further fair housing when applying for federal funds.
40. Congress might decide to narrow the requirements to only those housing providers that are of sufficient size to warrant imposing this expanded obligation, such as it has done in enforcing the accessibility requirements for new multifamily housing. 42 U.S.C. § 3604(f)(3)(C).

References

Abravanel, Martin D. 2002. "Public Knowledge of Fair Housing Law: Does It Protect against Housing Discrimination?" *Housing Policy Debate* 13: 469.
Adarand Constructors, Inc. v. Peña, 515 U.S. 200 (1995).
Allen v. Wright, 468 U.S. 737 (1984).
Baker v. Carr, 369 U.S. 186 (1962).
Board of Trustees of the University of Alabama v. Garrett, 531 U.S. 356 (2001).
Broome v. Biondi, Fair Housing/Fair Lending Reporter ¶ 16,240 (S.D.N.Y. 1997).
Brown v. Board of Education, 349 U.S. 294 (1955).
Carr, James H., and Nandinee K. Kutty. 2008. *Segregation: The Rising Costs for American Cities*. New York: Routledge.
Cashin, Sheryll. 2004. *The Failure of Integration: How Race and Class Are Undermining the American Dream*. New York: Public Affairs.
Chayes, Abram. 1976. "The Role of the Judge in Public Law Litigation." *Harvard Law Review* 89: 1281.
City of Boerne v. Flores, 521 U.S. 507 (1997).
City of Cuyahoga Falls, Ohio v. Buckeye Community Hope Foundation, 538 U.S. 188 (2003).
City of Richmond v. J.A. Croson Company, 488 U.S. 469 (1989).
Darst-Webb Tenant Ass'n Board v. St. Louis Housing Authority, 339 F.3d 702 (8th Cir. 2003).
Dean v. Martinez, 336 F. Supp.2d 477 (D. Md. 2004).
Fiss, Owen M. 1978. *The Civil Rights Injunction*. Bloomington: Indiana University Press.
———. 1979. "The Supreme Court 1978 Term, Foreword—The Forms of Justice." *Harvard Law Review* 93: 1.
Gautreaux v. Chicago Housing Authority, 690 F.2d 601 (7th Cir. 1982).
Gettman v. Drug Enforcement Administration, 290 F.3d 430 (D.C.Cir. 2002).
Gladstone Realtors v. Village of Bellwood, 441 U.S. 91 (1979).
Griggs v. Duke Power Co., 401 U.S. 424 (1971).
Grutter v. Bollinger, 539 U.S. 306 (2003).
Havens Realty Corp. v. Coleman, 455 U.S. 363 (1982).
Heifetz, Alan W., and Thomas C. Heinz. 1992. "Separating the Objective, the Subjective, and the Speculative: Assessing Compensatory Damages in Fair Housing Adjudications." *The John Marshall Law School Review* 26:3; reprinted at http://www.jmls.edu/fairhousingcenter/commentary.shtml (accessed September 19, 2008).
Hirsch, Arnold R. 1998. *Making the Second Ghetto—Race and Housing in Chicago 1949–1960*. Chicago: University of Chicago Press.
Huntington Branch, NAACP v. Town of Huntington, 844 F.2d 926 (2d Cir.), *aff'd, per curiam*, 488 U.S. 15 (1988).

Jones v. Alfred E. Mayer, 392 U.S. 409 (1968).

Kennedy v. City of Zanesville, Ohio, Civil No. 2:03-CV-01047 (S.D. Ohio 2008); http://www.relmanlaw.com (accessed September 19, 2008).

King v. Harris, 464 F. Supp. 827 (E.D.N.Y. 1979).

Massey, Douglas S., and Nancy A. Denton. 1993. *American Apartheid: Segregation and the Making of the Underclass*. Cambridge, MA: Harvard University Press.

Mayor and City Council of Baltimore v. Wells Fargo Bank, N.A., Case No. LO8 CV 062 (U.S. Dist. Md.) (Complaint filed on January 8, 2008).

Metropolitan Housing Development Corp., v. Village of Arlington Heights, 558 F.2d 1283 (7th Cir. 1977), *cert. denied*, 434 U.S. 1025 (1978).

Millilken v. Bradley, 418 U.S. 717 (1974).

Missouri v. Jenkins, 515 U.S. 70 (1995).

NAACP v. American Family Insurance Co., 978 F.2d 287 (7th Cir. 1992), *cert. denied*, 508 U.S. 907 (1993).

NAACP v. Secretary of HUD, 817 F.2d 149 (1st Cir. 1987).

Nationwide Mutual Insurance Co. v. Cisneros, 52 F.3d 1351 (6th Cir. 1995), *cert. denied*, 516 U.S. 1140 (1996).

O'Shea v. Littleton, 414 U.S. 488 (1974).

Otero v. New York Housing Authority, 484 F.2d 1122 (2d Cir. 1972).

Phillips v. Hunter Trails, 685 F.2d 184 (7th Cir. 1982).

Ritchie v. Simpson, 170 F.3d 1092 (Fed. Cir. 1999).

Schwemm, Robert. 1981. "Compensatory Damages in Fair Housing Cases." *Harvard Civil Rights/Civil Liberties Law Review* 16: 83.

Secretary v. Fung and Ho, 2008 WL 366380 (HUD ALJ 2008).

Secretary v. Gruzdates, Fair Housing/Fair Lending Reporter ¶ 25,137 (HUD ALJ 1998).

Seng, Michael P., Jay Einhorn, and Merilyn D. Brown. 1992. "Counseling a Victim of Racial Discrimination in a Fair Housing Case." *The John Marshall Law School Review* 26: 53; reprinted at http://www.jmls.edu/fairhousingcenter/commentary.shtml (accessed September 19, 2008).

Seng, Michael P. "Standing to complain in fair housing administrative investigations," The John Marshall Law School Fair & Affordable Housing Commentary (2008). http://www.JMLS.edu/fairhousingcenter/commentary.shtml (accessed April 20, 2009).

South Suburban Housing Center v. Greater South Suburban Board of Realtors, 935 F.2d 868 (7th Cir. 1992).

Thompson v. HUD, 348 F. Supp. 2d 398 (D.Md. 2005).

Trafficante v. Metropolitan Life Insurance Co., 409 U.S. 205 (1972).

United States v. Chevy Chase, Fair Housing/Fair Lending Reporter ¶ 19,385 (D.D.C. 1994) (Consent Decree).

United States v. City of Black Jack, 508 F.2d 1179 (8th Cir. 1974).

United States v. Decatur Federal, Fair Housing/Fair Lending Reporter ¶ 19,377 (N.D.Ga. 1992) (Consent Decree).

United States v. Yonkers Board of Education, 635 F. Supp. 1577 (S.D.N.Y. 1986), 837 F.2d 1181 (2d Cir. 1987), *cert. denied*, 486 U.S. 1055 (1988).

Village of Arlington Heights v. Metropolitan Housing Development Corp., 429 U.S. 252 (1977).

Village of Bellwood v. Dwivedi, 895 F.2d 1521 (7th Cir. 1990).

Washington v. Davis, 426 U.S. 229 (1976).

CHAPTER 6

Constitutional and Statutory Mandates for Residential Racial Integration and the Validity of Race-Conscious, Affirmative Action to Achieve It

FLORENCE WAGMAN ROISMAN

Recent decisions of the United States Supreme Court have narrowed the circumstances in which government agencies may take race-conscious action to promote racial integration in education, government contracting, and voting. (*Adarand* 1995; *Bush* 1996; *Gratz* 2003; *Grutter* 2003; *Miller* 1995; *Parents Involved* 2007; *Shaw* 1993). The effect of these decisions on housing integration is not clear. In 1976, in *Hills v. Gautreaux*, the U.S. Supreme Court authorized the development of a race-conscious remedy that would enable Black public housing residents to move from Chicago to the suburbs (*Gautreaux* 1976). In 1999, however, the Fifth Circuit Court of Appeals questioned the continuing authority of *Gautreaux* and invalidated a race-conscious remedy to redress past housing segregation (*Walker* 1999).

Those Supreme Court decisions and *Walker* do not doom race-conscious action to promote residential racial integration (*Adarand* 1995, 237; Tegeler 2009); indeed, in *Walker*, the Fifth Circuit endorsed some race-conscious remedies. There is, moreover, a strong case to be made that courts and other government agencies have especially wide authority to order or implement affirmative, race-conscious actions to promote racial integration in housing. This argument relies both on federal statutes that require "affirmative" action to achieve integration and the fact that those statutes are authorized by the Thirteenth Amendment.

Race-Conscious Remedies in General

Race-conscious actions by government agencies have been the subject of many fascinating—and not obviously consistent—judicial rulings. In *Hirabayashi v. United States,* in 1943, the Supreme Court said that "[d]istinctions between citizens solely because of their ancestry are by their very nature odious to a free people whose institutions are founded upon the doctrine of equality," and that "racial discriminations are in most circumstances irrelevant and therefore prohibited" (*Hirabayashi* 1943, 100). Nonetheless, the Court in *Hirabayashi* upheld a curfew applicable only to persons of Japanese ancestry. In 1944, in *Korematsu v. United States,* the Supreme Court said that "all legal restrictions which curtail the civil rights of a single racial group are immediately suspect" and "courts must subject them to the most rigid scrutiny," but upheld the exclusion of U.S. citizens of Japanese descent from the areas in which they lived (*Korematsu* 1944, 216). Shifting its inclination, in 1954, the Court held that confining Blacks to separate public schools violated both the Equal Protection Clause of the Fourteenth Amendment and the Fifth Amendment, which has no equal protection clause (*Bolling* 1954; *Brown* 1954). As courts undid the system of de jure racial segregation imposed by many government agencies, they established that racial classifications were subject to "strict scrutiny" and would be upheld only when necessary to serve a "compelling government interest" and "narrowly tailored" to do so (*Parents Involved* 2007, 11–12). Very much as a matter of course, courts often ordered race-conscious remedies in these cases (*Parents Involved* 2007, 13–14, Kennedy, J. concurring in part).

In the 1960s, some government agencies instituted voluntary, affirmative, race-conscious programs to undo past racial discrimination and segregation (Farber and Frickey 1991, 712–13; Graham 1990, 278–345). In the late 1970s, the Supreme Court, becoming less friendly to civil rights claims, held that the restrictions on race-conscious actions applied to benign as well as malevolent programs, to remedies as well as evils, to "affirmative action" as well as efforts to oppress minorities (*Adarand* 1995, 227; *Bakke* 1978; *Croson* 1989; *Johnson* 2005, 505; *Parents Involved* 2007, 34–35, plurality opinion). The Supreme Court also held that remediating general societal discrimination was not a compelling government interest (*Croson* 1989, 498–99; *Parents Involved* 2007, 23, plurality opinion; *Shaw* 1996, 909–10).

It became increasingly difficult for affirmative, race-conscious actions to survive judicial scrutiny. In 1993, 1995, and 1996, the Supreme Court invalidated race-conscious redistricting plans (*Bush* 1996; *Miller* 1995; *Shaw*

1993). In 2003, the Supreme Court struck down race-conscious admission policies of the University of Michigan's undergraduate college, but—by a vote of 5 to 4—upheld race-conscious admission policies of the University's law school (*Gratz* 2003; *Grutter* 2003). In 2007, after the retirement of Justice Sandra O'Connor, who had been the swing vote in the Michigan cases, and her replacement by the more conservative Justice Samuel Alito, the Court, by a 5 to 4 vote, invalidated the voluntary, race-conscious pupil assignment plans of the Louisville and Seattle school boards (*Parents Involved* 2007).

These recent cases challenging race-conscious actions were brought by white people who argued that they had been deprived of their rights under the Equal Protection Clause of the Fourteenth Amendment or the equal protection guarantees that the Court had found in the Fifth Amendment. In all of these cases, the issue was whether the lower courts or other government agencies had established that the racial classifications were necessary and narrowly tailored to serve a compelling government interest.

Affirmative, Race-Conscious Actions to Promote Housing Integration

While there has been far less litigation against housing segregation than against school segregation, courts frequently have ordered race-conscious remedies for housing segregation. In the seminal public housing desegregation litigation, *Gautreaux v. Chicago Housing Authority and HUD*, the district court and court of appeals ordered a series of race-conscious remedies, including interdistrict relief that extended to the suburbs of Chicago. By the time the issue of interdistrict remedy reached the Supreme Court, the Court had taken its conservative turn, and had held that school desegregation remedies in city school cases could not reach into the suburbs (Chemerinsky 2003, 1607; *Milliken* 1974, 757). Nonetheless, the Supreme Court held in *Gautreaux* that a race-conscious, interdistrict remedy was appropriate in the housing context.

Race-conscious remedies for segregation were not favored by the Reagan and Bush I Administrations (Briggs 2003). During the Reagan Administration, the Department of Justice successfully challenged the use of race-conscious tenant admission policies that had been created to promote racial integration. In *U.S. v. Starrett City*, the Second Circuit Court of Appeals invalidated the challenged admission policy, but emphasized that it did "not intend to imply that race is always an inappropriate consideration under Title VIII in efforts to promote integrated housing" (*Starrett* 1988, 1103). The court said that it held "only that Title VIII does not allow [the]… use [of] rigid racial quotas of indefinite duration to maintain a fixed level of integration…by restricting minority access to scarce and desirable rental accommodations…" (*Starrett* 1988, 1103).

Through all recent Administrations, the courts, including the Second Circuit, continued to order race-conscious remedies in housing desegregation cases (e.g., *Raso* 1998; *Yonkers* 1987, 1996; *Young* 1995, 2003a, 2003b, 2004). During the Clinton Administration, HUD implemented affirmative, race-conscious programs to settle pending desegregation cases and in other contexts (Roisman 1999, 172–73).

In 1999, however, the Fifth Circuit invalidated a race-conscious remedy in *Walker v. City of Mesquite*, a challenge brought by white homeowners to a district court's order that public housing be constructed in a "predominantly white" neighborhood of Dallas (*Walker* 1999). The court of appeals acknowledged that "Blacks were purposefully segregated for decades" and that the order served the compelling government interest of undoing the past intentional segregation (*Walker* 1999, 976, 982). The court held, however, that the race-conscious remedy must be a "last resort," and would not be considered "narrowly tailored" unless race-neutral remedies had been tried without success (*Walker* 1999, 982–83). The court of appeals acknowledged that in *Hills v. Gautreaux* (1976) the Supreme Court had approved (in the court of appeal's language, "did not disapprove") a race-conscious remedial order, but the court of appeals said that in *Hills v. Gautreaux* the Supreme Court had not focused on race consciousness and, the court of appeals said, "*Hills* predates significant changes that have occurred both in HUD's approach to public housing and in the scrutiny afforded race-conscious remedies" (*Walker* 1999, 983 n. 20).

The Fifth Circuit's decision in *Walker* may be a "legal outlier" (Tegeler 2009), but concerns that were raised by *Walker* have been given more weight by the new appointments to the Supreme Court and the decision in *Parents Involved*. Philip Tegeler has very usefully analyzed the *Walker* and *Parents Involved* decisions to identify the kinds of race-conscious remedies for housing segregation that would meet the legal standards established in those two cases (Tegeler 2009). He points out that *Walker* and *Parents Involved* do not prohibit all race-conscious remedies, and perhaps do not even require that all race-conscious remedies be subjected to strict scrutiny. He concludes that "[t]here may be more cases like *City of Mesquite*, but if our policies are well designed and properly documented, we need not fear the courts" (Tegeler 2009, 165).[1] This chapter adds to the Tegeler analysis consideration of the Thirteenth Amendment and statutes enacted pursuant to its authority.

The Thirteenth Amendment and Housing-Related Legislation Enacted Pursuant to Its Authority

Congress has enacted two principal laws regarding discrimination and segregation in housing. The first is the single sentence of the 1866 Civil Rights

Act now codified at—and generally known as—42 U.S.C. § 1982. It provides that "[a]ll citizens of the United States shall have the same right, in every State and Territory, as is enjoyed by white citizens thereof to inherit, purchase, lease, sell, hold, and convey real and personal property" (U.S. Code 1866). The second is Title VIII of the 1968 Civil Rights Act. The following section discusses both statutes and their application to racial residential segregation and affirmative action to end it.

Section 1982

The 1866 Civil Rights Act was enacted to implement the Thirteenth Amendment, which had been adopted by Congress on January 31, 1865 and declared ratified on December 18, 1865 (Hoemann 1987, 129–30, 1; *Jones* 1968, 431–56; tenBroek 1965, 174). The Thirteenth Amendment has two sections. The first declares that "[n]either slavery nor involuntary servitude...shall exist within the United States..."; the second, that "Congress shall have power to enforce this article by appropriate legislation" (U.S. Const. amend XIII).

The 39th Congress convened on December 5, 1865 (tenBroek 1965, 174). When it learned that the Thirteenth Amendment had been ratified, Congress proceeded to implement the Amendment with a change to the Freedmen's Bureau Act and the legislation that became the 1866 Civil Rights Act (*Jones* 1968, 433; tenBroek 1965, 177). The work of the Reconstruction Congress then was completed by adoption of the Fourteenth and Fifteenth Amendments and enactment of the Civil Rights Acts of 1870, 1871, and 1875 (Kaczorowski 2005, xiii–xiv).

Although the 1866 statute and the Thirteenth and Fourteenth Amendments initially were applied generously by the lower federal courts, by 1873 the Supreme Court began to "interpret...Congress's power to enforce the rights these amendments secured more narrowly than had lower federal court judges" (Kaczorowski 2005, 4–5, xvi; Vorenberg 2001, 240–41). A century after enactment of the 1866 Act, courts and commentators generally believed that the 1866 statute banned only government, not private, acts of discrimination; the Supreme Court had as much as said that this was the case (*Hurd* 1948, 31; *Jones* 1966, 43). In 1968, however, the Supreme Court rejected that understanding, holding, in *Jones v. Mayer*, that "§1982 bars all racial discrimination, private as well as public, in the sale or rental of property..." (*Jones* 1968, 413).

The Court also held in *Jones* "that the statute, thus construed, is a valid exercise of the power of Congress to enforce the Thirteenth Amendment" (*Jones* 1968, 413). The Court defined very broadly the authority of Congress under the Thirteenth Amendment, holding that the Amendment's second section "clothed 'Congress with power to pass all laws necessary and proper for abolishing all badges and incidents of slavery in the United States'" (*Jones*

1968, 21–22, quoting *The Civil Rights Cases* 1883, 20), and that "Congress has the power under the Thirteenth Amendment rationally to determine what are the badges and the incidents of slavery, and the authority to translate that determination into effective legislation" (*Jones* 1968, 440). The Supreme Court said that "the majority leaders in Congress—who were, after all, the authors of the Thirteenth Amendment—had no doubt that its Enabling Clause contemplated the sort of positive legislation that was embodied in the 1866 Civil Rights Act" (*Jones* 1968, 339–40). The Court said it is for Congress to determine "what that appropriate legislation is to be" (*Jones* 1968, 440).[2]

The Supreme Court had said in *The Civil Rights Cases* of 1883 that "the Thirteenth Amendment authorizes Congress not only to outlaw all forms of slavery and involuntary servitude but also to eradicate the last vestiges and incidents of a society half slave and half free…" (*Jones* 1968, 443, quoting *The Civil Rights Cases* 1883, 22, 35, dissenting opinion). The Supreme Court held in *Jones v. Mayer* that it was rational for Congress to determine that a private individual's refusal to sell a home to a Black man was a "badge or incident" of slavery. The Court said that the seller's refusal to sell is a restraint upon "those fundamental rights which are the essence of civil freedom, namely, the same right * * * to inherit, purchase, lease, sell and convey property, as is enjoyed by white citizens" (*Jones* 1968, 441). The Court continued:

> Just as the Black Codes…were substitutes for the slave system, the exclusion of Negroes from white communities became a substitute for the Black Codes. And when racial discrimination herds men into ghettos and makes their ability to buy property turn on the color of their skin, then it too is a relic of slavery. (Jones 1968, 441–43; see also tenBroek 1965, 173)

It always had been clear that §1982 prohibits not only racial discrimination but also racial segregation. A central goal of the 1866 Act was invalidating the Black Codes which had, among other things, reincarnated slavery's control by whites over where Blacks could live.[3] When states and cities turned to explicit racial zoning in order to impose residential racial segregation, the Supreme Court relied in part on § 1982 to hold that race could not be used as a basis for determining where people may live or own property (*Buchanan* 1917, 78–79).[4] As the Court said in *Jones v. Mayer*, it unquestionably is unlawful for "the State and its agents [to] lend…support to those who wish to exclude persons from their communities on racial grounds" (*Jones* 1968, 421). What *Jones v. Mayer* added to that was the holding that it also is unlawful for private persons to exclude persons from their communities on racial grounds.

Jones v. Mayer made clear that § 1982 prohibits racial segregation imposed by private as well as by public actors. While *Jones v. Mayer* was directly concerned with the refusal to sell a home because of the race of one potential purchaser, the Supreme Court stated in that decision that part of Congress' purpose in enacting § 1982 was to eliminate whites' ability to control where Negroes could live, either by prohibiting Negroes from moving into certain areas or by driving them out of areas where they already resided. The Supreme Court specifically mentioned, for example, references in the legislative history to "white citizens...who combined to drive [Negroes] out of their communities" (*Jones* 1968, 427–28) and actions "virtually prohibiting Negroes from owning or renting property in certain towns" (*Jones* 1968, 428; see also tenBroek 1965, 181). The Court noted that

> Opponents of the bill [that became the 1866 Civil Rights Act] charged that it would...directly "determine the persons who (would) enjoy * * * property within the States," threatening the ability of white citizens "to determine who (would) be members of (their) communit(ies) * * *." The bill's advocates did not deny the accuracy of those characterizations. Instead, they defended the propriety of employing federal authority to deal with "the white man * * * (who) would invoke the power of local prejudice" against the Negro. (*Jones* 1968, 443)

The Court said that the statute applies to "those who wish to exclude persons from their communities on racial grounds" and to private as well as "officially sanctioned segregation in housing" (*Jones* 1968, 421–22). The statute was to assure Negroes "the right to live wherever a white man can live..." (*Jones* 1968, 443). Thus, while *Jones v. Mayer* was a case in which racial discrimination was not distinguished from racial segregation, the Court made clear that § 1982 prohibits segregation as well as discrimination. There can be no doubt that action to end residential segregation is specifically authorized by Section 1982.[5]

Title VIII of the 1968 Civil Rights Act

In 1968, Congress made even more clear its determination to end residential racial segregation when it enacted Title VIII of the Civil Rights Act of 1968 (U.S. Code 1968). Although the words *segregation* and *integration* do not appear in the statute, the Supreme Court long has recognized that opposing segregation and promoting integration are two of the statute's goals. Furthermore, the Act requires HUD and other federal agencies "affirmatively to further" the purposes of the statute, which include promoting integration (*U.S. Code* 1968 §§ 3608(d)(5),(e)), and Congress,[6] the Executive Branch,[7] and courts have extended that duty to other federal, state, and local agencies (*Otero* 1973, 1133–34; *In re Adoption of Qualified Allocation Plan* 2004 369 N.J. Super., 21–22, 848 A.2d:12–13).

The legislative history of the 1968 Act clearly expressed a strong interest in achieving integration (Roisman 2007, 372–76; Schwemm 2007,§ 2.3; U.S. Senate Hearings 1967, 2, 4, 82).[8] In a statement later quoted by the Supreme Court and other courts, Senator Walter Mondale, a principal sponsor of the bill, said that the bill's purpose was to replace the ghettos "by truly integrated and balanced living patterns" (*U.S. Cong. Rec.* 1968). Robert Schwemm, the leading scholar of the statute, concludes that "[t]his legislative history makes clear that residential integration is a major goal of the Fair Housing Act, separate and independent of the goal of expanding minority housing opportunities" (Schwemm 2007, 2–8).

In its first decision interpreting the Fair Housing Act of 1968, *Trafficante v. Metropolitan Life Insurance Company*, the Supreme Court adopted this view of the legislative purpose. The Court held that the statute authorized relief for the loss of the "benefits of living in an integrated community…" (*Trafficante* 1972, 208). The Court repeated the explanation of Senator Mondale that "the reach of the proposed law was to replace the ghettos 'by truly integrated and balanced living patterns'" (*Trafficante* 1972, 211). Specifically, the Court held that the plaintiffs, who were white, had standing to seek relief if

> (1) they had lost the social benefits of living in an integrated community; (2) they had missed business and professional advantages which would have accrued if they had lived with members of minority groups; (3) they had suffered embarrassment and economic damage in social, business, and professional activities from being "stigmatized" as residents of a "white ghetto." (*Trafficante* 1972, 208)

Other decisions of the Supreme Court and federal courts of appeals also have identified as goals of the statute both undoing segregation and achieving integration. In *Linmark Associates, Inc. v. Township of Willingboro*, for example, the Supreme Court said that "Congress has made a strong national commitment to promoting integrated housing" (*Linmark* 1977, 95; see also *Gautreaux* 1976; *NAACP, Boston Chapter* 1987; *Otero* 1973; *Shannon* 1970). Professor Schwemm writes that "[t]he courts have regularly cited this legislative history and the *Trafficante* opinion to conclude that the goal of the Fair Housing Act is not only to advance minority housing rights but to achieve integration as well" (Schwemm 2007, 7–5 and cases there cited).

The integration mandate of the 1968 Act is implicit throughout the statute, but most of the judicial decisions acknowledging the mandate have involved either of two particular provisions: § 3604(a)'s prohibition of conduct which "otherwise makes unavailable" a dwelling because of race (or another protected characteristic) or § 3608's requirements that agencies "affirmatively… further" the policies and purposes of Title VIII.[9]

"Otherwise Make Unavailable...."

The seminal decision establishing that Title VIII prohibits the "perpetuation of segregation" is *Metropolitan Housing Development Corp. v. Village of Arlington Heights*, decided in 1977 by the Seventh Circuit Court of Appeals (*Arlington Heights II* 1977). *Arlington Heights II* held that Title VIII can be violated by actions that have discriminatory impact even when there is no proof of discriminatory intent, and specifically identified the perpetuation of segregation as a prohibited discriminatory impact. The court said that "[c]onduct that has the necessary and foreseeable consequence of perpetuating segregation can be as deleterious as purposefully discriminatory conduct in frustrating the national commitment 'to replace the ghettos "by truly integrated and balanced living patterns"'" (*Arlington Heights II* 1977, 1289–90, quoting *Trafficante* 1972, 211). Again citing *Trafficante*, the court said that a distinct, separate, independent, prohibited disparate impact is "the effect which the decision has on the community involved; if it perpetuates segregation and thereby prevents interracial association it will be considered invidious under the Fair Housing Act independently of the extent to which it produces a disparate effect on different racial groups" (*Arlington Heights II* 1977, 1290). Discussing earlier cases, the court said that "the effect of the municipal action in both cases was to foreclose the possibility of ending racial segregation in housing within those municipalities" (*Arlington Heights II* 1977, 1291). The court also noted that in this case, "plaintiffs are seeking to effectuate the national goal of integrated housing..." (*Arlington Heights II* 1977, 1294).

Arlington Heights II has been followed by every federal court of appeals that has addressed the issue. "Their opinions vary somewhat, but all of the circuits that have considered the matter now agree that Title VIII may be violated by an action that has the effect of perpetuating segregation in a community" (Schwemm 2007, 10–55 and cases cited *infra* at note 15). After *Arlington Heights II*, perhaps the most important case in this regard is the Second Circuit's decision in *Town of Huntington, N.Y. v. Huntington Branch, NAACP*, a decision that is significant both for its own substance and because the U.S. Supreme Court affirmed part of the decision (*Huntington* 1988). In *Huntington*, the Second Circuit endorsed and strengthened the Seventh Circuit's holdings that Title VIII can be violated by actions that have discriminatory effect and that one form of unlawful discriminatory effect is "harm to the community generally by the perpetuation of segregation" (*Huntington* 1988, 937). The Second Circuit said that "recognizing this second form of effect advances the principal purpose of Title VIII to promote 'open, integrated residential housing patterns'" (*Huntington* 1988, 937). Reviewing the decision because part of it was within the Supreme Court's mandatory appellate jurisdiction, the Supreme Court said that, without reaching the question whether the disparate impact test was appropriate, the Court was "satisfied on this record that disparate impact was shown…," thus apparently endorsing the lower courts' consistent view that perpetuation of segregation is a discriminatory impact forbidden by the statute (*Huntington* 1988, 488 US, 18).

"Affirmatively...Further"

The 1968 statute contains two explicit requirements of affirmative action. Sections 3608(e)(5) and (d) direct the Secretary of HUD and all other federal agencies and departments administering housing and urban development programs "affirmatively to further" the policies and purposes of Title VIII (*U.S. Code* 1968 §§ 3608(e)(5), 3608(d)).[10] Since achieving integration has been identified as one of the purposes of Title VIII, courts uniformly have held that HUD and other federal agencies are obligated to act affirmatively to achieve integration.

One of the most significant of these cases is *NAACP, Boston Chapter v. Secretary of HUD*, a 1987 decision of the Court of Appeals for the First Circuit. In an opinion written by Judge Stephen Breyer before he ascended to the Supreme Court, the First Circuit held that Title VIII embodies "an intent that HUD do more than simply not discriminate itself; it reflects the desire to have HUD use its grant programs to assist in ending discrimination and segregation, to the point where the supply of genuinely open housing increases" (*NAACP, Boston Chapter* 1987, 155).

Another important landmark in this regard is *Otero v. New York City Housing Authority*, in which the Second Circuit Court of Appeals held that the statute and the Constitution impose on the New York City Housing Authority the duty "to take affirmative steps to promote racial integration," and noted that "affirmative action to erase the effects of past discrimination and desegregate housing patterns may be ordered" (*Otero* 1973,1133). The court held that:

> Action must be taken to fulfill, as much as possible, the goal of open, integrated residential housing patterns and to prevent the increase of segregation, in ghettos, of racial groups whose lack of opportunities the Act was designed to combat. (*Otero* 1973, 1134)

The court spoke of honoring "Congress' desire to prevent segregated housing patterns and the ills which attend them" and said that housing officials could not be permitted "to make decisions having the long range effect of increasing or maintaining racially segregated housing patterns" lest the officials become "willing, and perhaps unwitting, partners in the trend toward ghettoization of our urban centers" (*Otero* 1973, 1134).

In the most recent "affirmatively further" case, District Judge Marvin Garbis held that HUD violated § 3608(e)(5) by failing adequately to consider regional approaches to ameliorating racial segregation in Baltimore City's public housing (*Thompson* 2005, 451, 458–65). Following past case law, the court held that the "policies" of Title VIII include "the dual goals of preventing the increase of segregation in housing and attaining open, integrated residential housing patterns" (*Thompson* 2005, 458). It also held that HUD had "failed to achieve significant desegregation in Baltimore City" and had failed, "over time, to take seriously its minimal Title VIII obligation to consider alternative courses of action in light of their impact on open housing" (*Thompson* 2005, 461).

The Significance of the Thirteenth Amendment and the Fair Housing Statutes Enacted Pursuant to Its Authority with Respect to Race-Conscious, Affirmative Action to Achieve Residential Racial Integration

Jones v. Mayer held that the Thirteenth Amendment authorized Congress to enact legislation prohibiting private as well as public racial discrimination and segregation with respect to the sale and rental of housing. *Jones v. Mayer* involved the Civil Rights Act of 1866, but its reasoning applies equally to the racial provisions of Title VIII of the Civil Rights Act of 1968 insofar as that applies to race (Schwemm 2007, 6-1 to 6-2).[11]

Just as the Thirteenth Amendment justifies Congress' banning racial discrimination in housing, it also justifies Congress' directing federal agencies "affirmatively to further" the goals of ending racial discrimination and segregation in housing. As noted above, the Court held in *Jones* that the second clause of the Amendment "clothed 'Congress with power to pass all laws necessary and proper for abolishing all badges and incidents of slavery in the United States'" and that "Congress has the power under the Thirteenth Amendment rationally to determine what are the badges and the incidents of slavery, and the authority to translate that determination into effective legislation" (*Jones* 1968, 439–440).

It certainly was rational for Congress to determine that affirmative action by federal agencies was necessary to achieve the goal of allowing African Americans to have the same rights as whites to live where they choose.[12] A central point of the 1866 Civil Rights Act was "that the way to implement the Thirteenth Amendment and secure liberty was to protect men in their 'civil rights and immunities' and to do so directly through the national government…" (tenBroek 1965, 178). "[T]he federal government alone was to be the agency of enforcement. Thus was effected a complete nationalization of the civil or natural rights of persons" (tenBroek 1965, 179).[13]

The rationality of Congress' decision to impose an affirmative obligation on federal agencies is particularly clear in light of the roles that federal agencies had played in excluding African Americans from particular kinds of housing and housing locations.[14] Knowledge of the federal role in imposing racial discrimination and segregation in housing and related programs was a significant part of the Congressional discussion of the 1968 Act (Roisman 2007, 375–80). The validity of Congress' enactment of the "affirmatively further" requirement fits well within the Court's conclusion in *Jones v. Mayer* that the validity of Congress's enactment of the 1866 Act banning private discrimination was settled by "the celebrated words of Chief Justice Marshall in *McCulloch v. State of Maryland*:

> Let the end be legitimate, let it be within the scope of the constitution, and all means which are appropriate, which are plainly adapted to that end, which are not prohibited, but consist with the letter and spirit of the constitution, are constitutional. (Jones 1968, 443)

Thus, it appears that not only § 1982 but also Title VIII, including the "affirmatively...further" provisions of Title VIII (and the "affirmatively further" provisions of other federal statutes) are authorized by the Thirteenth Amendment. Recognizing the role of the Thirteenth Amendment brings new elements to consideration of the validity of race-conscious, affirmative actions taken pursuant to these statutes.[15] The discussion that follows is preliminary and suggestive only; full analysis is essential.

First, *Jones v. Mayer* established that the Thirteenth Amendment and the 1866 Civil Rights Act apply to private as well as government action, and this determination has been reconsidered and affirmed by the Supreme Court (*Patterson* 1989; *Runyon* 1976). Thus, very importantly, not only de jure but also de facto segregation has been held permissibly invalidated by legislation enacted by Congress pursuant to section 2 of the Thirteenth Amendment.

This should inform and change the consideration of what constitutes a compelling government interest sufficient to justify the use of racial classifications—even racial classifications that give benefits to particular people based on race.[16] The Court has held that under the Fourteenth Amendment remediating general societal discrimination is not a compelling government interest. But the Thirteenth Amendment is directed at every private action of racial discrimination that "herds men into ghettos and makes their ability to buy property turn on the color of their skin..." (*Jones* 1968, 442–43; see also tenBroek 1965, 173). There is a strong argument to be made that remediating societal discrimination is a compelling government interest under the Thirteenth Amendment.

Second, it is not clear whether, or to what extent, whites' equal protection claims under the Fourteenth or Fifth Amendments ought to outweigh actions taken pursuant to such legislation authorized by the Thirteenth Amendment. At the very least, it would seem that action taken pursuant to such legislation ought to be entitled to high deference. The Supreme Court has said that the "history of racial classifications in this country suggests that blind judicial deference to legislative or executive pronouncements of necessity has no place in equal protection analysis" (*Croson* 1989, 501; *Parents Involved* 2007, 37, plurality opinion; 9–11 (Kennedy opinion). But that "suggestion," condemning "blind" deference, may well be overborne by this long-standing legislation that implements a Constitutional condemnation of private and public acts that impose residential racial segregation.

Third, the relevance of the Thirteenth Amendment may undermine the principle that race-conscious remedies must be tested against the individual claims of white people. While the Fifth and Fourteenth Amendments "protect *persons,* not *groups*" (emphasis added) (*Adarand* 1995, 227), the Thirteenth Amendment seems to have been intended to protect groups: "[i]t was meant to be a direct ban against many of the evils radiating from the system of slavery as well as a prohibition of the system itself":

> the slavery which the Thirteenth Amendment would abolish [was]…
> the involuntary personal servitude of the bondsman; the denial to
> blacks, bond and free, of their natural rights through the failure of the
> government to protect them and to protect them equally; the denial
> to whites of their natural and constitutional rights through a similar
> failure of government (tenBroek 1965, 168–69).

Fourth, the Thirteenth Amendment may be significant with respect to a separate, very important issue under Title VIII—the extent to which disparate impact alone may constitute a violation of the statute. Professor William Carter has noted that, "while the Equal Protection Clause is limited to instances of intentional or purposeful discrimination, the Court has not so limited the Thirteenth Amendment. Thus, applying the Thirteenth Amendment to unintentional or 'disparate impact' discrimination remains possible" (Carter 2007, 1328; see also Carter 2004, 85–87).[17]

Detailed analysis of the implications of the Thirteenth Amendment is beyond the scope of this chapter, but it certainly is possible that the authority of that Amendment and Congressional legislation enacted pursuant to it authorize affirmative, race-conscious actions that might not satisfy standards imposed without consideration of the Thirteenth Amendment.[18] Further exploration of this certainly is warranted. The "strong national commitment to promoting integrated housing" (*Linmark* 1977, 95) requires no less.

Acknowledgments

I am grateful to Laura Beshara, Esq., Michael M. Daniel, Esq., Philip Tegeler, Esq., and my colleagues Professors George Wright, Michael Pitts, and Allison Martin for invaluable substantive advice; to librarian Richard Humphrey, research assistant Ravinder Singh Deol, and faculty assistant Mary Deer for research and other help. I have benefitted substantially from reading, rereading, and discussing with its author Philip Tegeler's "The Future of Race Conscious Goals in National Housing Policy."

I dedicate this chapter to my beloved granddaughter Madeline Jonna Roisman, in the hope that she and her generation will come to maturity in a much more just and peaceful world than the one into which they were born.

Notes

1. It is noteworthy that the Fifth Circuit's opinion expressly endorsed a race-conscious Section 8 plan (*Walker* 1999, 986–88). Furthermore, after the Fifth Circuit's decision in *Walker*, the district court and court of appeals approved a public housing development for one of the challenged locations; and the project has in fact been built. See Horner 2008; Ragland 2008; *Walker* 2005; http://www.danielbesharalawfirm.com/walkervhud.aspx (Accessed July 20, 2008).
2. *Jones* 1968, 440 ("Who is to decide what that appropriate legislation is to be? The Congress of the United States; and it is for Congress to adopt such appropriate legislation as it may think proper, so that it be a means to accomplish the end.").
3. See Foner 1988, 244 (stating that "[t]he shadow of the Black Codes hung over these debates, and [Senator Lyman] Trumbull began his discussion of the Civil Rights Bill with a reference to recent laws of Mississippi and South Carolina, declaring his intention 'to destroy all these discriminations'"); see also id., 200, 209 (stating that under Mississippi's Black Code of 1865, freedmen "were forbidden to rent land in urban areas" and that "[a]larmed by the reaction to the early codes, Mississippi Governor Sharkey declared the measure barring blacks from renting real estate 'palpably in violation of the constitution, and therefore void'...").
4. See Higginbotham 1996, 119–26 for a discussion of ways in which racial zoning laws replicated concepts of slavery, particularly "the assumptions of whites in power that African Americans were too inferior to be their neighbors" (119).
5. The Supreme Court has not made clear to what extent the Thirteenth Amendment of its own force prohibits not only slavery and involuntary servitude but also the "badges and incidents" of slavery. Involuntary residential racial segregation may be an element of slavery itself as well as a "badge and incident" of slavery. In light of the fact that Congress has addressed residential racial segregation in § 1982, it has not been necessary to consider to what extent the Thirteenth Amendment itself invalidates segregatory action (but see *City of Memphis* 1981, 124–25).

   The central characteristic of slavery was dominance, the lack of freedom. With respect to housing and residence, this meant that slaves could not decide where they would live. "To most Northerners," as well as Southerners, "segregation constituted... simply the working out of natural law, the inevitable consequence of the racial inferiority of the Negro. God and Nature had condemned the blacks to perpetual subordination" (Litwack 1961, 98). Free Blacks as well as slaves were confined to particular areas and excluded from desirable neighborhoods.

   The vigorous exclusion of Negroes from white residential neighborhoods made escape from the ghetto virtually impossible. The fear of depreciated property values overrode virtually every other consideration. As early as 1793, the attempt to locate "a Negro hut" in Salem, Massachusetts, prompted a white minister to protest that such buildings depreciated property, drove out decent residents, and generally injured the welfare of the neighborhood. Some years later, New Haven petitioners complained that the movement of Negroes into previously white neighborhoods deteriorated real estate values from 20 to 50 per cent; an Indianan asserted that the proposed establishment of a Negro tract would reduce the value of nearby white-owned lots by at least 50 per cent. Obviously, then, the Negro had to be contained in his own area. Thus when a Boston Negro schoolmistress considered moving to a better neighborhood, the inhabitants of the block where she proposed to settle resolved either to eject her or to destroy the house. (Litwack 1961, 169–70).

6. See 42 U.S. Code §§ 12872, 12873,12892, 12893, 1437aaa-1,2 (HOPE [Home Ownership for People Everywhere] programs); 42 U.S.C. § 12705 (Comprehensive Housing Affordability Strategy) 42 U.S.C. §§ 5304(b), 5306(d) (Community Development Block Grant [CDBG] program; 42 U.S.C. § 11386 (supportive housing); 42 U.S.C. § 11394 (Safe Havens for Homeless Individuals Demonstration program).

7. See, e.g., 24 C.F.R. §§ 91.225, 91.235, 91.325, 91.425, 91.520 (CDBG generally); 92.207, 92.508 (HOME Investment Partnerships Program); 115.309 (Fair Housing Assistance Program); 903.1, 903.2, 903.7(o), 960.103, 982.53, 983.8 (public housing); 570.411, 570.421, 570.440, 570.487, 570.601, 570.704, 570.904 (CDBG); 511.14 (Rental Rehab Grant Program); 585.502 (YouthBuild Program); 598.210 (empowerment zones).

Also, President Clinton issued an Executive Order regarding "Affirmatively Furthering Fair Housing" (*Federal Register* 1994), and the Department of Defense issued a regulation to enforce the requirement that fair housing be "affirmatively" furthered (32 CFR § 192.4).

8. The 1968 Act resulted from an unorthodox legislative process and was not preceded by authoritative House or Senate reports or a conference report (see Dubofsky 1969; Roisman 2007, 360–63; Schwartz 1970, 1629–32; Schwemm 2007, § 5.2, 5.4; *Trafficante* 1972).

9. Some of these cases also involve allegations of violation of 42 U.S.C. § 3617, which makes it "unlawful to coerce, intimidate, threaten, or interfere with any person" with respect to exercise of any right "granted or protected by sections 3603, 3604, 3605, or 3606," but the decisions usually do not discuss § 3617 separately because, as the Seventh Circuit said in *Arlington Heights II*, "[s]ince the violation of section 3617…depends upon a finding that the Village interfered with rights granted or protected by § 3604(a)," the decision with respect to § 3604(a) will resolve the question with respect to ' 3617 (*Arlington Heights II* 1977, 1288).

10. 42 U.S.C. § 3608(e)(5) directs the Secretary of HUD to "administer the programs and activities relating to housing and urban development in a manner affirmatively to further the policies" of Title VIII; 42 U.S.C. § 3608(d) directs that "[a]ll executive departments and agencies shall administer their programs and activities relating to housing and urban development…in a manner affirmatively to further the purposes of this subchapter…." The commentary and cases uniformly treat "purposes" and "policies" as synonymous. See Roisman 1998, 1025 n. 78.

11. When the legislation that became Title VIII was being considered by Congress, what little discussion there was of Constitutional authority for the legislation seems to have focused on the Commerce Clause and the Fourteenth Amendment. See, e.g., Schwartz 1970, 1807, reproducing a memorandum prepared by staff of the House Committee on the Judiciary and included in the debate in the House of Representatives in 1968. Comparing the 1966 House bill to the Senate bill then pending before the House, the Committee staff wrote:

> whereas the 1966 House bill fell within the Congressional power over interstate commerce, the more far-reaching Senate bill probably does not and must look to section 5 of the Fourteenth Amendment as its constitutional basis. Since section 1 of the Fourteenth Amendment focuses only on "State" action, it has long been doubted that Congress could reach private discriminatory action through legislation to "enforce" section 1 of the Fourteenth Amendment…. However, six Justices of the Supreme Court…, in the case of *United States v. Herbert Guest*, 383 U.S. 745 (1966), stated in *dictum* that section 5 of the Fourteenth Amendment empowers Congress to enact laws which reach private discrimination.

Of course, this was written before the Supreme Court's decision in *Jones v. Mayer* gave prominence to Thirteenth Amendment analysis. See also Graham 1990, 258 (quoting Attorney General Nicholas Katzenbach as warning in 1965 that fair housing legislation presented "many constitutional problems…").

Consideration of nonracial discrimination is beyond the scope of this chapter.

12. See Tsesis 2004, 86 ("The rationality standard is a low one that Congress can meet by examining the historical landmarks of slavery, evaluating what existing practices perpetuate it, and promulgating laws to end them," 93); ("Congress has virtually plenary federal power under that section [section 2] to protect freedom against arbitrary infringements").
13. See also tenBroek 1965, 167–68, 188–89; 195, 197.
14. The sorry tale of intentional racial discrimination and segregation by federal agencies has been told many times, by scholars and by courts (Jackson 1987, 190–230; Massey and Denton 1993, 26–59; *Thompson* 2005, 466–70; *Young* 1985, 1045–56).
15. As a matter of linguistics, "affirmative action" and "race-consciousness" are not necessarily synonyms: one could, for example, describe "class-conscious" actions as "affirmative action." Since the 1960s, however, "affirmative action" has been understood to mean "using membership in those groups that have been subject to discrimination as a consideration [in decision-making or allocation of resources]" Edley 1996, 17. In enacting Title VIII, Congress was focused on race, particularly on "Negroes." See Roisman 2007, 371–75.
16. See Tegeler 2009 (suggesting that classifying individuals on the basis of race may face a particularly challenging burden under *Parents Involved*).
17. The Supreme Court has held that intent is needed to establish a violation of 42 U.S.C. § 1981 (*General Building Contractors* 1982).
18. See Aleinikoff 1991, 1120; Carter 2004, 36 (proposing an "amendment shift" "away from the Fourteenth Amendment's commitment to equal treatment based on race and toward reliance on the Thirteenth Amendment for a call to an end of second-class status for racial minorities." Professor Carter adds that "[s]uch an 'amendment shift' would recognize that the Fourteenth Amendment's protection of *ad hoc*, irrational, racialized decision-making by governmental actors, standing alone, will not eliminate the lingering effects of the slave system in the United States." See also Amar 1992, 157 n. 181 (stating that the Thirteenth Amendment evokes "vivid images of asymmetric social, political, and economic power—images of masters and slaves, images more congenial to openly asymmetric attempts to right past imbalances").

References

Adarand 1995. Adarand Constructors, Inc. v. Peña, 515 U.S. 200 (1995).
Aleinikoff, Alexander. 1991. "A Case for Race-Consciousness." *Columbia Law Review* 91(5): 1060–1126.
Amar, Akhil Reed. 1992. "The Case of the Missing Amendments: R.A.V. v. City of St. Paul." *Harvard Law Review* 106(1): 124–62.
Arlington Heights II 1977. Metropolitan Housing Dev. Corp. v. Village of Arlington Heights, 558 F.2d 1283 (7th Cir. 1977), cert. denied, 434 U.S. 1025 (1978).
Bakke 1978. Regents of the Univ. of Cal. v. Bakke, 438 U.S. 265 (1978).
Bolling 1954. Bolling v. Sharpe, 347 U.S. 497 (1954).
Briggs, Xavier de Souza. 2003. "Housing Opportunity, Desegregation Strategy, and Policy Research." *Journal of Policy Analysis and Management* 22(2): 201–06.
Brown 1954. Brown v. Board of Education of Topeka, KS, 349 U.S. 294 (1954).
Buchanan 1917. Buchanan v. Warley, 245 U.S. 60 (1917).
Bush 1996. Bush v. Vera, 517 U.S. 952 (1996).
Carter, William M. 2004. "A Thirteenth Amendment Framework for Combating Racial Profiling." *Harvard Civil Rights–Civil Liberties Law Review* 39(1): 17–94.
———. 2007. "Race, Rights, and the Thirteenth Amendment: Defining the Badges and Incidents of Slavery." *UC Davis Law Review* 40(4): 1311–80.
Chemerinsky, Erwin. 2003. "The Segregation and Resegregation of American Public Education: The Courts' Role." *North Carolina Law Review* 81(4): 1597–1622.
City of Memphis 1981. City of Memphis v. Greene, 451 U.S. 100 (1981).
Civil Rights Cases 1883, The. Civil Rights Cases, 109 U.S. 3 (1883).
Croson 1989. City of Richmond v. J.A. Croson Co., 488 U.S. 469 (1989).
Dubofsky, Jean E. 1969. "Fair Housing: A Legislative History and a Perspective." *Washburn Law Journal* 8(2): 149–66.
Edley, Christopher. 1996. *Not All Black and White: Affirmative Action, Race, and American Values*. New York: Hill & Wang.
Farber, Daniel A., and Philip P. Frickey. 1991. "Reflections on Affirmative Action and the Dynamics

of Civil Rights Legislation." *California Law Review* 79(3): 685–728.
Federal Register 1994. Executive Order 12892, Leadership and Coordination of Fair Housing in Federal Programs: Affirmatively Furthering Fair Housing. 59 Fed. Reg. 2939 (Jan. 20, 1994).
Foner, Eric. 1988. *Reconstruction: America's Unfinished Revolution, 1863–1877*. New York: Harper & Row.
Gautreaux 1976. Hills v. Gautreaux, 425 U.S. 284 (1976).
General Building Contractors 1982. General Building Contractors Ass'n., Inc. v. Pennsylvania, 458 U.S. 375 (1982).
Graham, Hugh Davis. 1990. *The Civil Rights Era: Origins and Development of National Policy.* New York: Oxford University Press.
Gratz 2003. Gratz v. Bollinger, 539 US. 244 (2003).
Grutter 2003. Grutter v. Bollinger, 539 U.S. 306 (2003).
Higginbotham, Leon. 1996. *Shades of Freedom: Racial Politics and Presumptions of the American Legal Process.* New York: Oxford University Press.
Hirabayashi 1943. Hirabayashi v. United States, 320 U.S. 81 (1943).
Hoemann, George H. 1987. *What God Hath Wrought: The Embodiment of Freedom in the Thirteenth Amendment.* New York: Garland.
Horner, Kim. 2008. "Far North Dallas Project to Soon Open." *Dallas News,* http://www.dallasnews.com/sharedcontent/dws/news/localnews/stories/DN-hillcrest_14met.ART.State.Edition2.4d726f7.html (August 5, 2008)
Huntington 1988. Huntington Branch, NAACP v. Town of Huntington, 844 F.2d 926 (2d Cir. 1988), affirmed per curiam in part, 488 U.S. 15 (1988).
Hurd 1948, Hurd v. Hodge, 334 U.S. 24 (1948).
In re: Adoption of Qualified Allocation Plan 2004. In re: Adoption of 2003 Low Income Housing Tax Credit Qualified Allocation Plan, 369 N.J. Super. 2, 848 A.2d 1 (N.J. Super. Ct. App. Div. 2004), certification denied, *In re New Jersey Housing and Mortg. Finance Agency,* 182 N.J. 141 (N.J. 2004).
Jackson, Kenneth T. 1987. *Crabgrass Frontier: The Suburbanization of the United States.* New York: Oxford University Press.
Johnson 2005. Johnson v. California, 543 U.S. 499 (2005).
Jones 1966. Jones v. Mayer, 379 F.2d 33 (8th Cir. 1966), reversed by *Jones v. Mayer,* 392 U.S. 409 (1968).
Jones 1968. Jones v. Mayer, 392 U.S. 409 (1968).
Kaczorowski, Robert. 2005. *The Politics of Judicial Interpretation: The Federal Courts, Department of Justice, and Civil Rights, 1866–1876.* New York: Fordham University Press.
Korematsu 1944. Korematsu v. United States, 323 U.S. 214 (1944).
Linmark 1977. Linmark Associates, Inc. v. Township of Willingboro, 431 U.S. 85 (1977).
Litwack, Leon F. 1961. *North of Slavery: The Negro in the Free States 1790–1860.* Chicago: University of Chicago Press.
Massey, Douglas S., and Nancy A. Denton. 1993. *American Apartheid: Segregation and the Making of the Underclass.* Cambridge, MA: Harvard University Press.
Miller 1995. Miller v. Johnson, 515 U.S. 900 (1995).
Milliken 1974. Milliken v. Bradley, 418 U.S. 717 (1974).
NAACP, Boston Chapter 1987. NAACP, Boston Chapter v. Secretary of H.U.D., 817 F.2d 149 (5th Cir. 1987).
Otero 1973. Otero v. New York City Hous. Auth., 484 F.2d 1122 (2nd Cir. 1973).
Parents Involved 2007. Parents Involved in Community Schools v. Seattle School Dist. No. 1, 127 S.Ct. 2738 (2007).
Patterson 1989. Patterson v. McLean Credit Union, 491 U.S. 164 (1989).
Ragland, James. 2008. "Rich and Poor to Live Side by Side in North Dallas Housing Project." *Dallas News.* http://www.dallasnews.com/sharedcontent/dws/dn/latestnews/stories/071608dnmetragland_hp.5c7f78e2.html. (August 5, 2008)
Raso 1998. Raso v. Lago, 135 F.3d 11 (1st Cir. 1998), cert. denied, 525 U.S. 811 (1998).
Roisman, Florence Wagman. 1998. "Mandates Unsatisfied: The Low Income Housing Tax Credit Program and the Civil Rights Laws." *University of Miami Law Review* 52(4): 1011–49.
———. 1999. "Long Overdue: Desegregation Litigation and Next Steps to End Discrimination and Segregation in the Public Housing and Section 8 Existing Housing Programs." *Cityscape* 4(3): 171–96.
———. 2007. "Affirmatively Furthering Fair Housing in Regional Housing Markets: The Baltimore

Public Housing Desegregation Litigation." *Wake Forest Law Review* 42(2): 333–92.

Runyon 1976. Runyon v. McCrary, 427 U.S. 160 (1976).

Schwartz, Bernard. 1970. *Statutory History of the United States: Civil Rights Part II*. New York: Chelsea House.

Schwemm, Robert G.. 2007. *Housing Discrimination: Law and Litigation*. Rochester, NY: Thompson/West.

Shannon 1970. Shannon v. U.S. Dept. of Housing and Urban Development, 436 F.2d 809 (3rd Cir. 1970).

Shaw 1993. Shaw v. Reno, 509 U.S. 630 (1993).

Shaw 1996. Shaw v. Hunt, 517 U.S. 899 (1996).

Starrett 1988. U.S. v. Starrett City Associates, 840 F.2d 1096 (2d Cir. 1988), cert. denied, 488 U.S. 946 (1988).

Tegeler, Philip. 2009. "The Future of Race-Conscious Goals in National Housing Policy." In *Public Housing Transformation: Confronting the Legacy of Segregation*, ed. Margery Turner, Susan J. Popkin, and Lynette Rawlings. Washington, DC: The Urban Institute Press, 145–69.

tenBroek, Jacobus. 1965. *Equal Under Law* (originally published as *The Antislavery Origins of the Fourteenth Amendment)*. New York: Collier Books.

Thompson 2005. Thompson v. U.S. Dept of Hous. & Urban Dev., 348 F. Supp. 2d 398 (D. MD 2005).

Trafficante 1972. Trafficante v. Metro. Life Ins. Co., 409 U.S. 205 (1972).

Tsesis, Alexander. 2004. *The Thirteenth Amendment and American Freedom: A Legal History*. New York: New York University Press.

U.S. Code 1866. Civil Rights Act of 1866, ch.31, 14 Stat. 27 (1866) as amended, 42 U.S.C. §1982.

U.S. Code 1968. Civil Rights Act of 1968, Title VIII, Pub. L. 90-284, 82 Stat. 81 (1968) as amended, 42 U.S.C. §§ 3601 et seq.

U.S. Cong. Rec. 1968 114 Cong. Rec. 3422.

U.S. Const. amend. XIII.

U.S. Senate Hearings 1967: Fair Housing Act of 1967, Hearings Before the Subcomm. On Housing & Urban Affairs of the Senate Comm. on Banking and Currency, 90th Cong.

Vorenberg, Michael. 2001. *Final Freedom: The Civil War, the Abolition of Slavery, and the Thirteenth Amendment*. Cambridge, UK: Cambridge University Press.

Walker 1999. Walker v. City of Mesquite, 169 F.3d 973 (5th Cir. 1999), cert. denied, 528 U.S. 1131 (2000).

Walker 2005. Walker v. U.S. Dept. of HUD, 326 F.Supp.2d 780, 781 (N.D. TX 2004), aff'd, 402 F.3d 532 (5th Cir. 2005).

Yonkers 1987. U.S. v. Yonkers Board of Education, 837 F.2d 1181 (2d Cir. 1987), cert. denied, 486 U.S. 1055 (1988).

Yonkers 1996. U.S. v. City of Yonkers, 96 F.3d 600 (2d Cir. 1996).

Young 1985. Young v. Pierce, 628 F. Supp. 1037 (E.D. TX 1985).

Young 1995. Young v. Cisneros & Young v. Martinez, Civil Action No. P-80-8-CA, E.D. TX, Final Judgment and Decree (1995). http://danielbesharalawfirm.com/Documents/final%20judgement%201995.pdf (August 7, 2008)

Young 2003a. Young v. Cisneros & Young v. Martinez, Civil Action No. P-80-8-CA, Settlement Agreement and Release (March 20, 2003). http://danielbesharalawfirm.com/Documents/state%20agreement.pdf (August 7, 2008).

Young 2003b. Young v. Cisneros & Young v. Martinez, Civil Action No. P-80-8-CA , Settlement Stipulation and Order Modifying Final Judgment (October 23, 2003). http://danielbesharalawfirm.com/Documents/settlement%20stip%20and%20order.pdf (August 7, 2008)

Young 2004. Young v. Cisneros & Young v. Martinez, Civil Action No. P-80-8-CA, Order Modifying Final Judgment (Jan. 13, 2004). http://danielbesharalawfirm.com/Documents/settlement%20stip%20and%20order.pdf (August 7, 2008)

CHAPTER 7

Housing Mobility

A Civil Right

ELIZABETH K. JULIAN AND DEMETRIA L. MCCAIN

All Citizens of the United States shall have the same right, in every State and Territory, as is enjoyed by white citizens thereof to inherit, purchase, lease, sell, hold, and convey real and personal property. (Civil Rights Act of 1866 [42 U.S. Code § 1981])

Be it enacted by the Senate and House of Representatives of the United States of America in Congress assembled, That no applicant for or resident of federally-assisted housing shall be required to accept a housing unit in a development or in a census tract in which his/her race/ethnicity predominates as a condition of receiving said federal low-income housing assistance, either as a temporary or permanent placement.

Sec. 2, And be it further enacted, That if an applicant/resident exercises his/her right under this provision, then the administering agency shall, at the individual's election, provide all assistance necessary for that individual to obtain a desegregated housing opportunity, including a housing voucher, and counseling and supportive services. This provision shall be enforceable by the individual applicant for or recipient of such assistance. (2009 Federal Assisted Housing Civil Rights Enforcement Act [proposed])

The role the government has played in creating and perpetuating racially segregated housing patterns in our country has been documented to the point of absurdity (Briggs 2005; Goering 1986; Kerner Commission 1968; Massey and Denton 1993). Nowhere is that condition more pronounced or is the government more responsible than in government-assisted low-income housing (Roisman 2007, 336–46). Whatever progress we have made in affording middle- and upper-income people of color the same opportunities to access housing in locations of their choice as middle- and upper-income white people have, we have been markedly ineffectual in affording those opportunities to lower-income people of color.

Poor people live where the powers that be, of whatever color, decide they should. And historically those powers have decided that poor people should live in a racially segregated condition. The modern-day public housing program was built upon a foundation of de jure segregation dating back to the 1930s (Kerner Commission 1968, 246). The assisted housing programs that followed years later utilized the blatantly discriminatory private housing market to continue that pattern (Goering 1986, 245–48). The most recent low-income housing production program continues the practice of funding low-income housing developments in a way that perpetuates segregation and allows private market discrimination to reinforce it (Massachusetts Law Reform Institute et al. 2004; Poverty & Race Research Action Council 2004). De jure segregation may no longer be the law, but the reality of our low-income housing programs continues to produce segregation in fact (Julian and Daniel 1989).

Those who believe that low-income people of color should choose to remain in predominantly minority[1] neighborhoods and communities are free to make that case. However, they should not be free to: (1) hold people hostage by using governmental housing programs to control where low-income people of color can live, or (2) limit federal housing assistance to those who agree to accept racial segregation as a principle of social organization for themselves and their families, or who agree to accept the conditions that often exist in many low-income communities due to the legacy of segregation (Julian 2008, 2007).

While we continue to debate whether, how and when such segregated conditions will be effectively addressed systemically and institutionally, it is the thesis of this chapter and our argument that, regardless of the outcome of this "Integration Debate," Congress should take steps to recognize and enforce the existing right of every low-income person of color who seeks and receives federally-funded housing assistance to be afforded the opportunity to receive such assistance on a non-segregated basis. Such a right is imbedded in our Constitution and the laws passed to effectuate that Constitution.[2] The Constitutional violation of forced racial segregation demands such a remedy and is the minimum imposed by the "affirmatively furthering" duty on federal housing programs under the Fair Housing Act.[3] Giving effect to this long-neglected right requires a clear understanding of its nature, as well as the remedy for its violation.[4] It involves a commitment of resources and a resolve to make securing the right to federal housing assistance on a non-segregated basis a priority of housing and civil rights advocates. We know how to do this, and we must.

Housing Mobility as a Right and Remedy

What Housing Mobility Is

The term *housing mobility* developed in the context of our history of racial segregation in low-income housing. The landmark public housing desegregation litigation, *Gautreaux v. HUD*, used the term *housing mobility* to describe a particular part of the remedy for the Constitutional violation of racial segregation in Chicago's public housing program. (*Gautreaux v. Pierce* 1981; Polikoff 2006, 246). In that context, it refers to the ability of low-income people of color to choose to live in other than low-income, predominantly minority communities. It is often associated with giving people access to communities of "high opportunity." Certainly one of the reasons people of color may choose to live in such a location is that they believe that it offers greater opportunities for them and their children. However, *housing mobility* as used in this context refers simply to the right of low-income people of color not to be limited to predominantly minority communities as a condition of receiving federal housing assistance. The goal of accessing "high opportunity," however that may be defined, is consistent with that definition but not required.

What Housing Mobility is Not

Housing Mobility Is Not a "Policy Experiment." Researchers at Northwestern University have documented the generally positive outcomes over decades for those who chose and were able to obtain the Gautreaux housing mobility remedy; that research has informed much of the discussion about the value of housing mobility as a policy choice (Institute for Policy Research n.d.). While the Moving to Opportunity (MTO) "experiment" was born out of the Gautreaux research, MTO did not involve housing mobility as defined above, and it should not be confused with it (Goering 2005, 149).[5] As ultimately designed and implemented, MTO did not even pretend to address the Constitutional violation of governmentally-imposed racial segregation. Research which suggests that both Gautreaux movers and MTO movers experienced some degree of positive outcomes by society's standards is certainly worth knowing and, at least in the case of Gautreaux research proves relevant to the issue of racial segregation (Turner and Acevedo-Garcia 2005, 17).

However, our position is that low-income families of color should not have to prove anything to anyone to exercise the right to live in areas that are occupied predominantly by white people. We note that as a society we did not experiment with racial segregation to determine if it would be good for people of color before it was imposed, and it should not be a prerequisite to housing mobility before people are allowed to make that choice. In this regard, generally speaking, people who exercise their right to housing mobility should not be studied as if they are guinea pigs or laboratory rats. They are people who have historically had their life opportunities limited because of their race. We recognize the value of understanding how government might more effectively ensure the right to housing mobility, but to the extent that research is done it must be accomplished purely with the voluntary participation of the individuals involved, and the receipt of housing assistance should not be conditioned upon participation in, cooperation with, or results of such research.

No Coercion into Research

Housing Mobility Is Not In Conflict With the "Right to Stay. The right to choose to continue to live in a minority community is important and in many ways is just as dependent on the presence of decent affordable housing and redress for discrimination. We support those who prefer to focus their energies on more "place-based" strategies in addressing the vestiges of segregation and urge them to do so in a manner that addresses the systemic and institutional racism that is at the core of the difficulties facing those communities. That work presents its own set of challenges and difficult trade-offs, and it is sometimes tempting to see housing mobility work and community revitalization work as conflicting visions. However, they are really two sides of the same coin. Both must be advanced with a respect for and not at the expense of each other.

Let us be clear: The statutory provision proposed at the beginning of this chapter would provide an *individualized* remedy for low-income families who choose to avail themselves of it. It does not address the institutional and systemic vestiges of Jim Crow and segregation and is not a substitute for doing so. It does not directly increase the supply of affordable housing for low-income families. Indeed, it puts the burden of asserting and enforcing the right to such housing on the individuals who are perhaps the least able and should be the last required to bear it. It is indeed a modest proposal.

We understand that for many people housing mobility is a choice that makes no sense. Why go where you are not wanted? Why not stay with your own kind, and work to build and improve the community where you already belong? We do not know the answers to those questions for everyone, but we do know that for any number of reasons there are low-income people of color who make such decisions every day. Given our failure to effectively address our history of segregation systemically and institutionally, the least we can do is insure that, individually, those who would make those choices have the ability to secure them.

Making the Right Real

At a minimum, insuring the right of low-income people of color not to be subjected to segregation as a condition of receiving housing assistance will involve a comprehensive assessment of assisted housing resources in order to determine the extent to which the creation of new housing is necessary and where it should be located. It will involve resources for counseling and supportive services that include housing search assistance and financial assistance to fund the gaps created by discrimination in the housing market (e.g., HUD Fair Market Rents that reflect the true cost of living in whiter, more affluent areas that have historically excluded people of color and affordable housing). It will involve retooling existing housing production programs to insure that affordable housing is not limited in terms of location by race or income. It will involve aggressive and multifaceted fair housing advocacy and enforcement activity. In short, it will involve making the provision of housing mobility as important as the provision of the housing itself.

How It Can Work in the Real World

> "I love it out here. The kids love it." (*Walker* Program participant, mother of two, and six-year resident of north suburban Dallas)

The Dallas-based Inclusive Communities Project (ICP) operates a housing mobility program that is based upon the proposition that housing mobility is a civil right. It was created to support implementation of the final part of the remedy developed in *Walker v. HUD*, a public housing desegregation case. The remedial scope in *Walker* was extensive and involved both "in place" and "mobility" provisions (*Walker v. HUD* 1989).

The aspect of the remedy with which ICP is currently involved deals with the use of Section 8 Housing Choice Vouchers (HCVs) by families who choose the opportunity to live in areas that are predominantly nonminority and are not poverty-concentrated, as defined by the Court (known as "Walker Targeted Areas" or WTAs). As part of the final settlement in the litigation, HUD provided an allocation of special remedial vouchers (known as Walker Settlement Vouchers or WSVs). Walker Settlement Vouchers have a somewhat higher purchasing power than regular Housing Choice Vouchers (125% of HUD's Fair Market Rent level) and come with first-time move-related financial assistance, such as application fees and security deposits to help mitigate the costs of moving to the higher-income, whiter areas. Once a family makes the first mobility move under the program, ICP is available to assist the family if they move again but want to stay in a WTA. The Inclusive Communities Project also works with families who are not moving but have other issues that may impact their ability to take full advantage of the benefits of their housing choices.

There are approximately 2,500 African-American families (*Walker* class members) who have chosen to participate in the WSV program since 2002, and an additional approximately 3,000 class members who have used their regular HCV to move into WTAs without the additional mobility assistance during the period when there were no WSVs available.[6]

The housing mobility program that ICP runs is not a model. It is a work in progress, a *design build*, to use an architectural term, and ICP makes adjustments to its program based upon experience and client feedback. Our goal is to support families who make the sometimes difficult choice to move to an unfamiliar place where they are not sure they are wanted, which they are not sure they can afford, but where for a number of reasons they want to go. This means that we do not try to be all things to all people. Our clients are Black voucher holders or applicants for vouchers who, after a thorough briefing about their options, say they want to try living in the suburbs or in areas within the City of Dallas where low-income Black people have not historically lived. Because we are assisting our clients in obtaining fundamental civil rights, our housing mobility counseling program is more advocacy-oriented than social services providers tend to be and is supported by a team of lawyers who have significant experience with the issues of race and housing. There are a multitude of barriers to the effective exercise of a housing mobility choice, and it is ICP's job to identify and remove those barriers. We do that on an individual, systemic, and institutional basis.

Identifying and Removing Barriers to Housing Mobility

While theoretically vouchers offer families an opportunity to obtain housing in a location of their choice, the reality is that many local housing authorities do not support and are not administratively designed to foster nonsegregative housing. The effect of such an institutional antimobility attitude should not be minimized. For example, the voucher briefing process offers a fertile opportunity to steer families to places that are known, that are assumed to be where low-income people of color want/ought to live, and that will cause the least political headaches for an institution that is usually not beloved in the local community. Those locations are usually not predominantly white areas of above average income. To address those barriers, ICP counselors attend all briefings, make presentations about the services available for those wishing to make a mobility move, monitor Dallas Housing Authority presentations for accuracy and attitude, and engage in ongoing communication with Housing Authority personnel at the appropriate level to address concerns.

For families to be able to take advantage of the theoretical choice the voucher offers, they must have information about housing located outside traditional low-income minority areas, information and resources that a public housing authority (PHA) may not have nor be inclined to develop. Most PHAs have established relationships with landlords in more traditional low-income communities, and may experience resistance if they seek to expand the pool of housing opportunities for families outside those areas. To counter that dynamic, ICP counselors do extensive outreach in nonminority, low-poverty areas to acquaint landlords with the program and recruit them to work with ICP clients.

Administrative responsibilities related to the voucher program, such as housing quality inspections and rent reasonableness determinations, are made more complicated if housing mobility is involved and require PHA staff effort and expertise beyond traditional services. Housing mobility advocates can play a crucial role in educating PHA staff and working with landlords to facilitate the use of vouchers in nontraditional areas that promote expanded housing choice.

The inherent barrier presented by limited personal financial resources and the higher costs often associated with rental units in whiter areas (i.e., application fees, security deposits, as well as rents) can steer families of color to historically minority segregated areas. Families who do make mobility choices can be subjected to a rent burden due to the market-driven rent realities in the higher-opportunity communities. ICP mobility counselors work with landlords to educate them about the voucher program, recruit their participation, and assist them in dealing with the Housing Authority. The Inclusive Communities Project can provide a bonus to create an incentive for a landlord to try the program or to enable a family to obtain or remain in tenancy by convincing the landlord to keep the rent voucher-eligible. On the systemic front, ICP has sued HUD in federal court, challenging the process for setting Fair Market Rents in the Dallas area, alleging that the process has the purpose and effect of steering low-income families of color into low-income minority areas and making rental housing in more affluent white areas unavailable (*ICP v. HUD* 2007).

Once achieved, a move to a higher-opportunity area often means moving into an environment with limited or difficult-to-find services for low-income families. The Inclusive Communities Project counselors identify financial and social service resources and make appropriate referrals on a wide range of matters. Families are given information about schools, support services, amenities, and activities/events in their new communities. Regular geographic-based "Focus Group" meetings with groups of clients and ICP-sponsored group outings for clients and their children help them connect with each other and their new community.

Although many of our clients who choose to move have their own cars, transportation is always a barrier to housing mobility, as people move to locations that are not served by good public transportation (Abell Foundation 2006; see website for information regarding funding to the Baltimore Housing Authority's Vehicles for Change program toward the purchase of 60 low-cost used cars for participants in the Special Housing Mobility Voucher program).

The Inclusive Communities Project is exploring ways to provide access to used cars for families, as well as working with its attorneys to examine the exclusionary impact of transportation policies in some larger suburbs.

The policies of the private rental market can be a barrier to effective housing mobility due to their ignorance of or hostility to the program. While it is not illegal in Texas for a landlord to refuse to accept a voucher, it is clear that race discrimination is at the heart of some potential landlords' refusals. In those instances, ICP can undertake testing, more aggressive landlord outreach that seeks to eliminate any legitimate nondiscriminatory reasons for refusing to participate in the program, and ultimately fair housing enforcement activity. Even in the Low Income Housing Tax Credit (LIHTC) program, which prohibits discrimination against voucher holders, constant vigilance is required to ensure that the owners of such developments do not violate that provision.

Unfortunately, one of the causes, as well as the byproducts, of our nation's legacy of segregation is bigotry and prejudice toward those who are of a different race. Clients of ICP have sometimes encountered hostile neighbors and insensitive school personnel when they move into a neighborhood or community in which African Americans have not resided in any significant numbers. Inclusive Communities Project counselors work with the affected families to address the issue, which, depending upon the circumstances, can involve relocating, facilitating communication between the parties, communicating with local officials regarding race relations in the community, requesting or attending parent/teacher conferences, or other interventions with school personnel.

Often families believe that a mobility move will give them access to better schools, and ICP counselors use the most current school accountability information when assisting families in their housing searches in order to inform parents about the schools to which their children will be assigned. This has uncovered a practice reminiscent of the sort of tactics used to perpetuate segregation after *Brown vs. Board* outlawed overtly segregated schools:

suburban areas using the attendance zone process to segregate children who live in multifamily developments (as opposed to neighboring single-family houses) into schools that are overcrowded and underperforming. It is important to pursue advocacy activities designed to attack this practice because it can effectively deny a child one of the benefits of his or her family's move. The Inclusive Communities Project is in the process of analyzing the relationship between multifamily housing and attendance zone assignments in various suburbs to see if more systemic advocacy is suggested. These types of actions by local authorities expose them to the same legal challenges that characterized early post-*Brown* desegregation cases 40 years ago.

Another more individualized barrier encountered by families who seek to realize the benefits of higher-opportunity areas involves the costs of participating in social events like school extracurricular and graduation activities. To help meet this need, ICP counselors engage in ongoing research and outreach to find existing resources, and develop new sources of assistance.[7] Many schools in higher-opportunity areas have scholarship and grant programs that go unadvertised and unused until ICP counselors make inquiries that unearth them. Such efforts have resulted in students having access to resources such as band instruments and sports uniforms to allow them to more fully participate in activities in their new schools, and play a more active part in their new community. Finally, identification of these kinds of needs creates an opportunity for individuals and organizations who might not otherwise be interested in supporting ICP's work to make contributions specifically targeted for such activities.

On the institutional side, exclusionary local land use and housing policies are time-honored barriers to effective housing mobility for low-income people of color. "Don't Build It and They Won't Come" might be the motto of many suburban cities and certain parts of urban areas. "You are not welcome" is clearly the message sent by such actions as: (1) adopting local zoning and other land use policies that eliminate or make it virtually impossible to develop affordable housing, and (2) engaging in or supporting NIMBY responses to efforts to build such housing.

Even where there is some affordable housing in a suburb, it is often in the older parts of town where people of color were historically relegated to live. While this situation may give a city an appearance of having a greater supply of affordable housing than some of its neighbors, the location of that housing only reinforces the segregation along racial and class lines that characterizes the broader community.

In addition to traditional litigation pursued under our civil rights laws, an initiative currently being undertaken by ICP to address some of these development issues involves acquisition of land in several suburban communities that would be suitable for multifamily housing development. This sort of suburban land-banking will put ICP in a position to address any potential barriers, such as zoning or other land use issues, prior to partnering with a developer to get affordable housing built on the site.

Another institutional barrier to effective housing mobility involves decisions about where federally-funded project-based housing for low-income people, including replacement public housing and housing developed using the LIHTC Program, should be located. The *Walker* litigation challenged the way that public housing had historically been sited to perpetuate segregation in Dallas and has resulted in the construction of 474 new units of public housing in predominantly white areas (*Walker v. City of Mesquite* 2005). Because the LIHTC Program is currently the more prolific producer of housing for low-income families, and because tax credit developments cannot legally refuse a family if they have a housing voucher, tax credit units are a valuable source of housing mobility opportunities for low-income families who participate in the voucher program. Unfortunately, in the Dallas Metro Area, as in many places throughout the country, LIHTC developments have been disproportionately concentrated in low-income minority areas, as were their public housing predecessors.[8]

In an attempt to address the LIHTC siting barrier, ICP has recently sued the state housing finance agency, which administers Texas' LIHTC program, for perpetuating segregation through its administration of the program. The suit alleges that a disproportionate number of tax credit developments for families (as opposed to those for the elderly) have been sited in predominantly minority areas, including developments that were located in areas with high crime, near environmentally degraded sites like landfills, or otherwise inappropriate locations (*ICP v. Texas Department of Housing & Community Affairs* March 28, 2008). Additionally, ICP has petitioned the IRS for rule-making that would implement the Fair Housing Act's requirements that federal housing and community development programs affirmatively further fair housing (ICP Letter of Petition for Rule Making 2008).

These examples of housing mobility-related advocacy underscore the wide range of local advocacy activities that can be undertaken to foster and support housing mobility as a civil right of low-income people of color. The advocacy can be as systemic and institutionally focused as the tax credit litigation, and it can be as individually and personally focused as the effort to get a student a horn to play in his or her school band. It can address ignorance and misinformation with education and outreach activities, and it can realistically assess the need for more adversarial efforts when resistance is encountered from a landlord, a housing authority employee, a hostile neighbor, or a governmental entity.

An Unfinished Agenda

There is work left to do. Those who were involved in the Administration at HUD during the Clinton years rightly point to the fact that the administration reversed the positions taken by the Bush I Administration in the pending civil rights lawsuits that challenged public housing segregation. They are proud of the fact that most of those lawsuits were settled in a manner that tried to further fair housing, rather than defend the indefensible, and rightly so.

However, they blinked when it came to taking on the issue of housing segregation in a more comprehensive, systemic, and institutional way. Given what they knew, the Clinton Administration at HUD could have chosen to undertake an examination of all of its housing programs through the magnifying glass of race to see where the segregated patterns could be laid at the feet of policy or practice that was engaged in or allowed by the federal government, not just where victims of discrimination had access to legal advocates who can bring a lawsuit to protect their rights. That could have been followed by development and implementation of a systematic plan of action that would eliminate those policies and practices, and more importantly, effectuate remedial policies and practices that would undo their vestiges. *That* would have been transformative. But it would have also meant that the important agendas and the budgets of too many people in positions of authority at HUD would have been diverted to that end. So the "good guys" stepped up when lawyers came calling, but otherwise opted to leave in place many of the conditions that they knew were caused by the institution of which they were now a responsible part. There is no doubt that good things came out of those legal settlements and other efforts to further fair housing and civil rights during those eight years, as there should have been. However, the failure to address *fundamentally* the issue of racial segregation in low-income housing programs continues to stand as one of our greatest policy failures.

Looking to the future, those currently in the midst of their early careers of advocacy and civil rights involvement must recognize the very real interests of those who may be the quieter "squeaky wheels" but retain Constitutional rights that have been and continue to be marginalized by the legacy of governmental low-income housing policy. Many of us commit to do good work and fight the fight of the disenfranchised, but the disenfranchised are not a monolith. Time must be taken to analyze local and national policy, as well as information that goes beyond the immediate neighborhoods in which advocates work, in order to see the interconnectedness that impacts various populations of low-income people of color. While the plight of residents who choose to remain in segregated areas where they feel invested is compelling, the plight of those who seek to assert their right to make immediate differences in their own and their families' lives by moving to desegregated, low-poverty areas should not be muted by broad sweeping policy positions that leave no room for such moves. The emerging generation of advocacy leaders must decide whether to learn from its baby-boomer predecessors who fell short of going the distance, or to continue to promote the false choice between housing and desegregation (Rubinstein et al. 1956; Seicshnaydre 2007). Sixty years ago, liberal low-income housing advocates argued "housing now, desegregation later." Will our theme for our lifetime be "housing now, desegregation never"?

Conclusion

On June 29, 1949 the Congress of the United States defeated an amendment to the 1949 Housing Act that would have prohibited segregation in federally-funded public housing.[9] The legacy of that unconscionable decision continues to this day. The time is long overdue for Congress to remove the stain from the federally-funded low-income housing programs of our nation.

The authors, who span the generational divide, argue for a renewed commitment for zealous advocacy to remove that stain and push to undo all vestiges of historical segregation for low-income people of color at both the individual and systemic levels.

This includes recognizing and supporting housing mobility as a civil right of low-income people of color. Affirmative action is required.

Acknowledgments

The authors wish to acknowledge the efforts of the families with whom the Inclusive Communities Project (ICP) works, the ICP staff, and Mike Daniel and Laura Beshara and their staff as we push this rock called Civil Rights up the hill.

Notes

1. The authors use the term *minority* as consistent with its use by the Court in *Walker v. HUD*, in describing nonwhites or whites of Hispanic or Latino origin, and in no way implies any negative connotation through its usage.
2. U.S. Const. amend. XIII; U.S. Const. amend. XIV (ensuring, through The Civil Rights Act of 1868, that citizenship extended to former enslaved Africans and other blacks for whom equal protection of the law should be provided); 42 U.S.C.S. § 1981 (enforcing the right of all citizens of every race and color through The Civil Rights Act of 1866 to make and enforce contracts, inherit, purchase, lease, sell, hold, and convey real estate and personal property, among other things); 42 U.S.C. § 1983 (providing, through the Civil Rights Act of 1871 *also known as* the Klu Klux Klan Act of 1871, an enforcement mechanism against governmental entities).
3. Fair Housing Act, Pub. L. No. 90-284, 82 Stat. 73 (1968) (codified as amended at 42 U.S.C.S. § 3608. [Lexis 2008]).
4. Low-income housing advocates have long supported the right of individual public housing tenants to enforce statutory rights afforded under Section 1437 of the U.S. Housing Act of

1937 (42 U.S.C.S. 1437p). The right to desegregated housing should be no less an enforceable right of individual participants in federal programs.

5. The Moving to Opportunity (MTO) program, a short-lived metropolitan-wide federal experiment in Boston, New York, Baltimore, Los Angeles, and Chicago, was authorized by Congress in 1991 to assist families with children to move out of areas with high concentrations of persons living in poverty. Although inspired by the *Gautreaux* litigation, the demonstration program did not use race as a factor, as did the Chicago demonstration; therefore, many movers relocated to neighboring communities with moderately higher incomes and similar concentrations of people of color. MTO was authorized under § 152 of the Housing & Community Development Act of 1992 and jointly administered by HUD's Office of Policy Development and Research, Office of Fair Housing and Equal Opportunity, and Office of Public and Indian Housing. Housing and Community Development Act of 1992 § 152, Pub. L. No. 102-550, 106 Stat. 3672, 3716–17 (1992).

6. In response to ICP advocacy, the Dallas Housing Authority is in the process of giving those HCV families the opportunity to exchange their HCVs for WSVs, which will give those families the benefits of the program, and free up a HCV for another family on the waiting list.

7. For example, we found that Balfour, the company that provides graduation materials for many high schools which our children attend, has a program that assists families who cannot afford the costs of invitations, caps and gowns, etc. Because the company was not accustomed to families needing their program in the high schools in more affluent areas, they do not advertise the program's availability, but ICP now has the information and provides it to our clients on a regular basis.

8. When the *Walker* case was filed in 1985, over 95% of family public housing was located in overwhelmingly minority, historically segregated, high-poverty communities. Today, as a result of *Walker* and other litigation, 64% of the units are in that category. In the LIHTC program, approximately 3% of tax credit units are in 70 to 100% white census tracts; 85% of tax credit units are in 0 to 30% white census tracts.

9. The amendment was made by Representative Vito Marcantonio, who challenged the chamber during debate about the 1949 Housing Act. At issue was whether to permit racial segregation in the public housing which would be created by the bill. Liberal Democrats, fearful that to do so would cause the bill to fail, rejected his plea. The bill passed, and segregation in federally-funded low-income housing was the result. Housing Act of 1949, Pub. L. No. 81-171, 63 Stat. 413 (codified as amended 42 U.S.C.S § 1441).

References

Abell Foundation. 2006 Grant Recipients. http://www.abell.org/grantmaking/2006grants/2006.html (Accessed July 18, 2008)

Briggs, Xavier de Souza, ed. 2005. *The Geography of Opportunity: Race and Housing Choice in Metropolitan America*. Washington, D.C.: Brookings Institution Press.

Brown v. Board of Education, 34 U.S. 483 (1954).

Gautreaux v. Pierce, 690 F.2d 616, 622-24 (7th Cir. 1981) (affirming the lower court's approval of the settlement).

Goering, John M. 1986. *Housing Desegregation and Federal Policy*. Chapel Hill: University of North Carolina Press.

———. 2005. "Expanding Housing Choice and Integrating Neighborhoods: The MTO Experiment." In *The Geography of Opportunity*, ed. Xavier de Souza Briggs. Washington, D.C.: Brookings Institution Press, 127–49.

Inclusive Communities Project v. HUD, 3-07 CV 0945-L (N.D. Tex. Complaint filed May 29, 2007).

Inclusive Communities Project v. Texas Department of Housing & Community Affairs, 308CV-546-D (N. Dist. Tex. Complaint Filed March 28, 2008).

Inclusive Communities Project v. TDHCA (Defendant's Motion to Dismiss filed June 27, 2008).

Inclusive Communities Project Letter of Petition for Rule Making Involving the Qualified Allocation Plan to the Internal Revenue Service. Filed March 12, 2008. On file with authors.

Institute for Policy Research, Northwestern University. n.d. "IPR Research on Gautreaux and other Housing Mobility Programs." http://www.northwestern.edu/ipr/publications/Gautreaux.html (Accessed July 18, 2008)

Julian, Elizabeth. 2007. "An Unfinished Agenda." *Shelterforce* (Winter): 20.

———. 2008. "Fair Housing and Community Development: Time to Come Together." *Indiana Law Review* 41: 555.

———, and Michael Daniel. 1989. "Separate and Unequal—The Root and Branch of Public Housing Segregation." *Clearinghouse Review* (October): 666.

Kerner Commission. 1968. *Report of the National Advisory Commission on Civil Disorders*. New York: Bantam Books.

Massachusetts Law Reform Institute et al. 2004. Letter to the Internal Revenue Service. March 30, 2004. http://www.prrac.org/pdf/IRSLetter.pdf (Accessed July 18, 2008)

Massey, Douglas S., and Nancy A. Denton. 1993. *American Apartheid: Segregation and the Making of the Underclass*. Cambridge, MA: Harvard University Press.

Montgomery County v. Glenmont Hills Associates, Privacy World at Glenmont Metro Centre, 936, A.2d, 345 (Md. Ct. of App. 2007), *cert. denied* 128 S.Ct. 2914, 2008 Lexis 4793 (June 9, 2008).

Polikoff, Alexander. 2006. *Waiting for Gautreaux: a Story of Segregation, Housing, and the Black Ghetto*. Evanston, IL: Northwestern University Press.

Poverty & Race Research Action Council. 2004. "Civil Rights Mandates in the Low-Income Housing Tax Credit Program: An Advocate's Guide." http://www.prrac.org/pdf/crmandates.pdf (Accessed July 18, 2008)

Roisman, Florence Wagman. 2007. "Affirmatively Furthering Fair Housing in Regional Housing Markets: The Baltimore Public Housing Desegregation Litigation." *Wake Forest Law Review* 42: 333–91.

Rubinstein, Annette T., and Associates, ed. 1956. " The Eighty-first Congress 1949–1950" in *I Vote My Conscience*. New York: The Vito Marcantonio Memorial, 307–08.

Seicshnaydre, Stacy E. 2007. "In Search of a Just Public Housing Policy Post-Katrina." *Poverty & Race* 16 (September/October): 3–6.

Turner, Margery Austin, and Dolores Acevedo-Garcia. 2005. "The Benefits of Housing Mobility: A Review of the Research Evidence." In *Keeping the Promise*, ed. Poverty & Race Research Action Council. Washington, D.C., 9–23.

Walker v. HUD, 734 F. Supp. 1231, 1247-61 (N.D. Tex. 1989).

Walker v. City of Mesquite, 402 F.3d 532 (Fifth Cir. 2005).

CHAPTER 8

Desegregated Schools With Segregated Education

WILLIAM A. DARITY, JR. AND ALICIA JOLLA

A comparatively less remarked aspect of two of the heretical economist John Kenneth Galbraith's works, *The Affluent Society* (1958) and *The New Industrial State* (1967), was his prescient discussion of "the New Class." Of particular importance in this context is Chapter 25 of *The New Industrial State*, "The Educational and Scientific Estate." Galbraith, the quintessential modern American liberal, actually praised the work of the iconoclastic Trotskyist James Burnham, who turned into an early neoconservative, and whose book *The Managerial Revolution* (1941) provided a foundation for Galbraith's discussion.

Galbraith's "educational and scientific estate" constitutes the highly educated or credentialed members of contemporary society, also often called the intellectuals and intelligentsia. These individuals collectively overlap with the segment of the population that Robert Reich (1992, 208–24) has called "the symbolic analysts." They can be found working directly for the industrial or corporate system, or they can be found working for centers comparatively independent from the industrial or corporate sector, such as, colleges, universities, research institutes, think tanks, foundations, art centers, museums, and the like.

Galbraith posed this development as the emergence of a "New Class" distinct from capital and labor, a New Class whose very existence leveled a critique of both left and right orthodoxy. According to Galbraith, albeit a bit simplistically, both procapitalist and procommunist doctrines saw all persons who receive wages as laborers or as members of the working class.[1]

Nevertheless, Galbraith was broadly correct that highly credentialed workers typically were treated as entirely a part of the working class as long as they receive salaried compensation—and, accordingly, there was no fundamental alteration in our understanding of the world.

In Galbraith's analysis, the boundaries of the New Class are set by educational credentials and the presumption of the possession of expert knowledge. The New Class also plays a critical role as the arbiter of taste or cultural norms (Bourdieu 1984); what is in fashion—what is fashionable—becomes the purview of the New Class. The requisite rite of passage for entry into the New Class customarily is a successful journey through the college and university system and attainment of the appropriate degrees. Moreover, for this social class, work should be both entertaining and well paid. As Galbraith (1967, 267) observed, education is intended for acquiring "an interesting and rewarding occupation, not merely for income."

Galbraith also had an intensely optimistic view of the long-term consequences of the rise of the "educational and scientific estate," unlike, for example, the dark vision embodied in Burnham's *Managerial Revolution* of the New Class as, in essence, a force that will subvert democratic possibilities. Believing that American education is at base an open system, Galbraith anticipated that there would be free access to the New Class. For Galbraith, finally, here was an elite that any could enter by dint of talent and motivation. Indeed, as society came to value educational credentials more and more, the elite itself might grow to encompass all members of society.

Unfortunately, here is where Galbraith was incorrect. American education is not an open system. Indeed, one of the major consequences of the closed nature of American education is differential access to the New Class based upon race. Differential access arises because talent and ability is selectively constructed in our nation's schools on racial grounds. To demonstrate this argument, our analysis begins with the segregated South of the pre-Civil Rights era, when racially unequal education was blatant and transparent.

Dangers of School Desegregation

The most famous fictional depiction of the segregated South is probably Harper Lee's novel *To Kill a Mockingbird* (Lee 1960). Widely used in our nation's public schools, it has become the iconic novel enabling teachers to say their literature curriculum addresses race in America in a manner similar to the way in which *The Diary of Anne Frank* functions as *the* Holocaust text (Frank 1952). The central problem with *To Kill a Mockingbird*—a problem not shared by *The Diary of Anne Frank* where the voice we hear is the voice of the victim herself—is the novel's embodiment of the colonial gaze. The experience of blacks in the small Southern community is seen through the eyes of whites, looking in on the "natives" with either sympathy or hostility but always paternalistically.

The narrator is a young girl, Scout, whose father, Atticus Finch (played by Gregory Peck in the film version of the nove)l, is the good, courageous bwana, but a bwana nonetheless. The "natives" never really speak for themselves. We never hear directly what they think about the social system in which they are compelled to live nor what they believe they can do about it.

Prince Edward, a more recent novel by Dennis McFarland (2004), for all its merits, repeats the *Mockingbird* conceit. Set in Farmville, Virginia, a community where a white school board shut down the public schools altogether in 1959 rather than desegregate, from its opening passages the novel also epitomizes the colonial gaze directed at "the Negro."

A rare exception to this pattern is Thulani Davis' novel *1959* that explores school desegregation in the same region of Virginia during the same time period. Davis' novel is written entirely from the interior perspective of the black community. Her readers hear the debates that took place among black parents as school desegregation loomed on the horizon—their reservations, aspirations, plans, and strategies. The reservations described by Davis in her novel include the following:

1. The danger from white hostility to black families' livelihoods. Whites could threaten black parents with job loss or worse if they pursued enrolling their sons and daughters in previously all-white schools. Constance Curry's (1996) moving study of the efforts of the solitary black family in Sunflower County, Mississippi to desegregate the public schools there reveals the full range of possible white retaliatory terror.
2. Threats to the job status of black teachers and administrators.
3. Fear that their children would be maltreated, physically harmed, or badly educated in formerly all-white schools, particularly since desegregation generally operated in one direction—black students moving into previously all-white schools.

While Davis reveals these issues in the context of a fictional account, W. E. B. DuBois (1935) raised the same issues in a controversial essay published in *The Journal of Negro Education* during the mid-1930s. Critical of both "mixed" and "separate" schools, DuBois argued that there was no reason to presume black students necessarily would get a better education in the previously all-white schools.

School choice plans in Sunflower County—and throughout the South in the aftermath of the *Brown v. Board* (1954) decision—were mechanisms to evade school desegregation. The Farmville strategy was to close the public schools altogether while white families received subsidies to attend segregated private academies, an early uniracial voucher plan. But long prior to enforced desegregation, a school choice plan was implemented in Cincinnati, Ohio. During the late 1920s and early 1930s, Cincinnati officially gave black families a fully sanctioned opportunity to send their children to either all-black or "mixed" (predominantly white) schools in the city. Apropos of DuBois' discussion, Crowley (1932) found no significant difference in academic outcomes for black students in either type of school. The key was both sets of schools were similarly resourced, and the black teachers in the all-black schools had qualifications at least the equivalent of the white teachers in the mixed schools.

On the surface, one route toward implementation of the intent of *Brown v. Board of Education* was to utilize residential desegregation to promote school desegregation. Both before and after the *Brown* decision, particularly in Northern cities, the combination of residential segregation and district assignment by neighborhoods led to de facto school segregation. "Indeed, among other factors, such as the size of the metropolitan area, per capita income, and average school enrollment size, research suggests that residential segregation is the most important factor in determining the level of school segregation" (Rickles et al. 2001, 7–8). But, as we demonstrate in detail, desegregation of schools at the site or facility level—whether by residential desegregation, busing, or through magnet programs—generally does not translate into internal desegregation of schools at the level of curriculum and instruction.

A paradigmatic example of this phenomenon is found in the integrated suburban Shaker Heights community of Ohio where Ronald Ferguson (2001) investigated how a desegregated residential community still produces racially uneven education. This occurs despite the fact that there is only one prestigious, public high school that all students attend. Ferguson found, in particular, that black students had strikingly low levels of enrollment in Advanced Placement (AP) courses at Shaker Heights High School. Indeed, although the high school was about half black, black students were only 31% of those in honors classes and only 11% of those taking at least one AP class (Ferguson 2001).

Historically, as a matter of dignity and principle, black America went forward with the pursuit of school desegregation, but eliminating American educational apartheid has had its costs. Tragically, all the dangers anticipated by the black parents in Davis' novel and in DuBois' essay have been realized fully. At the heart of matters is the sustained process of racially uneven talent development in our nation's schools. Neither residential desegregation nor school desegregation has led to racially equal schooling. Within the "mixed" school, separate curricula frequently are delivered to black and white students; a condition persists of segregated education within desegregated schools (Donelan, Neal, and Jones 1994).

Racialized Tracking

Internal segregation within schools has substituted for segregation at the facility level.[2] During slavery times, the rule of thumb was no schooling for blacks. Under Jim Crow, schooling for blacks was separate and unequal. Horace Mann Bond (1934)) documented the magnitude of the inequality when he demonstrated that by the 1930s in most of the states of the "Old Confederacy," per pupil resources were five to six times greater for students in white schools than for students in black schools. There were times when white school boards did not allocate any local tax revenue to black schools, although black households paid taxes. Black parents then would pay not only the local property taxes but also find a way to build a school for their children and pay the teachers (Anderson 1988, Williams 2005). Today, although schools generally are desegregated, the content of education remains separate and unequal. Consequently, the achievement gap is fundamentally a curriculum gap: Black children are disproportionately tested on material they never have been taught.

Segregated education under school desegregation operates primarily through racialized tracking within schools. Consider Columbia High School in Maplewood, New Jersey. In 2005 (Gettleman 2005), the school had over 2,000 students, with the following racial/ethnic composition: 58% black, 35% white, 4% Latino, and 3% Asian. The school assigned students to mathematics classes ranging from Levels 2 through 5, with 2 as the lowest tier and 5 as the highest tier. Close to 90% of the students in Level 2 math were black, while close to 80% of the students in Level 5 math were white (Gettleman 2005).

This pattern is the long-term outcome of a process of systematic under-education of black students following the *Brown* decision via the mechanism of educational tracking. In the mid-1960s—when the District of Columbia's public schools still had a racially mixed student population—compelling evidence emerged that curriculum and student classroom assignments were being structured to miseducate black children deliberately.

Black children were labeled uneducable due to "cultural deprivation" or an alleged tendency to learn more slowly than other children "because they were from broken or unwed homes or their parents spend long hours away from that home at work"; black children were viewed as "...too often [being] so hopelessly handicapped that a great number of them are not ready to be exposed to normal tools of knowledge offered a typical first grader" (Mazique 1965, 2). Thus, a presumption of black cognitive inferiority was being embedded into the operations of the school system from the point when black children first began school. The contradiction with the history of the black march toward literacy and learning was transparent for one critic of the D.C. public schools:

If "cultural deprivation" and "economic underprivileged" conditions were the bar to literacy, as maintained, Negroes would not have made the progress they did during the latter [half of the] 19th century. Who among them had parents who were literate? That number was few indeed. If broken or unwed homes constitutes the barrier to learning, as proclaimed today, there would have been no need or demand for education of Negroes in the South following Emancipation, for broken homes or an unwed condition was the rule...not the exception. But Negroes, however they were conceived, did learn and still learn whether they have an intact home or not. (Mazique 1965, 3)

A track system was introduced in the District's schools, an ability grouping scheme where students were placed in Basic, General, Regular, or Honors tracks. The Basic track was for students identified as "mentally retarded" and was a wholly remedial curriculum. The General track was a technical training curriculum for students who did not intend to pursue higher education after high school. The Regular and Honors tracks were for the college-bound, with the Honors track offering the most challenging curriculum (Hansen 1965, 9–11). There were negligible numbers of black students in either of the two upper tracks in the integrated schools, and their presence was disproportionately lower in the schools with majority black student bodies.

Moreover, in the District's school system "uptracking" (moving from a lower to a higher track) was rare, while "downtracking" was commonplace. Not only were the numbers of students in the Basic and General tracks rising, but so were the numbers of dropouts (Hansen 1965). Black students were increasingly testing poorly in the system, but it was apparent that their poor test performance was because, under the structure of the track system, they had not been taught the material that was being evaluated (Mazique 1965, 2).

Moreover, teachers of black children were being pushed to dilute the content of what they were teaching their pupils. In 1961, a teacher assigned to a junior primary group was warned not to teach her "culturally deprived" six-year-olds numbers or the alphabet. Instead, she was told to entertain them rather than give them the first-grade course of study. Finally, one of her students stood up after a month of these empty activities and asked when they would start to do what they had come to school to do—learn? The teacher then set about giving them challenging work, to which they took with enthusiasm. At the close of the school year, her class, which had been expected to repeat first grade, tested at the second-grade level, and her job was in danger. By responding to her students' desires to learn, she had undermined an intended self-fulfilling prophecy. Because of the actions of a citizens' advocacy group seeking to restore quality education in the schools and concerns expressed by members of the House Appropriations Committee, the teacher was not fired. But her students still had to repeat first grade (League for Universal Justice and Goodwill 1965 and 1966, 270).

Another teacher at a different school was assigned a middle track of a five-section second grade. Her group tested far ahead of the first group, the gifted honors class. She was rebuked for pushing her students and told she must slow their pace of study. After all, they never should have performed ahead of the students in group one, since they were in group three (League for Universal Justice and Goodwill 1965 and 1966, 270).

There was a strong correlation between a child's family income and his or her assignment to tracks in the system. Lower-income children fell into the lower tracks, higher-income children rose into the higher tracks. Race, however, was more decisive than class in track assignments. Middle-class black children were liable to be assigned to tracks with negligible academic challenge and also were subjected to being labeled inaccurately as "retarded."

Consider the case of Edward Mazique, a black youngster from an affluent family with highly educated parents. In the late 1950s, he entered the DC public schools as a second grader, having transferred from a private school where he was reported as performing two grades above his classification. In public school, he did not qualify for the top section of second graders and was placed in the middle section. In third grade, "he was placed in the slow group and soon developed or showed signs of retardation, such as holding his mouth open and walking with a gait usually associated with severely mentally retarded children" (Mazique 1965, 4). By fourth grade, the young man received a report card replete with failing grades in all subjects except deportment.

His parents, having the resources, had him tested privately, establishing that he was actually gifted. He applied to and was accepted at St. Anselm's, a prestigious boys' middle and high school, well-known throughout the DC area for high academic standards. His grades for the balance of the year were all Bs. He became an A student thereafter. Following the exams, he was among the 28 students chosen for St. Anselm's seventh-grade class. He maintained his excellent performance at St. Anselm's, starting Latin in seventh grade, adding French in eighth grade, along with Greek as a third language, second-year algebra, biology, religion, and English. He also played on the school basketball team (Mazique 1965, 4). Today, he is a successful physician in Houston, Texas.

Edward Mazique's case was not unique among the children of the District's black middle class. Mrs. Wendell Lucas of the Rock Creek Estate Neighborhood League moved her ten-year-old son to a private school after recognizing that he simply was not being taught in the public schools. Similar problems were described by Woodrow Wilson, secretary of the Citizens Committee of the District, who transferred his children to parochial schools (Lindsay 1961, A1, A7). Still more cases emerged in the Congressional hearings held on the District schools in 1965 and 1966 (League for Universal Justice and Goodwill, 1965 and 1966, 255–306). Those black families who could manage to pay for private education exited from the District's public schools.

Programmed Retardation

Today, the extent of black miseducation can be gauged by black students' participation and performance in Advanced Placement courses that ostensibly offer a college-level learning experience. Of the roughly 750,000 students who took more than 1.2 million AP exams in May 2000, only 36,000 were African-American (Burdman 2000, note 18). There are now a total of 37 different AP courses and examinations (College Board 2008, 2). University students who have taken at least one AP course in high school significantly outperform those who had not taken an AP course but have had the college-level prerequisites (Jeong 2008). Participation in AP classes also is associated with bigger gains for students from underrepresented groups once they reach the university (Jeong 2008). Furthermore, in general, achievement test performance tends to rise with exposure to more challenging courses, including AP courses (Sorenson and Hallinan 1997).

Despite a marked increase in the numbers of black students taking AP courses during the past two decades (some states, like North Carolina, received federal Advanced Placement Incentive Grants to expand access to AP courses for students underrepresented in the courses ("North Carolina Receives" 2006)), black students still are underrepresented among AP course-takers. By 2006, blacks were 13% of all high school students in the United States, 11% of SAT test-takers, but still only 5.6% of all AP test-takers. The highest share of black test-takers for any AP exam was 7.6% for English literature. Exams where black students constituted less than 5% of test-takers included calculus AB and BC, statistics, physics, Spanish language, European history, and computer science A and AB ("Black Enrollment" 2007, 86–87). In 2007, there were only 86 black students who took the Spanish literature AP exam nationwide (College Board 2008, 49).

Among those black students who took the AP exams, their scores typically are markedly lower than those attained by students from other racial/ethnic groups, especially white and Asian students. Advanced Placement exams are graded on a 1 to 5 scale from low to high. Students have to receive a score of at least a 3 to have the prospect of receiving college credit for having taken the course in high school. Nationally in 2007, black students were 14% of the student population, but only 3.3% of the students receiving scores of 3 or higher on at least one AP exam.

In the District of Columbia, black students were about 84% of the student population but only 24% of the students who scored a 3 or higher on at least one AP exam. In New Jersey, the state where Columbia High School is located, black students comprised 15% of the student population but less than 3% of the students scoring a 3 or better on at least one AP exam. In our home state of North Carolina, black students were 28% of the student population but only about 6% of the test-takers scoring a 3 or better.

The only states where there was near parity between the share of black students in the high school population and the black share of all test-takers scoring a 3 or better on at least one test were those where black students were about 1% or less of the state's student body—states like Hawaii, Vermont, and Idaho (College Board 2008, 10). We speculate that in those states the threshold presence of black students is so low that they are less exposed to systematic exclusion from the most challenging curricula offered in the public schools.

High school outcomes like these are foreordained by what happens earlier in the students' school experience. Patterns of high school course-taking and performance are best understood by examining a student's trajectory of course-taking from the earliest years of schooling. The process of segregated education even in desegregated schools starts in the primary school years with the process of gifted and talented (G&T) identification. Black students are grossly underidentified for G&T programs nationwide. Typically, this is the first important stage of racialized tracking in the nation's public schools.

Across Census Region 3 (Pennsylvania, Delaware, the District of Columbia, Maryland, Virginia, and West Virginia), data from the Center for Educational Performance and Information indicate that in 2000 black students were 14.4% of the K-12 population but only 7.5% of the students who had been G&T-identified. A similar pattern of underidentification occurred as well for Latino students, who were 4.4% of the K-12 population but 1.7% of the G&T-population. In contrast, Asian students were 2% of the student population and 3.6% of the G&T population, and white students were 79% of the student population and 87% of the G&T population. In Michigan, in 2006, blacks were 20% of the K-12 student population but only 7.5% of the G&T population. Again, similarly, Latinos were 4.1% of the student population but a mere 1% of G&T students, and American Indian students were 1% of all K-12 students but only 0.5% of G&T students. Again, in contrast, Asian students were 2.2% of the student population and 5.6% of G&T students, while white students were 72.6% of all students and 85% of G&T students.

In 2005, in North Carolina, 4.5% of black, 3.9% of Latino, and 6.9% of American Indian students were G&T-identified by the start of middle school, while 19% of white students and 20% of Asian students were G&T-identified at the same stage. Therefore, for black, Latino, and American Indian students, odds were approximately 1 in 20 that they would have been deemed eligible for the G&T curriculum; for white and Asian students, odds were 1 in 5. On the flip side of the curricular hierarchy, 5% of black students were labeled uneducable and mentally handicapped versus only 1% of white students. Black students had a 1 in 20 chance of being classified in this most extreme "slow learner" category, but white students only had a 1 in 100 chance (Zhang 2005).

There are a host of devastating consequences of underidentification of black students for G&T curricula. First, black students are disproportionately denied the benefits of such identification. They are denied the enrichment effect, the anointment effect, and the cumulative learning effect. The enrichment effect is the intellectual gain from exposure to more challenging and interesting content and the development of critical thinking skills.

Following Lauren Resnick's (1995) pedagogical stance, aptitude is constructed—in short, students can be taught how to be "smart"—rather than something that is fixed and immutable. For Resnick, ability is the product of educational nurturing. An engaging and substantive curriculum from the earliest years of school enhances students' ability to master complex material later in school. Students can benefit from both an anointment and a cumulative learning effect.

The anointment effect is the confidence and validation that students receive by being identified as "gifted." The cumulative learning effect is the increased capacity to take harder courses later in schooling as a result of exposure to and mastery of relevant preparatory material in the earlier years of schooling. Some preliminary evidence in North Carolina indicates that students who were G&T-identified in elementary school are three to four times more likely to take AP and Honors courses in high school than those who were not.

Thus, the uneven process of G&T identification sustains conditions of programmed retardation of black students. Programmed retardation constitutes that nexus of educational "policies, programs and instructional practices designed to guarantee educational failure" (Hayes 2008, 525). Other scholarly reports have referred to the same set of policies as "designed racial gaps" for black students (Hubbard and Mehan 1999).

Second, the underidentification of black students for G&T programs reinforces deeply held beliefs about black cognitive and cultural inferiority. It gives aid and comfort and seemingly confirming evidence to those who believe that racial academic disparities can be explained by black genetic endowments or by black collective cultural dysfunctionality. The latter allegedly results in the adoption of self-defeating behavior on the part of black students. Representative of this type of argument is the Fordham–Ogbu (1986) charge, that black students are bedeviled by a culturally based "burden of acting white."

The exclusion of black students from G&T curricula makes race-thinking become racist-thinking. The pattern of classroom assignment itself can construct an equation between being black and being an inferior student, particularly in white students' minds. Perhaps the most invidious circumstance occurs when G&T instruction is conducted on a pull-out basis, and all the students who get up to leave for the G&T class are white while all the students who stay in the home classroom for "regular" instruction are black.

In a doctoral dissertation completed at the University of North Carolina at Chapel Hill, Timothy Diette (2005) found that middle schools with the most white students are also the schools with the most students who are G&T-identified and have the highest End of Grade state examination mathematics scores. They also are the schools where black students have the lowest odds of taking Algebra 1 during the middle school years.

Third, racialized tracking beginning with G&T selection during the elementary years can produce conditions where the one or two black students taking AP or Honors courses in a desegregated school may be subjected to the charge by their black peers that they are trying to be white. This form of apparent opposition to educational achievement is *not*, as Fordham and Ogbu (1986) would have had it, a cultural import from the black community at-large born of the group's status as involuntary minority. The long history of the black struggle for quality education runs directly counter to that claim (Anderson 1988, Williams 2005). When this type of racialized harassment occurs, it is born of attitudes that are produced by a school context where school policies have disproportionately excluded black students from the "smart kids" curriculum since they were in elementary school. The "acting white" sentiment does not generally arise independent of school context; it is created by the school context.

Note that nonracialized harassment of high achievers is the norm in American schools. "Geeks," "nerds," "brainiacs" are commonplace slurs applied to strong students that do not associate their high achiever status with a particular racial identity. The slurs may actually signal a form of subconscious anti-intellectual class warfare, since the geeks, nerds, and brainiacs are on their way into Galbraith's educational and scientific estate. Essentially, the question remains: When do high-achieving black students get accused of being race traitors when they try to do well in school?

An ethnographic study of schools in North Carolina leads to a hypothesis that the most toxic environment is a high school that is 25 to 75% black, with only one or two black students in the most challenging classes. The situation becomes worse if those students convey an impression that they feel superior to their black peers (Tyson, Darity, and Castellino 2005). No evidence of a "burden of acting white" was detected in all-black schools, i.e., high schools with a student body that is 90% or more black. Black student underrepresentation in the most challenging classes does not become a visible issue in those schools. No evidence of a "burden of acting white" was found in schools with a critical mass of black students in the high-level curriculum that provides access to the "New Class."

Indeed, contra-Galbraith, racialized tracking limits access to the New Class; it maintains the exclusivity of the New Class. American education remains a closed system. Furthermore, evidence of a "burden of acting white" is not always found even in mixed schools where black students are grossly underrepresented in the most challenging classes, but they are the most likely sites. The key point is that in the absence of programmed retardation of black students, there probably would be no evidence of the "burden of acting white" whatsoever in our nation's schools. There would be no racial achievement gap in the first place.

Desegregating Education

What are the effects of desegregating the educational content provided for students? During the course of conducting a Spencer Foundation-funded research initiative titled "Effective Schools, Effective Students," our research team discovered the story of Southwest Elementary in Durham, North Carolina. In 1999, David Snead, a white male, became principal at Southwest. He served there through the 2003–2004 academic year (when he was "kicked upstairs" to serve as head of all middle school programs in the Durham public school system). When he became principal at Southwest, he immediately made a key observation: Both a disproportionately and absolutely small number of black students were in the school's G&T program. Snead saw this pattern as a mechanism for achieving within-school segregation or what he described as "indirect segregation."

In 1997–1998, prior to Snead becoming principal, 98% of the white students in the school had been G&T-identified, while only 7% of the black students had been. The school's overall student body was about 30% white and 70% black. By 1999–2000, when Snead arrived, 18 out of 39 white students in third grade were G&T-identified, but only 2 out of 90 black students were so identified. In the school's fifth grade, 31 out of 33 white students were in the G&T program, in comparison with 12 out of 90 black students. By 2003–2004, Snead's final year as principal, the fifth-grade class consisted of 35 out of 90 black students and 23 out of 35 white students in the G&T program. At that stage, school-wide, 60% of the G&T students were black and 40% were white, a dramatic change in the composition of the gifted population (Snead 2006).

Snead recognized that the teachers were the key gatekeepers in the gifted and talented selection process, that their assessment triggered full consideration of each child for the program. Snead focused on the following initiatives to close the achievement gap at Southwest Elementary School:

- *Exploratory Guest Program:* The core principle in using the G&T program to eliminate the achievement gap is found in the effectiveness of the "guest" program. The guest program was designed to assist students who showed potential and came close to being identified as G&T. This program provided an opportunity for those students to partake in the challenging curricula despite the fact that they were not officially designated as academically gifted students. The "guest" program did not modify identification criteria, but simply provided even more students with exposure to more rigorous coursework. While the "guests" were taking these courses, their progress was monitored closely. Subsequent to receiving these enrichment opportunities as well as other types of support, the students were encouraged to take the G&T test. At Southwest, "guests" were disproportionately black students who had high test scores in reading and math but still had not qualified for G&T identification. This "nurturing giftedness" technique was based upon the idea that exposure to rigorous academic courses will lift student expectations and improve student performance, thus increasing test scores.
- *Early Expectations:* Snead personally believed the key to closing the achievement gap was challenging students early in their schooling. Throughout the interviews, teachers emphasized that Snead lifted the "expectancy level" and consistently argued that all students can succeed regardless of socioeconomic or racial/ethnic background. For instance, all kindergarten children were expected to be at a certain reading level prior to entering the first grade.
- *Reading & Math Remediation:* Many parents and teachers recognized the "Reading Recovery" program at Southwest as an important element for closing the achievement gap. To support this effort, Snead hired a retired schoolteacher to provide one-on-one tutoring in both reading and math for first-grade students.
- *Professional Development:* Snead held professional development retreats during his tenure at Southwest in order to help the faculty members focus on planning for the school year, creating a school theme, and addressing critical issues. One parent said: "After observing the professionals at Southwest, I can attest that when you enroll your child at Southwest, you are guaranteed 100% of the staff's efforts. They do their utmost to nurture every student in the school." Further, the school organized a "diversity training" assessment that aimed to broaden teachers' perceptions of talent in minority students.

- *End of Grade (EOG) Training Early:* Two months before EOG tests were given, the third-, fourth-, and fifth-grade class schedules were modified to accommodate EOG practice sessions. Since EOG testing starts in the third grade, mock EOG exams have been administered to all second-grade students to familiarize them with the test-taking process.

The impact of Snead's leadership at Southwest was remarkable. In 1999–2000, 41% of Southwest's fifth-grade black students did not pass the state's reading test, in comparison with 12% of the white students, and 23% of the black students did not pass the state's mathematics test in comparison with 9% of the white students. By 2002–2003, only 10% of both the black and white students did not pass the reading test and less than 3% of both black and white students did not pass the mathematics test. Southwest Elementary had virtually eliminated the racial achievement gap by eliminating the racial instructional gap (Jolla 2005).

The gap was eliminated despite the fact that white students at Southwest Elementary on average are more affluent and are more likely to come from two-parent families than black students. In fact, during the interval of Snead's tenure as principal, the proportion of students at the school eligible for free and reduced lunch rose from 30% to 47%, increasing from 61% to 68% for black students and decreasing from 33% to 22% for white students (Snead 2006).

One facet of the Snead approach to desegregating education at Southwest Elementary was to upgrade the content of K-2 instruction for all the students at the school. Project Bright IDEA, a demonstration project now under way in North Carolina, funded by the Javits Program of the U.S. Department of Education, that "begins in kindergarten and tailors gifted methodologies for regular classroom teachers to use with all children," focuses on K-2 instruction as well. Project Bright IDEA is predicated on the view that all students can learn gifted behaviors, or, as Lauren Resnick might put it, learn how to be "smart" (Resnick 1995). Located in elementary schools that typically have some 900 students, about 60% of their students eligible for free and reduced lunch, and at least 35% of their population black or Latino, students are chosen at random for Bright IDEA classrooms (classrooms where the teachers have been trained to provide the Bright IDEA curriculum). Students from Bright IDEA classrooms now are qualifying for G&T programs at higher rates than students in their schools who are not in Bright IDEA classrooms (Project Bright IDEA 2).[3]

The experience at Southwest Elementary and with Project Bright IDEA suggests that a preferred initial policy to desegregate education is to universalize access to a G&T-quality curriculum. If that is not possible, then, at minimum, access to a G&T-quality curriculum should be equalized by race. The barrier toward achieving a more inclusive curriculum is white political resistance under the guise of merit, maintenance of "standards," and "true" ability. Recently, in the Chapel Hill-Carrboro Schools in North Carolina, as momentum built toward having a more inclusive program of G&T instruction, some white parents were promoting introduction of a Tier One program. This would constitute a still higher level of curriculum for the truly exceptionally gifted, and would reproduce the conditions perpetuating segregated education.

Of course, it is easier to make changes in the early years that affect children who have not been scarred by racialized tracking, but there is no need to perform triage on students who already have been badly served during their previous years of schooling. Advancement Via Individual Determination (AVID) is a programmatic intervention that has been utilized at both the high school and middle school levels as an effective device for detracking toward excellence:

> ...[AVID is] a reform program...designed to help low-income and minority children prepare for college.... It promises to improve the achievement of low-income and minority students and increase their chances of attending college by offering them a more rigorous college preparatory high school curriculum accompanied by an elective class in which study skills are taught.... [C]ollege students are employed to tutor AVID students in their academic work, and teachers are shown how to provide social supports to better facilitate learning. (Hubbard and Mehan 1999, 214–15)

Hubbard and Mehan (1999, 215) have shown that AVID was highly effective for the students who participated in San Diego, California and the pseudonymously named East Oakwood High School in Oakwood, North Carolina.

Despite its success, expansion of the program to include more students at East Oakwood ran into funding limitations attributable to the following obstacles:

> ...long-standing and deep-seated beliefs about the intellectual inferiority of Black students and some resistant White educators' use of the discourse of meritocracy to shield their advanced and college preparatory classes from minority students. The belief that intelligence is disparately distributed by race is another idea engrained in these educators' practices that negatively affected reform efforts aimed at preparing the African American students at Oakwood for college. (Hubbard and Mehan 1999, 215)

In direct contrast with Lauren Resnick's (1995) perspective, these educators saw "[a]cademic achievement...as static, unchanging and supportive of tracking practices (Hubbard and Mehan 1999, 220)."[4] The program has not been scaled upward because of the opposition of politically powerful white parents. Hubbard and Mehan (1999, 224) observe that in many of the schools where AVID has been implemented it enrolls less than 10% of the students, ensuring that only a small number of black students get access to AP and Honors courses.

Affluent white parents, in an act of blatant racial tribalism, are protecting turf for their own children in the New Class. Educators and teachers frequently can act as their de facto agents.

About two years ago, the then-Superintendent of Schools in Forsyth County, North Carolina told us the following story when he heard our co-authored presentation on the effectiveness of Southwest Elementary's efforts to desegregate their G&T program. He told us that a couple of years earlier at Mt. Tabor High School, the freshman class had 50 black students whose middle school End of Grade mathematics scores indicated they should be placed in Honors geometry. But none of their middle school math teachers had recommended them for an Honors placement. In some cases, they were not even recommended to take geometry, although all of them had completed Algebra 1!

In this instance, the principal, in consultation with the superintendent, decided to ignore the middle school teachers' recommendations and did not let the high school teachers know that the students had not been recommended for Honors geometry. The students were doing fine; there was no problem—until some of the teachers eventually learned what had been done. Resistance to desegregating education in America is profound, because it is resistance to desegregating the educational and scientific estate. The central prop to this resistance is the enduring belief in black cognitive inferiority, a belief that is maintained by many, no matter how strong the evidence to the contrary.

More than 70% of Americans believe that the achievement gap between black and Latino students vis-à-vis white students "is primarily due to factors unrelated to the quality of schooling that children receive." This absolves the actual system of education that is practiced in the United States from responsibility for producing the "designed gaps" (Burris and Welner 2005). But the evidence presented in this chapter places the blame squarely on what happens in schools themselves for creating the racial achievement gap. And the solution is to detrack toward providing a high-track curriculum for all students (Burris and Welner 2005).[5] Now the political battle must be waged to make that happen.

Acknowledgments

Portions of the research reported here were supported by a Spencer Foundation grant to support the "Effective Schools, Effective Students" project.

Notes

1. Of course, Galbraith never was particularly enthusiastic about the perspectives of Karl Marx on the left or Walt Rostow on the right (although he and Rostow were fairly close personal friends). Still, there is a compelling analysis of the professional managerial class that can be linked to the rise of unproductive labor in Marxist analysis (Darity 1996) and a parallel interpretation of the position of the highly credentialed in studies like *The New Right Papers* (Whitaker 1982)—both roughly consistent with Galbraith's take on the New Class.
2. This is not to deny that the issue of facility-level segregation is an ongoing issue. Indeed, Charles Clotfelter (2004) has documented carefully the process of resegregation of public schools across the country. Nevertheless, the nation—and especially the South—is nowhere near the condition that existed in 1950. The level of public school segregation in the South in 1950 was virtually 100%.
3. In Guilford County's two schools with Project Bright IDEA classrooms, six students from those classrooms qualified for G&T placement, while none did from the control classrooms. In Hickory County, 25 Bright IDEA students qualified for G&T placement versus 14 in non-Bright IDEA classrooms. In Lenoir County, 13 Bright IDEA students were approved for G&T placement versus only 2 from the control classrooms. And in Moore County, 38 Bright IDEA students qualified for G&T, while 11 qualified from the control classrooms. In the remaining two districts, the ratios favored the control classrooms. In Roanoke Rapids Graded District, 3 students from Bright IDEA classrooms qualified for G&T placement, while 7 qualified from the control classrooms, and in Wake County, 13 Bright IDEA students qualified for G&T, while 20 non-Bright IDEA students qualified for G&T.
4. It should be noted that many white teachers simply do not want to teach classes consisting of black students. A study in Georgia indicates that white teachers flee predominantly black schools after controlling for student poverty and test scores (Freeman, Scafidi, and Sjoquist 2005, 159; Scafidi et al. 2007).
5. Burris and Welner (2005) report on the dramatically positive effects of universal acceleration of the curriculum on New York State Regents exams performance of black students at Rockville Center High School, where Burris was principal, For example, prior to adoption of the detracking strategy, in the 2000 graduating class, 32% of black and Latino students and 88% of white and Asian students earned Regents diplomas. In the first cohort to experience the detracked high-level curriculum for the full four years—the class that graduated in 2003—82% of black and Latino students and 97% of white and Asian students earned Regents diplomas.

References

Anderson, James. 1988. *The Education of Blacks in the South, 1860–1935*. Chapel Hill: University of North Carolina Press

"Black Enrollment in Advanced Placement Programs: The News Is Mixed." 2007. *The Journal of Blacks in Higher Education* 55(Spring): 85–89.

Bond, Horace Mann. 1934. *The Education of the Negro in the American Social Order*. Englewood Cliffs, NJ: Prentice-Hall.

Bourdieu, Pierre. 1984. *Distinction: A Social Critique of the Judgment of Taste*. London: Routledge.

Brown 1954. Brown v. Board of Education of Topeka, KS, 349 U.S. 294 (1954).

Burdman, Pamela. 2000. "Extra Credit, Extra Criticism." *Black Issues in Higher Education* 17 (October 26): 28–33.

Burnham, James. 1941. *The Managerial Revolution: What Is Happening in the World*. New York: John Day.

Burris, C. C., and K. G. Welner. 2005. "Closing the Achievement Gap by Detracking." *Phi Delta Kappan* 86 (April): 8.

Clotfelter, Charles. 2004. *After Brown: The Rise and Retreat of School Desegregation* Princeton, NJ: Princeton University Press.

College Board AP. 2008. *The Fourth Annual AP Report to the Nation.* http://www.collegeboard.com/ appress (Accessed February 13, 2008)

Crowley, M. R. 1932. "Cincinnati's Experiment in Negro Education: A Comparative Study of the Segregated and Mixed School." *Journal of Negro Education* 1(1): 25–33.

Curry, Constance. 1996. *Silver Rights.* New York: Harvest Books.

Darity, William, Jr. 1996. "'The Undesirables, America's Underclass in the Managerial Age: Beyond the Myrdal Theory of Racial Inequality." In *An American Dilemma Revisited: Race Relations in a Changing World,* ed. Obie Clayton, Jr. New York: Russell Sage Foundation, 112–37.

Davis, Thulani. 1992. *1959: A Novel.* New York: Grove Press.

Diette, Timothy. 2005. "The Algebra Obstacle: Access, Race and the Math Achievement Gap." Ph.D. diss., The University of North Carolina at Chapel Hill.

Donelan, R. W., G. A. Neal, and D. L. Jones. 1994. "The Promise of Brown and the Reality of Academic Grouping: The Tracks of My Tears." *Journal of Negro Education* 63(3): 376–87.

DuBois, W. E. B. 1935. "Does the Negro Need Separate Schools?" *Journal of Negro Education* 4 (July): 328–35.

Ferguson, Ronald. 2001. "A Diagnostic Analysis of Black-White GPA Disparities in Shaker Heights, Ohio." *Brookings Papers on Education Policy* 4: 347–414.

Fordham, Signithia, and John U. Ogbu. 1986. "Black Students' School Success: Coping with the Burden of 'Acting White.'" *The Urban Review* 18(3) September: 176–206.

Frank, Anne. 1952. *Anne Frank: The Diary of a Young Girl.* New York: Doubleday.

Freeman, Catherine, Benjamin Scafidi, and David Sjoquist. 2005. "Racial Segregation in Georgia Public Schools, 1994–2000: Trends, Causes, and Impact on Teacher Quality." In *School Resegregation: Must the South Turn Back?* ed. John Boger and Gary Orfield. Chapel Hill: University of North Carolina Press, 148–63.

Galbraith, John Kenneth. 1958. *The Affluent Society.* Boston: Houghton Mifflin

———. 1967. *The New Industrial State.* Boston: Houghton Mifflin.

Gettleman, Jeffrey. 2005. "The Segregated Classrooms of a Proudly Diverse High School." *New York Times Education Section,* April 3.

Hallinan, M. T., and A. B. Sorenson. 1977. *The Dynamics of Learning: A Conceptual Model,* Discussion Paper 444–77. Madison, WI: Institute for Research on Poverty.

Hansen, Carl F. 1965. "No Retreat in the Drive to Excellence: A Reply to the Critics of the Track System." *Report to the Board of Education, Public Schools D.C.* April 22.

Hayes, Floyd. 2008. "Programmed Retardation." In *The International Encyclopedia of the Social Sciences,* ed. William Darity, Jr. Detroit: Thomson-Gale, 6: 525–27.

Hubbard, Lea, and Hugh Mehan. 1999. "Race and Reform: Educational 'Niche Picking' in a Hostile Environment." *Journal of Negro Education* 68(2): 213–26.

Jeong, Dong Wok. 2008. "The Effects of the Advanced Placement Program on College-Level Outcomes." Unpublished typescript, Teachers College, Columbia University.

Jolla, Alicia. 2005. "Closing the Achievement Gap By Increasing Access to AIG (Academically and Intellectually Gifted) Program: A Case Study of Southwest Elementary School." Master's thesis, Public Administration, University of North Carolina at Chapel Hill.

League for Universal Justice and Goodwill. 1965 and 1966. Statement to the *Investigation of the Schools and Poverty in the District of Columbia of the Committee on Education and Labor, House of Representatives,* 89th Congress, October 7, 8, 12, 26, 1965 and January 13, 1966.

Lee, Harper. 1960. *To Kill a Mockingbird* New York: Harper and Collins.

Lewis, Ronald L'Heureux. 2008. "Educational Inequality in an Affluent Setting: An Exploration of Resources and Opportunity." Ph.D. diss., University of Michigan at Ann Arbor.

Lindsay, John J. 1961. "Fund Given to Extend Amidon Idea: Rabaut Provides $157,000 for Basic School Instruction." *The Washington Post,* June 16, A1, A7.

Mazique, Jewell. 1965. "Public Schools in the District of Columbia." Testimony at *Public Hearing on the District of Columbia's Public Schools,* July 27.

McFarland, Dennis. 2004. *Prince Edward.* New York: Henry Holt.

"Movement Between Tracks, June 1963–June 30, 1964 High Schools (appendix table)." In *Report to the Board of Education, Public Schools D.C.,* April 22, 1965.

"North Carolina Receives AP Incentive Grant: Funds Benefit Low Wealth Districts." http://www.ncpublicschools.org/newsroom/news/2006-07/20060929-01

"Project Bright IDEA 2: Interest Development Early Abilities, A Javits K-2 Nurturing Program funded by the US Department of Education, 2004–2009, 2009. http://www.aagc.org/BrightIdeaDescription.pdf

Reich, Robert. 1992. *The Work of Nations: Preparing Ourselves for 21st Century Capitalism.* New York: Vintage Books.

Resnick, Lauren. 1995. "From Aptitude to Effort: A New Foundation for Our Schools." *Daedalus* 124: 55–62.

Rickles, Jordan, Paul Ong, Shannon McConville, and Doug Houston. 2001. *Relationship between School and Residential Segregation at the Turn of the Century.* UCLA, The Ralph and Goldy Lewis Center for Regional Policy Studies. June 11.

Scafidi, Benjamin, David L. Sjoquist, and Todd R. Stinebrickner. 2007. "Race, Poverty, and Teacher Mobility." *Economics of Education Review* 26: 145–59.

Snead, David. 2006. "Closing the Gap at Southwest." Presentation at the Youth and Race Conference, Duke University and the University of North Carolina at Chapel Hill, October.

Sorenson, A. B., and M. T. Hallinan. 1997. "The Effects of Ability Grouping on Growth in Academic Achievement." *American Educational Research Journal* 23(4): 510–42.

Tyson, Karolyn, William Darity, Jr., and Domini Castellino. 2005. "It's Not a 'Black Thing': Understanding the Burden of acting White and Other Dilemmas of High Achievement." *American Sociological Review* 70 (4): 582-605.

Whitaker, Robert. ed. 1982. *The New Right Papers.* New York: St. Martin's Press.

Williams, Heather. 2005. *Self-Taught: African American Education in Slavery and Freedom.* Chapel Hill: University of North Carolina Press.

Winerip, Michael. 2005. "How One Suburb's Black Students Gain." *New York Times AP,* December 14.

Zhang, Gongshu. 2005. "How Do High-Achieving Students Perform in North Carolina?" North Carolina Department of Public Instruction, June 2.

CHAPTER 9

The Effects of Housing Market Discrimination on Earnings Inequality

SAMUEL L. MYERS, JR., WILLIAM A. DARITY, JR.,
AND KRIS MARSH

This chapter explores the impact of racial disparities in housing market outcomes on earnings inequality. Racialized housing patterns in metropolitan areas can affect labor market outcomes for any number of reasons. Patterns of housing can affect wealth creation and the intergenerational transmission of economic status which, in turn, can influence the skills and productivity-related characteristics of workers.

Thus, the surface impression that human capital characteristics "explain" racial gaps in earnings might be linked to other factors—such as disparities in housing markets—that themselves are rooted in racially discriminatory processes. "Pre-market factors" can, themselves, be the products of market processes. We know that there is evidence pointing to a link between residential segregation and test scores (Card and Rothstein 2005), perhaps helping to explain the racial gap in skills and human capital acquisition. We also know, for example, that racial lending disparities are pronounced and persistent across metropolitan areas and that lending disparities affect homeownership and intergenerational transmission of wealth. But do these lending disparities also affect earnings inequality?

Finally, there is a linkage between residential segregation and lending disparities. Could any observed relationship between either lending disparities and earnings inequality or residential segregation and earnings inequality arise spuriously as a result of the correlation between lending disparities and residential segregation? This chapter is an exploratory exercise designed to bring these questions to the forefront of policy debate.

Background

There are wide and persistent racial gaps in loan denial rates. These gaps cannot be explained by observed measures of creditworthiness or risk of default (Goering and Wienk 1996; Munnell et al. 1992). Although this conclusion has been subjected to challenges (Berkovec et al. 1994), replication of the original findings produced by the Boston Federal Reserve suggest that the racial gap in loan denial rates remain largely unexplained even after controls are introduced for credit risk and other relevant predictors of a borrower's default risk (Carr and Megbolugbe 1993; Myers and Chan 1995). Audit studies also confirm the findings of loan data demonstrating that disparities cannot be explained by differences in characteristics of borrowers (Ross and Yinger 2002; Yinger 1995).

High levels of residential segregation persist in America's largest metropolitan areas (Charles 2003; Massey and Denton 1993). Blacks are most heavily concentrated in the lowest-income neighborhoods in aging sections of cities in the Northeast and Midwest. These patterns of residential apartheid continue long after the passage of laws banning official forms of housing segregation, including "protective" covenants in real estate contracts. Furthermore, residential segregation is inextricably linked, according to many sociologists, to the lack of social mobility and the lack of accumulated social capital (Iceland and Wilkes 2006).

There is an empirical relationship/association between residential segregation in a metropolitan area and racial wage disparities in the same metropolitan area. There is also a correlation between loan denial rates and racial wage disparities in MSAs. A fairly direct measure of residential segregation is the Dissimilarity Index.[1] A conventional measure of lending disparities is the ratio of black-to-white loan denial rates. Earnings gaps are measured by the ratio of black-to-white wage and salary incomes.

Figure 9.1 plots the ratio of black-to-white loan denial ratio against the ratio of black-to-white wage and salary incomes for the 50 largest MSAs in the United States. Figure 9.2 plots a measure of residential segregation, the Dissimilarity Index, against the ratio of black-to-white wage and salary incomes. The horizontal axes measure the degree of racial earnings equality. For example, a rise in the ratio of black-to-white earnings signals greater parity between black and white incomes. The vertical axes measure the degree of racial lending inequality in Figure 9.1 and the degree of racial residential segregation in Figure 9.2. A rising ratio of the black-to-white loan denial rate indicates greater racial disparities in lending. A rise in the Dissimilarity Index scores indicates an increase in the degree of residential segregation.

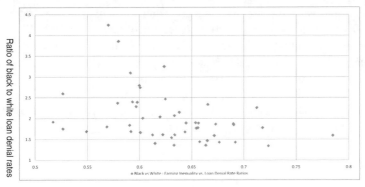

Ratio of black to white wage and salary income

Figure 9.1 Earnings inequality vs. loan denial ratios: Black vs. White.

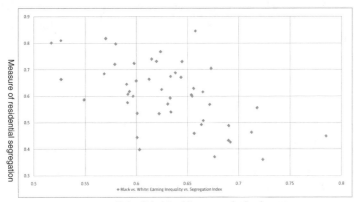

Ratio of black to white wage and salary income

Figure 9.2 Earnings inequality vs. segregation index: Black vs. White.

In both Figures, there is a sharp inverse relationship: first, between racial earnings equality and loan disparities, and next, between racial earnings inequality and residential segregation. The underlying data from which Figure 9.1 were constructed reveal that in 2000, the Milwaukee, Wisconsin MSA experienced the highest ratio of black-to-white loan denial rates among the top 50 MSAs in the United States. Blacks in Milwaukee were 4.25 times more likely to be denied home purchase mortgages than whites. Milwaukee had the seventh lowest ratio of black-to-white wage and salary incomes in 2000, with blacks earning 57 cents for every dollar earned by whites. In contrast, Salt Lake City was the bottom-ranked MSA in terms of loan denial disparities. In the Salt Lake MSA, the ratio of black-to-white loan denial rates was 1.37. It was also the MSA with the second highest black-to-white earnings ratio; blacks earned 72 cents for every dollar that whites earned.

A similar ranking of cities emerged when the Dissimilarity Index was used instead of lending inequality as a measure of racial disparity. Milwaukee was the second most segregated MSA among the top 50 MSAs, with a Dissimilarity Index of .82, while Salt Lake City was the least segregated with a Dissimilarity Index of .36. Rankings of the top- and bottom-ranked MSAs by loan denial disparities, earnings inequality, and Dissimilarity Indices are provided in Table 9.1, which reveals why there is such a sharp downward slope in both Figures 9.1 and 9.2. There could be a threshold effect that affects this pattern. Salt Lake City obviously does not have as large a black population in terms of share and absolute numbers as Milwaukee—or most other major cities, for that matter. So Salt Lake City may look better because the black population is too small to elicit higher degrees of discrimination.

The key question of interest is: Why would such an association exist between lending practices, housing segregation, and racial earnings gaps? There are at least two possible reasons: (1) residential segregation and/or the lack of access to home loans reduces spatial access to better (higher-paying) jobs for blacks, or (2) there is a general citywide climate of discrimination that pervades all arenas of life.

The analysis below does not test specifically between these two alternative explanations. Rather, the analysis attempts to determine, controlling for other relevant factors, whether housing discrimination "explains" some or all of our estimates of earnings discrimination. To do this, we estimate individual earning equations with and without controls for MSA residential segregation and lending disparities. The hypothesis is that if residential segregation and/or lending disparities "explain" earnings gaps, then measured discrimination (the "unexplained" effect of race on earnings) should diminish when one controls for MSA residential segregation and/or lending disparities.

Data

Home Mortgage Disclosure Act (HMDA) data for the year 2000 provide information on loan denial rates for individual loan applicants. From the original Loan Application Register files (LARs), which report every individual mortgage loan application, we computed loan denial rates for single-family, owner-occupied home mortgage applications. For the 50 largest MSAs, the loan denial rates are computed for each race. Excluded from the calculation of the denial rates were applications that were incomplete or where the applicant withdrew the application. A file was created assigning the ratio of black-to-white denial rates to each MSA for home mortgage loans. The 50 MSAs were sorted from the highest ratio of black-to-white loan denial rates to the lowest and divided into quintiles. Quintile 1 (the top quintile) is com-

Table 9.1 MSA's Ranked by Loan Denial Ratio, Earnings Ratio, and Dissimilarity Index

Rank	MSA	Black versus White Loan Denial Ratio 2000	MSA	Black versus White Earning Ratio 2000	MSA	Black versus White Dissimilarity Index 2000
1	Milwaukee, WI	4.2486	Miami, FL	0.4789	Detroit, MI	0.8456
2	Chicago, IL	3.8564	Newark, NJ	0.5173	Milwaukee, WI	0.8178
3	Cleveland, OH	3.2528	New York, NY	0.5266	New York, NY	0.8100
4	Minneapolis-St. Paul, MN	3.0987	Houston, TX	0.5268	Newark, NJ	0.8010
5	Boston, MA	2.7984	Dallas, TX	0.5490	Chicago, IL	0.7973
6	Raleigh, Durham, NC	2.7420	New Orleans, LA	0.5689	Cleveland, OH	0.7678
7	New York, NY	2.5949	Milwaukee, WI	0.5704	Cincinnati, OH-KY-IN	0.7395
8	Washington, DC	2.4657	Philadelphia, PA	0.5792	Saint Louis, MO-IL	0.7307
9	Oakland, CA	2.3978	Chicago, IL	0.5801	Nassau-Suffolk, NY	0.7302
10	Bergen-Passaic, NJ	2.3893	Atlanta, GA	0.5906	Bergen-Passaic, NJ	0.7232
41	Nashville, TN	1.5882	Nashville, TN	0.6717	Seattle, WA	0.4885
42	Greensboro, NC	1.5386	Indianapolis, IN	0.6730	Portland, OR	0.4636
43	Columbus, IH	1.4666	Orange County, CA	0.6765	Norfolk, VA Beach, VA	0.4598
44	Detroit, MI	1.4381	Phoenix, AZ	0.6902	Riverside, CA	0.4494
45	Las Vegas, NV-AZ	1.4295	Seattle, WA	0.6904	Raleigh-Durham, NC	0.4445
46	Orange County, CA	1.4290	Las Vegas, NV-AZ	0.6921	Phoenix, AZ	0.4328
47	Cincinnati, OH-KY-IN	1.4034	Portland, OR	0.7125	Las Vegas, NV-AZ	0.4264
48	Forth Worth, TX	1.3596	Sacramento, CA	0.7180	San Jose, CA	0.3986
49	San Antonio, TX	1.3558	Salt Lake City, UT	0.7236	Orange County, CA	0.3714
50	Salt Lake City, UT	1.3409	Riverside, CA	0.7848	Salk Lake City, UT	0.3611

prised of the MSAs with the highest ratios; Quintile 5 (the bottom quintile) is comprised of the MSAs with the lowest ratios.

The Census 2000 Residential Housing Patterns database was used to retrieve Dissimilarity Index measures of segregation for the 50 largest MSAs in 2000. The Integrated Public Use Microdata Series database was used to measure characteristics of individual householders in the 50 largest MSAs in 2000. The sample was restricted to both non-Hispanic blacks and whites.

Model

Earnings (log-earnings) were estimated using Ordinary Least Squares (OLS) regression analysis. The unit of observation is the household head. Independent variables included: number of children in household; whether the household is female-headed; age of the household head; education; occupation; and race. The estimated coefficients on the race variable are interpreted as the "discriminatory" component of the wage gap. The model is estimated with and without controls for the MSA-level Dissimilarity Index and the loan denial disparity. The model was estimated for all MSAs and also for each quintile.

Results

The key descriptive result evident in Figures 9.1 and 9.2 shows an inverse relationship between the ratio of black-to-white earnings and loan disparities or measures of residential segregation. The Figures indicate that the higher the lending disparity or degree of segregation, the lower the ratio of black-to-white wage and salary incomes. Table 9.2 computes the wage and salary incomes for household heads for the most and least segregated MSAs and for the MSAs with the highest and lowest ratios of black-to-white loan denial rates. Consistent with the inverse relationship in the Figures, the black-to-white earnings ratios were higher in the least segregated MSAs (62.74%) than they were in the most segregated MSAs (59.03%). When ranked according to loan denial rates, MSAs with the highest disparity had black-to-white earnings ratios of 60.35%. Those with the lowest loan denial disparities had earnings ratios of 64.54%.

What also is apparent from Table 9.2 is that the difference in mean earnings for blacks in the most segregated ($33,374) and least segregated ($31,142) MSAs is much smaller ($2,232) than the difference in mean earnings for whites ($6,904). The difference in mean earnings for blacks in the MSAs with the highest lending disparities ($34,521) and the lowest lending disparity ($31,518) is also smaller ($3,003) than the difference in mean earnings for whites ($8,369). Moreover, the MSAs with the largest difference in earning

Table 9.2 Difference of Means of Salary for Household Heads by Segregation Index and Loan Disparity Rankings

	Quintile	Whites	Blacks	B/W Ratio
	Segregation Index Ranking			
Most segregated	1	$56,538	$33,374	0.5903
Least segregated	5	$49,634	$31,142	0.6274
	Loan Disparity Ranking			
Highest Loan Denial Disparity	1	$57,205	$34,521	0.6035
Lowest Loan Denial Disparity	5	$48,836	$31,518	0.6454

between blacks and whites (and thus the lowest black-to-white earnings ratios) are the MSAs with the highest mean earnings. The average wage and salary income of a white householder in the most segregated MSAs was $56,538. The average wage and salary income of a white household in the least segregated MSAs was $49,634. The average wage and salary income of black householder in the most segregated MSAs was $33,374, while the average wage and salary income of black householder in the least segregated MSAs was $31,142.

A similar pattern is found with respect to the ranking of MSAs by loan denial ratios. Thus, although racial earnings gaps are wider in the most segregated MSAs and in metropolitan areas with the highest loan denial disparities, mean earnings are also higher for both whites and blacks.

Table 9.3 reveals that there is little substantive change in the race coefficients when lending disparities and measure of residential segregation are and are not taken into account.[2] All of the coefficients reported are statistically significant.

Contrary to the expectation that the coefficients on the race variable would become zero (or at least get smaller), in the full sample coefficients on the race variable get slightly larger (in absolute value) when one controls for lending disparities for all MSAs and the top quintile. There is a nontrivial increase (in absolute value) in the race coefficient when the Dissimilarity Index is introduced as a control. Only for the bottom quintile do the coefficients

Table 9.3 Estimated Measures of Discrimination in Earnings Equations

	All MSAs	Top Quintile	Bottom Quintile
No control for lending disparity	-0.1863	-0.1787	-0.1810
With lending disparity	-0.1877	-0.1853	-0.1799
No control for Dissimilarity Index	-0.1863	-0.1939	-0.2248
With segregation index	-0.1962	-0.1997	-0.2146

diminish. In short, only in the least segregated MSAs or metropolitan areas with the lowest lending disparities do segregation or lending disparities "explain" earning disparities and/or discrimination. Otherwise, the omission of these place-based measures produces a downward bias in measured discrimination.[3]

Conclusion

The underlying premise of this empirical analysis is that spatial aspects of racial discrimination or segregation influence individual outcomes in the labor market. Place-based measures, such as the degree of residential segregation or the extent of racial disparities in loan denial rates in a MSA, capture a notion of racialized outcomes in a spatial context. Where these racialized outcomes are more adverse, one could expect that individual black household heads fare less well than in places where these outcomes are less adverse. An alternative and equally plausible explanation for an association between residential segregation and employment discrimination is the John F. Kain (1992) spatial mismatch thesis relating residential segregation to transportation costs and job access.

The central difference between these two competing explanations for an association between residential segregation (or lending disparities) and employment discrimination is that the former posits that the place-based measure of racialized outcomes captures something akin to the "racial climate" in a location that affects all market and nonmarket activities. Thus, locations that exhibit more adverse racialized outcomes in the housing market are also likely to exhibit more racialized outcomes in the labor market. There is no direct causal linkage between these two markets. Rather, individuals participating in the labor market are affected by the area's overall racial mood that is captured by the location-based measure of segregation or lending disparities. The latter explanation posits a causal link between housing segregation and employment disparities attributable to a mismatch between where black workers live (the ghetto) and where the good jobs are (the suburbs).

Therefore, the descriptive evidence leads to a continuing puzzle. The broad patterns are clear: There is an inverse relationship at the aggregate level between black–white earnings ratios and measures of residential segregation and lending disparities. The descriptive evidence is fully consistent with the view that earnings disparities are wider in areas with greater segregation and higher racial disparities in lending.

However, greater disparities in earnings do not always mean that there are greater levels of market discrimination in employment. In our attempts to measure discrimination, we account for age, education, family structure, and occupation. When we account for place-based measures of residential segregation or loan denial disparities, there is no major change in our results, at least not for the models with the specifications adopted here. This does not necessarily mean there is no connection between residential segregation and employment discrimination. Rather, it suggests that the connection between residential segregation and employment discrimination in recent years is more complex than the simple descriptive profiles suggest.

More likely, and, perhaps more plausibly, the reason for the inverse relationship between various measures of housing market disparities with black-white earnings ratios is that within locations racialized outcomes are interdependently influenced by similar factors. The factors that explain the higher ratio of black-to-white loan denial rates might be exactly the factors that explain the lower ratio of black-to-white earnings in a given area. The same factors that explain the high levels of residential segregation might be exactly the factors explaining the low ratio of black-to-white earnings in a given area. The fact that those places with the highest individual-level earnings are also the places with greatest segregation and highest ratios of black-to-white loan denials works to obscure these aggregate or macro patterns that are revealed in the descriptive evidence.

What might these factors be? Further analysis, of course, would be required to offer more than mere speculation. However, we do know that many of the locations with the highest degree of residential segregation and/or loan denial disparities are locations with significant black political representation. Newark, Washington, DC, Minneapolis, Detroit, and Chicago either had black mayors or significant presence of black elected officials in 2000. These locations also appeared among the most segregated or among locations with the highest loan denial ratios in the country. The black political representation, while possibly a byproduct of racially segregated residential patterns, also could work to suppress or diminish the most overt forms of employment discrimination. Further analysis, therefore, should investigate whether the connection between residential segregation and employment discrimination is mitigated by political representation.

On a practical policy level, though, the implication is that eradicating residential segregation or diminishing racial gaps in loan denials will not have any immediate impact on narrowing earnings gaps. If anything, the pathway towards reducing earnings disparities extends beyond simply location or housing outcomes. The pathway must account for how schools in even integrated residential areas fail to produce African-American children equipped to score well on basic standards examinations and to matriculate into colleges and universities. The pathway must account for the fact that segregated neighborhoods are not the only neighborhoods where there are huge racial disparities in arrest and incarceration rates. In short, the route towards narrowing earnings gaps is likely to be far more complex than the simple descriptive profile linking housing market disparities to labor markets.

Notes

1. The Dissimilarity Index (Dxy) is calculated to compare the extent to which different types of households are spatially separate from one another: $Dxy = 0.5\Sigma|(xi / X)—(yi / Y)|$. X and Y represent the total number of households of a particular type in the metropolitan area as a whole; xi and yi are the number of these household types within census tract i. When the index is converted to a percentage, it varies from zero (no separation or complete integration) to 100 (complete separation). Dxy, then, can be understood as the percentage of a given household type that would have to move to another census tract to make their distributions proportionally equal (Jakubs 1977). Generally, scores below 30 are considered low, between 30 to 60 are moderate, and above 60 are high (Kantrowitz 1973).
2. Table 9.3 presents the results of estimating log-earnings equations for all 50 MSAs and for the top and bottom MSAs as measured by segregation or loan denial disparities. If metropolitan area segregation or lending disparities "explains" racial wage discrimination, then when one accounts for these aggregate indicators one would expect the overall measure of discrimination to decline. The coefficient on the race variable captures the independent influence of race on earnings, once one has accounted for measurable human capital (or productivity-linked) characteristics. The race coefficient is the unexplained portion of the racial earnings gap. The race coefficient measures labor market discrimination. In the absence of controls for place-level variables, such as residential segregation or loan denial ratios, one would expect that the race coefficient would be negative. If all of the racial gap in earnings can be explained by human capital factors plus place-based factors, then the coefficients on race should converge to zero.
3. There are several caveats to these findings. The aforementioned results come about using ordinary least squares as the method of estimating the log-earnings equations. Typically, in multilevel models one uses fixed-effects estimates. It is conceivable that the failure to account for fixed effects masks the true impacts of segregation and loan denial disparities. The models estimated also do not account for zero earners or possible selection bias arising from differential labor force participation. Moreover, the models do not consider alternative directions of causation between residential segregation and loan disparities on the one hand and earnings disparities on the other. Future work will explore the impacts of undertaking these alternative model specifications and estimation techniques.

References

Berkovec, James A., Glenn B. Canner, Stuart A. Gabriel, and Timothy H. Hannan. 1994. "Race, Redlining, and Residential Mortgage Loan Performance." *Journal of Real Estate Finance, and Economics* 9(3): 263–94.

Card, David, and Jesse Rothstein. 2005. *Racial Segregation and the Black-White Test Score Gap.* National Bureau of Economic Research. Working Paper No. 12078.

Carr, James H., and Issac F. Megbolugbe. 1993. "The Federal Reserve Bank of Boston Study on Mortgage Lending Revisited." *Journal of Housing Research* 4(2): 277–313.

Charles, Camille Zubrinsky. 2003. "The Dynamics of Racial Residential Segregation." *Annual Review of Sociology*, 29: 167–207.

Goering, John, and Ron Wienk. (1996). *Mortgage Lending, Racial Discrimination, and Federal Policy.* Washington, DC: Urban Institute Press.

Iceland, John, and Rima Wilkes. 2006. "Does Socioeconomic Status Matter? Race, Class, and Residential Segregation." *Social Problems* 52(2): 248–73.

Jakubs, John F. 1977. "Residential Segregation: The Taeuber Index Reconsidered." *Journal of Regional Science* 17: 281–303.

Kain, John F. 1992 "The Spatial Mismatch Hypothesis." *Housing Policy Debate* 3(2): 381–92.

Kantrowitz, Nathan. (1973). *Ethnic and Racial Segregation in the New York Metropolis.* New York: Praeger.

Massey, Douglas, and Nancy Denton. 1993. *American Apartheid.* Cambridge, MA: Harvard University Press.

Munnell, Alicia H., Lynn E. Browne, James McEneaney, and Geoffrey M. B. Tootell. 1992. *Mortgage Lending in Boston: Interpreting HMDA Data.* (Working Paper Series No. 92-7). Boston: Federal Reserve Bank of Boston.

Myers, Samuel L., and Tsze Chan. 1995. "Racial Discrimination in Housing Markets: Accounting for Credit Risk," *Social Science Quarterly* 76(3): 543–61.

Ross, Stephen L., and John Yinger. 2002. *The Color of Credit: Mortgage Discrimination, Research Methodology, and Fair-Lending Enforcement.* Cambridge, MA: MIT Press.

Yinger, John. 1995. *Closed Doors, Opportunities Lost: The Continuing Costs of Housing Discrimination.* New York: Russell Sage Foundation.

CHAPTER 10

Racial/Ethnic Integration and Child Health Disparities

DOLORES ACEVEDO-GARCIA, THERESA L. OSYPUK,
AND NANCY MCARDLE

Racial/ethnic health disparities across the life course are both a stark indicator of the lack of integration in our society, as well as a reflection of racial inequities—or lack of integration—in other areas, for example, neighborhood environment. This is particularly the case when we look at health disparities among children, since they signal an uneven playing field that starts before children are born and has implications across the life course. In this chapter, we argue that racial/ethnic health disparities can serve as a marker of racial integration. We then examine how the lack of residential integration—resulting in a highly unequal geography of neighborhood opportunity—is a root cause of racial/ethnic health disparities in childhood and beyond. We conclude by showing that despite the severity of racial/ethnic health disparities, an encouraging sign is that, unlike in other areas where we see "race fatigue," in recent years public health has experienced an increasing recognition of the magnitude of such disparities, their causes, and the urgent need to address them. Increasing evidence on the extent of racial/ethnic health disparities and their origins may serve to renew the national debate on racial integration.

Health as a Measure of Racial Integration

In 1967, Martin Luther King referred to the large racial disparity in infant mortality as an example of the willingness of the nation to reduce blacks "to

50% of a citizen." The black infant mortality rate was then, and continues to be, about twice as large as the white infant mortality rate (Mathews and MacDorman 2007). Indeed, we could use racial disparities as an indicator of integration in one area of life—health—that is essential for our well-being and for functioning in many other areas, such as education and employment. Baubock (1994, cited in Fix, Passel, and Zimmerman 2001, 33) suggested that

> ...social integration refers to the distribution of particular groups over positions in social and economic life and the stability of such distributions over time. Such positions may be arranged vertically (as is, for example, the case with hierarchies of income, of professional prestige, of education etc.) or horizontally (residential areas, spatial location of organizations of the same kind such as firms, schools etc.). When measuring how well a society is integrated with respect to a particular group, one may use segregation indices, which compare the proportional distribution of one group over all relevant positions with that of the rest of the population. Systematic group deviation from the average patterns be it a concentration in certain residential areas or segments of the labour market or by a lower position in the hierarchies of education, income and wealth would then count as social disintegration.

Although single indicators communicate part of the story of lack of racial integration, viewing racial disparities across multiple life domains is not only more compelling, but constitutes a starting point for examining the links between inequalities across domains of life. As articulated by Baubock (1994), performance across *multiple* domains is the litmus for social integration, and although he did not explicitly articulate health as one of the domains used to gauge integration, we argue that health should be included. The positions or hierarchies in the health domain are various levels of health status, or the number of years people from different racial/ethnic groups can expect to live—or live in a healthy state. We can examine—and epidemiologists routinely do so—these health positions across racial/ethnic groups and over time.

In the United States, the magnitude, persistence, and implications of racial/ethnic health disparities are stark, both at the individual and at the population level. At the individual level, for instance, life expectancy is over six years higher for white men than for black men (75.7 vs. 69.5), and over four years higher for white women than for black women (80.8 vs. 76.5) (National Center for Health Statistics 2005). At the population level, former U.S. Surgeon General David Satcher and colleagues (Satcher et al. 2005) estimated that 83,570 excess black deaths each year could be prevented in the United States if the black–white mortality gap could be eliminated. One of the most striking features of racial/ethnic health disparities in the United States is their persistence over time, as they have not changed much in the last 50 years (Satcher et al. 2005; Williams and Jackson 2005).

Common explanations of racial/ethnic health disparities include individual-level factors such as health behaviors (e.g., diet, physical activity, substance use); psychosocial factors (e.g., stress); access to health care; experience of discrimination (e.g., unequal treatment in health care); genetics; and differential socioeconomic position (e.g., income, education, occupation, wealth). Although most of these explanations likely contribute to racial health disparities, their relative importance is unclear (Williams 2001).

In some cases, adjustment for racial/ethnic differences in socioeconomic status accounts for health disparities. In other cases, though, racial/ethnic disparities in health persist after accounting for socioeconomic status, suggesting that the health returns of income, education, and wealth in our society are lower for minorities than for whites. For example, even after taking into account maternal age, education, and health behaviors, as well as medical risk factors during pregnancy, black babies are more likely to be low birthweight or preterm (Acevedo-Garcia, Soobader, and Berkman 2005; Osypuk and Acevedo-Garcia 2008). Yet this disparity may not be attributed to genetic differences, as black babies born to immigrant mothers are significantly less likely to be low birthweight than their counterparts born to (presumably genetically similar) U.S.-born black mothers (Acevedo-Garcia, Soobader, and Berkman 2005). To address the limited explanatory power of individual-level factors, public health experts have also explored contextual factors that may influence health and differentially affect racial/ethnic minorities (LaVeist 2003). Such contextual factors include neighborhood environment and residential segregation.

Residential Segregation and Health Disparities

In addition to being a telling indicator of social integration, racial disparities in health reflect lack of integration in other domains of life. Growing evidence suggests that residential segregation is a key determinant of racial inequalities for a broad range of societal outcomes and a fundamental cause of health disparities. Racial/ethnic residential segregation is not in itself detrimental to health, because living in neighborhoods with people from certain racial/ethnic groups is not what affects health per se. The adverse effects of segregation arise because segregation is associated with racial/ethnic inequality in socioeconomic status and in neighborhood environment (Acevedo-Garcia and Lochner 2003; Acevedo-Garcia et al. 2003;

Acevedo-Garcia and Osypuk 2008; Carr and Kutty 2008; Williams and Collins 2001).

Residential segregation between the white and the black populations continues to be very high in America's metropolitan areas. Although residential segregation of Hispanics/Latinos is not yet as high as that of African Americans, it has been increasing over the last few decades, while black segregation has modestly decreased (Iceland et al. 2002), and patterns of neighborhood inequality between Hispanics and whites are nearly as stark as those between blacks and whites (Acevedo-Garcia et al. 2007; Acevedo-Garcia et al. 2008; Osypuk et al., 2009).

While sociologists and demographers have theorized about and measured segregation in metropolitan areas since the beginning of the twentieth century, public health research only began to establish a link between segregation and poor health among blacks starting in the late 1980s. Conceptual and methodological refinements on the relationship between segregation and health have come about since 2000 (Acevedo-Garcia 2000, 2001; Acevedo-Garcia and Lochner 2003; Acevedo-Garcia et al. 2003; Bell et al. 2006; Collins and Williams 1999; Grady 2006; Grady and Ramirez 2008; Hearst and Oakes 2008; Masi et al. 2007; Osypuk and Acevedo-Garcia 2008; Subramanian, Acevedo-Garcia, and Osypuk 2005; Williams and Collins 2001).

Residential segregation affects health through a variety of pathways (Acevedo-Garcia and Lochner 2003; Williams and Collins 2001). First, segregation constrains the socioeconomic advancement of minorities by limiting educational quality and employment (Cutler and Glaeser 1997), as well as by diminishing the returns to homeownership because school quality, job opportunities, and property values are lower in disadvantaged neighborhoods. In turn, the distribution of good health in society is strongly related to socioeconomic position, with those at the top of the socioeconomic ladder having better health than those at the middle and those at the bottom (Berkman and Kawachi 2000).

Second, segregation increases the exposure of minorities to unfavorable physical and social neighborhood environments, including high exposure to crime, environmental hazards, inferior municipal services, "food deserts" (i.e., limited availability of healthy food outlets), and scarce venues for physical activity (Acevedo-Garcia et al. 2003; Acevedo-Garcia, Osypuk, McArdle, and Williams 2008; Williams and Collins 2001).

Third, residential segregation leads to segregation in health care settings, which is in turn associated with disparities in quality of treatment. Even eliminating unequal treatment within health care settings would not eliminate racial disparities in health care because of the large disparities between health care facilities, which result from segregation (Baicker, Chandra, and Skinner 2005; Smith et al. 2007).

Segregation and Racial Disparities in Child Health and Development

Increasingly, social epidemiologists advocate for a life course perspective, because health and developmental outcomes are often the result of trajectories that start early in life (Hertzman and Power 2003; Knudsen et al. 2006; Palloni 2006; Shonkoff and Phillips 2000). There is consensus that experiences in early childhood are critical for the promotion of healthy development throughout the life course (Poulton et al. 2002), and that childhood health matters for adult socioeconomic achievement because it has indirect effects on occupational standing, earnings, and wealth via educational attainment and adult health status (Case and Paxson 2006). Economists, moreover, have urged investment in early childhood because it yields large economic returns to society in terms of increased health and productivity, and decreased crime and dependency over the life course (Hertzman and Power 2003).

Racial/ethnic disparities in child development emerge at young ages. For example, racial differences in academic readiness emerge prior to school entry (Rock and Stenner 2005). Therefore, childhood is a critical period to intervene in order to correct inequality, the effect of which resonates throughout the life course (Acevedo-Garcia et al. 2007; Acevedo-Garcia et al. 2008; Shonkoff and Phillips 2000).

One of the most powerful ways to assess the costs of the lack of racial integration is to examine its effects on children. Racial disparities in child health and development reflect racial/ethnic disparities in socioeconomic conditions across multiple contexts—e.g., families, neighborhoods, schools, which are contributed to by residential segregation.

An Example of the Association between Segregation and Child Health: The Effect of Hypersegregation on Black Infant Preterm Birth

The persistent racial disparity in birth outcomes—i.e., low birthweight (less than 2,500 grams), preterm birth (babies born before 37 weeks of gestation), and infant mortality (death during the first year of life)—is one of the most startling health trends in the United States. For these three health indicators, there is a large racial disparity disfavoring blacks, which concerned Dr. King four decades ago and continues to concern public health experts. For example, infants born to black women are 260 grams lighter on average, and are over 50% more likely to be born preterm than infants born to non-Hispanic white women, and over twice as likely to die in the first year of life (Martin et al. 2006; Mathews and MacDorman 2007).

Health and developmental trajectories throughout the life course are influenced by child health at birth. Low birthweight and short gestation are leading causes of infant mortality (Kington and Nickens 2001; U.S. Department of Health and Human Services 2000). They are also related to worse health and developmental outcomes later in life, including school-age disabilities, behavioral problems, cognitive function, and educational attainment. (Behrman, Butler, and Committee on Understanding Premature Birth and Assuring Healthy Outcomes 2006).

The causes of preterm birth and of the racial disparity in birth outcomes are poorly understood (Behrman, Butler, and Committee on Understanding Premature Birth and Assuring Healthy Outcomes 2006). Although maternal individual-level risk factors—including age, marital status, and cigarette smoking—account for only half of the racial risk in low birthweight (Buka et al. 2003), the explanations for social inequalities in infant health have generally focused on individual risk factors, directing attention away from structural explanations (Roberts 1997).

To identify factors accounting for the large and persistent black–white disparities in health, it is necessary to focus on factors that either differentially influence blacks versus whites, or uniquely impact blacks (or whites). Residential segregation is such a phenomenon (LaVeist 2003). The pathways from racial segregation to birth outcomes are not entirely clear, yet existing evidence indicates the importance of individual and neighborhood deprivation acting through health behavior and stress pathways (Behrman, Butler, and Committee on Understanding Premature Birth and Assuring Healthy Outcomes 2006). For instance, those living in black neighborhoods are exposed to higher rates of crime and neighborhood poverty (Massey 2001), and such exposure to chronic or acute stressors has been linked to worse birth outcomes through immune and neuroendocrine pathways (Behrman, Butler, and Committee on Understanding Premature Birth and Assuring Healthy Outcomes 2006; Massey 2004).

Individual-level stressors are more prevalent in deprived neighborhoods, and four distinct pathways link individual-level stressors with preterm delivery: adverse health behaviors (e.g., smoking, poor nutrition); psychosocial factors (e.g., depression, social support); stress hormones that may initiate labor, and depressed immune functioning that causes increased susceptibility to infection (Misra, O'Campo, and Strobino 2001; O'Campo and Schempf 2005). For example, women living in higher-crime and lower-socioeconomic neighborhoods exhibit worse birth outcomes, even after controlling for individual-level factors (Messer et al. 2006; Morenoff 2003; O'Campo et al. 1997; Pearl, Braveman, and Abrams 2001; Rauh, Andrews, and Garfinkel 2001, see comment; Roberts 1997).

Additionally, the effects of disadvantaged neighborhood contexts may be stronger among older black women. According to the "weathering" hypothesis, black women may experience worse birth outcomes with age, reflecting the cumulative effects of psychosocial and environmental hazards associated with population-level patterns of racial inequality (Geronimus 1996). For example, prior work has documented that risk of adverse birth outcomes may rise with increasing age among disadvantaged women, or in areas with greater poverty (Geronimus 1996; Rauh, Andrews, and Garfinkel 2001; Rich-Edward et al. 2003).

Osypuk and Acevedo-Garcia (2008) found that black women living in hypersegregated metropolitan areas had a higher probability of preterm birth than their counterparts in nonhypersegregated areas, and the associations were worse among older black women. The racial disparity in preterm birth was also larger for older mothers and in hypersegregated areas, which provides support for the weathering hypothesis (Osypuk and Acevedo-Garcia 2008).

In multilevel statistical models adjusted for demographic, socioeconomic, health-behavior, medical-risk, and regional factors, black infants living in hypersegregated areas, compared to white infants, had nearly 83% significantly higher odds of being born preterm; but the odds were only 69% higher for blacks in nonhypersegregated areas.

Figure 10.1 depicts the racial disparity in preterm birth (e.g., the adjusted predicted probability of preterm birth for black infants minus that of white infants) by hypersegregation and maternal age. The racial disparity in preterm birth is considerably higher among older mothers, regardless of segregation. Moreover, the preterm birth racial disparity is higher in hypersegregated areas vs. nonsegregated areas at nearly all ages. But the racial disparity in hypersegregated areas is higher compared to that in nonhypersegregated areas among older women vs. younger women. For example, among women age 45, the racial preterm birth disparity is 14.1 percentage points in hypersegregated areas, versus 10.6 points in nonhypersegregated areas. In other words, hypersegregated areas exhibit a racial disparity that is 3.5 points (or 33%) larger than the disparity in nonhypersegregated areas among the oldest women (Osypuk and Acevedo-Garcia 2008).

Although Osypuk and Acevedo-Garcia (2008) found a detrimental effect of hypersegregation on preterm birth for blacks, hypersegregation accounted only partially for the racial disparity in preterm birth. Importantly, we would expect small effects for a cause such as segregation that operates through multiple mediators to ultimately influence birth outcomes. Birth outcomes, like preterm birth and infant mortality, may be associated with maternal exposures prior to the birth of the infant, such as smoking in pregnancy, teenage childbearing, and low socioeconomic status (Kraus, Greenland, and Bulterys 1989; Little and Peterson 1990). Those earlier maternal exposures

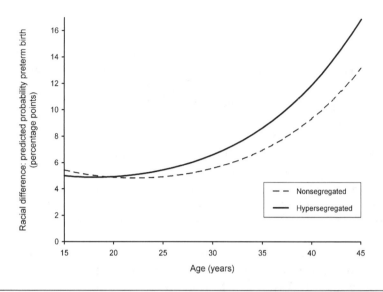

Figure 10.1 Adjusted racial disparity in predicted probability of preterm birth by metropolitan area hypersegregation and maternal age. Note: Racial difference calculated as the black minus white predicted probability of a preterm birth, output from logistic regression model of preterm birth, adjusted for mother's age, race/ethnicity, education, marital status, prenatal care, smoking and drinking alcohol during pregnancy, infant's sex, birth order, MA (metropolitan area) median income, median income, MA population size, MA % in poverty, MA % black, and Census region. Data from 237 metropolitan areas, Year 2000 Detail Natality Dataset. Hypersegregation defined as a metropolitan area that exhibits high segregation on at least 4 of 5 dimensions of racial residential segregation. Source: Osypuk, T. and D. Acevedo-Garcia (2008). "Are Preterm Birth Racial Disparities Larger in Hypersegregated Areas?" *American Journal of Epidemiology* 167(11): 1295-1304.

might be where the action is with respect to segregation effects. For instance, segregation may result in different distributions of variables, such as education or teenage childbearing (Cutler and Glaeser 1997) that may be on the causal pathway between segregation and health outcomes. Thus, the statistical models in Osypuk and Acevedo-Garcia (2008) may have underestimated the effect of segregation, since we adjusted for variables that have been conceptualized as mediators between segregation and birth outcomes (Ellen 2000), including education, health behaviors, and medical conditions.

Racial Disparities in Birth Outcomes across Metropolitan Areas

Nationwide, 14% of black infants are born low birthweight, compared with 7% of white infants (Martin et al. 2006). However, there is considerable geographic variability in the racial/ethnic patterns of low birthweight. Patterns by metropolitan area may be particularly revealing about causes of low birthweight that might be operating through neighborhood environment. The distribution of the low birthweight rate for each racial/ethnic group for the largest 100 metro areas is presented in Figure 10.2. The distribution of the low birthweight rate for black babies is distinctly worse than for white and Latino babies. In 95% of metro areas, the low birthweight rate for white babies was 3 to 6%. This level is close to or better than the low birthweight rate target (5%) set in the health objectives for the nation in *Healthy People 2010* (U.S. Department of Health and Human Services 2003). In 70% of metro areas, the low birthweight rate for Hispanic babies was also 3 to 6%. The most prevalent rate for black babies was much higher, 9 to 12% in 66% of metros.

The distribution of the preterm birth rate is better for white babies (i.e., lower rates of preterm birth) than for minority babies. The distribution for black babies is the worst—higher preterm birth rates. While in 60% of metro areas, the preterm birth rate for black babies is over 15%, there are virtually no metros with that high a rate for white or Latino babies (Acevedo-Garcia et al. 2007).

In contrast to many adverse indicators of family and neighborhood

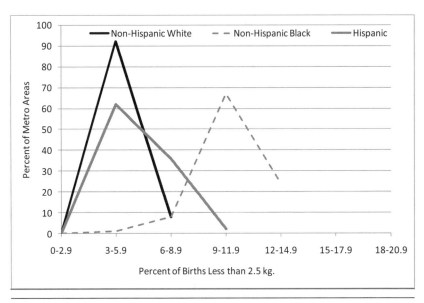

Figure 10.2 Low-birthweight rates: Distributions by race/ethnicity 100 largest metro areas: 2001–2002. Note: Excludes metro areas with less than 100 births to mothers in the specified subgroup over the 2001–2002 time period. Excludes plural births and births that occurred abroad, in Puerto Rico, or in the U.S. Territories. Source: D. Acevedo-Garcia et al., Children Left Behind: How Metropolitan Areas Are Failing America's Children. DiversityData Reports no. 1 (Boston, MA: Harvard School of Public Health, and Center for Advancement of Health, January 2007).

socioeconomic disadvantage, for health at birth Latino children have favorable outcomes relative to white children. This is related to the so-called "Hispanic health paradox" (Acevedo-Garcia and Bates 2007; Acevedo-Garcia, Soobader, and Berkman 2005, 2007). Hispanic infants, especially those born to immigrant mothers, have better birth outcomes than would be expected, given the low socioeconomic status of their mothers and families. Although public health experts are still uncovering the reasons for this paradox, it is undoubtedly good news that Hispanic children start off their lives with a healthy birthweight profile.

Black children are more likely to be low birthweight and preterm than children of other racial/ethnic groups. Thus, many black children are at a disadvantaged position from the start. Ideally, the conditions they face in their families, neighborhoods, and schools would ameliorate this initial health disadvantage. Hispanic children start with a better health picture than black children, comparable to that of white children. Ideally, the conditions they face later in childhood would help preserve and further this initial health advantage. However, across metropolitan areas, the actual conditions facing black and Latino children work to compound the initial health disadvantage of black children, and to undermine the initial health advantage of Latino children.

Beyond their effect on infant health outcomes such as preterm birth, residential segregation and the associated racial/ethnic disparities in neighborhood environment may continue to influence health and development during childhood and beyond.

Neighborhoods Affect Child Health and Development

The rapidly growing evidence on "neighborhood effects" finds that after taking into account individual-level factors, disadvantaged neighborhood environments (e.g., poverty concentration) have a detrimental effect on health outcomes, including mortality, child and adult physical and mental health, and health behaviors (Diez-Roux 2003; Ellen, Mijanovich, and Dillman 2001; Kawachi and Berkman 2003). Poor neighborhood conditions may put children at risk for developmental delays, mental health and behavior problems, teen parenthood, and academic failure (Brooks-Gunn, Duncan, and Aber 1997; Caughy, Nettles, and O'Campo 2008; Xue et al. 2005). Children growing up in disadvantaged neighborhoods may face difficult challenges, including a hazardous physical environment, a poor social environment, low-quality schools, and lack of public safety.

Although neighborhood conditions may influence health outcomes in all age groups, exposure to neighborhood disadvantage during childhood may be particularly harmful, as the effects of this exposure may continue into adolescence and adulthood. For example, children's exposure to disadvantaged environments, such as poor neighborhoods, may compromise brain development (Knudsen et al. 2006). In other words, getting children back on track is much more difficult than starting them out (and keeping them) on track.

Health researchers continue to investigate why and how neighborhoods matter for child health and development, and seem to agree that the answer depends on the health outcome in question. For example, for child mental health and behavioral outcomes, some hypothesize that neighborhood social processes such as social capital (i.e., the trust, mutual understanding, and shared values and behaviors that make cooperative action possible) and collective efficacy (i.e., a group's shared belief in its capability to organize and execute the actions required to attain its collective goals) may mediate the effect of neighborhood socioeconomic disadvantage. Others argue that parenting behavior may act as a mediator. For instance, evidence from the Project on Human Development in Chicago Neighborhoods suggests that children's mental health—i.e., clinical levels of internalizing behavior problems (depression, anxiety, withdrawal, and somatic problems)—is associated with concentrated disadvantage, independent of family demographic characteristics, maternal depression, and earlier child mental health scores (Xue et al. 2005). In the Chicago study, "concentrated disadvantage" comprised the poverty rate, the percentage of residents receiving public assistance, the percentage of female-headed families, the unemployment ratio, and the percentage of African-American residents. Neighborhood collective efficacy mediated the effect of concentrated disadvantage. Similarly, Caughy, Nettles, and O'Campo (2008, 47) reported that both neighborhood socioeconomic impoverishment and negative social climate contribute to child behavior problems. They concluded that there is increasing evidence that "child behavior problems are not only a function of processes at the individual and family level but are also influenced by characteristics of the neighborhoods in which children live."

In sum, the available evidence suggests that neighborhoods matter for child health and development. Research to uncover the mechanisms through which neighborhoods influence the health of their residents is valuable and should continue. However, in addition to research on the mechanisms through which neighborhoods impact health, we need to examine the implications of large racial disparities in the population-wide distributions of neighborhood environments. The social reality of our metropolitan areas is one of stark segregation between non-Hispanic white and minority children. The question then is how large are the racial/ethnic disparities in neighborhood environment, and what may be their implications for racial health and developmental disparities among children.

Children Face a Highly Unequal Geography of Opportunity: Black and Latino Children Experience Multiple Environmental Risks

We refer to "opportunity neighborhoods" to denote neighborhoods that support healthy development (Acevedo-Garcia et al. 2008; Osypuk et al. 2009). Characterizing opportunity neighborhoods requires selecting variables that are indicative of high (or low) opportunity. High-opportunity indicators include access to high-quality health care, adequate transportation, quality child care, neighborhood environmental and public safety, sustainable employment, high-performing schools, and institutions that facilitate civic engagement. Because it is challenging to characterize neighborhoods in such a comprehensive manner across all metropolitan areas, other more available indicators are often used to define opportunity, most commonly the neighborhood poverty rate, but also the unemployment rate, the proportion of single female-headed households, and the proportion of adults without a high school diploma (Acevedo-Garcia et al. 2007; Galster and Killen 1995). The central premise of a "geography of opportunity" framework is that residents of a metropolitan area are situated within a context of neighborhood-based opportunities that shape their quality of life. Thus, the location of housing is a powerful impediment to or asset for accessing these opportunities (Briggs 2005; powell 2005), including opportunities for healthy development.

Racial residential segregation continues to be very high (Iceland et al. 2002), and has been deemed a fundamental cause of racial health disparities (Williams and Collins 2001). As a result of segregation, minority children have limited access to neighborhoods with opportunities, such as good schools and after-school programs, safe streets and playgrounds, and positive role models. Neighborhood quality is considerably worse for racial minority children than for non-Hispanic whites, independent of socioeconomic status.

Not only are the average values of most neighborhood indicators worse for black and Hispanic children, but both across metropolitan areas and within metropolitan areas, the entire neighborhood distribution is shifted in a worse direction for black and Hispanic children (Acevedo-Garcia et al. 2007; Acevedo-Garcia et al. 2008; Osypuk et al. 2009.

Within metropolitan areas, black and Hispanic children are concentrated at the worst end of the neighborhood quality distribution (e.g., neighborhoods with the highest poverty, unemployment, disability rates), while white children are concentrated at the best end of the neighborhood quality distribution. Analyses of the 2000 Census found extremely limited overlap between the black and white distributions of neighborhood poverty. Neighborhoods with the highest poverty rates for whites overlapped neighborhoods with the lowest poverty rates for blacks, while the middle part of the distributions for whites and blacks did not overlap at all (Acevedo-Garcia et al. 2008; Osypuk et al. 2007; Osypuk et al. 2009). On average, in metropolitan areas there is only a 24% overlap between the distribution of neighborhood poverty for black children and the one for white children. In other words, on average, the lowest-poverty neighborhoods for black children have poverty rates equivalent to those found in the 24% poorest neighborhoods for white children. This lack of overlap is not due to racial differences in the distribution of family poverty. When the analysis is limited to children living in poor families, on average, the extent of overlap in the racial distributions of neighborhood poverty is only 26%.

The above data are average overlap figures for the 100 largest metropolitan areas. However, as shown in Figures 10.3 and 10.4, in many metropolitan areas there is virtually no overlap in the racial distributions of neighborhood poverty (Acevedo-Garcia et al. 2008; Osypuk, Galea, McArdle, and Acevedo-Garcia 2007; Osypuk et al. 2009). Again, these disparities are not accounted for by differences in family poverty. Even poor white children are likely to live in low-poverty neighborhoods, while the majority of poor black and Latino children live in high-poverty neighborhoods. On average, while only 1% of poor white children in metropolitan areas live in poor neighborhoods, 17% of poor black children and 21% of poor Latino children do (Acevedo-Garcia et al. 2008).

We also found that in metropolitan areas, the overlap in the racial/ethnic distributions of neighborhood poverty is significantly patterned by the extent of residential segregation—i.e., there is less overlap in areas that have higher levels of racial/ethnic segregation (Acevedo-Garcia et al. 2008; Osypuk et al. 2007; Osypuk et al. 2009).

From a perspective of child health and development, exposure to neighborhood poverty is troubling because child development experts agree that the accumulation of multiple environmental risks, rather than a singular risk exposure, may be an especially pathogenic aspect of childhood poverty (Knudsen et al. 2006; Shonkoff and Phillips 2000). However, not all poor children experience multiple environmental risks. Given that in the majority of school districts across the U.S. children attend neighborhood-based schools, patterns of residential segregation and associated disparities in neighborhood quality translate into school segregation and disparities in school quality (Acevedo-Garcia et al. 2007).

In sum, not only are black and Latino children more likely to live in poor families than other children, but, due to segregation, they also experience neighborhoods (and schools) with unfavorable socioeconomic environments—a kind of double (or triple) jeopardy (Acevedo-Garcia et al. 2007; Acevedo-Garcia et al. 2008).

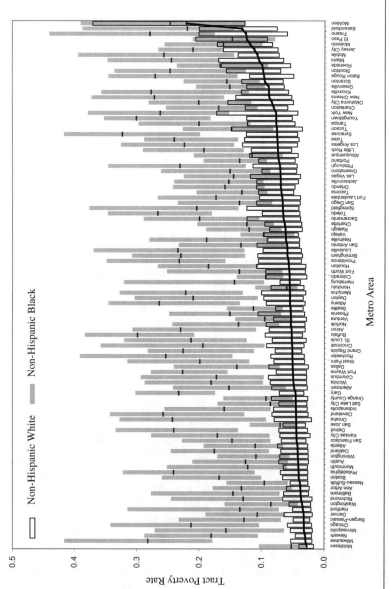

Figure 10.3 White and Black children overlap for neighborhood poverty: 2000. Notes: The boxplots show the distribution of children's exposure to neighborhood (census tract) poverty by race/ethnicity in each metropolitan area.. The first and third quartiles of race/ethnic-specific distributions of neighborhood poverty correspond to the bottom and top lines of each box. The median of neighborhood poverty for each MA was marked by a heavy line in the center of the box. The metropolitan areas along the horizontal axis are ranked according to the metropolitan median neighborhood poverty rate of non-Hispanic whites. Source: Analysis of 2000 Decennial Census, Summary Files 1 and 3.

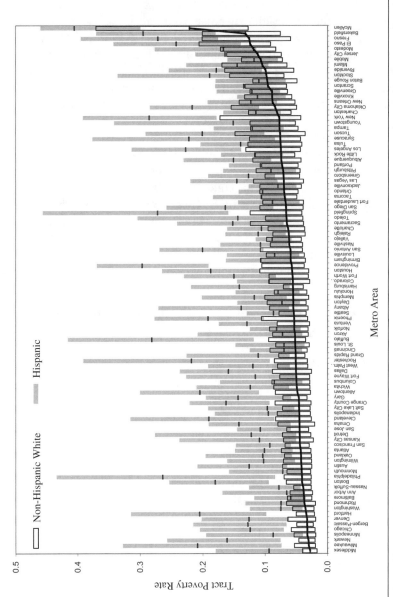

Figure 10.4 White and Hispanic children overlap for neighborhood poverty. 2000. Notes: The boxplots show the distribution of children's exposure to neighborhood (census tract) poverty by race/ethnicity in each metropolitan area. The first and third quartiles of race/ethnic-specific distributions of neighborhood poverty correspond to the bottom and top lines of each box. The median of neighborhood poverty for each MA was marked by a heavy line in the center of the box. The metropolitan areas along the horizontal axis are ranked according to the metropolitan median neighborhood poverty rate of non-Hispanic whites. Source: Analysis of 2000 Decennial Census, Summary Files 1 and 3.

In addition to the association between neighborhood and school poverty, there are other reasons why high-poverty neighborhoods may offer fewer resources for healthy child development. Possible mechanisms through which neighborhoods influence health may range from direct physical influences such as exposure to toxic waste to the cumulative stress associated with living in unsafe neighborhoods with limited resources (Flournoy and Yen 2004; Kawachi and Berkman 2003). Since disadvantaged neighborhoods may limit opportunities for upward social mobility, neighborhoods may also influence health status by shaping socioeconomic attainment throughout the life course.

America's children are more racially and ethnically diverse than the total population. Eighteen million of the 45 million children in the largest metro areas live in "majority-minority" metros, where nonwhite or Hispanic children make up more than half of the child population. Given this increasing diversity, major racial/ethnic disparities among children are of particular concern. The landscape of diversity and opportunity in metropolitan areas has a substantial impact on the well-being of America's children. And, in turn, the health and development of these children will have a strong influence on the economic and social prospects of these regions.

Can the Evidence on Racial/Ethnic Health Disparities Help Renew the Interest in Residential Integration?

In many areas of our social life, we have witnessed a retrenchment of racial integration goals. Addressing racial/ethnic disparities in access to opportunity neighborhoods and schools is becoming more difficult in a political and policy environment in which race-based solutions are being challenged. The Supreme Court recently ruled against school integration programs that seek to improve access of minority children to quality schools by trying to balance racial composition across schools within school districts. School segregation experts anticipate that it is only a matter of time before there are legal challenges against school integration across school districts. Although very limited in scope, given the small number of children they affect, school integration programs are one of very few policy tools based on the premise that residential segregation is at the root of disparities affecting children.

An awareness of how segregation affects minority Americans across the income spectrum, and not just those who are poor, is an important piece of the discussion about integration (Cashin 2005). Therefore, the evidence of racial/ethnic health disparities beyond socioeconomic differences may serve as an important tool to renew our national dialogue about the importance of race. Additionally, we may be able to estimate the health-related costs of lack of integration. For example, we could estimate the costs of excess obesity and diabetes prevalence among minorities both in terms of health care costs and decreased productivity.

Research on both racial/ethnic disparities and on the health effects of unfavorable neighborhood environments has considerably increased in the last two decades. Both the public and the private sectors have developed initiatives to address health disparities. For example, reducing health disparities is one of the two major objectives for the nation, per our national public health plan, Healthy People 2010 (U.S. Department of Health and Human Services 2000). In 1993, the federal government created the National Center on Minority Health and Health Disparities to promote minority health and coordinate the National Institutes of Health's effort to reduce health disparities. While in other areas such as education our policies seem to be shying away from race and integration, in public health the increasing awareness of racial/ethnic health disparities and their roots in social determinants appears to be running counter to this current trend.

Also, gradually, there has been an effort to communicate the magnitude and seriousness of health disparities to a wider audience. In 2003, the *New York Times Magazine* featured an article, "Ghetto Miasma" (Epstein 2003), arguing that "there are many different types of disadvantaged neighborhoods in America, but poor urban minority neighborhoods seem to be especially unhealthy. Some of these neighborhoods have the highest mortality rates in the country, but this is not, as many believe, mainly because of drug overdoses and gunshot wounds. It is because of chronic diseases." In the Spring of 2008, PBS released a documentary on health disparities titled *Unnatural Causes: Is Inequality Making Us Sick* (California Newsreel 2008). This documentary features researchers as well as real-life stories of how damaging social environments and social factors affect health (including an episode focused on neighborhoods and health). Around the same time, a study showing that in neighborhoods crowded with fast-food and convenience stores (instead of grocery or produce stores), residents are at higher risk of obesity and diabetes (California Center for Public Health Advocacy, PolicyLink, and UCLA Center for Health Policy Research 2008) was featured in major news outlets across the country.

An important caveat is that, although public health research on disparities can provide a powerful way to monitor the extent and implications of racial/ethnic health disparities, the search for explanations and appropriate interventions should be informed by work in other sectors (e.g., housing, education) with a better understanding of upstream structural causes. In the last two decades, social epidemiologists have increasingly turned to the health effects of "place" above and beyond the health effects of individual-level factors, since the latter do not fully account for black/white health disparities (Macintyre, Ellaway, and Cummins 2002; Williams and Jackson 2005). Public health research on place influences on health, though, has largely focused on neighborhoods. However, a focus exclusively on neighborhoods limits our understanding of health disparities. Individual neighborhoods—and their qualities, risks, and resources—are part of metropolitan area-wide neighborhood distributions. Neighborhoods are influenced by the larger economic and social context (e.g., housing and labor markets) of their metropolitan area (Briggs 2005; Galster and Killen 1995). Although this metropolitan context has been well documented in sociology, demography, and urban studies, the health literature remains focused primarily on the health effects of individual neighborhoods. For example, we have a burgeoning literature on methods to characterize neighborhood walkability and neighborhood food environment, but it remains to be seen whether disparities in population health across multiple health outcomes can be reduced by interventions such as improving the walkability/food environment in a few disadvantaged neighborhoods.

A needed complementary focus in public health should be on policies to address the vast disparities in access to opportunity neighborhoods, which underlie disparities in health and well-being (Acevedo-Garcia et al. 2008). However, such policies do not fall within the range of conventional public health interventions. Therefore, we advocate for a broader view of what is considered "health policy." Several professional and advocacy communities (e.g., regional equity, affordable housing, fair housing) are committed to reducing racial/ethnic disparities in access to opportunity neighborhoods. And although the public health community has prioritized reduction of racial/ethnic health disparities, traditional public health strategies do not address disparities in access to opportunity neighborhoods. Despite the increasing evidence on social determinants of health, most public health interventions address proximal risk factors but not social determinants. We suggest that improving access to neighborhoods of opportunity should be regarded as a public health intervention. Undoubtedly, racial/ethnic disparities in neighborhood environment are a matter of concern in their own right. Their effect on health makes them even more unjustifiable, and the need to address them even more urgent.

Acknowledgments

We gratefully acknowledge support from the W. K. Kellogg Foundation (*Diversity Data*, Dolores Acevedo-Garcia, PI).

REFERENCES

Acevedo-Garcia, Dolores. 2000. "Residential Segregation and the Epidemiology of Infectious Diseases." *Social Science and Medicine* 51: 1143–61.

———. 2001. "Zip Code Level Risk Factors for Tuberculosis: Neighborhood Environment and Residential Segregation, New Jersey, 1985–1992." *American Journal of Public Health* 91: 734–41.

———, 2007. "Low Birthweight among US Hispanic/Latino Subgroups: The Effect of Maternal Foreign-Born Status and Education." *Social Science & Medicine* 65: 2503–16.

———, and Lisa M. Bates. 2007. "Latino Health Paradoxes: Empirical Evidence, Explanations, Future Research, and Implications." In *Latino/as in the United States: Changing the Face of America*, ed. H. Rodriguez, R. Saenz, and C. Menjivar. New York: Springer, 101–13.

———, Kimberly A. Lochner. 2003. "Residential Segregation and Health." In *Neighborhoods and Health*, ed. I. Kawachi and L. F. Berkman. New York: Oxford University Press, 265–87.

———, Nancy McArdle, and David R. Williams. 2008. "Towards a Policy-Relevant Analysis of Geographic and Racial/Ethnic Disparities in Child Health." *Health Affairs* 27: 321–33.

———, Nancy McArdle, Theresa L. Osypuk, Bonnie Lefkowitz, and Barbara Krimgold. 2007. *Children Left Behind: How Metropolitan Areas Are Failing America's Children*. Boston, MA: Harvard School of Public Health, and Center for the Advancement of Health.

———, Theresa L. Osypuk. 2008. "Impacts of Housing and Neighborhoods on Health: Pathways, Racial/Ethnic Disparities, and Policy Directions." In *Segregation: The Rising Costs for America*, ed. J. Carr and N. Kutty. New York: Routledge, 197–235.

———, Theresa L. Osypuk, and S. V. Subramanian. 2003. "Future Directions in Residential Segregation and Health Research: A Multilevel Approach." *American Journal of Public Health* 93: 215–21.

———, Mah-J. Soobader, and Lisa F. Berkman. 2005. "The Differential Effect of Foreign-Born Status on Low-Birthweight by Race/Ethnicity and Education." *Pediatrics* 115: e20–e30.

Baicker, Katherine, Amitabh Chandra, and Jonathan S. Skinner. 2005. "Geographic Variation in Health Care and the Problem of Measuring Racial Disparities." *Perspectives in Biology and Medicine* 48: s42–s53.

Baubock, Rainer. 1994. *The Integration of Immigrants*. Strasbourg, France: The Council of Europe.

Behrman, R. E., A. S. Butler, and Committee on Understanding Premature Birth and Assuring Healthy Outcomes. 2006. *Preterm Birth: Causes, Consequences, and Prevention*. Washington, DC: National Academies Press.

Bell, Janice F., Frederick J. Zimmerman, Gunnar R. Almgren, Jonathan D. Mayer, and Colleen E. Huebner. 2006. "Birth Outcomes among Urban African-American Women: A Multilevel Analysis of the Role of Racial Residential Segregation." *Social Science & Medicine* 63: 3030–45.

Berkman, Lisa, and Ichiro Kawachi. 2000. *Social Epidemiology*. New York: Oxford University Press.

Briggs, Xavier de Souza. 2005. *The Geography of Opportunity: Race and Housing Choice in Metropolitan America*. Washington, DC: Brookings Institution Press.

Brooks-Gunn, Jeanne, Greg J. Duncan, and J. Lawrence Aber. 1997. *Neighborhood Poverty*. New York: Russell Sage Foundation.

Buka, Stephen L., Robert T. Brennan, Janet W. Rich-Edwards, Stephen W. Raudenbush, and Felton Earls. 2003. "Neighborhood Support and the Birth Weight of Urban Infants." *American Journal of Epidemiology* 157: 1–8.

California Center for Public Health Advocacy, PolicyLink, and UCLA Center for Health Policy Research. 2008. "Designed for Disease: The Link Between Local Food Environments and Obesity and Diabetes."

California Newsreel. 2008. *Unnatural Causes: How Inequality Is Making Us Sick*. ed. Larry Adelman: California Newsreel.

Carr, J., and N. Kutty. 2008. *Segregation: The Rising Costs for America*. New York: Routledge.

Case, Anne, and Christina Paxson. 2006. "Children's Health and Social Mobility." *The Future of Children* 16: 151–73.

Cashin, Sheryl. 2005. *The Failures of Integration: How Race and Class Are Undermining the American Dream*. New York: Public Affairs.

Caughy, M. O., S. M. Nettles, and P. J. O'Campo. 2008. "The Effect of Residential Neighborhood on Child Behavior Problems in First Grade." *American Journal of Community Psychology* 42: 39–50.

Collins, C., and D. R. Williams. 1999. "Segregation and Mortality: The Deadly Effects of Racism." *Sociological Forum* 14: 495–523.

Cutler, David M., and Edward L. Glaeser. 1997. "Are Ghettos Good or Bad?" *The Quarterly Journal of Economics* 112: 827–72.

Diez-Roux, Ana V. 2003. "The Examination of Neighborhood Effects on Health: Conceptual and Methodological Issues Related to the Presence of Multiple Levels of Organization." In *Neighborhoods and Health*, ed. I. Kawachi and L. F. Berkman. New York: Oxford University Press, 45–64.

Ellen, Ingrid Gould. 2000. "Is Segregation Bad for Your Health? The Case of Low-Birth Weight." In *Papers on Urban Affairs, Brookings-Wharton Papers on Urban Affairs*, ed. W. G. Gale and J. R. Pack. Washington, DC: Brookings Institution Press, 203–38.

Ellen, Ingrid Gould, Tod Mijanovich, and Keri-Nicole Dillman. 2001. "Neighborhood Effects on Health: Exploring the Links and Assessing the Evidence." *Journal of Urban Affairs* 23: 391–408.

Epstein, Helen. 2003. "Ghetto Miasma: Enough to Make You Sick?" *New York Times Magazine*, October 12.

Fix, M. E., Passel, J. S., & Zimmermann, W. 2001. *The Integration of Immigrant Families in the United States*. Washington, DC: The Urban Institute.

Flournoy, Rebecca, and Irene Yen. 2004. *The Influence of Community Factors on Health. An Annotated Bibliography*. Oakland, CA: PolicyLink and the California Endowment.

Galster, George C., and Sean P. Killen. 1995. "The Geography of Metropolitan Opportunity: A Reconnaissance and Conceptual Framework." *Housing Policy Debate* 6: 7–43.

Geronimus, A. T. 1996. "Black/White Differences in the Relationship of Maternal Age to Birthweight: A Population-Based Test of the Weathering Hypothesis." *Social Science & Medicine* 42: 589–97.

Grady, Sue C. 2006. "Racial Disparities in Low Birthweight and the Contribution of Residential Segregation: A Multilevel Analysis." *Social Science & Medicine* 63: 3013–29.

Grady, Sue C., and Ivan J. Ramirez. 2008. "Mediating Medical Risk Factors in the Residential Segregation and Low Birthweight Relationship by Race in New York City." *Health & Place* 14(4): 661–77.

Hearst, Mary, and J. Michael Oakes. 2008. "The Effect of Racial Residential Segregation on Black Infant Mortality." *American Journal of Epidemiology*, 168: 1247–54.

Hertzman, C., and C Power. 2003. "Health and Human Development: Understandings from Life-Course Research." *Developmental Neuropsychology* 24: 719–44.

Iceland, J., D. H. Weinberg, E. Steinmetz, and U.S. Census Bureau. 2002. "Racial and Ethnic Residential Segregation in the United States: 1980–2000." U.S. Census Bureau. Washington, DC: U.S. Government Printing Office.

Kawachi, Ichiro, and Lisa F. Berkman. 2003. *Neighborhoods and Health*. New York: Oxford University Press.

King, Martin Luther Jr. 1967. "Speech on the Casualties of the War in Vietnam February 25, 1967." http://www.aavw.org/special_features/speeches_speech_king02.html (July 28, 2008).

Kington, Raynard S., and Herbert W. Nickens. 2001. "Racial and Ethnic Differences in Health: Recent Trends, Current Patterns, Future Directions." In *America Becoming: Racial Trends and Their Consequences*, ed. N. J. Smelser, W. J. Wilson, F. Mitchell, and National Research Council. Washington, DC: National Academy Press, 253–310.

Knudsen, E. I., J. J. Heckman, J. L. Cameron, and J. P. Shonkoff. 2006. "Economic, Neurobiological, and Behavioral Perspectives on Building America's Future Workforce." *Proceedings of the National Academy of Sciences* 103: 10155–62.

Kraus, J. F., S. Greenland, and M. Bulterys. 1989. "Risk Factors for Sudden Infant Death Syndrome in the US Collaborative Perinatal Project." *International Journal of Epidemiology* 18: 113–20.

LaVeist, T. A. 2003. "Racial Segregation and Longevity among African Americans: An Individual-Level Analysis." *Health Services Research* 38: 1719–33.

Little, R. E., and D. R. Peterson. 1990. "Sudden Infant Death Syndrome Epidemiology: A Review and Update." *Epidemiologic Reviews* 12: 241–46.

Macintyre, Sally, Anne Ellaway, and Steven Cummins. 2002. "Place Effects on Health: How Can We Conceptualise, Operationalise and Measure Them?" *Social Science & Medicine* 55: 125–39.

Martin, Joyce A., Brady E. Hamilton, Paul D. Sutton, Stephanie J. Ventura, Fay Menacker, and Sharon Kirmeyer. 2006. "Births: Final Data for 2004." In *National Vital Statistics Reports*. Atlanta, GA: Centers for Disease Control, 55: 102.

Masi, Christopher M., Louise C. Hawkley, Z. Harry Piotrowski, and Kate E. Pickett. 2007. "Neighborhood Economic Disadvantage, Violent Crime, Group Density, and Pregnancy Outcomes in a Diverse, Urban Population." *Social Science & Medicine* 65: 2440–57.

Massey, Douglas S. 2001. "Residential Segregation and Neighborhood Conditions in U.S. Metropolitan

Areas." In *America Becoming: Racial Trends and Their Consequences*, ed. N. J. Smelser, W. J. Wilson, F. Mitchell, and National Research Council. Washington, DC: National Academy Press, 1: 391–434.

———. 2004. "Segregation and Stratification: A Biosocial Perspective." *Du Bois Review* 1: 1–19.

Mathews, T. J., and Marian F. MacDorman. 2007. "Infant Mortality Statistics from the 2004 Period—Linked Birth/Infant Death Data Set." *National Vital Statistics Reports* 55. Atlanta, GA: Centers for Disease Control, 55.

Messer, Lynne C., Jay S. Kaufman, Nancy Dole, David A. Savitz, and Barbara A. Laraia. 2006. "Neighborhood Crime, Deprivation, and Preterm Birth." *Annals of Epidemiology* 16: 455–62.

Misra, Dawn P., Patricia O'Campo, and Donna Strobino. 2001. "Testing a Sociomedical Model for Preterm Delivery." *Paediatric and Perinatal Epidemiology*, 15: 110–22.

Morenoff, Jeffrey D. 2003. "Neighborhood Mechanisms and the Spatial Dynamics of Birth Weight." *American Journal of Sociology* 108: 976–1017.

National Center for Health Statistics. 2005. "Table 27. Life Expectancy at Birth, at 65 Years of Age, and at 75 Years of Age, by Race and Sex: United States, Selected Years 1900–2005." Hyattsville, MD: NCHS.

O'Campo, Patricia, and Ashley Schempf. 2005. "Racial Inequalities in Preterm Delivery: Issues in the Measurement of Psychosocial Constructs." *American Journal of Obstetrics and Gynecology* 192: S56–63.

———. Xiaonan Xue, Mei-Cheng Wang, and Margaret O'Brien Caughy. 1997. "Neighborhood Risk Factors for Low Birthweight in Baltimore: A Multilevel Analysis." *American Journal of Public Health* 87: 1113–18.

Osypuk, Theresa L., and D. Acevedo-Garcia. 2008. "Are Preterm Birth Racial Disparities Larger in Hypersegregated Areas?" *American Journal of Epidemiology* 167: 1295–1304.

Osypuk, Theresa L., Sandro Galea, Nancy McArdle, and Dolores Acevedo-Garcia. 2007. "The Distribution of Neighborhood Poverty and Racial Disparities in Neighborhood Context: The Unequal American Geography of Opportunity." Presentation at Population Association of America Annual Meeting, New York, NY.

———. 2009. "Quantifying Separate and Unequal: Racial/Ethnic Distributions of Neighborhood Poverty in Metropolitan America." *Urban Affairs Review*, [Epub 2009 Feb 4].

Palloni, Alberto. 2006. "Reproducing Inequalities: Luck, Wallets, and the Enduring Effects of Childhood Health." *Demography* 43: 587–615.

Pearl, Michelle, Paula Braveman, and Barbara Abrams. 2001. "The Relationship of Neighborhood Socioeconomic Characteristics to Birthweight among 5 Ethnic Groups in California." *American Journal of Public Health* 91: 1808–14.

Poulton, R., A. Caspi, B. J. Milne, W. M. Thomson, A. Taylor, M. R. Sears, and T. E. Moffitt. 2002. "Association between Children's Experience of Socioeconomic Disadvantage and Adult Health: A Life-Course Study." *Lancet* 360: 1640–45.

powell, john. 2005. "Expert Remedial Report in *Thompson v. HUD.*" Kirwan Institute for the Study of Race & Ethnicity, Columbus, OH.

Rauh, V. A., H. F. Andrews, and R. S. Garfinkel. 2001. "The Contribution of Maternal Age to Racial Disparities in Birthweight: A Multilevel Perspective." *American Journal of Public Health* 91: 1815–24.

Rich-Edwards, J. W., S. L. Buka, R. T. Breman, and F. Earls. 2003. "Diverging Associations of Maternal Age with Low Birthweight for Black and White Mothers." *International Journal of Epidemiology* 32: 83–90.

Roberts, E. M. 1997. "Neighborhood Social Environment and the Distribution of Low Birthweight in Chicago." *American Journal of Public Health* 87: 597–603.

Rock, Donald A., and A. Jackson Stenner. 2005. "Assessment Issues in the Testing of Children at School Entry." *The Future of Children* 15: 15–34.

Satcher, D., G. E. Fryer, Jr., J. McCann, A. Troutman, S. H. Woolf, and G. Rust. 2005. "What If We Were Equal? A Comparison of the Black-White Mortality Gap in 1960 and 2000." *Health Affairs* 24: 459–64.

Shonkoff, Jack P., and Deborah A. Phillips. 2000. *From Neurons to Neighborhoods: The Science of Early Childhood Development*. Washington, DC: National Academies Press.

Smith, David Barton, Zhanlian Feng, Mary L. Fennel, Jacqueline S. Zinn, and Vincent Mor. 2007. "Separate and Unequal: Racial Segregation and Disparities in Quality across U.S. Nursing Homes." *Health Affairs* 26: 1448–58.

Subramanian, S. V., Dolores Acevedo-Garcia, and Theresa L. Osypuk. 2005. "Racial Residential Segregation and Geographic Heterogeneity in Black/White Disparity in Poor Self-Related Health
in the US: A Multilevel Statistical Analysis." *Social Science & Medicine* 60: 1667–79.
U.S. Department of Health and Human Services. 2000. *Healthy People 2010: Understanding and
Improving Health.* U.S. Department of Health and Human Services. Washington, DC: Government Printing Office.
———. 2003. *Healthy People 2010.* 2nd ed., vol. 2. *Understanding and Improving Health.* U.S. Department of Health and Human Services, Washington, DC: Government Printing Office.
http://www.healthypeople.gov/document/tableofcontents.htm (June 17, 2004).
Williams, David R. 2001. "Racial Variations in Adult Health Status: Patterns, Paradoxes, and Pros-
pects." In *America Becoming: Racial Trends and Their Consequences*, ed. N. J. Smelser, W. J.
Wilson, F. Mitchell, and National Research Council. Washington, DC: National Academy
Press, 2: 371–410.
Williams, David R., and Chiquita Collins. 2001. "Racial Residential Segregation: A Fundamental
Cause of Racial Disparities in Health." *Public Health Reports* 116: 404–16.
Williams, D. R., and P. B. Jackson. 2005. "Social Sources of Racial Disparities in Health." *Health
Affairs* 24: 325–34.
Xue, Y., T. Leventhal, J. Brooks-Gunn, and F. J. Earls. 2005. "Neighborhood Residence and Mental
Health Problems of 5- to 11-Year-Olds." *Archives of General Psychiatry* 62: 554–63.

CHAPTER **11**

Integration, Segregation, and the Racial Wealth Gap

GEORGE LIPSITZ AND MELVIN L. OLIVER

Housing equity is an important component of the wealth portfolio of most American families. Especially for minorities, particularly African Americans, advances in accumulating wealth depend heavily on housing wealth. Home equity is the most important reservoir of wealth for average American families, and disproportionately for African Americans. For Black households, home equity accounts for 63% of total average net worth. In sharp contrast, home equity represents only 38.5% of average white net worth (Oliver and Shapiro 2006, Shapiro 2004). However, given the lower rate of homeownership among African Americans and the "segregation" tax that Black homeowners face, their homes appreciate far slower in segregated and racially changing neighborhoods (Flippen 2004; Krivo and Kaufman 2004; Oliver and Shapiro 2006). This chapter examines how segregation has limited the ability of African Americans to accumulate wealth and the ways in which government and financial institutions have conspired to limit and even "strip" hard-gained home equity from Black and other minority communities. Because wealth is historically constituted—that is, it is passed from generation to generation—the processes of wealth accumulation that have produced cumulative disadvantages for African Americans and locked in positions for whites, have led to the current situation where Blacks possess just 7 cents for every dollar of net worth that whites possess (Kochar 2004; Oliver and Shapiro 2006).

The Historical Background of Segregation

The long history of housing discrimination has allowed whites to "lock in" advantages of homeownership and its attendant subsidies (Roithmayr 2007). They receive transformative assets that fund education, business start-ups, and home purchases by inheriting assets that their families obtained originally in an expressly racist and exclusionary housing market (Shapiro 2004). Over generations, these assets appreciate in value. They lock in advantages across generations that make it harder for new competitors to enter the housing market. Legal scholar Daria Roithmayr (2007) describes the long history of restrictive covenants, racial zoning, redlining, steering, block-busting, and mob violence between 1866 and 1948 as part and parcel of other concerted actions by a racial cartel that monopolized the benefits of favored access to homeownership, employment, education, and political power for whites. These cumulative locked-in advantages and vulnerabilities stemmed from direct action by government bodies, as well as from private acts of discrimination by white individuals and organized groups. The Black children who salute the flag in U.S. classrooms every morning are not likely to come from families that include the 46 million adults who can trace the core of their family's assets to the 1862 Homestead Act. That legislation gave 1.5 million families some 246 million acres of land, yet only whites could receive these lands. Similarly, the families to which Black children belong are unlikely to have been major beneficiaries of the 1934 Federal Housing Act, which put the full faith and credit of the federal government behind the home mortgage industry, creating the largest redistribution of wealth and assets in U.S. history (Shapiro 2004, 190). The expressly racist categories required by the Act's appraisal manuals made sure that between 1934 and 1968, 98% of FHA loans went to whites (Jackson 1985; Logan and Molotch 1987, 130).

Oliver and Shapiro (2006, 18) note that:

> The FHA's actions have had a lasting impact on the wealth portfolios of Black Americans. Locked out of the greatest mass-based opportunity for wealth accumulations in American history, African Americans who desired and were able to afford homeownership found themselves consigned to central city communities where their investments were affected by the self-fulfilling prophecies of the FHA appraisers: cut off from sources of new investment their homes and communities deteriorated and lost value in comparison to homes and communities that FHA appraisers deemed desirable.

We sometimes pass too quickly over the long-term effects of the FHA's expressly discriminatory loan policies. Scholars acknowledge that discrimination by the FHA deprived the Black community of millions of dollars, but only rarely do we ask the questions that should proceed from that fact. If the Black community has lost billions and even trillions of dollars, we need to ask: Who Took It? How Did They Take It? Where Did It Go? Where Is It Now? Why is it so easy for us to see Black communities as disadvantaged but seemingly so difficult to describe them as taken advantage of? Why do we fail to connect the unfair and unjust impediments against asset accumulation imposed on Blacks to the realization of unfair gains and unjust enrichments by whites?

From the 1930s through the 1970s, federal urban renewal and highway construction subsidized the rewards of whiteness. Federally-assisted urban renewal projects demolished 20% of the central-city housing units occupied by African Americans during the 1950s and 1960s (Logan and Molotch 1987). People of color made up more than 60% of the population displaced by urban renewal (Zarembka 1990, 104). Ninety percent of the low-income housing units destroyed by urban renewal were never replaced (Duster 1987, 308–09; Quadrango 1994, 91–92; Zarembka 1990, 104). Urban renewal demolished some 1,600 Black neighborhoods in cities North and South (Fullilove 2005, 20). Clinical psychiatrist and public health specialist Mindy Thompson Fullilove (2005) argues that urban renewal in the mid-twentieth century was of sufficient scale and scope that it destroyed the emotional ecosystems of Black communities, inducing a profound alienation, a collective traumatic stress reaction that she describes as "root shock." Urban renewal destroyed housing stock, property values, community networks, and business opportunities in Black communities all across the country, but it also entailed yet another seizure of Black property. Like the white riot that destroyed $1.8 million in property and most of the Black business district in Tulsa in 1921, urban renewal programs punished Black home and business owners for their economic success. It provided an urban corollary to the pattern of rural Black dispossession revealed by the reduction of farm land owned by Blacks from 15 million acres in 1920 to less than 1 million acres in 2000 (Gilbert and Quinn 2000). There were nearly 1 million Black farmers in the United States in 1920, but that number dropped to fewer than 20,000 by 1992. Federal policies played a direct role in this decline. The Department of Agriculture routinely excluded Black farmers from a broad range of subsidies and benefits. As recently as the Reagan presidency, the Department loaned $1.3 billion to some 16,000 farmers to buy more land. Only 209 of these recipients were Black, at a time when consolidation by agribusiness and farm foreclosures caused thousands of Black farmers to lose their land entirely. In approving a 1999 consent decree designed to redress some of the injustices perpetrated by this program, federal judge Paul Friedman noted the "well-founded and deep seated mistrust of the USDA" because of the agency's "long history of racial discrimination" (A. King 2008, A3).

Wealthy and powerful corporations have long carved out advantages for themselves by shaping public policies that exploit the cumulative vulnerabilities of communities of color. Lobbyists for the banking industry in 1968 exploited concerns about urban rebellions and racial strife in drafting that year's Housing and Urban Development Act. This legislation created a lucrative unregulated home mortgage market for lenders while making the attendant risks the responsibility of the federal government. An investigation by the U.S. Commission on Civil Rights later found that government officials conspired with local real estate agents and lenders who engaged in blockbusting and racial steering while offering Black home-seekers mortgages on substandard housing. Lenders and real estate agents profited from making unsound loans and from the 200% increase in prices of inner-city homes that this program provoked. When borrowers could not pay back the loans, however, and the substandard homes could not be resold, HUD responded essentially by redlining inner cities, destroying home values in those areas for many years (Logan and Molotch 1987, 13).

It would be naïve to think that the designers of urban renewal or the 1968 Housing and Urban Development Act were unaware of the racial consequences of their actions. Yet they did not need to express any intentional racial animus. The cumulative vulnerabilities of communities populated by the victims of housing discrimination meant that the neighborhoods slated for destruction had large numbers of absentee landlords, suffered from political isolation and powerlessness, and occupied locations near downtown desirable for creating centralized convention facilities, museums, concert halls, and subsidized hotel and office developments. Although large-scale urban renewal programs now seem to be a thing of the past, the logic that guided racialized urban renewal persists in a wide range of public policies, including tax abatements, tax increment financing, and issuance of industrial development revenue bonds (Lipsitz 2002).

The Racial Costs of Segregation for Housing Equity

As noted above, home equity plays a crucial role in the wealth accumulation process of the average American household. Di, Belsky, and Liu (2007, 288) examined households that were renters in 1989 and became homeowners, and demonstrated that "it is homeownership itself that results in greater future household net wealth," rather than other factors like initial levels of wealth (e.g., wealthier households become owners). For African Americans and other minorities who manage successfully to get into the housing market, racial segregation takes a heavy toll on their development of home equity.

In *Black Wealth/White Wealth*, Oliver and Shapiro (2006) noted that racial segregation dampens demand in the housing market, as integrated and African-American neighborhoods increasingly become markets only for other Black buyers. This artificially lowers housing values and decreases home equity accumulation for Black homeowners. On the other hand, whites pay a "premium" to preserve their homogeneous communities. Examining home equity for homeowners who purchased homes in the years 1967 to 1988, Oliver and Shapiro found that whites had an average increase in their home value of $53,000, compared to only $31,100 for Black homebuyers. The $21,900 difference is a "compelling index of bias in housing markets that costs Blacks dearly" (Oliver and Shapiro 2006, 150).

To further understand this difference, the authors divided the sample into two different time periods, 1967 to 1977 and 1978 to 1988, to reflect the differing impact of housing inflation which started in the 70s and increased during the 80s. They also looked at less expensive homes (priced below the median) and more expensive homes (priced above the median). The results for the latter period, where inflation was highest, demonstrated that for homes with a median-Blacks' first mortgage of less than $52,000, whites' homes increased $13,200 more than Blacks' homes. The less expensive homes of whites increased during this period by 122% compared to 79% for comparable Black homes. For more expensive homes, the difference continues to be significant and of similar magnitude: For whites, their homes appreciated $47,800 or by 56%, while for Blacks the increase was only $34,900 or 44%. The index of bias, $12,900, is quite similar to what was uncovered for less expensive homes.

For the earlier period, homeowners have had far longer time to accumulate home equity, including the high-inflation 80s. White homeowners who purchased less expensive homes (priced less than $28,000) in the years 1967 to 1977 saw their homes increase by $60,000, compared to a $28,000 increase for Blacks who bought similarly priced homes. Thus, the index of bias was $32,000. Whites enjoyed a 325% increase in housing appreciation compared to only 175% for Blacks. Among buyers of expensive homes, white homes went up $78,000, compared to only $38,700 for Blacks. While the increase for both groups was impressive, whites had a 148% increase, compared to 88% for Blacks, leading to an index of bias of $39,300. A regression analysis confirmed "the importance of race in housing appreciation, even when non-race-related factors affecting home values are taken into account" (Oliver and Shapiro 2006, 152).

In a more sophisticated analysis, Flippen (2004) demonstrates convincingly that housing in predominantly minority and integrated neighborhoods appreciates more slowly than comparable housing in predominantly white communities. This analysis goes beyond others in examining the extent to which this inequality is due to "nonracial socioeconomic and housing structure factors," with a particular emphasis on the poverty composition of communities (Filppen 2004, 1523). The focus on both Blacks and Hispanics provides an important contribution to the literature on racial differences in housing values. Her findings represent the best analysis we have on this issue.

Using a unique and rich set of data from the Health and Retirement Study (HRS)—a survey conducted every two years by the University of Michigan of more than 22,000 Americans over the age of 50 and sponsored by the National Institute of Aging—Flippen is able to gain an impressive portrait of an aging America's physical and mental health, insurance coverage, financial status, family support systems, labor market status, and retirement planning. Combining those data with the 1970, 1980, and 1990 Census of Housing and Population, Flippen conducts a hedonic analysis of current home prices that "produce readily interpretable results" and allow comparable prices of a "constant-quality house across different housing markets," as well as allowing assessment of "the effect of previous neighborhood characteristics as well as neighborhood change" (Flippen 2004, 1532). Focusing on the cohort of homeowners born between 1930 and 1941, her results confirm and deepen the analysis conducted by Oliver and Shapiro (2006). First, she finds that the "current value of minority-owned homes is substantially below that of white-owned homes" and "levels of appreciation are also markedly lower for Blacks than for whites and are somewhat lower for Hispanics." Most telling is the fact that "mature Black homeowners experience depreciation more often than appreciation" (Flippen 2004, 1535). Second, the more expensive the home and the earlier it was purchased, the lower the appreciation for Black homeowners. Third, and most importantly, the degree of segregation is highly related to housing appreciation. This result requires greater explication.

Because of the unique nature of the data set, Flippen was able to identify the racial composition and poverty context of each household's home. Thus, she was able to identify how housing appreciation was related to racial segregation, the dynamics of racial change, and the dynamics of a changing poverty context. Figure 11.1 summarizes the basic relationship of housing appreciation and racial segregation for Blacks and Hispanics. For African Americans, housing appreciation is monotonically related to the percent of Blacks in the neighborhood: The lower the initial level of the Black population, the higher the level of home appreciation. In neighborhoods with 0 to 2% initial Black population, the amount of housing appreciation is approximately five times more ($24,993) than if the neighborhood was initially 65% or greater Black ($4,726). For Hispanics, the pattern is somewhat different and not as monotonic in structure.

With a growing concern about poverty, some critics contend that this strong finding is not about racial segregation, but about poverty. Flippen per-

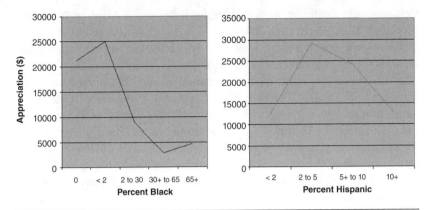

Figure 11.1 Percent Black and Hispanic and housing appreciation (for 1930–1941 Cohort). Source: Flippen, Chenoa, "Unequal Returns to Housing Investments? A Study of Real Housing Appreciation among Black, White, and Hispanic Households," *Social Forces*, June 2006, 82(4):1536.

forms several similar analyses using percent poverty, and changes in poverty and racial composition over time. The resulting analyses "clearly establish that neighborhood minority composition exerts a large effect on housing appreciation, both directly at high levels of concentration and indirectly through the association between minority and poverty compositions." To illustrate how this works, Flippen (2004, 1543) performs a simulation that examines the disparate effects of neighborhood experiences on housing appreciation inequality for African Americans and Latinos "if they lived in neighborhoods comparable to those of whites" (2004, 1543). Her findings are that if the average Black HRS respondents lived in the same neighborhoods as the average white HRS respondents, their home would be worth $24,500 more in 1992 than if they lived in the typical Black neighborhood. This would represent a 39% increase for Black housing appreciation. Interestingly enough, Flippen finds that the results for Hispanics show an even greater undermining of home equity, resulting in a difference of $59,300, or a 76% increase, were Hispanics to live in neighborhoods similar to whites.

Stripping Minority Home Equity: The Subprime Meltdown

The most important contemporary set of institutional forces to dispro-portionally affect the ability of African Americans and other minorities to achieve parity in home equity has been the subprime mortgage crisis. African Americans, along with other minorities and low-income populations, have been the targets of the subprime mortgage system. Blacks received a disproportionate share of these loans, leading to a "stripping" of their hard-won home equity gains of the recent past and the near future (California

Reinvestment Coalition 2008; Center for Responsible Lending 2006; Immergluck 2008; Rivera et al. 2008).

Changes in the mortgage market, of which the current subprime meltdown is the most visible part of a larger pattern, were not racially neutral. The initial foray into subprime loans targeted mainly Black and other elderly minority homeowners. The 1990 to 2000 period was known for its predatory loans, primarily refinancing, which flew under the radar of the wider society, but were fought tooth and nail by local communities. These practices were refined and sharpened by the financial services industry during this period and rolled out as the more exotic and legal subprime loans we are familiar with today (high hidden costs, exploding adjustable rates, prepayment penalties to preclude refinancing) (Immergluck 2008). With the recognition that average American families were accumulating trillions of dollars in housing wealth, these "financial innovations" and new financial instruments relaxed (and sometimes ignored) rules and regulations and became the market's preferred method of broadening homeownership.

Minority communities received a disproportionate share of subprime mortgages. As a result, they are suffering a disproportionate burden of the harm and losses.

Households of color were more than three times as likely as white households to end up with riskier loans containing features like exploding adjustable rates, deceptive teaser rates, and balloon payments (Center for Responsible Lending 2006). Good credit scores often made no difference, as profit incentives trumped sound policy. Similarly, sociologist Jesus Hernandez proves that the physical locations of foreclosures of homes owned by Blacks and Latinos in Sacramento between 1998 and 2008 can be identified precisely by finding the areas in Sacramento in 1939 that were redlined as white but did not have restrictive covenants. Even though the individuals who shaped and profited from the patterns of 1939 were long gone, their actions determined that the home foreclosure crisis of the turn of the twenty-first century would have disproportionate impact on minority borrowers (Hernandez 2008). Thus, the line from redlining to the subprime crisis is direct. Even many upper-income African Americans were steered into subprime mortgages. The Center for Responsible Lending (among others) projects that 2.2 million borrowers who bought homes between 1998 and 2006 will lose their homes and at least $164 billion of wealth in the process. African-American and Latino homeowners are twice as likely to suffer subprime-related home foreclosures as white homeowners. Foreclosures are projected to affect 1 in 10 African-American borrowers. In contrast, only about 1 in 25 white mortgage-holders will be affected. African Americans and Latinos are not only more likely to have been caught in the subprime loan trap; they are also far more dependent, as a rule, on their home as a financial resource (Center for Responsible Lending 2006).

Home equity, at its present (2008) total value of $20 trillion (Demos 2008, 7), represents the biggest source of wealth for most Americans, as we have noted, and it is even more important for African Americans. The comparatively little amount of wealth accumulation in the African-American community is concentrated largely in housing wealth. One recent estimate places the total loss of wealth among African-American households at $72 to $93 billion for subprime loans taken during the past eight years (Rivera et al. 2008).

This devastating impact is not confined to just those foreclosed, because there is a spillover effect in addition to the direct hit of the estimated 2.2 million foreclosures. An additional 40.6 million neighboring homes will experience devaluation because of subprime foreclosures that take place in their community. The Center for Responsible Lending (2008) estimates that the total decline in house values and tax base from nearby foreclosures will be $202 billion. Homeowners living near foreclosed properties will see their property values decrease $5,000 on average (Center for Responsible Lending 2008).

It is not possible to analyze specifically the full spillover impact of subprime foreclosures on African Americans or Latinos, largely because these data are not available yet, but communities of color will be especially harmed, since these communities receive a disproportionate share of subprime home loans. This lost home value translates into a decrease in the tax base, consumer expenditures, investment opportunities, and money circulating in communities of color. Already, United for a Fair Economy estimates the total loss of wealth among households of color at between $164 billion and $213 billion for subprime loans taken between 2000 and 2008 (Rivera et al. 2008).

Whatever the exact figures, the bottom line is clear: After centuries of being denied any opportunity for accumulating wealth, after a few decades of having limited opportunities, after a generation during which a significant amount of wealth was accumulated by middle-class African-American and Latino families, the African-American and Latino community now faces the greatest loss of financial wealth in its history. Institutional processes and racialized policy are trumping hard-earned educational, job, and income advances.

Transforming Racial Inequality in Home Equity

Forty years after passage of the Fair Housing Act and the Supreme Court's ruling in *Jones v. Mayer* (cited in Lamb 2005); more than four decades after Dr. King's Open Housing marches in Chicago, and nearly a century and a half after adoption of the Fourteenth Amendment, and one hundred forty-three years after the signing of the 1866 Civil Rights Law, people of different races in the United States today remain relegated to different spaces. Each year, more than 4 million instances of housing and lending discrimination work insidiously to skew opportunities and life chances along racial lines (National Fair Housing Alliance 2008). We would make enormous progress toward racial justice if fair housing laws were strengthened; if they included cease and desist orders or penalties sufficient to deter lawbreakers; if governments at all levels honored their affirmative fair housing obligations; if the Office of the Comptroller of the Currency and the Federal Reserve Board pursued cases against mortgage lenders based on evidence of policies with disparate racial impacts; if the property insurance industry was required to provide the kind of data that the Home Mortgage Disclosure Act requires from housing lenders; and if government agencies and officials at all levels enforced the law more actively and aggressively.

Yet stronger laws and better law enforcement alone will not be enough to counter the ways that race skews opportunities and life chances in our society. The patterns of the past impede the attainment of equality in the present and will continue to do so until we come to grips with the ways in which present policies increase the value of past and present discrimination by exploiting the cumulative vulnerabilities of aggrieved racialized groups. Imbalances of power offer opportunities for profiteering and exploitation. Sites of cumulative violation and vulnerability yield unusually high profits.

As organizers in the Civil Rights Movement used to say, "water flows to the low places." Local, state, and federal governments do not do enough to combat discrimination, to be sure, but even worse, they add to existing injustices and inequality by providing subsidies for segregation and rewards for racism through putatively race-neutral policies that have disparate racial impacts and frequently expand rather than narrow racial gaps in assets, wealth, opportunities, and life chances.

At all levels, government policies today produce unearned advantages and unjust enrichments for whites while imposing unfair impediments to asset accumulation, education, employment, and health care for people of color. These policies actually increase the rewards of past discrimination by extending favored treatment to the descendants of its perpetrators. In addition, they make victims of past discrimination pay a disproportionate share of the burdens of social change by exploiting the accumulated weaknesses incurred by aggrieved communities. The cumulative and collective vulnerabilities of communities of color create collective unfair and unearned advantages for whites.

Today, a broad range of putatively race-neutral tax policies consistently subsidize those forms of income most likely to be inherited as a result of successful discrimination in the past. Public and private housing, home loan, and tax policies inhibit the entry of new competitors into the housing market. They add to the locked-in advantages and wealth of those who inherit the assets originally secured on a discriminatory basis from the Homestead Act and the FHA. For example, the home mortgage interest deduction—and the favored tax treatment given to income derived from inheritance and capital gains income—all work to augment the value of the unfair gains secured through direct discrimination in previous eras. Segregated suburban schools and neighborhoods provide whites with assets that appreciate in value and with privileged access to insider information and personal networks that give them decided advantages in securing the 80 to 90% of jobs in U.S. society that are never openly advertised (Skrentney 1996; Sullivan 1989).

The "locked-in" gains of past discrimination also secure subsidies in the present. Homeowners generally deduct the costs of local property taxes from their federal income tax. This lowers their federal tax obligations and makes it financially desirable for them to support property tax increases that fund local schools. Similarly, the home mortgage interest deduction increases property values, which add to the income of wealthy districts. In contrast, school districts whose constituents include large numbers of renters or less affluent homeowners who do not itemize deductions do not secure similar funding for their schools. A study in 2001 showed that while the poverty-stricken city of Camden, New Jersey received $1,140 per student in federal aid (mostly from Title 1 grants), property tax and mortgage interest deductions funneled $2,399 per student to the wealthy suburban city school system in Princeton, New Jersey (Rothstein 2001).

Because of the cumulative imbalances of wealth and power created by policies that funneled assets that appreciated in value and could be passed down to whites while denying them expressly to Blacks and other people of color, nearly any policy adopted today is likely to have a disparate racial impact. Debates over the 1999 banking reform law or the 1996 telecommunications reorganization act rarely touched on race. Yet these legislative acts played major roles in creating the preconditions for the above-cited loss of $164 to $213 billion by people of color as a result of the subprime crisis and the destruction of local Black radio news and public affairs programs as a result of corporate monopolization of radio air waves (Center for Responsible Lending 2006; Rose 2008).

We cannot eliminate every policy that has a disparate racial impact. Yet we can face up to the reality of cumulative vulnerability by drawing on the best traditions of abolition democracy and use government funds and programs to support the emergence of new democratic institutions and practices. We can revive the original intent of the Fourteenth Amendment to serve as an antisubjugation measure and rescue it from the right-wing judicial activists who have hijacked it and misrepresented it as a measure that requires us to pretend that we do not see the racial—and racist—realities that are right before our eyes. The proposed resolution of the *Thompson v. HUD* case in Baltimore offers us an exemplary model of democratic institution-building. The U.S. Department of Housing and Urban Development (HUD) has been found guilty of deliberately segregating public housing in Baltimore. The remedial phase expert report in the case by john anthony powell explained that the expressly racial injury in the case required a race-conscious remedy. As a result, the court explored a plan that entails building new housing for Blacks in integrated communities of opportunity. This kind of "remedy" would be constructive and valuable in other cases, even where a de jure violation of law by a single perpetrator cannot be established (powell 2005).

The emphasis in *Thompson v. HUD* on expressly race-based remedies presents the only way we can reckon fairly and adequately with the long history of race-based locked-in advantages and market exclusions in housing and homeownership. At every level of income and wealth, race remains the crucial variable in determining opportunities and life chances in the United States. Housing discrimination concentrates poverty, but it also racializes it. Even middle- and upper-income Blacks suffer from concentrated poverty. A 2003 sociological study disclosed that while 10% of whites are likely to live some part of their lives in a poor neighborhood in any given decade, a majority of African Americans will live in poor neighborhoods at some point in the same decade (Quilian 2003, 221–49). The overwhelming majority of white and Asian students attend schools where fewer than 30% of the students come from impoverished households, but 60% of Black and Latino students are enrolled in schools where more than half of the students' families have incomes below the poverty line. In the Washington, DC area, more than a quarter of the region's poor Blacks live in neighborhoods where at least 30% of the people are poor, but only 2% of poor whites live in areas where poverty is highly concentrated (Acevedo-Garcia and Osypuk 2008, 197).

In addition to programs like those outlined in *Thompson v. HUD* designed to move people to communities of opportunity, we also need investment and development policies that spread opportunities to communities that lack them. We need programs that acknowledge the importance of the racial wealth gap and that enable aggrieved racial groups to determine their own destinies through democratic deliberation and decision-making.

Segregation into different neighborhoods relegates people of different races to different sectors of the banking industry. In white neighborhoods, residents rely on providers of mainstream financial services: savings and checking accounts, certificates of deposit, prime rate mortgages, individual retirement accounts, and automobile and home improvement loans. Minority communities, however, find themselves riddled with second-rung financial service providers: payday lenders, pawn shops, check-cashing establishments, rent-to-own shops, and subprime mortgage lenders.

Corporations that pollute land near homes inhabited by whites pay penalties 500% higher than those assessed on firms that pollute sites near Black neighborhoods. Penalties for all violations of federal environmental laws have been 46% lower in minority communities than in white neighborhoods. Superfund cleanups begin faster and are more extensive in areas populated by whites than in comparable sites inhabited by Blacks or Latinos (Bullard 1993, 21). National studies reveal that poor Black children have a far greater likelihood of suffering from lead poisoning than poor white children. Medical authorities in St. Louis in 1998 announced the existence of 1,833 new cases of childhood lead poisoning. These health officers estimated that 20 to 25% of local youths had toxic levels of lead in their bloodstreams, a percentage nearly six times the national average. In some Black neighborhoods, the figure was even higher, nearly 40%. Even after controlling for income and education, the health of Black people seems worth less than the health of whites to the decision-makers in our society (Higgins 2000, 17).

Addressing the skewing of opportunities and life chances along racial lines in the society requires stronger fair housing laws and better law enforcement. But we also need to end those practices and policies that widen racial disparities and instead create new programs designed to promote equal opportunity through asset accumulation, educational equity, and environmental justice. These remedies should include asset-building strategies for individuals, but they also necessitate the kinds of government investments in Black communities adequate for addressing the cumulative, collective, and continuing costs of discrimination and segregation. But these measures will only work in a context of expanding democratic opportunity, of progressive rather than regressive taxation, educational equity, environmental justice, and full employment.

The desegregation of public accommodations and public schools needs to be accompanied by the desegregation of the dollar. In "Where Do We Go From Here? From Chaos to Community," Martin Luther King Jr. (1991) compared the passage of the 1964 Civil Rights Act and the 1965 Voting Rights Act to a stage in a football game. Dr. King said it was as if Black people started with possession of the ball deep in their own territory. Through tireless struggle they made it out to the 50-yard line. But then, their opponents told them to pretend they had scored a touchdown and to give them back the ball. We still need to complete the work that remains undone today, just as it was in Dr. King's day.

Our problems did not begin yesterday, and they will not be solved tomorrow. But every day we delay, the cost of justice grows higher. Addressing and redressing the long legacies of history requires us to mobilize degrees of courage, conviction, and commitment that we have not seen in the United States in many years. But people of all embodied identities suffer from the neglect of talent and misallocation of resources that discrimination creates. Unfair impediments to asset accumulation undermine the economy and make a mockery out of the allegiance that children pledge every school day to "one nation, indivisible, with liberty and justice for all."

References

Acevedo-Garcia, Dolores, and Theresa L. Osypuk. 2008. "Impacts of Housing and Neighborhoods on Health: Pathways, Racial/Ethnic Disparities, and Policy Directions." In *Segregation: The Rising Costs for America*, ed. James H. Carr and Nandinee K. Kutty. New York: Routledge, 197–235.

Bullard, Robert D. 1993. "Anatomy of Environmental Racism and the Environmental Justice Movement." In *Confronting Environmental Racism: Voices from the Grass Roots*, ed. Robert D. Bullard. Boston: South End, 15–40.

California Reinvestment Coalition. 2008. "Paying More for the American Dream: The Subprime Shakeout and Its Impact on Lower-Income and Minority Communities." http://www.nedap.org/resources/reports.html (accessed March 17, 2009).

Center for Responsible Lending. 2008. "Subprime Spillovers: Foreclosures Cost Neighbors $202 Billion; 40.6 Million Homes Lose $5,000 on Average." http://www.responsiblelending.org/pdfs/subprime-spillover.pdf (accessed March 17, 2009).

———. 2006. "Losing Ground: Foreclosures in the Subprime Market and Their Cost to Homeowners." http://www.responsiblelending.org/pdfs/foreclosure-paper-report-2-17.pdf (accessed March 17, 2009).

Demos. 2008. "Beyond the Mortgage Meltdown: Addressing the Current, Avoiding a Future Catastrophe." http://demos.org/pubs/housingpaper_6_24_08.pdf (accessed March 17, 2009).

Di Zhu Xiao, Eric Belsky, and Xiadong Liu. 2007 "Do Homeowners Achieve More Household Wealth in the Long Run?" *Journal of Housing Economics* 16: 274–90.

Duster, Troy. 1987. "Crime, Youth, Unemployment and the Underclass" *Crime and Delinquency* 33 (2): 308–09.

Flippen, Chenoa A. 2004. "Unequal Returns to Housing Investments? A Study of Real Housing Appreciation Among Black, White, and Hispanic Households." *Social Forces* 82 (4): 1523–55.

Fullilove, Mindy Thompson. 2005. *Root Shock: How Tearing Up City Neighborhoods Hurts America and What We Can Do About It*. New York: Ballantine.

Gilbert, Charlene, and Quinn Eli 2000. *Homecoming: The Story of African-American Farmers*. Boston: Beacon Press.

Hernandez, Jesus. 2008. "Redlining Revisited: Mortgage Patterns in Sacramento, 1930–2004." Presentation at Policy Mentor Conference, Irvine, California, July 12.

Higgins, Laura. 2000 "The Lead Menace." *Riverfront Times*, April 12–18, 17.

Immergluck, Dan. 2008. "From the Subprime to the Exotic: Excessive Mortgage Market Risk and Foreclosures." *Journal of the American Planning Association*, 74 (1): 59–76.

Jackson, Kenneth. 1985. *Crabgrass Frontier: The Suburbanization of the United States*. New York: Oxford University Press.

King, Alan 2008. "Newly-Passed Bill Plugs Loophole for Black Farmers." *The Baltimore Afro-American*, May 24–30, A3.

King, Martin Luther Jr. 1991. "Where Do We Go From Here: Chaos or Community." In *A Testament of Hope: The Essential Writings and Speeches of Martin Luther King Jr.*, ed. James M. Washington. New York: HarperCollins, 555–633.

Kochar, Rakesh. 2004. *The Wealth of Hispanic Households: 1996–2002*. Washington, D.C.: Pew Hispanic Center.

Krivo, Lauren, and Robert Kaufman. 2004. "Housing and Wealth Inequality: Racial-Ethnic Differences in Home Equity in the United States." *Demography* 41(3): 585–605.

Lamb, Charles. 2005. *Housing Segregation in Suburban America Since 1960*. New York: Cambridge University Press, 208–10.

Lipsitz, George. 2002 "The Silence of the Rams: How St. Louis School Children Subsidize the Super Bowl Champs." In *Sports Matters: Race, Recreation, and Culture*, ed. John Bloom and Michael Nevin Willard. New York: New York University Press, 225–45.

Logan, John, and Harvey Molotch. 1987. *Urban Fortunes: The Political Economy of Place*. Berkeley: University of California Press.

National Fair Housing Alliance. 2008. *2008 Fair Housing Trends*. Washington, D.C.: Author.

Oliver, Melvin, and Thomas Shapiro. 2006. *Black Wealth/White Wealth: A New Perspective on Racial Inequality*. New York: Routledge.

powell, john anthony. 2005. *Remedial Phase Expert Report in Thompson v. HUD* http://www.structuralracism.org/publications/partnerpub.-kl.htm (accessed March 17, 2009).

Quadrango, Jill. 1994. *The Color of Welfare: How Racism Undermined the War on Poverty*. New York: Oxford University Press.

Quilian, Lincoln. 2003, "How Long Are Exposures to Poor Neighborhoods? The Long Term Dynamics of Entry and Exit from Poor Neighborhoods." *Population Research and Policy Review* 22: 221–49.

Rivera, Ammad, Brenda Cotto-Escalera, Anisha Desai, Jeannette Huezo, and Dedrick Muhammad. 2008. *Foreclosed: State of the Dream 2008*. Boston: United for a Fair Economy.

Roithmayr, Daria. 2007 "Racial Cartels." *University of Southern California Law and Economics Working Papers Series*. Working Paper 66.

Rose, Tricia. 2008. *The Hip Hop Wars: What We Talk About When We Talk About Hip Hop—And Why It Matters*. New York: Basic Books.

Rothstein, Richard. 2001 "How the U.S. Tax Code Worsens the Education Gap," *New York Times*, April 25, A-17.

Shapiro, Thomas. 2004. *The Hidden Cost of Being African American: How Wealth Perpetuates Inequality*. New York: Oxford University Press.

Skrentney, John David. 1996. *The Ironies of Affirmative Action*. Chicago: University of Chicago Press.

Sullivan, Mercer.1989. *Getting Paid: Youth, Crime, and Work in the Inner City*. Ithaca, NY: Cornell University Press.

Thompson v. HUD. http://www.Kirwaninstitute.org/research/projects/ThompsonHud.php (accessed March 17, 2009).

Zarembka, Arlene. 1990. *The Urban Housing Crisis: Social, Economic, and Legal Issues and Proposals*. Westport, CT: Greenwood.

CHAPTER 12

Two-Tiered Justice

Race, Class, and Crime Policy

MARC MAUER

For more than a half century since the promise of an integrated society occasioned by the historic *Brown v. Board of Education* decision (1954), opportunities for people of color have expanded significantly. Since 1954, a thriving black middle class has emerged, along with growing numbers of Latinos and other groups who are reaping the rewards of a multicultural society. And, of course, the ascent of the nation's first black President only accentuates the achievements of many African-American professionals in recent decades.

Lurking not far below the surface, though, is the grim reality of a society that in many respects is as segregated as ever, and arguably one with declining opportunities for those left behind in the changing economic climate. In many of the nation's urban areas, large numbers of the generation that grew up after the Civil Rights Movement now toil in low-wage or underground economies, with only distant connections to the national, let alone global, economy. And in the most profound betrayal of the promise of integration and opportunity, the United States has created a world-record prison population, fueled by policies that have exposed substantial portions of African Americans to the life-changing consequences of the criminal justice system.[1]

These policies and outcomes are intimately tied in with the dynamics of a segregated society in several ways. First, through law enforcement practices and the development of criminal justice policy, residential segregation patterns contribute to an expanding prison system. Second, segregation ensures that the presumed purpose of incarceration—producing public safety—inevitably will be seriously compromised. Finally, these developments come together to produce a vicious cycle of declining political influence for the communities most affected by mass incarceration, thus resulting in misguided and racially skewed policies becoming entrenched.

The Development of Mass Incarceration

For about 50 years prior to 1972, the rate of imprisonment in the United States remained relatively steady. The prison population rose during the Depression years and declined during World War II, but the rate of imprisonment hovered in the range of 110 per 100,000 population throughout this period, or about 160 per 100,000, adding the local jail population. By the standards of other industrialized nations, this was a high figure, roughly two to three times the rate in Canada and Western Europe. By 1972, the total incarcerated population stood at about 330,000 (Mauer 2006).

In the more than three decades since then, the United States has been engaged in what I have elsewhere termed a "race to incarcerate" (Mauer 2006). This has produced a six-fold increase in the number of people behind bars, now totaling 2.3 million (Sabol and Couture 2008). The rate of incarceration, 762 per 100,000 as of 2007, is the highest in the world and generally five to eight times that of other industrialized nations (International Centre for Prison Studies 2008).

The racial/ethnic disparities produced by this prison explosion have been profound. Nearly 60% of the prison and jail population is African-American or Latino, far out of proportion to their overall share of the national population. As of 2001, 16.6% of adult black males had spent time in prison, as had 6% of Latino males. And if current trends continue, one in three black males born today can expect to go to prison in his lifetime, as can one in six Latino males. Rates for women of color are lower overall, but the racial/ethnic disparities are similar (Bonczar 2003).

Many scholars have analyzed the proximate causes of this prison expansion, and there is a strong consensus among them that this has primarily been a function of changes in policy, and not crime rates. In this analysis, I will examine the ways in which racial segregation has contributed to the development of those policy changes and is in turn exacerbated by mass incarceration.

Segregation and the Growing Prison System

Some theorists have suggested that the U.S. prison system is the new Jim Crow, functioning as the most recent means of the several centuries-long control of America's black population. Loic Wacquant (2001), for example, asserts that the rise in the carceral state follows immediately upon the gains of the Civil Rights Movement, and that once the legal barriers for social control had eroded, another institutional form of control was necessary to accomplish that objective.

How intentional these developments may have been is subject to debate, but we can trace these trends as an outgrowth of demographic, economic, and political changes in the 1960s which influenced both crime and its political positioning. Beginning in the mid-1960s, crime rates rose in the United States for a period of about ten years. The reasons for this are complex, but in part relate to the rise of the "baby boom" generation, essentially a greater number of young males in the 15 to 24 age group, a group that historically has been disproportionately involved in crime. In addition, increasing urbanization—with a rapid increase during this time—has often been associated with higher rates of crime. But the racial context for these changes was critical. Despite a general decline in unemployment rates in the 1960s, economists Llad Phillips and Harold Votey document that unemployment rates for nonwhite youth were rising during this period, along with a decline in their overall labor force participation (Currie 1985). They contend that these labor market changes alone were "sufficient to explain increasing crime rates for youths" in the 1960s (Currie 1985, 111).

So, crime rates were rising, but *how* to respond to such a problem was still a matter of political negotiation, and one framed by racial perceptions. Bruce Western describes a process whereby "Elevated crime rates and the realigned race relations of the post-civil rights period provided a receptive context for the law-and-order themes of the national Republican Party," (2006, 60), themes that would be picked up by many Democratic political leaders as well.

These initiatives were advanced in a nation where residential segregation had persisted despite the changes in public policy brought about by the Civil Rights Movement. As Douglas Massey has documented, since 1970 "Metropolitan areas…with large black communities (Chicago, Detroit, Philadelphia) remain segregated at extremely high levels that have hardly changed since the passage of the Fair Housing Act…. therefore, race remains a dominant dimension of stratification in American housing markets" (2007, 75). The confluence of these political and environmental dynamics virtually ensured that the policy initiatives growing out of this framework would become dramatically punitive in their orientation.

This political characterization immediately preceded the dramatic shifts in the U.S. economy that would alter the life prospects of many African Americans. While these economic changes did not necessarily *require* the development of a massive prison system, in combination with the racialization of crime and the absence of a sustained opposition movement, they made such a development almost inevitable.

In broad terms, these economic changes included the oil crisis of 1973, the declining influence of the United States on the world stage, and a shift in the economy from a manufacturing state to a technical and financial services economy. These shifts presaged a growing divide in wealth and income since the early 1980s, one where the rich have done very, very well and the poor have become increasingly marginalized.

These economic dynamics have been overlaid with racial patterns that in turn influenced the development of penal policy in several ways. First, the geographical areas left behind in the emerging economy were by and large those urban communities that had long been dependent on the manufacturing boom of the post-World War II era. The enormous decline in manufacturing employment in urban areas during the 1970s included a loss of 170,000 blue-collar jobs in New York, 120,000 in Chicago, and 90,000 in Detroit (Kasarda 1989). These declines hit young African Americans particularly hard, with a 30% decline in employment among high school dropouts and 20% decline for high school graduates in metropolitan areas (Western 2008). Thus, working-class blacks (and whites as well) in Detroit, Akron, and elsewhere who had gained good union-wage jobs in the auto and steel industries now saw their sons and daughters more likely to be working at jobs in the fast-food industry at wages that could not support a family or homeownership. And those people who were increasingly left behind as a result of these shifts essentially became a "surplus population." As William Julius Wilson documents, it was not just a question of poverty, but "Something far more devastating has happened that can only be attributed to the emergence of concentrated and persistent joblessness and its crippling effects on neighborhoods, families, and individuals" (1997, 17). He concludes: "Since no other group in society experiences the degree of segregation, isolation, and poverty concentration as do African-Americans, they are far more likely to be disadvantaged when they have to compete with other groups in society...." (1997, 24).

As legitimate economic opportunities declined in these overwhelmingly segregated African-American neighborhoods, it should not have been surprising that at least some residents would become engaged in criminal behaviors. By the late 1980s, we would see the toll that crack cocaine, and in particular the violent drug markets that developed around the drug, exerted on many communities. The response to the crack epidemic only reinforced the strong interplay between race and the development of public policy. The mandatory sentencing laws passed by Congress in 1986 and 1988 imposed far harsher penalties on persons convicted of crack cocaine offenses than powder cocaine, despite the fact that the two drugs are pharmacologically identical, and crack is merely a derivative of powder cocaine (U.S. Sentencing Commission 2007). The combined effect of skewed federal law enforcement practices with the new sentencing laws resulted in African Americans constituting more than 80% of the people subsequently sentenced to mandatory five- and ten-year prison terms (U.S. Sentencing Commission 2007).

As we have seen with the experience of crack cocaine policy, so was it the case that in the nation's overall approach to crime the policy of choice was one of heavy-handed law enforcement and incarceration policy, despite the fact that a variety of other strategies could have been pursued. These might have included economic development, school reform, homeownership programs, and job placement—all sorely needed by low-income communities and demonstrated to be effective in promoting public safety. But by defining the issue as a "criminal justice" problem, these alternative approaches vanished from the political landscape.

The growing race and economic divide also exacerbated the scale of incarceration. All nations have prison systems, but these vary enormously in the degree to which they employ incarceration. Some research suggests that the scale of incarceration is related to the degree of inequality in a society (Wilkins and Pease 1987). That is, the greater the inequality, the higher the overall rate of incarceration. The theory behind this is that societies provide a variety of positive and negative rewards to their populations. In the United States, where the positive economic rewards are most extreme, so too, are the negative consequences—in this case, imprisonment. One can also see how this plays out in the world of public policy. In recent decades, legislators at both the state and federal level have increasingly adopted a host of mandatory and determinate sentencing policies that have reduced the discretion of sentencing judges in favor of across-the-board sentencing policies based primarily on the offense of conviction and prior criminal record. While these factors are clearly relevant at sentencing, so too have been background characteristics of the defendant, such as a history of substance abuse, domestic violence, or limited educational attainment. But given the social distance between most legislators and the defendant population, the less empathy there is likely to be, thus making it easier to adopt such punishments. Thus, the social divisions produced by segregation further disadvantage people of color by making it more likely they will be sentenced to prison rather than having their life circumstances taken into consideration as mitigating factors.

The racial dynamics of drug policy illustrate this most starkly. In the early decades of the twentieth century, marijuana was viewed as a drug largely used by blacks and Mexican Americans, with popular references to it being used in jazz clubs and "racy" parts of town. Whether or not this perception was entirely accurate, it no doubt contributed to such policies as the Boggs Act of 1951, which penalized first-time possession of marijuana or heroin with a sentence of two to five years in prison (Schlosser 1994). By the 1960s, though, marijuana began to be widely used by white middle-class college students, and public attitudes began to change quickly. Marijuana came to be seen by many as a relatively harmless drug, with broad calls for its decriminalization. Nothing had changed about the drug, of course, only the public perception of the user, but as that racial perception changed so too did public policy.

Segregation Contributes to Unfair and Ineffective Crime Control Policies

A growing body of literature documents that mass incarceration has had, at best, a modest impact on controlling crime (Tonry 2004; Western 2006). A variety of factors explain this limited impact, including: deterrence is more a function of the certainty of punishment (apprehending more offenders) than the severity of punishment (increasing the length of prison terms); the "replacement" effect, by which convicted drug offenders and auto thieves are replaced by others on the street; and, the "aging out" of the prison population beyond the high crime-rate years. Further, whatever incapacitating or deterrent effect has been achieved is now long past the point of diminishing returns, as prisons are increasingly filled with nonviolent drug and property offenders. But in addition to these prison-crime dynamics, persistent segregation also plays an enhancing role in limiting whatever crime control impact might otherwise be achieved.

These effects begin with the concentration of low-income communities of color in highly segregated neighborhoods in urban areas across the United States. Policing practices over time have underserved, and subsequently overpoliced, these communities. For much of the early twentieth century, communities of color were largely an afterthought in the practices of many urban police departments. Crime was viewed as nothing to worry about so long as it did not spill over into more affluent areas of the city, and the overwhelmingly white police forces hardly reflected the composition of low-income communities of color. Needless to say, such practices and attitudes did not engender good relations between communities of color and law enforcement.

Changes in urban policing in the latter part of the century brought about some notable improvements, although they simultaneously reinforced some of the preexisting tensions. Most significantly, the changes included opening up many police departments to officers of color, including in leadership positions. By the 1990s, a significant number of police chiefs of big-city police departments were African American or Latino. Heightened public dialogue also produced greater attention and concern to the needs of communities of color, although varying broadly in the approaches that were taken.

In some cities, community policing approaches emphasized law enforcement agencies developing partnerships with communities as a means of resolving problems and underlying tensions in those communities. Operation

Ceasefire in Boston, for example, was credited with helping to reduce the spate of juvenile homicides of the early 1990s through a partnership between law enforcement, churches, and social service workers. But in many other areas, the renewed law enforcement presence was experienced as little more than a heavy-handed infusion of police with little regard for community input. New York City under the combined administration of Mayor Rudy Giuliani and Police Commissioner William Bratton is the prime example in this regard. With a strong commitment to the "broken windows" style of policing, under which any type of disorder, no matter how minor, would be treated as evidence of potential for more serious harm, the new regime launched a virtual onslaught on minority neighborhoods. Street stops and arrests by police all rose precipitously in the first several years after the policy was adopted. At the same time, and not coincidentally, so too did civilian complaints to the police review board, along with a widespread perception among minority youth that they were being targeted merely for being black or brown.

Proponents of these strategies argue that these neighborhoods are challenged by high rates of crime and therefore welcome this police presence. But as thoughtful law enforcement leaders have long known, the police can only be as effective as their relationship with the community. Rarely are police fortunate enough to witness a crime being committed. The vast majority of the time they are dependent on the community to report crimes, provide information, and serve as witnesses in court. When the police–community relationship becomes strained—as clearly evidenced by civilian complaints—cooperation and coordination suffer, and with that crimes are less likely to result in arrests, and arrests less likely to result in convictions.

U.S. District Judge Reggie Walton of Washington, DC, a self-described former "hard-charging prosecutor," describes the consequences of these frayed relations in the context of the "war on drugs," and in particular its impact on African-American communities.

> And I've had jurors come up during the voir dire process and say that they just will not be a part of sending another black man to jail in a system that they believe is racist because of the disparity regarding crack as opposed to powder cocaine sentencing. (U. S. Sentencing Commission 2006, 115)

Segregation affects the utility of the criminal justice system in other ways as well. The very nature of a prison—an institution that involuntarily houses hundreds of thousands of persons against their will—inevitably creates tension between staff and prisoners. In many instances, this atmosphere is exacerbated by the presence of race-identified gangs, largely functioning as an outgrowth of racially and ethnically formed gangs in segregated neighborhoods. As substantial numbers of their groups have become incarcerated, the gangs merely extend their reach behind the prison walls. California exhibits the most extreme form of this dynamic, so much so that for many years prison officials had a policy of segregating new prisoners by race and ethnicity so as to reduce intergroup conflict. This policy was ultimately struck down by the U.S. Supreme Court in 2005 with a finding that segregation was not necessary to create a safe environment in the prison system. But even as of 2008, on the eve of implementing the changes required by the Supreme Court, the California system was described as "One of the last bastions of racial segregation" (Arnoldy 2008, 119–120).

Segregation also reduces the effectiveness of criminal justice practice by limiting the impact of reentry programming, designed to connect people leaving prison with institutions in the community that can aid in reducing recidivism. In this regard, the challenges posed by the highly segregated, and poor, neighborhoods that most prisoners return to means that those institutions critical to reentry success are very fragile. Job markets are limited, social services poorly funded, and treatment programs for substance abuse or mental health sorely inadequate. No matter how motivated an individual may be to lead a legitimate lifestyle, the paucity of supportive services places great odds against his or her ultimate success.

As a result of this environment, along with the stigma attached to a prison record, incarceration produces a significant effect on the earnings potential of people who have been incarcerated. Bruce Western estimates that there is about a 15% reduction in hourly wages for former prisoners, as well as a substantial reduction in annual hours worked. Thus, for a black male high school dropout, an average annual income of about $9,000 would be reduced by about $3,300 (Western 2006).

Segregation and the Drug War

As noted, there has been a long history of tension between police and communities of color. In many instances, these relations have become strained since the inception of the drug war, beginning in the early 1980s. Here we can trace both the unprecedented ways in which drug policy has contributed to the prison population expansion and the resulting deleterious effects on communities of color.

The scale of the drug war's effects are enormous, with an increase in the number of people awaiting trial or serving a sentence for a drug offense in the nation's prisons and jails rising from 41,000 in 1980 to 500,000 by 2008 (Mauer and King 2007). Within state prisons, nearly 80% of drug offenders are African-American or Latino, a figure far out of proportion to the degree that these racial/ethnic groups use or sell drugs (Mauer and King 2002).

The means by which the "war" has been waged has been very much a two-tiered approach. For communities with resources, treatment and public health approaches remain the policies of choice. With only rare exceptions do we see large-scale drug busts or major police investigations into suburban drug rings. Instead, families suffering from a loved one's substance abuse attempt to cope with the problem by identifying treatment providers who can address the addiction.

Conversely, in low-income communities of color, the drug war has been waged relentlessly as a criminal justice war, involving a large police presence and record numbers of arrests, with only limited treatment interventions. This has come about as a result of segregated communities being vulnerable to politically inspired punitive policing strategies. Police officials will often justify these approaches by contending that open-air drug markets are more prevalent in inner-city neighborhoods, as compared to drug-selling behind closed doors in more affluent communities; these markets hurt neighborhood cohesion and public safety; and, heavy-handed policing tactics are supported by residents of these communities as a means of removing negative influences.

These statements are all true, but only half true. With such high concentrations of low-income people in relatively isolated communities, open-air drug markets do indeed become more prevalent, and of course such markets would not be welcomed in any community. But how to cope with these problems becomes a policy question, one that is framed by considerations of politics and race. There is certainly no foregone conclusion that addressing drug problems through massive displays of law enforcement is the most effective, let alone compassionate, possible response. Indeed, a broad body of research suggests that proactive investments in prevention and treatment would be far more cost-effective in reducing drug abuse and related crime (Caulkins et al. 1997; Currie 1998). But these have been given little space in a political environment that has promoted "tough on crime" approaches at the expense of exploring alternative options.

Impact on Communities

Mass incarceration, focused as it is on largely segregated communities, produces a variety of consequences that limit the potential of the community to promote public safety and build strong institutions. While scholars are beginning to assess the ways in which this comes about, it is important to note that, given the relatively recent nature of these developments, in some respects we can only speculate about the long-term effects, since the situation is essentially unique in the history of democratic nations.

One possible effect of segregation is the limit it places on the deterrent effect of incarceration. While the impact of deterrence is often overstated in the political world, clearly the threat of a criminal justice sanction or prison term for violating the law plays at least some role in causing potential law-breakers to consider the consequences of their actions. But as prisons fill up and incarceration becomes almost a commonplace experience for people in certain neighborhoods, newcomers to prison are likely to be housed with many people they already know. And as offenders cycle from prison back to the community, the experience of prison becomes well known, and therefore the "mystery" attached to it may diminish. Along with this, there is likely to be a diminishing of any deterrent effect that imprisonment may impose.

The concentrated nature of incarceration also affects community cohesion and trust in social institutions. Robert Crutchfield investigated the impact of high rates of incarceration in neighborhoods in Seattle, Washington on attitudes among those residents who had not been to prison. He found a diminution of social cohesion and trust that was "due in part to sentencing patterns and correctional policies" (Clear 2007, 113).

A key area of community life that is affected by mass incarceration can be seen in the realm of family formation and child-rearing. Mass incarceration creates a severe gender imbalance in many urban communities of color. One study in Washington, DC found that in neighborhoods of high incarceration there were only 62 adult men for every 100 adult women (Braman 2002). Some of the "missing" men had died or were in the military, but many were behind bars. The implications of these distorted gender ratios are quite dramatic. They clearly contribute to high numbers of single-parent households, and thus to the economic disadvantages that ensue to those families. Emerging research also suggests that these gender imbalances may contribute to higher rates of HIV infection, as men are more likely to have multiple sexual partners than in neighborhoods with a more balanced gender ratio (Clear 2007).

The concentration of incarceration also results in a loss of social capital, and thus reduced ability by which communities can address public safety through informal social controls. This comes about due to the fact that persons sentenced to prison are not "24/7 criminals." They may commit crimes once a day or once a year, but they also interact with their communities in socially productive ways. These include functioning as parents, consumers, workers, and other roles that contribute to community cohesion. Thus, when someone is sent to prison the community may gain some degree of public safety through incapacitation but it also loses the benefits provided through these other roles. This dynamic may explain the "tipping point" phenomenon of crime control observed by researchers in Tallahassee, Florida (Clear 2007). Looking at low-income, primarily African-American neighborhoods, the study's authors found that at modest rates of incarceration there were gains in reducing crime in the affected communities. But once these rates reached high levels, levels of crime actually increased. The researchers suggest that this outcome may be a function of the diminishing of parental controls, the community stress brought on by the large numbers of people returning from prison, and the fact that the accelerating incarceration of successively lower-level offenders produces increasingly smaller incapacitation effects. So, the loss of social capital, particularly when offset against the limited utility of the incarceration of low-level drug offenders, may result in overall negative consequences.

Related to the loss of social capital are the negative health consequences, and their racial dynamics, for people who have experienced incarceration. Michael Massoglia, for example, develops findings that show a "significant effect of incarceration on later health outcomes and indicate that the penal system accounts for a sizeable proportion of racial disparities in general health functioning" (2008, 277). He suggests that the negative health indicators may result from greater exposure to infectious diseases in prison and the stigmatizing of "ex-cons" that results in lowered social standing and an "inability of individuals to exercise control over their lives and participate fully in society" (2008, 296). Given the concentration effects of mass incarceration in black communities, these individual health indicators are then magnified to produce communities with high levels of health problems.

Finally, the concentration effect is likely to contribute to distortions in the role models available to young people. Currently, one of every fourteen African-American children has a parent in prison on any given day (Mumola 2000), and, as previously noted, one in three black male children born today can expect to go to prison if current trends continue (Bonczar 2003). While young black children may not know these precise figures, they can no doubt witness the cycle of people leaving their communities and returning from prison in great numbers, and doing so to a much greater extent than young people leaving for college. So as prison seems to become a virtual norm in some communities, it can come to be seen as almost an inevitable part of the life cycle for young men, and increasingly for young women.

These effects are exacerbated by the shift in resources that has been occasioned by the development of mass incarceration and its impact on affected communities. The irony of this situation is that taxpayers in fact are spending substantial funds on low-income communities of color, but these resources are increasingly devoted to incarceration. For example, researchers have identified "million dollar blocks" in densely populated Brooklyn, New York, in which taxpayers spend that sum each year to imprison people just from that one block alone (Cadora, Swartz, and Gordon 2003). Therefore, it is not so much a question about investment in these neighborhoods, but rather what form that investment takes. One could envision an investment of $1 million annually that might be put toward tutoring programs, summer job development, or substance abuse treatment as competing ways of strengthening families and communities so as to reduce overall levels of crime in a more proactive and compassionate way than the back-end response of incarceration.

Impact on Political Power and Efficacy

The combined impact of mass incarceration and segregation contributes to a vicious cycle whereby the racially skewed nature of the drug war in particular leads to distorted use of incarceration and in turn to declining political and economic power in communities of color. This comes about not necessarily through a conscious strategy designed to produce these effects, but rather through a set of policy initiatives developed over time and with little regard or analysis of any collateral racial effects.

Mass incarceration results in diminished black voting strength through the mechanism of felony disenfranchisement, the denial of the right to vote for people with felony convictions. Arising initially at the time of the founding of the nation—along with prohibitions on voting by women, African Americans, illiterates, and poor people—these policies have also been revised over time, often with the specific intent of disenfranchising black voters. In the post-Reconstruction era, at the time Southern legislators were imposing poll taxes and literacy requirements, lawmakers in states such as Alabama and South Carolina revised their disenfranchisement policies to target the newly freed black male voters. They did so by imposing disenfranchisement for crimes believed to be committed by blacks, but not for those offenses believed to be committed by whites. Thus, a man convicted of beating his wife would lose the right to vote, while a man convicted of killing his wife would not. Such was the racial logic of the time.

Today, 48 states and the District of Columbia ban voting by people serving a felony sentence in prison, 35 of these states also prohibit persons on probation or parole from voting, and in 11 states, a felony conviction can result in the loss of voting rights even after completion of sentence, and often permanently (The Sentencing Project 2008). As of 2004, an estimated 5.3 million Americans were disenfranchised by a felony conviction. Of this total, 4 million were not incarcerated, but were living in the community, either under probation or parole supervision, or, in the case of 2 million, had completed their felony sentence but lived in one of the states with post-sentence disenfranchisement (Manza and Uggen 2006).

Whether or not intended under current policies, the clear impact of disenfranchisement today is a dramatic disparity in the loss of voting rights for African Americans. Because of highly disparate rates of incarceration (a result of both greater involvement in crime and racially biased criminal justice practices), African Americans are disenfranchised at a rate of 8.25%, compared to a rate of 2.42% for all Americans (Manza and Uggen 2006). Thus, one of every twelve adult African Americans is currently not eligible to vote.

These figures take on meaning for black communities due to segregated housing patterns, whereby it is not only persons with a felony conviction who are affected but communities of African Americans as a whole whose voting power is diluted through the presence of large numbers of legally disenfranchised citizens. A study of Atlanta, Georgia, for example, found that in eleven highly segregated neighborhoods in the city, more than 10% of black males were ineligible to vote. For the city as a whole, black males were eleven times more likely to be disenfranchised than other males (Mauer and King 2004). Beyond that, there may be less incentive and pressure to vote on the part of those eligible if so many of their neighbors are not voting. The irony of these dynamics is that as black communities have been hard hit by the implementation of the war on drugs, this then results in the dilution of their voting strength, and thereby gives them less ability to express their political will on these and other issues. The reduced number of voters also provides disincentives to political candidates to campaign in these communities.

Political influence, and financial support, is further eroded through policies of the U.S. Census Bureau regarding how people in prison are enumerated for Census purposes. People in prison are counted in the counties in which the prison is located, not in their home districts. This practice is sometimes defended on the grounds that it is similar to the method used for enumerating college students who attend school away from home. There are key differences between these constituencies, though. College students are well integrated into their communities. They rent apartments, buy food, clothing, and gas at local establishments, and generally function as an integral part of the local economy. People in prison, on the other hand, have virtually no direct connection with the local economy or community. They are housed in state or federal prisons which purchase food and healthcare services from vendors often far away, they do not directly utilize any local services such as educational or cultural institutions, and of course, do not have the right to vote for local representatives.

The impact of segregation on these developments is that in most states the prison population consists disproportionately of people of color from a relative handful of urban neighborhoods who are then housed disproportionately in prisons that are far from home and in rural, largely white, areas. An analysis of 2000 Census data found that in 18 counties across the United States, more than 20% of the county population consisted of people in prison (Lotke and Wagner 2004). Since the Census count then influences political apportionment and certain federal and state funding streams, a transfer of wealth and power takes place from (black) urban areas (the homes of those incarcerated) to (white) rural areas.

Conclusion

The advent of mass incarceration has brought about profound changes to the ways in which we conceptualize problems of crime, disorder, and social intervention. These changes have been primarily experienced in communities of color, with imprisonment now becoming a common aspect of the life cycle in many low-income neighborhoods. The policies and practices that have produced these outcomes have set in motion a vicious cycle whereby the failure to invest in communities leads to higher rates of incarceration, which in turn contribute to frayed social relations and declining economic prospects. Throughout this process, residential segregation sets the stage for a punitive orientation in public safety policies as well as diminishing the effectiveness of the criminal justice system. Challenging segregation will not in itself reverse these trends, but it would set the stage for a more constructive dialogue on how best to approach these complex issues.

Note

1. Many of the dynamics described in this chapter may apply to Latinos as well, but the relative scarcity of data and analysis regarding Latinos and the criminal justice system makes it difficult to draw firm conclusions.

References

Arnoldy, Ben. 2008. "In California, a Segregation Bastion Falls." *Christian Science Monitor*, June 12.

Bonczar, Thomas P. 2003. *Prevalence of Imprisonment in the U.S. Population, 1974–2001*. Washington, DC: Bureau of Justice Statistics.

Braman, Donald. 2002. "Families and Incarceration." In *Invisible Punishment: The Collateral Consequences of Mass Imprisonment*, ed. Marc Mauer and Meda Chesney-Lind. New York: New Press, 117–135.

Brown v. Board of Education, 34 U.S. 483 (1954).

Cadora, Eric, Charles Swartz, and Mannix Gordon. 2003. "Criminal Justice Health and Human Services: An Exploration of Overlapping Needs, Resources, and Interests in Brooklyn Neighborhoods." In *Prisoners Once Removed: The Impact of Incarceration and Reentry on Children, Families, and Communities*, ed. Jeremy Travis and Michelle Waul. Washington, DC: Urban Institute Press, 285–311.

Caulkins, Jonathan, C. Peter Rydell, William Schwabe, and James Chiesa. 1997. *Mandatory Minimum Drug Sentences: Throwing Away the Key or the Taxpayers' Money?* Santa Monica, CA: RAND Corporation.

Clear, Todd. 2007. *Imprisoning Communities: How Mass Incarceration Makes Disadvantaged Neighborhoods Worse*. New York: Oxford University Press.

Currie, Elliot. 1985. *Confronting Crime—An American Challenge*. New York: Pantheon.

———. 1998. *Crime and Punishment in America*. New York: Metropolitan Books.

International Centre for Prison Studies, School of Law, King's College, London. *Prison Brief, Highest to Lowest Rates*. http://www.kcl.ac.uk/depsta/law/research/icps/worldbrief/wpb_stats.php (July 8, 2008).

Kasarda, John D. 1989. "Urban Industrial Transition and the Underclass." *Annals of the American Academy of Political and Social Science* 501: 26–47.

King, Ryan S., and Marc Mauer. 2002. *Distorted Priarities: Drug Offenders in State Prisons.* Washington, DC: The Sentencing Project.

———. 2004. *The Vanishing Black Electorate: Felony Disenfranchisement in Atlanta, Georgia.* Washington, DC: The Sentencing Project.

Lotke, Eric, and Peter Wagner. 2004. "Prisoners of the Census: Electoral and Financial Consequences of Counting Prisoners Where They Go, Not Where They Come From." *Pace Law Review* 24: 587–607.

Manza, Jeff, and Christopher Uggen. 2006. *Locked Out: Felony Disenfranchisement and American Democracy.* New York: Oxford University Press.

Massey, Douglas S. 2007. *Categorically Unequal: The American Stratification System.* New York: Russell Sage Foundation.

Massoglia, Michael. 2008. "Incarceration, Health, and Racial Health Disparities." *Law & Society Review* 42: 275–305.

Mauer, Marc. 2006. *Race to Incarcerate.* New York: The New Press.

———, and Ryan S. King. 2007. *A 25-Year Quagmire: The War on Drugs and Its Impact on American Society.* Washington, DC: The Sentencing Project.

Mumola, Christopher J. 2000. *Incarcerated Parents and Their Children.* Washington, DC: Bureau of Justice Statistics.

Sabol, William J., and Heather Couture. 2008. *Prison Inmates at Midyear 2007.* Washington, DC: Bureau of Justice Statistics.

Schlosser, Eric. 1994. "Reefer Madness." *Atlantic Monthly,* August, 45–63.

The Sentencing Project. 2008. *Felony Disenfranchisement Laws in the United States.* Washington, DC: Author.

Tonry, Michael. 2004. *Thinking About Crime.* New York: Oxford University Press.

U.S. Sentencing Commission. 2006. *Public Hearing on Cocaine Sentencing Policy.* Washington, DC.

———. 2007. *Report to the Congress: Cocaine and Federal Sentencing Policy.* Washington, DC :

Wacquant, Loic. 2001. "Deadly Symbiosis: When Ghetto and Prison Meet and Mesh." In *Mass Imprisonment: Social Causes and Consequences,* ed David Garland. Thousand Oaks, CA: Sage, 82–120

Western, Bruce. 2006. *Punishment and Inequality in America.* New York: Russell Sage Foundation.

———. 2008. "The Prison Boom and the Decline in American Citizenship." In *What Do We Owe Each Other?* ed. Howard L. Rosenthal and David J. Rothman. New Brunswick, NJ: Transaction, 101–115.

Wilkins, Leslie T., and Ken Pease. 1987. "Public Demand for Punishment." *International Journal of Sociology and Social Policy* 7: 16–29.

Wilson, William Julius. 1997. *When Work Disappears.* New York: Vintage Books.

CHAPTER 13

Residential Mobility, Neighborhoods, and Poverty

*Results from the Chicago Gautreaux Program
and the Moving to Opportunity Experiment*

STEFANIE DELUCA AND JAMES E. ROSENBAUM

Over the past few decades, researchers have become increasingly interested in the effects of neighborhood context on the lives of families and young people, and communities have become even more relevant in light of recent public policy developments. Theoretically, neighborhoods are important contexts for socialization and development, as well as places where we see structures of inequality and opportunity in action. Neighborhoods are also significant because they are closely tied to schooling opportunities, given the zoning of public schools. This connection is underscored by recent federal court cases that have considered whether to mandate racial or socioeconomic integration in housing and school settings (*Meredith v. Jefferson County Board* (2007); *Parents Involved in Community Schools v. Seattle School District No. 1* (2007); *Thompson v. HUD* (2006)). Residential mobility and housing policy have also garnered national attention after the hurricane disaster in New Orleans, and HOPE VI demolitions are prompting concerns about where families relocate after their housing projects are demolished.

Despite years of research on the connection between neighborhood characteristics and family and child outcomes, it is hard to know for sure if neighborhoods can be used as policy levers to improve youth and family well-being. This is due in large part to two related issues. First, despite relatively high levels of residential mobility in the United States, we see little variation in the types of communities low-income minority families inhabit. Often, poor families are trapped in dangerous neighborhoods, and their children are trapped in poor schools (Massey and Denton 1993; South and Crowder 1997; South and Deane 1993;). Therefore, we don't get the chance to observe how a different environment might affect their life chances. Second, families choose neighborhoods, and the characteristics of families that lead them to choose certain neighborhoods are also likely to affect family and child well-being. This leads to the selection problem (endogeneity), which plagues our attempts to recover causal estimates of environmental effects. However, there have been some opportunities to study what happens when parents and children experience moderate to radical changes in their neighborhood or schooling environments. Residential mobility programs, where poor families relocate to opportunity-rich communities via housing vouchers, provide one way we can begin to separate the effects of family background and neighborhood conditions. In this chapter, we review one particularly important mobility plan—Chicago's Gautreaux program—and examine a decade of research following the fortunes of the families who moved as a part of this intervention, and briefly consider Gautreaux in the context of some subsequent programs.

The Gautreaux Program

As a result of a 1976 Supreme Court decision, the Gautreaux program allowed low-income black public housing residents in Chicago to receive Section 8 housing vouchers and move to private-sector apartments either in mostly white suburbs or within the city. Between 1976 and 1998, over 7,000 families participated, and over half moved to suburban communities. Because of its design, the Gautreaux program presents an unusual opportunity: It allows us to examine whether individual outcomes change when low-income black families move to safer neighborhoods with better labor markets and higher-quality schools.

Gautreaux participants circumvented the typical barriers to living in suburbs, not by their jobs, finances, or values, but by acceptance into the program and quasi-random assignment to the suburbs. The program provided housing subsidy vouchers and housing support services, but not employment or transportation assistance. Unlike the usual case of working-class blacks living in working-class suburbs, Gautreaux permitted low-income blacks to live in middle- and upper-income white suburbs. Participants moved to more than 115 suburbs throughout the six counties surrounding Chicago. Suburbs with a population that was more than 30% black were excluded by the consent decree. A few very high-rent suburbs were excluded by funding limitations of Section 8 certificates.

In the 1970s, the national housing voucher experiment showed that if given vouchers, poor people choose familiar areas, segregated areas similar to the ones they left (Cronin and Rasmussen 1981). To ensure that families gained access to opportunity-rich communities, Chicago's Gautreaux program provided real estate staff to locate apartments in allowable neighborhoods, and housing counselors deeply committed to promoting racial integration to advise families about the benefits of moves into mostly white middle-class suburbs. As we shall see, these housing support services were crucial components of the program that cannot be overlooked.

Early Findings

Early research on Gautreaux had shown large and significant relationships between placement neighborhoods and subsequent gains in employment and education. A study of 330 Gautreaux mothers in the early 1990s found that suburban movers had higher employment than city movers, but not higher earnings, and the employment difference was especially large for adults who were unemployed prior to the move (Rosenbaum 1995). Another study found that, as young adults, Gautreaux children who moved to the suburbs were more likely than city movers to graduate from high school, attend college, attend four-year colleges (vs. two-year colleges), and if they were not in college, to be employed and to have jobs with better pay and with benefits (Rosenbaum 1995). These differences were very large.

Analyses indicated that children moving to suburbs were just as likely to interact with neighbors as city movers, but the suburban movers interacted with white children, while city movers interacted mostly with black children. The program seems to have been effective at integrating low-income black children into middle-class white suburbs. Although suburban schools were often far ahead of city schools in terms of curriculum level, mothers reported that suburban teachers often extended extra efforts to help their children catch up with the class. Initial concerns that these children would not be accepted were unsupported by the evidence.

Recent Research

To improve the design and data quality of the earlier work, recent research accounted for more pre-program characteristics and used administrative data to locate recent addresses for a random sample of 1,500 Gautreaux movers, as well as track residential and economic outcomes for mothers and children. Gautreaux was indeed successful in helping public-housing families relocate to safer, more integrated neighborhoods (Keels et al. 2005). These families came from very poor neighborhoods, with census-tract poverty rates averaging 40 to 60%, or three to five times the national poverty rate. Through the program, the suburb-movers moved to neighborhoods that were 5% poor. By the late 1990s, 15 to 20 years after relocating, these families often moved, but they lived in neighborhoods with poverty rates of 7% (DeLuca and Rosenbaum 2003, 323). *Gautreaux* also achieved striking success in moving low-income black families into more racially integrated neighborhoods (323). The origin communities were 83% black, while the program placed suburban movers in communities that averaged 28% black (most of the suburban moves were to communities that were more than 90% white). While some Gautreaux families later moved to neighborhoods that contained more blacks, suburban movers were living in areas that were about 36% black (323). Despite the increase, these levels were less than half of what they had been in the origin neighborhoods.

Parental economic outcomes, such as welfare receipt, employment, and earnings, were also influenced by the income and racial characteristics of placement neighborhoods. Women who moved to mostly black, low socio-economic status neighborhoods received welfare 7% longer, on average, than women placed in any other neighborhoods; women placed with few (0–10%) versus many (61–100%) black neighbors had employment rates that were 6 percentage points higher and earned $2,200 more annually than women placed in less affluent areas (Mendenhall, DeLuca, and Duncan 2006).

Another striking finding is that there seems to be a "second generation" of Gautreaux effects. Research on the children of the Gautreaux families has demonstrated that the neighborhoods where they resided in the late 1990s as adults were substantially more integrated than their overwhelmingly minority origin neighborhoods (Keels 2008a). With most Gautreaux children still too young for a reliable assessment of career successes, Keels (2008b) used administrative data on criminal justice system involvement to examine arrests and convictions for the young adults. Males placed in suburban locations experienced significantly lower odds of being arrested or convicted of a drug offense, compared with males placed within Chicago; specifically, there was a 42% drop in the odds of being arrested and a 52% drop in the odds of being convicted for a drug offense for suburban movers relative to city movers. Surprisingly, females placed into mostly white suburban neighborhoods had approximately three times the likelihood of being convicted of a drug, theft, or violent offense, compared to females placed within Chicago.

How Did Gautreaux "Work"?

The findings described above focus on the advances made in recent quantitative work. We had employed techniques to approximate the assessment of Gautreaux as a "treatment"—a social intervention with effects we might measure through statistical corrections and design comparisons. However, the stories Gautreaux participants tell about their experiences can also contribute greatly to our understanding. The long-term family outcomes we observed appear to be significantly linked to the mobility program and the characteristics of the placement neighborhoods. However, administrative data cannot tell us *how* these outcomes occurred or the mechanisms through which neighborhoods have their impact. This is a problem common to neighborhood research, and one that makes improving mobility programs especially difficult. However, in several qualitative studies (Rosenbaum, Reynolds, and DeLuca 2002; Rosenbaum, DeLuca, and Tuck 2005), we analyzed interviews with mothers who described how these neighborhoods helped improve their lives and the lives of their children. Was it a matter of just increasing access to better resources, or was it necessary to interact with neighbors to obtain the full benefit of these new resources?

We analyzed interviews with 150 Gautreaux mothers and found that after the move, they described a new sense of self-efficacy and reported that the major changes in their environments helped them to see that they had the ability to make improvements in their lives. Certain features of the new suburban neighborhoods changed their perception of what was possible. Specifically, the women reported that they felt better about having an address in the suburbs, and not having to put down a public housing address on job applications. Other women noted that by moving to areas with more white residents, they and their children got to know more white people, and racial stereotypes were debunked. One child whose only exposure to white people had been those she saw on TV reported that after moving, she discovered that not all whites looked like TV actors.

Social interactions with whites allowed some of these women to feel that they had more social and cultural know-how and feel much less intimidated by future contexts in which they might have to interact with whites. Additionally, working through some of the initial difficulties of the transitions to the suburbs allowed these women to realize that they could handle manageable challenges along the way to better jobs and more schooling. In comparison, the drugs or gang violence in their old city neighborhoods seemed to be forces too big for them to control and therefore permanent impediments to the advancements they were trying to make in their lives. These findings suggest to us that one's repertoire of capabilities can vary depending on the type of neighborhood one lives and works in.

Many of the mothers we interviewed also noted that they had to change their way of behaving to comply with the social norms of the new neighborhoods. Several women noted initial difficulties in adjusting to suburban norms, which were unfamiliar and intolerant of some of their prior behaviors. These mothers, who have lived all their lives in housing projects where these norms did not exist, saw benefits in complying with these expectations, and they decided to adopt them. For example, some of the women told us that they were less likely to go out at night or have parties in their yards, and that they were careful to monitor their sons' behaviors and not let them play music too loudly outside. One mother mentioned that she felt the need to keep her lawn free of any trash, so that she could prove to her neighbors she was a good housekeeper. Some of these normative constraints, such as low tolerance for drugs and parties, were liberating because the trade-off was community safety. This meant that mothers did not have to spend all their time watching their children, and these norms allowed mothers to give their children more freedom.

Similarly, mothers reported social responsiveness from their neighbors. They received the benefits of reciprocal relations related to child care and neighbor concern and watchfulness, which promoted the safety of their children, their property, and themselves. They were also given favors in terms of transportation and some acts of charity. It is remarkable that these new residents, who generally differed in race and class from their neighbors, were awarded this collective generosity, and the interviews suggest that it may have been conditional on their showing a willingness to abide by community norms.

Most important, the new suburban social contexts provided a form of capital that enhanced people's capabilities. Some mothers reported that they could count on neighbors if their child misbehaved or seemed at risk of getting into trouble, if their child was sick and couldn't attend school, or if there was some threat to their children, apartments, or themselves. This was not just interpersonal support, it was systemic, and enabled these mothers to take actions and make commitments that otherwise would be difficult or risky. For instance, some mothers reported a willingness to take jobs because they could count on a neighbor to watch their child in case they were late getting home from work. It is through some of these mechanisms—some social, some psychological—that we believe some Gautreaux families were able to permanently escape the contexts and consequences of segregated poverty and unsafe inner-city neighborhoods.

More recent interviews with Gautreaux mothers suggest that some aspects of the city–suburban divide were also important for shaping how the placement community affected their children's behavior (Keels 2008b; Mendenhall 2004). City movers placed in both moderate- and low-poverty neighborhoods found that although their immediate neighborhood was safe, the larger community to which their children had easy access continued to be dangerous. In comparison, children placed in the suburbs had less direct neighborhood exposure to drugs and illegal activities and attended higher-performing public schools with greater financial and teacher resources. Interviews revealed that affluent suburban neighborhoods also had substantially fewer opportunities for involvement in delinquent criminal activities and gangs.

Was Gautreaux a Social Experiment?

Methodologically, we often rely on observational data and regression analyses to provide estimates of the "effect" of neighborhood contexts and interventions. These approaches have their weaknesses. It is complicated, if not impossible, to infer causal effects when we know that there are unobservable characteristics of families that lead not only to their selection of neighborhood, but also to the outcomes of interest. As a result, there has been an increased push to employ experimental designs to assign social and economic "treatments," such as neighborhoods, school programs, or income subsidies.

Along these lines, the Gautreaux program resembled a quasi-experiment (Shadish, Cook, and Campbell 2002). Although the program was not designed as an experiment and families were not formally assigned randomly to different neighborhood conditions, aspects of the program administration break the link between family preferences and neighborhood placement. In principle, participants had choices about where they moved. In practice, qualifying rental units were secured by rental agents working for the Gautreaux program and offered to families according to their position on a waiting list, regardless of their locational preference. Although participants could refuse an offer, few did so, since they were unlikely to ever get another. As a result, participants' preferences for placement neighborhoods had relatively little to do with where they ended up moving, providing a degree of exogenous variability in neighborhood placement that undergirds Gautreaux research. Few significant differences were found between suburban and city movers' individual characteristics, but pre-move neighborhood attributes show small, but statistically significant differences on two of nine comparisons. This may indicate selection bias, although random assignment studies by the HUD-sponsored Moving to Opportunity (MTO) also find some substantial differences (Goering and Feins 2003, Table 7.1).

It is not clear whether the observed pre-move differences explain much of the outcome difference. For instance, while suburban movers came from *slightly* lower-poverty tracts than city movers (poverty rate of 40.6% vs. 43.8%), they moved to census tracts with *dramatically* lower poverty rates (5.3% vs. 27.3%; DeLuca and Rosenbaum 2003). While small (3 percentage points) differences in initial neighborhoods may account for a portion of the outcome differences, it is hard to dismiss the possible influence of the vast differences in placement neighborhoods. More recent papers have discussed these issues at length and examine multiple neighborhood-level indicators, detailed pre-program neighborhood differences, and intergenerational effects (DeLuca et al. 2009; DeLuca and Rosenbaum 2003; Keels 2008a, 2008b; Keels et al. 2005; Mendenhall, DeLuca, and Duncan 2006).

In contrast, MTO was an experiment, with the random assignment of low-income families to three conditions—an experimental group (who moved to low-poverty census tracts), an open-choice housing voucher group, and a "no move" control group. MTO was developed to formally test the Gautreaux findings, with more rigorous design and pre/postmove data collection.

Comparing Gautreaux and MTO

Unfortunately, while MTO was a stronger study, it was a weaker "neighborhood change treatment" (see Table 13.1). While the Gautreaux program

Table 13.1 Program Design Elements in MTO & Gautreaux

	MTO %	Gautreaux*%
Moving Distance		
Moves less than 10 miles	84	10
Neighborhood Placements (Census tract attributes)		
Placement average percent poverty (movers only)	12.4	5.3
Placement over 40% black areas	38	
Microneighborhoods		
Procedures to prevent enclaves?	No	Yes
Created enclaves?	Yes?	No
Social Contexts		
Schools		
School district change?	20	~100
Schools above-average test scores	10	88
Labor Markets		
Change labor market?	No?	Yes?
Labor market comparison	strong-->strong	weak-->strong
Social Interactions		
Contact with former peers?	Often?	Rare?
Safety Improvements	Yes	Yes
Duration		
Retention rate in placement neighborhoods**	56% after 4–7 yrs	66% after 15+ yrs

*These figures include the families who relocated to suburban communities outside of the city of Chicago. See DeLuca and Rosenbaum (2003) for a more detailed analysis of all Gautreaux program moves.
**For MTO, this means that the neighborhood at the follow-up survey was less than 10% poor; for Gautreaux, it means that the neighborhoods at last follow-up were less than 30% African-American. Note, however, that Gautreaux has a much longer follow-up period.
? indicates best estimate from qualitative or administrative data; the rest is based on systematic evidence.

moved nearly all families more than ten miles away from their original neighborhood (an average of 25 miles for the suburban movers), only 10% of MTO's treatment group moved ten miles or more. While Gautreaux procedures discouraged low-income enclaves within tracts, MTO did not. While virtually 100% of Gautreaux experimental group children (suburban movers) attended different school districts, only 20% of the MTO experimental group (and 30% of those who actually moved) changed school districts. While 88% of Gautreaux suburban movers attended schools with above-average achievement, only 10% of MTO experimental group children did.

The Gautreaux suburban movers moved to radically different labor markets, where nearly all children attended schools with above-average achievement and were too far away to interact with their old friends in the housing projects. The MTO moves were closer to the original neighborhoods and therefore created fewer barriers for children to maintain contact with old friends in the housing projects. While early Gautreaux analyses showed that suburban children attended much better schools and enjoyed improvements in educational outcomes relative to the city movers, the MTO program did not have such an effect on educational outcomes. The Interim Impacts study showed virtually no gains in academic performance or school engagement for the children from the experimental group, and only small increases in school quality (Sanbonmatsu et al. 2006). In part, the lack of educational effects could be explained by the fact that, by the time of the interim study, almost 70% of the MTO children were attending schools in the same district where they signed up for the program, and only 10% attended schools with above-average achievement (Orr et al. 2003).

While Gautreaux was associated with gains in mothers' employment, the MTO treatment group showed no benefits when compared to the control group—both groups showed large gains of comparable magnitude. However, MTO outcomes were measured in the late 1990s, during a strong labor market and strong welfare reform, so, although MTO found no difference between groups, it found an extraordinary 100% employment gain for the *control* group. One possible interpretation is that virtually everyone who could work was doing so, and residential moves had no additional effect for that reason. Large numbers of families in the control group had also moved out of highrise housing projects (and slightly less poor neighborhoods) through the federal HOPE VI program during the period of the MTO Interim Impacts evaluation. Therefore, the control group was experiencing unusual benefits and atypical circumstances which made it hard to see how the experimental group might have fared during a period with fewer factors affecting the control group. Despite the shorter moves and less change in social environment, both Gautreaux and MTO vastly improved mothers' and children's feelings of safety. MTO also showed significant reductions in depression and obesity among mothers and daughters (but no difference for sons; Kling, Liebman, and Katz 2007). Gautreaux studied neither of these outcomes.

When comparing the two programs, it is crucial to understand the nature of the comparisons being made. Social scientists and policymakers want to know how a family fares when given the opportunity to move to a lower-poverty or more integrated neighborhood, relative to what would have happened to that family had it not been given that opportunity. Gautreaux research studies can only compare subgroups of families who moved in conjunction with the program—there is no comparison group of similar families who did not move as part of the program. MTO's evaluation design is much stronger, since it tracked the fortunes of a randomly assigned control group of families who expressed interest in the program but, owing to the luck of the draw, were not eligible for it. At the same time, however, unlike MTO, Gautreaux can inform us about what happens when families move long distances to radically different neighborhoods, moves that changed their social context in many ways, in terms of racial integration, poverty, school quality, labor market strength, and safety.

Despite demographic similarities, families who volunteer for mobility vouchers also differ from other public-housing families. Thus, our findings generalize most readily to families voluntarily choosing to participate in residential-mobility programs. As the transformation of distressed public housing projects continues, families often involuntarily move to new communities; involuntarily relocating families may not result in the same outcomes as those found for Gautreaux or MTO participants. While studies from both programs indicate how powerful the effects of residential moves can be for some families, the differences in findings indicate the importance of program design features, historical context influences, and concurrent policy effects.[1]

Policy Implications

Both Gautreaux and MTO bet heavily that residential mobility and neighborhood change could alone promote families' self-sufficiency; neither provided family-based employment support, transportation help, or educational assistance. That's a tall order for a housing-only program to fill. Helping parents to acquire better jobs and transition off welfare may require coupling neighborhood change with services and supports tailored to individual families' needs. Of course, such support can also be provided independent of mobility programs. Recent research has shown that a number of experimental work-support programs in the 1990s boosted work, family income, and children's achievement (Morris et al. 2001). Some of these programs supplied poor parents with earnings supplements and center-based childcare assistance. Evidence from MTO also suggests that landlord problems figured prominently in distinguishing families who stayed in their placement units from those who moved on, often to higher-poverty and more segregated neighborhoods. Providing tenants with assistance in securing units or dealing with difficult landlords might help address these problems and might ensure that families remain in opportunity-rich communities, even after a second move. Yet it is noteworthy that while Gautreaux had extensive premove counseling and real estate staff assistance, the program provided minimal assistance of any kind after the move. Whether additional childcare, job-training, educational, transportation, and other support services have benefits if families are placed in very low-poverty areas with strong labor markets and good schools is really not known.

Many social policies also assume that low-income parents, if they had the resources, would approach opportunity the same way most middle-class families do. The MTO interviews in particular provide a reminder that poor families are not just wealthy families without a bank book. For example, poor parents often have less information about school-choice programs and may approach educational opportunities in different ways. It would be useful to test a program model in which mobility counselors were trained to inform parents about the new schooling choices in the area. While assisting with the sometimes disruptive effects of school transfers, counselors could help ensure that special needs are met, that receiving schools have information about the child, and that little instruction time is lost in the transition be-tween schools.

Currently, we have the chance to further examine some of these questions and the future viability of mobility programs. Researchers are planning a ten-year follow-up to MTO to see whether some of the early improvements have more substantial long-term benefits. For example, the reduction in stress among the MTO movers might translate over time into stable employment prospects and better outcomes for their children.

In Baltimore, the first-named author is following families who are mov-ing as part of a partial desegregation remedy to a court case filed in 1995—a case very similar to *Gautreaux*. In the *Thompson* case, a federal judge found the U.S. Department of Housing and Urban Development responsible for violating fair-housing laws by not looking beyond city limits for ways to house poor families, and awarded 2,000 vouchers for use in high-opportunity neighborhoods in the Baltimore region. With the help of housing counsel-ors and fair-housing lawyers, these *Thompson* families are relocating from public housing projects to low-poverty, nonsegregated neighborhoods all around the Baltimore metropolitan area. As of September 2008, over 1,200 former public-housing families have successfully relocated to safer, more opportunity-rich communities (DeLuca and Rosenblatt 2008). There are also extensive multipartner efforts in place to help connect these families to employment and education resources in their new communities. For example, the Baltimore Regional Housing Coalition (BRHC) is trying to expand a city-based job-counseling program to include suburban employers and a subset of the *Thompson* movers. Another program, funded by the Abell Foundation and the Baltimore Housing Authority, provides cars and low-cost financing for *Thompson* families working in the suburbs. Additionally, the BRHC is proposing a way for housing counselors to assess families' health needs and help them develop a plan for improvement. Time will tell whether these new programs and evaluations will make the implications of housing mobility programs clearer.

Many policy reforms have tried to improve individuals' education or employability while they remain in the same poor schools or labor markets, but these reforms have often failed. Such policies may be fighting an uphill battle as long as families remain in the same social contexts and opportunity structures. In contrast, Gautreaux findings suggest that housing policy is one possible lever to assist poor families, by moving them into much better neighborhoods, with much better schools and labor markets. The initial gains in neighborhood quality that many of the Gautreaux families achieved persisted for 15 years. The Gautreaux findings suggest that it is possible for low-income black families to make permanent escapes from neighborhoods with concentrated racial segregation, crime, and poverty, and that these moves are associated with large significant gains in education, employment, and racially integrated friendships, particularly for children. Indeed, some of these outcomes are ones that were extremely rare in the city sample: attending four-year colleges and having white friends. However, as the MTO findings suggest, there is much that we still need to learn about what kinds of moves are required to make major changes in outcomes, and, like MTO, strong research designs will be needed to remove alternative interpretations.

Note

1. Another program, Gautreaux II, was run by the agency that ran Gautreaux, but, by the late 1990s, the agency had different staff and a different philosophy, and the program had a very different design. Unlike Gautreaux, but like MTO, Gautreaux II had weak counseling and no real estate location staff. It relied on participants to find their own housing and let families live in high-poverty neighborhoods, as long as the larger census tract met program criteria. Unlike Gautreaux, but like MTO, children could continue attending the same school system and even the same schools, and adults often remained in the same labor market. For all practical purposes, Gautreaux II was designed to replicate MTO, not Gautreaux.

References

Cronin, Francis J., and David W. Rasmussen. 1981. Mobility. In *Housing Vouchers for the Poor: Lessons from a National Experiment*, ed. Raymond J.Struyk and Marc Bendick, Jr. Washington, DC: The Urban Institute, 107–128.

DeLuca, Stefanie, Greg Duncan, Ruby Mendenhall, and Micere Keels. 2009. "Gautreaux Mothers and Their Children: An Update." *Housing Policy Debate* 20: 2.

DeLuca, Stefanie, and James Rosenbaum. 2003. "If Low-Income Blacks Are Given a Chance to Live in White Neighborhoods, Will They Stay? Examining Mobility Patterns with Quasi-Experimental Data." *Housing Policy Debate* 14: 305–45.

———, and Peter Rosenblatt. 2008. "Residential Relocation in Baltimore's Thompson Housing Mobility Program." Report commissioned by the Maryland ACLU.

Goering, John, and Judith Feins. 2003. *Choosing a Better Life?* Washington, DC: Urban Institute Press.

Keels, Micere. 2008a. "Residential Attainment of Now-Adult Gautreaux Children: Do They Gain, Hold, or Lose Ground in Neighborhood Ethnic and Economic Segregation." *Housing Studies* 23: 541–64.

———. 2008b. "Second-Generation Effects of Chicago's *Gautreaux* Residential Mobility Program on Children's Participation in Crime." *Journal of Research on Adolescence* 18: 305–52.

———, and Greg J. Duncan, Stefanie DeLuca, Ruby Mendenhall, and James E. Rosenbaum. 2005. "Fifteen Years Later: Can Residential Mobility Programs Provide a Permanent Escape from Neighborhood Crime and Poverty?" *Demography* 42 (1): 51–73.

Kling, Jeffrey R., Jeffrey B. Liebman., and Lawrence F. Katz. 2007. "Experimental Analysis of Neighborhood Effects." *Econometrica* 75 (1): 83–119.

Massey, Douglas, and Nancy Denton. 1993. *American Apartheid*. Cambridge, MA: Harvard University Press.

Mendenhall, Ruby. 2004. "Black Women in Gautreaux's Housing Desegregation Program: The Role of Neighborhoods and Networks in Economic Independence." Ph.D. diss. Northwestern University.

Mendenhall, Ruby, Stefanie DeLuca, and Greg Duncan. 2006. "Neighborhood Resources and Economic Mobility: Results from the Gautreaux Program." *Social Science Research* 35: 892–923.

Meredith v. Jefferson County Board (05-915) (2007).

Morris, Pamela, Aletha C. Huston, Greg J. Duncan, Danielle A. Crosby, and Johannes M. Bos. 2001. *How Welfare and Work Policies Affect Children: A Synthesis of Research*. New York: MDRC.

Orr, Larry L. et al. 2003. *Moving to Opportunity Interim Impacts Evaluation*. Washington, DC: U.S. Dept. of Housing and Urban Development, Office of Policy Development and Research.

Parents Involved in Community Schools v. Seattle School District No. 1 (05-908) (2007).

Rosenbaum, James E. 1995. "Housing Mobility Strategies for Changing the Geography of Opportunity." *Housing Policy Debate* 6 (1): 231–70.

———, and Stefanie DeLuca, and Tammy Tuck. 2005. "Crossing Borders and Adapting: Low-Income Black Families in Suburbia." In *The Geography of Opportunity: Race and Housing Choice in Metropolitan America*, ed. Xavier de Souza Briggs. Washington, DC: Brookings Institution, 150–75.

———, and Lisa Reynolds, and Stefanie DeLuca. 2002. "How Do Places Matter? The Geography of Opportunity, Self-Efficacy, and a Look Inside the Black Box of Residential Mobility." *Housing Studies* 17: 71–82.

Sanbonmatsu, Lisa, Jeffrey R. King, Greg J. Duncas, and Jeanne Brooks-Gunn. 2006. "Neighborhoods and Academic Achievement: Results from the Moving to Opportunity Experiment." *The Journal of Human Resources* 41 (4): 649–91.

Shadish, William R., Thomas D. Cook, and Donald T. Campbell. 2002. *Experimental and Quasi-Experimental Designs*. Boston: Houghton Mifflin.

South, Scott, and Glenn D. Deane. 1993. "Race and Residential Mobility: Individual and Structural Determinants." *Social Forces* 72: 147–66.

———, and Kyle Crowder. 1997. "Escaping Distressed Neighborhoods: Individual, Community and Metropolitan Influences." *American Journal of Sociology* 102: 1040–84.

Thompson v. Department of Housing and Urban Development. Civil Action No. MJG-95-309 (2006).

CHAPTER 14

The Ghetto Game

Apartheid and the Developer's Imperative in Postindustrial American Cities

MINDY THOMPSON FULLILOVE,
LOURDES HERNÁNDEZ-CORDERO, AND ROBERT E. FULLILOVE

The names have changed, but the game's the same. (Malcolm X)

In the 1960s, open housing advocates feared that the United States might begin to play a "ghetto game," with whites moving away as blacks arrived, resulting in simply relocating but not abolishing American ghettos (Clark 1962). It turns out that these fears were justified, though the characteristics of the game differ substantially from what had been feared.

In 2001, our team, the Community Research Group, visited five cities that had leveled an African-American neighborhood as part of the federal urban renewal program funded by the Housing Act of 1949.[1] We realized, while doing that fieldwork, that many African Americans have moved because they were forced to do so. We also learned that forced displacement had a remarkably repetitive quality in the second half of the twentieth century (Fullilove 2004). These findings require, we believe, a reinterpretation of both the nature of American apartheid and the structure of the ghetto game.

We suggest that American apartheid is both a system of separation and of serial forced displacement. Angotti (2008, 82) has detailed African-American displacement in New York City, where "Blacks were consistent victims of displacement, first from their homes in Africa and then in America." Blacks moved north of Wall Street in the eighteenth century, then to Chelsea and the area that became Central Park, then to Hell's Kitchen, then to Harlem. As of this writing, they are on the move again, this time out of the city, to nearby suburbs and to the South (Angotti 2008, 2007). None of these upheavals has undone the system of segregation; each episode of forced relocation has found blacks confined to specified areas. The upheaval that has accompanied each of these forced displacements has had serious and unmitigated costs for the affected community, as well as for U.S. society as a whole.

Given this characterization of American apartheid, we propose that the ghetto game has four distinct parts: (1) churning of neighbors by developers; (2) dispersal of collective wealth; (3) restructuring of segregation; and (4) rendering invisible the new neighborhoods.

This chapter will describe the deleterious effects of displacement and present the history of serial displacement that we encountered in our fieldwork. In the course of that fieldwork, we also encountered a novel solution: using urban design as one tool for undoing the inattentional blindness that permits apartheid to thrive. We present that idea in the second part of the chapter.

The Ghetto Game

The Deleterious Effects of Displacement

Forced displacement of communities is profoundly harmful (Fullilove 2004). People who live together over time build up relationships that have worth that can be understood and measured in social, cultural, economic, political, and other ways. This worth is a collective asset and depends on the integrity of the group. These assets disappear when the group ceases to exist. However, it is these assets that are essential to completion of the tasks of group life, which include socializing the young, protecting the vulnerable, taking care of the material needs of the collective, and responding to external threats. These collective assets are not included in the price of an individual home, nor, indeed, can one put a simple monetary value on group assets like cultural capital.

The dispersion of social groups destroys these priceless assets and replaces an integrated social system with a disintegrated one. In his ground-breaking studies, Alexander Leighton (1959) established that disintegrated systems— those lacking capacity for group sustenance—were associated with higher levels of disease and disorder. The public health consequences are serious. Wallace and Wallace's (1998) detailed study of the South Bronx found increases in AIDS, substance abuse, violence, trauma-related mental illness, infant mortality, maternal mortality, tuberculosis, asthma, and obesity. Forced displacement of African-American communities must be taken very seriously as a factor in the remarkable disparities in health between blacks and whites in the United States.

In addition to noting the serious effects on the populations at most risk, Wallace and Wallace have found that the levels of health and social problems in the epicenter of the displacement set the levels of these problems for the greater New York region, and for the United States. Deleterious effects of forced displacement set the disease levels for the society as a whole and not simply for the group most obviously affected by the displacement. How important is that factor in shaping U.S. health? A remarkable study by Sir Michael Marmot's team (Banks et al. 2006) found that well-to-do white men in the United States had poorer health than poor white men in Britain. We interpret this finding as evidence that serial displacement is a very important factor in the health of all people in the United States, not just the African Americans who are most obviously injured.

The Policies of Serial Forced Displacement[2]

Segregation   Thomas Hanchett's (1998) study of Charlotte, North Carolina, provides an interesting window on the evolution of segregation. In the city's early history, black and white, rich and poor, lived in close proximity in this small city. Gradually, the population was "sorted out" by race and class, creating a highly segregated city. This was an active process in which people were pushed in pre-established directions. Once established in Charlotte, segregation has continued, though from time to time the African-American population has been shifted from one location to another.

Segregation, which took definitive form during the 1890 to 1910 era, was imposed by a mixture of laws, covenants, and practices. These have been the target of many attempts at reform over all the intervening decades. Segregation in residence continues to be a major force in American life. This represents both the legacy of past segregation and the continued operation of segregating forces like housing preferences, mortgage markets, and real estate steering.

The cities we visited in our study of urban renewal had segregated neighborhoods. The stories of how these neighborhoods came into being varied. African Americans had lived in the Hill District in Pittsburgh since the 1800s. By contrast, black settlement in the Fillmore District in San Francisco occurred in the 1940s, spurred by wartime employment and made possible by the internment of the Japanese people who had been earlier settlers in the area. These histories of settlement were entwined with the development of social, economic, political, and cultural organizations, largely confined within the boundaries of the segregated area. We were fascinated to learn that displacement by urban renewal tended to intensify rather than undo segregation by race, but also to fortify simultaneously segregation by class.

Redlining   Redlining was codified in 1937 by the Home Owners' Loan Corporation. It was intended to protect investment by indicating which areas offered the best potential for financial return. According the HOLC algorithm, new buildings with white inhabitants merited an "A" rating, while old buildings with nonwhite inhabitants received a "D." Redlining imposed serious hardship on ghetto neighborhoods because it created difficulties in getting money for investment. As pointed out by people we interviewed in 2004 who lived in the Central Ward of Newark, NJ, redlining made it difficult to get insurance or to borrow for repairs and remodeling. This meant that the built environment deteriorated more rapidly than it might have, given adequate and continuous maintenance. Redlining aggravated segregation in a very practical way: Having black people in a neighborhood literally did affect market values.

Urban Renewal   At the heart of setting up a 1950s urban renewal plan was a city's declaration that an area was "blighted." Dennis Gale, a professor of urban studies at Rutgers University in Newark when we interviewed him in 2001, explained:

> Part of the idea behind urban renewal is that the officials in Washington realized that you would never get private capital to invest back in the city, to build new office buildings, build shops, housing, etcetera—you could never encourage them to do that as long as there were these significant numbers of minorities and low-income people in the cities.... So the idea was, the only way that we can hope to get private capital back into the cities, because we can't do it alone without federal money, the only way to do it is to get rid of all the slums and deterioration. You label it as bad, you clear it all out. You have a featureless plain, and call it urban renewal. There is no longer any bad, there is nothing. And then you build from scratch.

Robert Pease, a planner who was involved in developing Pittsburgh's urban renewal plan for the Hill District, told us:

> There was a family there [in the Hill] who had a son the same age as my son. But I could look at the walls and see outside through the walls. And it was bitter cold.... Well, the conditions in the Hill, not every family lived that way, because there was some pretty decent housing there, not expensive but decent, with indoor plumbing and all the good things. But there were a lot of slums that were overcrowded and really needed to be cleared.

Sala Udin, who at the time of our interview was the City Councilman representing the Hill District, had grown up in the area Pease was describing. He commented:

> I think that the sense of community and the buildings are related within an old area. The buildings were old, the streets were cobblestone and old,

there were many small alleyways and people lived in those alleyways. The houses were very close together. There were small walkways that ran in between the alleyways—that was really a playground. So, the physical condition of the buildings helped to create a sense of community. We all lived in similar conditions and had similar complaints about the wind whipping through the gaps between the frame and the window, and the hole in the walls and the leaking fixtures, the toilet fixtures that work sometimes and don't work sometimes. But that kind of common condition bound us together.

Despite the existence of a sense of community and the mix of buildings in varying conditions, the neighborhoods were clear cut, creating the "featureless plain" that Dennis Gale described. This "new land" was used for many different purposes, ranging from low-income housing projects to cultural centers. The people who had lived in the neighborhoods were dispersed. The new places in which they settled—the resettlement neighborhoods— tended to be heavily black and less integrated by race and class than the old neighborhoods had been. Dense high-rise housing projects, such as those erected in the Central Ward of Newark, typified the extreme isolation of the very poor black people from others unlike themselves. Those housing projects were often poorly conceived and poorly built. They quickly became obsolete or dysfunctional, setting up future displacement, most recently in the form of the federal HOPE VI program. One of the most infamous examples of the rapid destruction of a failing housing project—the Pruitt-Igoe housing project—was just a few blocks away from the Mill Creek Valley urban renewal area in St. Louis. The land occupied by Pruitt-Igoe, which had been demolished in 1972, was still vacant when we visited in 2001.

People we interviewed delineated massive unmitigated losses that accompanied forced displacement by urban renewal (Fullilove 2004). They noted that social and family networks were shredded; businesses and organizations eliminated; economic and social capital lost; and confidence in government and the political process undermined. People also described their unremitting grief for their lost neighborhoods (cf. Fried 1963).

Planned Shrinkage or Catastrophic Disinvestment   Although the segregated neighborhoods had been undermined by redlining, the resettlement neighborhoods were undercut by a more catastrophic level of disinvestment. In New York City, this achieved the status of stated policy, as public services like fire protection were withdrawn from minority neighborhoods beginning in 1973 (Wallace and Wallace 1998). Not all cities used the term *planned shrinkage*, but the effects were the same. One such neighborhood was Gainsboro, a section of Roanoke, Virginia, which was marked for urban renewal, but never cleared. The declaration of urban renewal effectively blocked investment in the area. Slowly, the area deteriorated and the housing stock fell apart. Fires destroyed the buildings, and forced the population out. As people left, the businesses and other institutions suffered. As Evelyn Bethel, a resident of the Gainsboro area, pointed out:

> The small businesses that we had where people were self-sufficient to a degree, no matter how much or how little they made, they were self-sufficient, and they had a core of ready-made customers. When the people were forced out, your business could no longer survive, so it was a devastating loss to the residents as well as the business owners.

Dr. Walter Claytor, whose family lost substantial holdings in the area, took the City of Roanoke to court. He won a settlement based on making the link between the declaration of the area as a site for urban renewal and the loss of use of the family's property (Dickens 2003).

HOPE VI   Federal housing projects linked into this process in many ways. Housing projects were an important social reform when first introduced in the 1930s. They offered clean, decent housing for poor and working families. Indeed, housing projects developed in that era were often models of design, while those erected later were often poorly conceived and shoddily built. However they started, by the 1990s many housing projects were deemed "distressed communities," a label that was applied to an array of housing types and conditions. Problems of housing projects worked against their benefits. As Mohandas Salaam Allah of Roanoke pointed out, with some bitterness:

> I don't know whether the ultimate goal was to impoverish these black communities, but certainly anybody who has any understanding knows that if you spend thirty years in the project and you are not able to build equity, you are not going to be able to pass anything on to your children. And when you destroy a neighborhood where people own their own home, and replace it with a project, where people don't own nothing, then what is going to be the consequences in a thirty or forty year period? It's going to be that these people are going to be an impoverished group of people. And they are not participating in the American Dream. They are participating in the Housing Authority nightmare.

Reminiscent of urban renewal and the appellation of "blight," "distressed housing communities" were slated for destruction by the 1993 federal HOPE VI program. At the time of our fieldwork in 2001, HOPE VI projects were changing the face of public housing in the cities we visited. Among the justifications cited for the HOPE VI policy are data from the study of *Gautreaux v. Chicago Housing Authority*, a 1969 legal settlement that ordered the City of

Chicago to provide open housing for residents of Chicago housing projects ("Public Housing and Urban Policy: Gautreaux v. Chicago Housing Authority" 1969–70). This long-term follow-up study of people who volunteered to move out of public housing into selected communities in Chicago and at some distance away has provided evidence that housing mobility can work. The findings from the Gautreaux study have received confirmation from a more recent study of housing mobility, funded by the U.S. Department of Housing and Urban Development, called "Moving to Opportunity for Fair Housing" (Anderson et al. 2003).

Our data provide ample evidence that voluntary movement of a small number of people differs from the destruction of all or a substantial part of a residential community. In the former, people make a choice to move; they leave communities that continue to exist and to which they might return for visits or to live if they wished; and their original networks remain intact while they add new networks in their new homes. Forced displacement, by contrast, is not a choice of the individual or the individual's community, but rather of outside powers; destroys the home community so that the mover can never return; and shreds existing social networks and associated social capital. While the findings from these small research projects conducted with carefully selected volunteers provide hopeful evidence in support of housing mobility programs, the findings have been inappropriately used to justify large programs of forced displacement.

Ironically, we encountered people who had moved into the housing projects as a result of urban renewal and who were threatened by this new round of upheaval and resettlement due to HOPE VI. This was the case in Pittsburgh's Hill District, where Allequippa Terrace and Bedford Dwellings were slated for demolition when we first went to visit in 1997 (Robins et al. 1999). Ultimately, tenants of Bedford Dwellings organized and opposed the proposed plan. Rather than demolishing Bedford Dwellings first, they argued that the project would be more beneficial to current tenants if off-site housing were built first. Then people could move directly into their new homes, minimizing disruption of the community, limiting the number of people lost to follow-up, and offering people the opportunity to watch their new homes being built. This revised plan was carried out, with positive results (Murphy 2004).

Gentrification   During our fieldwork in 2001 and 2004, we examined the patterns of investment and disinvestment, with a particular focus on Newark and Pittsburgh. For example, we were able to discern a pattern of a moving front of catastrophic disinvestment that was moving away from the center of Newark, slowly destroying the neighborhoods—indeed, other cities—in its path. This wave of disinvestment was also pushing the black population from the center of the city toward the west. As the poor population was pushed west, some of the city's problems spilled over, destabilizing the nearby towns of Irvington, Elizabeth, and East Orange, New Jersey. Indeed, FBI Uniform Crime statistics for 2001 showed crime rates were higher in these cities than they were in Newark. These FBI data on violence are consistent with Rosin (2008), who reported on rising crime rates following displacement due to HOPE VI. The geography of Pittsburgh created a more complex pattern, but essentially similar observations about catastrophic disinvestment moving through space.

At the same time in both cities, investment had started to take place in areas closest to the center. Carlos Peterson, a resident of Lower Hill prior to urban renewal, had watched as disinvestment caused the next-over neighborhood to sag and disappear. This site was eventually cleared to make way for Crawford Square, an upscale townhome community. Peterson commented:

> I think the city government and urban developers waited twenty years for this area to kind of like, decline on its own, to make it easier for them to come in and redevelop the property. And I think some of the buildings could have been saved. It could have been more of what it was, but upgraded in terms of people, property, and so forth. Right now, I think that what they've developed in terms of Crawford Square, they basically razed everything. They just took everything down. And I used to call it the carcass of the Hill. You looked at the Hill and there was this carcass up there. I thought that they could have saved the structures, because there was so much character. Now it's like looking at some sort of cul-de-sac from suburbia, you know? People don't look out their windows, they don't sit on their porches, they don't barbecue and work on their cars. You know, it's just not black folks.

Frank Bolden, a reporter who spoke to us about Crawford Square at some length, concluded:

> Now even today, they still haven't done anything to beautify the Hill, except they put up the Civic Arena, and they put up Crawford Village, which has homes that are too expensive for the poor people to buy or rent. Now there are a few down there but I am talking about masses of the Negroes. Now they want to continue, they want to still beautify the Hill. They are hoping to bring white people back to the city to work, because those people living in Crawford Village and so forth now do not patronize anything in the Hill District. They patronize downtown. They are no use to us.

Mass Criminalization   In response to rising illegal drug use, the U.S. government launched a "war on drugs" which did not reduce drug use, but did greatly accelerate rates of incarceration, especially among African Americans. By 2004, 2.13 million people were incarcerated, 41% of them African American (Golembeski and Fullilove 2005). These high levels of incarceration undermined community life in many ways: destabilizing families; creating the need of women to share men, or be without a man, leading to increasing female disempowerment; increasing levels of infectious diseases; and creating a class of people who have lost their civil rights, including the right to vote. People interviewed in our study described in detail the ways in which deindustrialization and the collapse of neighborhood social controls shifted social functioning away from the tight control of earlier eras. In the small alleyways of the Hill District or the tight streets of Northeast Roanoke, adults were constantly watching the activities of the children. Furthermore, people had legitimate jobs, which brought money into the neighborhood where it was shared among networks of neighbors and friends. When these factors shifted, the whole culture changed and crime and violence flourished.

Making the Ghetto Invisible Mary Bishop, a reporter in Roanoke, who had drawn our attention to the story of urban renewal, also drew our attention to the process of making the ghetto invisible (Bishop 1995; Bishop and Harrington 1997). She reported that the poor neighborhoods in inner-city Roanoke had become invisible to the white population of the area. In Roanoke, the black Gainsboro neighborhood had been pushed back off the central thoroughfare, which was a major road to downtown from the western part of town. There was very little housing visible from the street. A number of devices were used, all obscuring the sight lines. It was possible to drive through without any sense that there were people of color living in the area. In Pittsburgh, the major roads went around the Hill District, thus eliminating the need for people who did not live there to enter the Hill's space. Spatial disconnections were amplified by media presentations of the ghetto as fearsome and impenetrable. In studies of consciousness, this creates visual neglect called "inattentional blindness" (Wallace and Fullilove 2008). The creation of inattentional blindness by distraction is a major tool of illusionists, and, we suggest, urban planners (Goodman 1971).

The Developers' Imperative

The urban renewal program set in motion by the Housing Act of 1949 had the interesting characteristic of transferring land from many small property owners to major developers (Rossi and Dentler 1961; Weiss 1985; Wilson 1966). As we traveled, we wondered why this was so. While our fieldwork was not designed to provide a full set of answers to this question, we could see evidence all around us that development is what developers do. This often means building large projects that need large tracts of land. Urban renewal provided large spaces; most of the sites we visited were on the order of 100 acres or more and they provided room for several large projects. But having developed a project on a large tract, the issue was not neighborhood stability or sustainability, but rather where to build next? We infer that developers operate under an imperative to find new land for new projects. If we assume that the desirable metropolitan area is finite and nearly built out, there is an inescapable need for developers to displace populations in order to do new projects. Among the many implications of this imperative is that it will continue to drive the ghetto game until the rules are changed.

Opening the Perspective

A French Urbanist in Pittsburgh

Michel Cantal-Dupart is an urbanist based in Paris and chair of the department of urbanism and the environment at the National Conservatory of Arts and Trades (Cantal-Dupart 1994). Known to one and all as Cantal, he is perhaps France's most important urbanist working from a human rights framework. His challenge to the status quo is rooted in ecology. He has been called to advise the presidents of France as they have grappled with the serious failures of French society in the face of growing multiculturalism. As an example, he joined with Jean Nouvel, one of the top architects in France and winner of the 2008 Pritzker Prize, to participate in President Nicholas Sarkozy's 2008 "Grand Pari"—The Big Bet—an effort to consider the future of the greater Paris region, the most culturally and socially complex region in the nation. While the thinking of the architects on the team turned immediately to the development of specific sites, Cantal turned his focus to the complex organization of the whole region.

In 1998, Cantal was invited to consult with a university–community partnership on displacement (Robins et al. 1999). A project of the University of Pittsburgh's Graduate School of Public Health Center for Minority Health, and led by Robert and Mindy Fullilove who were at the Center as visiting professors, the partnership examined HOPE VI projects that were then on the drawing boards.

One HOPE VI proposal discussed the fact that the housing project had been disconnected from the city street grid, making it difficult to get in and out. This very important observation about traffic was one of the factors to be addressed in the massive reconstruction of the area. Cantal, after examining the HOPE VI plan and visiting in the neighborhood, agreed that issues of reconnection were central to the reanimation of the neighborhood. He took the proposals much further, however, arguing for an intense focus on all the pathways in and out of the area. He asked people in the neighborhood, "How did people here get to work when the factories lined the riverbanks?"

Local people listed a number of lost routes, including an incline that used to link the Hill District to a riverside neighborhood called the Strip District. Cantal urged people in the Hill to "find the paths to the rivers." This slogan was adopted, and an organization was formed to take up the challenge. Given the isolation and invisible status of the Hill, Find the Rivers! had a most remarkable and immediate impact on the city of Pittsburgh by causing the Hill to show up on the map of a larger project reconnecting Pittsburgh neighborhoods to its rivers. Find the Rivers! explorations have led to a proposal called the "Kirkpatrick Greenway," a park to animate the center of the Hill District.

In 2002, Cantal invited Robert and Mindy Fullilove to visit the French city of Perpignan where he was in charge of major urban design projects. He was particularly interested in having the Fulliloves attend a ceremonial demolition of part of a housing project. The whole housing project was cut off from the city street system, reminiscent of the problems he had addressed in Pittsburgh. Prior to the demolition, the neighborhood was accessible only through two small underpasses, both at some distance from the housing project. The goal of the demolition was to reorganize the relationship to the street grid, creating a direct access to an important thoroughfare. In addition, architects had been selected to give each building a unique new look. The ensemble was completely transformed by these changes.

What was remarkable was the delicacy of the operation. Only small sections of the buildings were demolished. No one was displaced; the people who lived in the demolished sections were rehoused on the site. This stands in stark contrast to the massive demolition and displacement in Pittsburgh's HOPE VI project. Thus, while agreeing with Pittsburgh planners on the need for reconnection, he implemented that strategy first, thereby reknitting housing projects to the city as the solution. In Pittsburgh, the reconnection was implemented after the housing projects were destroyed and the minority inhabitants dispersed. Once there were new residents—who were both wealthier and more likely to be white—then the Pittsburgh planners reconnected the area to the city system. These are not trivial differences.

Rather than playing the ghetto game, Cantal's projects are intended to knit disconnected parts into a single, well-organized spatial entity. His principal tactic is a classic in French urbanism: creating perspective. First used by André Le Nôtre in 1663 to create the magnificent park at Vaux Le Vicomte, and later used to create the gardens of Versailles, perspective is often associated with the imposition of imperial will on territory (Orsenna 2000). This quality is derived from the opening of a long view permitting the lord to indicate the extent of his power and domain. André Le Nôtre's use of perspective has another property—creating a hierarchy in space—which brings the parts into relationship with each other. It is this second use that inspires the work of

Cantal. By bringing the parts of the city into a complex and tight interaction, he creates the spatial foundation for social solidarity.

Cantal applied this groundbreaking thesis to his design for the grounds of a new national school for prison guards (Fullilove 2001). The school authorities had proposed a design in which the school was surrounded by a wall. A restaurant that was to be shared with a neighboring university was to be situated just inside the gate of the prison-like complex. Cantal challenged that proposal, arguing that it ran counter to national prison policy, which intended to rehabilitate prisoners and return them to society. "Guards who are themselves in prison will not be prepared to show others the way back to free living. What is required is an open campus."

Cantal reorganized many aspects of the site plan, but three are critical to this discussion. First, his plan is completely open: There is no fence around the school. Second, he placed a canal in the center of school's park, creating a perspective between the major school building and a nearby church whose spire was visible from the school grounds. Third, he placed the shared restaurant at the far end of the park. Thus, the design replicated the best of free French society. As the school is a place to which French prison guards will return for continuing education, Cantal wanted them to have a home base from which they might draw inspiration and strength, as well as a love of freedom.

Conclusion

We opened this chapter with an examination of the dual nature of American apartheid: a continuity of separation but discontinuity in the location of the separation. This leads us to infer a set of rules for the ghetto game that we know have the effect of undermining the health of the whole American society. What are the alternatives? To expand the current debate, we have investigated the work of French urbanist, Michel Cantal-Dupart. His effort is to create continuity-in-space-and-in-time. This provides a strong foundation for society, as people are connected to each other across time and across space. Cantal-Dupart builds cities in this manner for reasons that are derived from a human rights perspective, coupled with principles of ecology. From this we learn that there is a socially and ecologically responsible way to reorganize marginal neighborhoods through a focus on reconnection.

The developers' imperative for a continuous supply of vacant land lies in direct opposition to what people need: stability in time and space. Citizens need to keep their communities fairly stable for centuries, even millennia. The ghetto game has terrible costs for U.S. society as a whole. We believe it is time to stop playing games with people's lives.

Note

1. The "Root Shock Project" was funded by an individual investigator award to Mindy Fullilove from the Robert Wood Johnson Foundation Health Policy Investigator Awards Program. In 2001, a team from the Community Research Group, of New York State Psychiatric Institute and Columbia University Mailman School of Public Heath, carried out situation analysis in five U.S. cities: Newark, NJ; Pittsburgh, PA; St. Louis, MO; Roanoke, VA; and San Francisco, CA. Additional fieldwork, called the "Transect Project," supported by Columbia University Health and Society Scholars Program, was carried out in the Newark metropolitan area in 2004. The interviews cited here are from these two studies; all quotes are from 2001 unless otherwise noted.
2. Serial forced displacement is explored in a number of other book chapters to which our team has contributed. For a detailed discussion, see Wallace and Fullilove (2008).

References

Anderson, Laurie M., Joseph St. Charles, Mindy T. Fullilove, Susan C. Scrimshaw, Jonathan E. Fielding, Jacques Normand, and Task Force on Community Preventive Services. 2003. "Providing Affordable Family Housing and Reducing Residential Segregation by Income: A Systematic Review." *American Journal of Preventive Medicine* 24 (3S): 47–67.
Angotti, Tom. 2007. "Burial Ground Bears Witness to a Segregated City." *Gotham Gazette*, http://www.gothamgazette.com/article/landuse/20071012/12/2318
———. 2008. *New York for Sale: Community Planning Confronts Global Real Estate*. Cambridge, MA: MIT Press.
Banks, James, Michael Marmot, Zoe Oldfield, and James P. Smith. 2006. "Disease and Disadvantage in the United States and England." *Journal of the American Medical Association* 295 (17): 2037–45.
Bishop, Mary. 1995. "Street by Street, Block by Block: How Urban Renewal Uprooted Black Roanoke," *The Roanoke Times* (January 29). Special Supplement.
Bishop, Mary, and S. D. Harrington. 1997. "The Invisible Inner City: Poverty, Crime and Decay in Roanoke's Oldest Neighborhoods," *The Roanoke Times* (October 30).
Cantal-Dupart, Michel. 1994. *Merci la Ville!* Bordeaux, France: Investigations Le Castor Astral.
Clark, Dennis. 1962. *The Ghetto Game: Racial Conflicts in the City*. New York: Sheed and Ward.
Dickens, Tad. 2003. "Claytor Lawsuit Sees Small Victory in Court." *The Roanoke Times*, June 19, A1.
Fried, Marc. 1963. "Grieving for a Lost Home." In *The Urban Condition*, ed. Leonard Duhl. New York: Basic Books, 151–71.
Fullilove, Mindy Thompson. 2001. "Links Between the Social and Physical Environments." *Children's Environmental Health* 48 (5): 1253–66.
———. 2004. *Root Shock: How Tearing Up City Neighborhoods Hurts America and What We Can Do About It*. New York: Ballantine/One World.
Golembeski, Cynthia, and Robert E. Fullilove. 2005. "Criminal (In)justice in the City and Its Associated Health Consequences." *American Journal of Public Health* 95: 1701–06.
Goodman, Robert. 1971. *After the Planners*. New York: Simon and Schuster.
Hanchett, Thomas W. 1998. *Sorting Out the New South City: Race, Class, and Urban Development in Charlotte, 1875–1975*. Chapel Hill: University of North Carolina Press.
Leighton, Alexander H. 1959. *The Stirling County Study of Psychiatric Disorder & Sociocultural Environment*. Vol. 1 of *My Name is Legion: Foundations for a Theory of Man in Relation to Culture*. New York: Basic Books.
Murphy, Patricia. 2004 *The Housing That Community Built*. November/December http://www.nhi.org/online/issues/138/bedford.html (Accessed December 2, 2008)
Orsenna, Erik. 2000. *Portrait d'un Homme Heureux*. Paris: Fayard.
"Public Housing and Urban Policy: Gautreaux v. Chicago Housing Authority." 1969/70. *The Yale Law Journal* 79 (4): 712–29.
Robins, Anthony, Terri Baltimore, Rich Brown, Mindy Fullilove, Robert Fullilove, and Tracy Myers. 1999. *Hillscapes: A Scrapbook, Envisioning a Healthy Urban Habitat*. Pittsburgh: University of Pittsburgh Press.

Rosin, Hanna. 2008. "American Murder Mystery." *The Atlantic*, July/August, http://www.theatlantic. com/doc/200807/memphis_crime
Rossi, Peter H., and Robert A. Dentler. 1961. *The Politics of Urban Renewal: The Chicago Findings*. New York: Free Press of Glencoe.
Wallace, Deborah, and Rodrick Wallace. 1998. *A Plague on Your Houses: How New York Was Burned Down and National Public Health Crumbled*. London: Verso.
Wallace, Rodrick, and Mindy Fullilove. 2008. *Collective Consciousness and Its Discontents: Institutional Distributed Cognition, Racial Policy and Public Health in the United States*. New York: Springer.
Weiss, Marc A. 1985. "The Origins and Legacy of Urban Renewal." In *Federal Housing Policy and Programs: Past and Present*, ed. J. P. Mitchell. New Brunswick, NJ: Rutgers University, 253–76.
Wilson, James Q., ed. 1966. *Urban Renewal: The Record and the Controversy*. Cambridge, MA: MIT Press.

CHAPTER **15**

The Myth of Concentrated Poverty

STEPHEN STEINBERG

All of us have stories that shape our worldview and lurk behind our scholarship. In 1996, I went to Chicago with my son, who was applying for admission to the University of Chicago. We stayed in the Marriott Courtyard on the edge of the Loop and took a taxi to campus. The driver told us that Lakeshore Drive was congested with traffic, and he made a detour through city streets. Within minutes, the window of the cab framed Cabrini-Green, identifiable by a massive rectangular sign in the middle of an open plaza. There it was—Cabrini-Green—the "project" that had achieved iconic notoriety through sensational press reports of anarchy and violence. The realization that Cabrini-Green was situated on the edge of Chicago's legendary Gold Coast provided an epiphanic moment: It was obvious why Cabrini-Green was slated for demolition. It occupied immensely valuable real estate that was in the way of the growth machine. As two geographers (Wyly and Hammel 1999, 711) put it, Cabrini was "an island of decay in seas of renewal."

Let me say up front that I am no housing expert or policy wonk. Had I been immersed in the social science literature, I would have known that Cabrini-Green was a shameful relic of a discredited policy that segregated blacks in soulless high-rise "projects" where the problems of concentrated poverty metastasized and took on a life of their own. No public housing had been built since the Nixon Administration, and under the Clinton Administration, HUD Secretary Henry Cisneros instituted a policy with a seductive (and hypocritical) acronym: HOPE VI (short for Housing Opportunities for People Everywhere). The stated policy objective was to replace "severely

214 • Stephen Steinberg

distressed" public housing with low-rise apartments that would be mixed-income and mixed-race. Architects and urban planners at the University of Chicago had advanced a "new urbanism," whose architectural features would blend residents of public housing into the surrounding neighborhood. Against the specter of crime-ridden, high-rise buildings that "warehoused" the poor and exacerbated their problems, we had the promise of decorous row houses that would foster integration in terms of both race and class. A compelling imaginary, to be sure.

Then again, if I had known still more, I would have known that my first instinct was correct: that there were grassroots groups fighting the Cabrini-Green demolition as a blatant land grab that served the interests of developers and politicians; that trampled over the rights and interests of the residents; and that would leave the displaced families worse off as they gravitated to other densely poor neighborhoods, further away from jobs, transportation, and services they relied upon (Bennett and Reed 1999; Goetz 2000; Wright 2006). To these critics, it was clear: HOPE VI was another instance of "Negro Removal," a term coined by James Baldwin in the early 1960s and embraced by Malcolm X to express opposition to the urban renewal projects of that period. This same charge was leveled by a few scholars who argued vociferously that the demolition of Cabrini-Green was a calamity for the 14,000 African Americans who would be forcibly evicted from their homes (Wright 2006, 169). For these critics, the promise of building mixed-race and mixed-income housing was only a smokescreen to conceal what amounted to the cleansing of cities of the black underclass.

So let me throw down the gauntlet: Does HOPE VI amount to Negro Removal by another name, one that would rid the urban landscape of the black nemesis and clear the way for the developers? This raises another necessary question: Were scholars and policy wonks complicit in providing indispensable legitimacy for this policy?

Let me be clear: I do not impugn the motives of those who imagine that HOPE VI and other mobility projects advance the cause of integration. Nor is it merely a question of unintended consequences. Rather, the thrust of my critique is on *the political uses* of scholarship for ends that may be disavowed by the scholars themselves. And if we are to follow the maxim made famous by Watergate, we have to follow the trail of money, which leads to government agencies and foundations that bankrolled and promoted knowledge production that is politically useful. Then, too, there are the subtle and pernicious ways in which social scientists share the racial mindset and worldview that spawn victim-blaming discourses and retrograde policy.

Negro Removal is an apt term, because it calls to mind another historical case where the state was implicated in ethnic cleansing: *Indian Removal*. Some will dismiss this claim as political hyperbole, if only because Indians were banished from white society, whereas the ostensible purpose of mobility projects is to enhance racial and class integration. Yet in the case of Cabrini-Green, the rule for one-to-one replacement of low-income housing was abrogated by Cisneros, the allotment of low-income housing was severely scaled back, and stringent tenant screening criteria, including strict work requirements, assured that only a handful of displaced residents would be allowed to return to the small allotment of public housing units in the new mixed-income development (Smith 2006; Wilen and Nayak 2006, 221). Cabrini-Green was relegated to oblivion, and the new development was refurbished with a new name: Parkside of Old Town. By September 2007, a local real estate blog offered this rhapsodic account of the neighborhood's transformation from slum to gold coast:

Parkside of Old Town Brings Development to Cabrini

Cabrini was once one of the most notorious neighborhoods in Chicago. When public housing was built in the neighborhood, many of the old homes were destroyed and families left the neighborhood.

During the 1980s and 1990s, crime and drugs levied a heavy cost on the neighborhood, making it one of the most dangerous in the city.

Today, Cabrini is the scene of one of the largest real estate redevelopment projects in all of Chicago. Most of the housing projects are gone now, replaced by cranes and new developments that offer a mix of luxury condominiums and affordable housing for former residents of public housing in the neighborhood.

One of the largest developments underway in Cabrini is Parkside of Old Town. Buyers can choose from condos and townhomes that start at $300,000. The townhomes sell for as much as $700,000.

This 18-acre development will offer park space with basketball courts and a playground. There are also several other new condo developments around the neighborhood that are attracting new families and bringing back the neighborhood feel that characterized Cabrini before the construction of public housing.

Many new residents choose Cabrini for the excellent location just minutes from downtown. Prices in the neighborhood are competitive when compared to other areas of north Chicago such as the Gold Coast and Streeterville.[1]

Efforts of community activists and years of litigation had all come to naught, and according to one estimate, 97% of dislocated families moved into areas that did not meet either the "low poverty or racial integration requirements set out in the relocation rights contract" (Wilen and Nayak 2006, 220). Broken promises: another similarity to the nation's treatment of Native Americans.

Indian Removal is commonly remembered as an event involving the infamous Trail of Tears, the forced movement of the Cherokees from their cultivated farms and communities in Georgia to wasteland in Oklahoma in 1837. Actually, this was the last of a series of removals of tribes to Indian Country, and the removal policy was contested in legislatures, courts, and public venues for many years. Indeed, the 1830 Indian Removal Act was the subject of contentious public debate, and the Removal Act passed by a slim margin (28 to 19 in the Senate, 102 to 97 in the House). Why, one might ask, didn't President Jackson, famous for having massacred Indians in battle, simply send in the cavalry and make removal a fait accompli? According to a recent history of Indian Removal:

> Jackson made certain that Indians knew he meant business, but he also wanted to avoid violent unrest. He had political worries as well. Realizing that many throughout the country would not approve unvarnished removal, he undertook to convince the public about the policy's wisdom. He recruited religious leaders and well-known proponents of Indian rights…to explain that removal was actually in the best interests of the Indians. In his first Annual Message he informed Congress of the pressing need for Indian removal and asked for money to accomplish it. As he habitually did in his public statements, Jackson framed his sentiments in humanitarian terms about the good effects removal would have on Indians. (Heidler and Heidler 2007, 23–4)

Thus, the first Moving to Opportunity program was born!

As with today's HOPE VI demolitions and mobility programs, a façade was erected to maintain the pretense that this was a legal program and that the Cherokees went voluntarily. In *Race, Racism, and American Law*, Derrick Bell (2008, 688) provides quite another account:

> The pressures from state and public officials created two factions among the Cherokee Nation: the Treaty Party, comprising the elite mixed bloods, and the Ross faction, supporters of Chief John Ross. Ross, who had the support of most of the Cherokee people, was incarcerated while the Treaty Party representatives negotiated the treaty. The treaty, ratified at New Echota, the capital of the Cherokee Nation, by only 20 persons, ceded all the tribal land in Georgia in exchange for 7 million acres of land in Indian Territory.

Some 16,000 of the 17,000 Cherokees signed a petition to Congress protesting the treaty, but to no avail. After gold was discovered in Georgia in 1829 (again inviting comparison to soaring real estate values in Chicago's post-industrial economy), pressures mounted to get rid of the Cherokees, the last of the so-called civilized tribes. With that ignominious act, the nation established a historical precedent for ethnic cleansing.

To my eye, HOPE VI looks like Negro Removal, and Negro Removal looks like Indian Removal, though dispossession and displacement are more ingeniously camouflaged today than in times past. Nobody accuses blacks of being "savages" incapable of being assimilated into white society. Well, that's not entirely true. We speak euphemistically of "the urban jungle," and social scientists who portray the inner city as a haven of pathology, disorder, and immorality are only a word away from declaring its inhabitants "uncivilized." Indeed, Dinesh D'Souza (1995, 554) made precisely this allegation in *The End of Racism*. According to D'Souza, racial disparities are due, not to racism, but rather to a "civilizational gap" between blacks and whites. It is precisely because the trope between "savage" and "civilized" endures that we have one African American "who is articulate and bright and clean and a nice-looking guy" who inhabits the White House, at the same time that we have another 1.1 million African Americans who are in the slammer!

Like Indian Removal, Negro Removal, especially in the post-civil rights era, required intellectual and moral justification. Enter the social scientist, with a new arrow in the quiver: "concentrated poverty." The concept of "concentrated poverty" has provided the crucial theoretical underpinning for HOPE VI and other mobility programs.[2] The hapless victims of these policies are not relocated west of the Mississippi, but they are removed from urban neighborhoods that are ripe for development. Dispossession and displacement are done in the name of deconcentrating poverty.

My purpose now is to subject the concept of "concentrated poverty" to critical scrutiny, and to examine the origins and evolution of this idea, its embedded assumptions, its consequences, and above all, its political uses.

Let us begin by distinguishing between concentrated poverty as fact and as theory. The fact of concentrated poverty—that poverty is spatially concentrated—is well known and easily documented. It is easy as well to chart trends, and to show that poverty, especially black poverty, has become more concentrated in recent decades (Jargowsky 1997; Massey and Denton 1993; Massey and Kanaiaupuni, 1993; Orfield 2002; Wilson 1987). But there is also a *theory* of concentrated poverty that postulates a causal relationship between concentrated poverty and a host of social ills. This is graphically portrayed in Edward Goetz's *Clearing the Way* (2003, 160). As can be seen in Figure 15.1, concentrated poverty is conceptualized as an intermediary factor between the structures that engender inequality and the "tangle of pathology" that is associated with the underclass (Clark 1965). Thus, structural factors are acknowledged as primary causes of concentrated poverty: economic restructuring, suburban exclusionism, disinvestment in central-city neighborhoods, discrimination in housing markets, and government policies (e.g., public housing). On the other hand, concentrated poverty takes on causal significance all its own, leading to the familiar litany of pathologies: drug use, violent crime, high school dropout rates/poor school

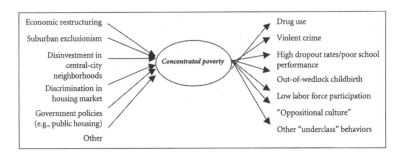

Figure 15.1 The cause and consequences of concentrated poverty. Source: Edward Goetz (2003, 22).

performance, out-of-wedlock childbirth, low labor force participation, and "oppositional culture."

I submit to you that this theory is deeply flawed: simplistic, misleading, pregnant with false or unsubstantiated assumptions, and dangerous as a predicate for social policy. In the first place, "concentrated poverty" may be new to social science, but it plays on the familiar image of "the huddled masses," generously portrayed as yearning to breathe free. It also plays on the trope of those "dangerous classes," corrupted by the city, mired in pathology, and a menace to civil society. Marx provides yet another perspective on urban concentration: It was precisely the density of the factory and of urban life that provided the ecological prerequisite for class consciousness and political action. Thus, as two housing advocates have noted, "It is debatable whether integration efforts bestow on poor African-Americans economic or sociological benefits or, rather, destroy nonwhite political power, sense of community, culture, and neighborhood-based support systems" (Wilen and Stasell 2006, 249).

As a theoretical construct, concentrated poverty entered academic discourse with William Julius Wilson's *The Truly Disadvantaged* (1987), though I think that Wilson gets too much credit—or blame, depending on your point of view—for this mistaken idea.[3] There are only three citations to "concentrated poverty" in the index of Wilson's book, mostly alluding to increases in concentrated poverty, followed by some speculation—and it is sheer speculation, without a shred of evidence—about the adverse consequences of "social isolation" or the putative "concentration effects." Moreover, in *The Truly Disadvantaged,* Wilson did not sever the relationship between concentrated poverty and the structural forces that engender it. His policy recommendations all pertain to addressing the root causes of concentrated poverty, through policies of full employment and a WPA-style jobs programs aimed for the ghetto poor. However, as concentrated poverty emerged as the latest rage in poverty research, Wilson got on the bandwagon, embracing both the theory of concentrated poverty and the idea that removal of the poor from neighborhoods of concentrated poverty is a policy desideratum.[4]

The chief exponents of removal policy have been a new breed of Moving to Opportunity (MTO) advocates and social capital theorists who make the fatal mistake of treating concentrated poverty as a factor sui generis—one that is a determinant of all these "urban" pathologies, and therefore one that can be remedied through targeted social policy.[5] Herein lies the epistemological fallacy. With a sleight of hand, all these powerful structural forces that involve major political and economic institutions are conflated into a single factor—concentrated poverty, which is now identified as *the* central problem in terms of analysis and social policy. As Goetz (2003, 160) shrewdly observed, "Over time, focus has shifted away from the causes of concentrated poverty toward the behavior of the poor in response to concentrated poverty." Thus, instead of dealing with the root causes of concentrated poverty, as Wilson did in his initial intervention, we have one study after another treating concentrated poverty as though it were an independent and self-sustaining factor, and thus the theoretical underpinning for policies whose central purpose is to deconcentrate poverty.

But what evidence is there that *concentrated* poverty has explanatory significance above and beyond the effects of poverty itself? Do we know that concentration magnifies or exacerbates poverty? Studies that advance the theory of concentrated poverty (e.g., Jargowsky 1997; Massey and Kanaiaupuni 1993) devote pages proving that poverty has become more concentrated, especially for African Americans, but they utterly fail to prove that concentration per se has an additive effect.[6] To demonstrate this, they would have to show that poor people who do not live in high-poverty census tracts—and who are not warehoused in soulless high-rise apartment buildings (like mine in New York City)—are far less prone to aberrant behavior than poor people who live in concentrated poverty. But we know from studies of rural poverty, whether in Appalachia or upstate New York or the farm belt, that all of these "urban" pathologies run rampant there. Alas, urbanists have fallen into the trap that Manuel Castells (1979) cautioned against long ago: of positing the reified "city" or aspects of urban ecology as the cause of "urban ills," rather than a political economy that engenders deep and persistent inequalities. And before we dynamite housing projects, obliterating the homes of 100,000 families, shouldn't there be convincing evidence that deconcentration will have the transformative effects that are presumed?

In short, the theory of concentrated poverty is based on a faulty theoretical premise—namely, that concentrated poverty can be severed from its root causes and projected as the focal point of social policy. It is rather like diagnosing a melanoma as a blemish and treating it with a palliative.

Therefore, it should not be surprising that follow-up studies of relocation programs have failed to provide convincing evidence that deconcentration has the expected outcomes. At least this was what Goetz (2003, 256) found, based on a rigorous and exhaustive review of the extensive body of MTO research. He concludes his book with a simple, categorical judgment: "The scattering of poor people, in itself, accomplishes little."[7]

Yet the cheerleaders of deconcentration turn a blind eye to the wide body of research that goes against their pet idea. This point is made forcefully in a recent article in which David Imbroscio (2008) challenges "the Dispersal Consensus" (DC for short). Imbroscio levels three criticisms:

1. The DCers trample over what Chester Hartman has called "the right [or ability] to stay put" (quoted in Imbroscio 2008, 114). Although the mobility programs typically recruit people whose participation is "voluntary," they can hardly be seen as exercising free choice when their only alternative is to live in neglected housing and underserved communities. Imbroscio writes (115): "Preferences for dispersal become nothing more than a desperate response to a set of desperate conditions, with little to do with any real notion of freedom of choice." Of course, in the case of HOPE VI demolitions, "choice" is a moot issue.
2. The DCers are guilty of overselling evidence, based mainly on studies of the Gautreaux program in Chicago and the MTO demonstration. Critics (Crump 2002; Goetz 2003) insist that these studies are flawed methodologically since participants are self-selected and heavily screened, vitiating comparisons to the people left behind. To make matters worse, the MTO studies typically report small findings that are wildly overstated as corroborating the claim that deconcentration has beneficial effects.
3. The DCers ignore or slight the evidence that points to viable alternatives to HOPE VI and mobility programs, such as the work of thousands of Community Development Corporations in providing affordable housing for low-income people and contributing to the revitalization of inner-city neighborhoods. Instead of contemplating strategies for ameliorating social problems where the poor live, the DCers obstinately cling to the idea that "opportunity" entails moving the poor as far as possible from the temptations and pathologies of the inner city. For all of their methodological sophistication, DCers seem oblivious to the fact that the efforts of the Community Development Corporations impact on entire communities, whereas MTO programs, at their very best, impact on the lives of a paltry number of individuals, deliberately scattered across the urban landscape. [See responses by Xavier de Souza Briggs (2008, 131–37), John Goering and Judith Feins (2008, 139–48), and rejoinder by David Imbroscio (2008,149–54).]

Not only do mobility programs fail to magically transform the lives of the small number of people who are delivered from "the 'hood," but studies find that relocatees are often worse off than before. With or without a Section 8 voucher, most relocatees gravitate to other poor neighborhoods where rents are low, thus moving the poor from one neighborhood of concentrated poverty to another, ironically validating the fears of the NIMBYs (Rosin 2008). Nor do the suburbs provide a magic solution. Xavier de Souza Briggs (2005, 36), a leading advocate of mobility programs, concedes that "many minority families that moved to the suburbs in the 1990s, even if they became home-owners, did not escape the pattern that contains poverty, school failure, and job isolation in particular geographic areas." In a study of a HOPE VI reloca-tion program in Tampa, Florida, Susan Greenbaum and her collaborators (in press) found that even when relocatees acknowledged that their housing was improved, "many…expressed feelings of loss and nostalgia for the neighborly relations they had in the public housing complexes where they used to live. In addition to enjoyment, patterns of mutual assistance and exchange among the residents had made survival easier on their very low incomes and offered a sense of community" (16–17).

There is an addendum to the narrative I began with. When my son was enrolled at the University of Chicago, living on Kimbark Avenue, his back porch provided a telescopic view of a strip of low-rise, subsidized housing that had been built on 55th Street. Architecturally, the houses were a New Urbanist nightmare: fortified bunkers, walled off to the street, with a small, internal courtyard. My son observed that on Sunday mornings, women dressed in their Sunday best would stand on the corner for a long time, waiting for a bus that would transport them, alas, back to "the 'hood" where their church was located.[8]

All of this raises the question of whether HOPE VI and mobility programs are predicated on a demonized image of the poor within those "severely distressed" housing projects. Implicitly and often explicitly, theorists and planners have in mind aberrant individuals who are the source of violence and disorder. Obviously, one can compile statistics that present a bleak picture of gangs, drugs, violence, et cetera, et cetera. But another picture emerges from ethnographic studies: of ordinary people, desperately poor and struggling to "survive"; of networks of resourceful women and extended families engaged in mutual support; of neighborhoods and churches that provide people with a sense of belonging and access to services and resources; and of activists and advocacy groups who valiantly represent the poor against the powerful institutions that seek their expulsion.[9] Why is it, one might ask, that social scientists valorize the solidarities of white ethnics as "Gemeinschaft," whereas in the case of racial minorities, these same solidarities are disparaged as "hypersegregation" whose only remedy is "deconcentration by demolition"

(Crump 2002, 581)? These scholars forget that when white ethnics were poor (like the Italians who were the first occupants of Cabrini-Green), they produced the same litany of "pathologies" associated with today's minorities. If these "pathologies" were not as prevalent or as enduring, this is because these white ethnics had the advantage of white privilege, were not encircled by discriminatory barriers, and consequently were not mired in poverty for generations (Marcuse 1997). As a result, they were able to fulfill the American Dream by moving to the very suburbs where the DCers want to place poor blacks who do not have the resources, and invariably encounter the bitter hostility of their neighbors (Moore 2008; Thompson 1998).

In short, a policy predicated on the claim that the demolition of their homes will advance the interests of the very people whose homes are being destroyed is a preposterous sham. And here we confront the cold reality: HOPE VI is not an antipoverty program, but on the contrary, one that stomps over the rights and interests of the poor and sacrifices them on the altar of political and economic power. This is how an agency whose historic mission was to provide housing of last resort for the poorest Americans is now responsible for the demolition of that very housing (Marcuse 1978). As with Indian Removal, this policy must be implemented in such a way as not to foment violent resistance or "political problems." This is where the theory of deconcentrated poverty comes into play, which is trotted out in Congressional hearings and in Congressional Research Service reports, to paste over the patent injustices and to make a virtue of the unconscionable.[10]

It is not my contention that, minus the theory of deconcentrated poverty, HOPE VI would not exist. Powerbrokers heed the sage advice of experts only when it is in their interest to do so. We have to be savvy about the political uses of the theory of concentrated poverty, which is invoked wherever the poor occupy valuable real estate that is coveted by developers, and which is part of the neoliberal agenda of reclaiming urban space that earlier was relinquished to the nation's racial and class pariahs. Neil Smith (1996, 45–47) has aptly called this "the revanchist city." Atlanta is in the process of demolishing most public housing, including housing occupied by stable families with regular employment.[11] And in New Orleans, even housing projects that escaped the ravages of Katrina were bulldozed despite the anguished protests of their residents.[12] While bodies were still being plucked from the floodwaters, William Julius Wilson and Bruce Katz (2005) appeared on the News Hour, declaring that Katrina presented a historic opportunity to break up concentrated poverty.[13] And when Xavier de Souza Briggs posted a petition on an urban sociology listserv under the title "Moving to Opportunity in the Wake of Hurricane Katrina," nearly 200 urban experts rushed to affix their signatures, oblivious to the political uses of their dogma.[14]

A final point. Let us concede for the sake of argument that deconcentration and mobility programs provide better housing and schools for some poor people, and advance the cause of racial integration. Even so, we have to ask whether the political appeal of such policies is that they divert attention away from the vastly greater problem: the plight of the millions of poor people who still inhabit ghettos and barrios, whose plight has been exacerbated by the dismantling of the welfare state, and who are now threatened with gentrification and other assaults of the neoliberal city. As Susan Greenbaum (2006, 111) has commented, "A poverty alleviation policy that excludes the majority cannot be judged a success." Not only do mobility programs provide relief only for a select few, they provide an ideological façade for the neoliberal war against the poor and for disinvestment in the inner city. As Goetz (2003, 252) writes: "When accepted as a political strategy, deconcentration justifies the redirection of community development efforts away from the declining housing stock of poor neighborhoods and/or away from poor residents." Thus, instead of comprehensive policies that would revitalize these communities, provide jobs—the sine qua non of antipoverty policy—and include grassroots organizations in the reconstruction of their communities, we have demonstration projects that, at best, can help a select few. Furthermore, as I suggested above, the dispersal of the minority poor makes it all the more difficult for them to mobilize politically and to put pressure on political and economic elites to live up to their responsibility to address the problems in their own back yard. Instead, in the name of deconcentrating poverty, they use dynamite as a remedy and transfer the problem to somebody else's back yard. And they do this with the indispensable sanction of urban experts who labor under the illusion that they are advancing the project of racial and economic justice.

Acknowledgments

Thanks to Greg Squires and Chester Hartman for welcoming a genuine and vigorous debate of housing policy. I first heard about the ravages of HOPE VI from Adolph Reed, who has provided me with invaluable perspective from both the ivory tower and the trenches on Chicago's extraordinary campaign to obliterate its public housing communities. Susan Greenbaum was immensely helpful as I delved into the literature on mobility programs. So too were Derrick Bell, Jane Collins, Mark Harvey, Micaela di Leonardo, Jeff Maskovsky, and Devah Pager. In writing this paper, I have profited from the incisive scholarship anthologized in *Where Are Poor People to Live? Transforming Public Housing Communities*, ed. Larry Bennett, Janet L. Smith, and Patricia Wright.

Notes

1. http://www.chicagorealestateblog.com/parkside-of-old-town-brings-development-to-cabrini/
2. Clearly, HOPE VI and the MTO programs are different policies. However, the logic, the embedded assumptions, and the overriding policy objective are the same: to deconcentrate poverty and to move people as far as possible (as Stefanie DeLuca and James Rosenbaum assert in their chapter in this volume) from the dense urban neighborhoods that putatively spawn pathology and prevent the poor from developing the social capital that would help them escape poverty.
3. For an incisive account of the origins of Wilson's "spatial turn," and the adoption and elaboration of the notion of "concentrated poverty" among urban specialists, see Crump 2002.
4. Despite the fact that Wilson's claims were altogether speculative and unsubstantiated, he provided indispensable authority and legitimacy to Chicago's plans to dismantle public housing. As far as I know, Wilson never took a public position during the acrimonious debates that raged around the decision to demolish Cabrini-Green, the Henry Horner Homes, and the Robert Taylor Homes. Yet his name and scholarship were frequently invoked by advocates of demolition. According to one account, his concept of concentrated poverty was "the ironclad precept" for housing officials and developers in enacting plans for the demolition of public housing (Bennett, Hudspeth, and Wright 2006, 195).

   In the debate over the 1999 Chicago Housing Authority's "Plan for Transformation," which contemplated the downsizing of public housing, Alexander Polikoff, the senior staff counsel of Business and Professional People for the Public Interest, made the following argument: "For me the case made by Harvard's William Julius Wilson is entirely persuasive.... Wilson speaks of the 'social pathologies' of ghetto communities and adds that, if he had to use one term to capture the differences in the experience of the ghetto poor from the poor who live outside, it would be 'concentration effect'—meaning social pathologies generated when a neighborhood is composed exclusively of ghetto poor.... [S]o persuaded am I of the life-blighting consequences of Wilson's concentrated poverty circumstances, that I do not view even homelessness as clearly a greater evil" (quoted in Wright 2006, 159–60). As far as I know, if Wilson objected to the use of his name and scholarship to justify the implosion of public housing in Chicago, he never made his dissent public.
5. There is a very large body of studies (extensively reviewed in Goetz 2003; Imbroscio 2008) that purport to evaluate the efficacy of mobility programs. By far, the most influential have been James Rosenbaum's studies of the Gautreaux program [for example, Rosenbaum and DeLuca (2000, 1–8); Rosenbaum, DeLuca, and Tuck (2005); coauthored chapter in this volume]. Other recent interventions include Briggs (2005); Goering (2005); and a recent symposium in the *American Journal of Sociology*, including Clampet-Lundquist and Massey (2008); Ludwig et al. (2008); and Sampson (2008). From the standpoint of the politics of knowledge production, the sheer amount of research on this dubious policy initiative is itself worthy of examination, as are the massive institutional subsidies. Clampet-Lundquist and Massey acknowledge support from no fewer than twelve foundations, governmental agencies, and research centers (including two grants from the National Institute of Mental Health and two from the National Science Foundation). Clampet-Lundquist and Massey begin by acknowledging that studies of the MTO housing mobility experiment "heretofore has not provided strong evidence to support the hypothesis of neighborhood effects on economic self-sufficiency among adults," and assert that selective bias casts a shadow of doubt on all these studies (2008, 107). However, instead of questioning the logic and assumptions, not to speak of the ideology, that undergird the MTO project, Clampet-Lundquist and Massey, like others before them, assume that their measures must be defective, and launch into yet another hairsplitting and word-parsing exercise to redeem the MTO concept.

   On the other hand, a number of studies have challenged the logic, methodology, and findings of the MTO canon. These include: Bennett and Reed (1999); Bennett, Smith, and Wright (2006); Crump (2002); Goetz (2003); Greenbaum (2006, 2008); Greenbaum, Spalding, and Ward (in press); Imbroscio (2008); Joseph, Chaskin, and Webber (2007); Reed and Steinberg (2006); Reingold, Van Ryzin, and Ronda (2001); Thompson (1998); and Tienda (1991).
6. See Tienda (1991) for a thoughtful analysis of the logic of "concentration effects." Tienda faults existing studies for failing to specify the mechanisms through which these putative effects

are enacted. She further argues that "if resource stock problems are the *root causes* of social dislocation observed in ghetto neighborhoods, then solutions focused on neighborhood revitalization might be more productive than those aimed at rehabilitation of individuals" (252, italics in original). Tienda concludes on a skeptical note: "Given the nature of available data, it is virtually impossible to determine with any degree of confidence the existence of neighborhood effects on poverty behaviors" (258).

7. The full passage reads: "A responsible antipoverty policy should not lead with the demolition of low-cost housing and the forced relocation of the poor. This nation's history with the urban renewal program suggests that without complementary actions to reduce exclusionary barriers and incentives that foster and facilitate growing socioeconomic disparities—and the geographic expression of those disparities—the scattering of poor people, in itself, accomplishes little."

8. Nor is this an anomalous event: see McRoberts (2005).

9. Early ethnographic studies that portray the poor or public housing in a more positive light are Liebow (1967); Stack (1974); Susser (1982); Williams and Kornblum (1985, 1994). For a review of recent ethnographic studies of poverty, see Morgen and Maskovsky (2003).

10. For example, Maggie McCarty (2007). "Reauthorization of the HOPE VI Program," Hearing Before the Subcommittee on Housing and Community Opportunity (June 21, 2007): http://frwebgate.access.gpo.gov/cgi-bin/getdoc.cgi?dbname=110_house_hearings&docid=f:37561.wais

11. Springston (2007) and Pearlstein (2007).

12. For a glimpse of the protest before the New Orleans City Council, see http://www.youtube.com/watch?v=cMBWAXfGsc4

13. http://www.pbs.org/newshour/bb/weather/july-dec05/rebuild_9-16.html

14. The petition can be found at http://www.newvisioninstitute.org/movingOppotunityScholarsPetition.pdf.

For critical commentary, see Imbroscio (2008); Reed and Steinberg (2006). Also, see the Symposium on Hurricane Katrina, including Susan Greenbaum, Sudhir Alladi Venkatesh, and Xavier de Souza Briggs (2006, 107–28), and Nicolai Ouroussoff's column in the *New York Times* (September 14, 2008) on the failure of planning in the reconstruction of New Orleans. http://www.nytimes.com/2008/09/14/weekinreview/14ouroussoff.html?pagewanted=print

References

Bell, Derrick. 2008. *Race, Racism, and American Law*. Boston: Little, Brown.
Bennett, Larry, Nancy Hudspeth, and Patricia Wright. 2006. "A Critical Analysis of the ABLA Redevelopment Plan." In *Where Are Poor People to Live?* ed. Larry Bennett, Janet L. Smith, and Patricia A. Wright. Armonk, NY: M.E. Sharpe, 185–215.
Bennett, Larry, and Adolph Reed Jr. 1999. "The New Face of Urban Renewal: The Near North Redevelopment Initiative and the Cabrini-Green Neighborhood." In *Without Justice for All*, ed. Adolph Reed Jr. Boulder, CO: Westview Press, 175–211.
———, and Janet L. Smith, and Patricia A. Wright, ed. 2006. *Where Are Poor People to Live?* Armonk, NY: M.E. Sharpe.
Briggs, Xavier de Souza. 2005. "Introduction" and "*More* Pluribus, *Less* Unum? The Changing Geography of Race and Opportunity." In *The Geography of Opportunity*, ed. Xavier de Souza Briggs. Washington, DC: Brookings Institution Press, 1–41.
———. 2006. "After Katrina: Rebuilding Places and Lives." *City & Community* 5 (2): 119–28.
———. 2008. Maximum Feasible Misdirection: A Reply to Imbroscio. *Journal of Urban Affairs* 30 (2): 131–37.
Castells, Manuel. 1979. *The Urban Question: A Marxist Approach*. Cambridge, MA: MIT Press.
Clampet-Lundquist, Susan, and Douglas S. Massey. 2008. "Neighborhood Effects on Economic Self-Sufficiency: A Reconsideration of the Moving to Opportunity Experiment." *American Journal of Sociology* 114 (1): 107–43.
Clark, Kenneth. 1965. *Dark Ghetto*. New York: Harper Torchbooks.
Crump, Jeff. 2002. "Deconcentration by Demolition: Public Housing, Poverty, and Urban Policy." *Environment and Planning D: Society and Space* 20: 581–96.

D'Souza, Dinesh. 1995. *The End of Racism*. New York: Free Press.

Geering, John, and Judith Feins. 2008. "Social Science Housing Policy, and the Harmful Effects of Poverty." *Journal of Urban Affairs* 30 (2): 139–48.

Goering, John. 2005. "Expanding Housing Choice and Integrating Neighborhoods: The MTO Experiment." In *The Geography of Opportunity*, ed. Xavier de Souza Briggs. Washington, DC: Brookings Institution Press, 127–49.

Goetz, Edward G. 2000. "The Politics of Poverty Deconcentration and Housing Demolition." *Journal of Urban Affairs* 22 (2): 167–73.

———. 2003. *Clearing the Way: Deconcentrating the Poor in Urban America*. Washington, DC: The Urban Institute Press.

Greenbaum, Susan. 2006. "Comments on Katrina." *City & Community* 5(2): 109–13.

———. 2008. "Poverty and the Willful Destruction of Social Capital: Displacement and Dispossession in African American Communities." *Rethinking Marxism*. 20(1): 42–54.

———, and Ashley Spalding, and Beverly G. Ward, "Scattering Urban Poverty: Hidden Results and Unintended Consequences." In press.

Heidler, David S., and Jeanne T. Heidler. 2007. *Indian Removal*. New York: Norton.

Imbroscio, David. 2008. "United and Actuated by Some Common Impulse of Passion": Challenging the Dispersal Consensus in American Policy Research." *Journal of Urban Affairs*, 30 (2): 111–30

———. 2008. "Rebutting Nonrebbutals: A Rejoiner to My Critics." *Journal of Urban Affairs* 30 (2), 149–54.

Jargowsky, Paul. 1997. *Poverty and Place: Ghettos, Barrios, and the American City*. New York: Russell Sage.

Joseph, Mark L., Robert J. Chaskin, and Henry S. Webber. 2007. "The Theoretical Basis for Addressing Poverty Through Mixed-Income Development." *Urban Affairs Review* 42 (3): 369–409.

Liebow, Elliot. 1967. *Tally's Corner: A Study of Streetcorner Men*. Boston: Little, Brown.

Ludwig, Jens, Jeffrey B. Liebman, Jeffrey R. Kling, Greg J. Duncan, Lawrence F. Katz, Ronald C. Kessler, and Lisa Sanbonmatsu. 2008. "What Can We Learn about Neighborhood Effects from the Moving to Opportunity Experiment?" *American Journal of Sociology* 114 (1): 14–88.

Marcuse, Peter. 1978. "Housing Policy and the Myth of the Benevolent State." *Social Policy* 8 (4): 21–26.

———. 1997. "The Enclave, the Citadel, and the Ghetto: What Has Changed in the Post-Fordist U.S. City." *Urban Affairs Review* 33 (2): 228–64.

Massey, Douglas S., and Nancy A. Denton. 1993. *American Apartheid: Segregation and the Making of the Underclass*. Cambridge, MA: Harvard University Press.

———. Shawn M. Kanaiaupuni. 1993. "Public Housing and the Concentration of Poverty." *Social Science Quarterly* 74 (1): 109–22.

McCarty, Maggie. 2007. "HOPE VI Public Housing Revitalization Program: Background, Funding, and Issues." *CRS Report for Congress*. Order Code RL32236.

McRoberts, Omar M. 2005. *Streets of Glory: Church and Community in a Black Urban Neighborhood*. Chicago: University of Chicago Press.

Moore, Solomon. 2008. "As Program Moves Poor to Suburbs, Tensions Follow." *New York Times*. http://www.nytimes.com/2008/08/09/us/09housing.html?scp=1&sq=as%20program%20for%20poor%20moves%20to%20the%20suburbs&st=cse (August 9, 2008)

Morgen, Sandra, and Jeff Maskovsky. 2003. "The Anthropology of Welfare 'Reform': New Perspectives on U.S. Urban Poverty in the Post-Welfare Era." *Annual Review of Anthropology* 32: 315–38.

Orfield, Myron. 2002. *American Metropolitics: The New Suburban Reality*. Washington, DC: Brookings Institution Press.

Pearlstein, Alex. 2007. "Atlanta to Demolish Nearly All Its Public Housing," *Planetizen: The Planning & Development Network*. http://www.planetizen.com/node/22899

Reed, Adolph, and Stephen Steinberg. 2006. "Liberal Bad Faith in the Wake of Hurricane Katrina." *The Black Commentator* http://www.blackcommentator.com/182/182_cover_liberals_katrina.html

Reingold, David A., Gregg G. Van Ryzin, and Michelle Ronda. 2001. "Does Urban Public Housing Diminish the Social Capital and Labor Force Activity of Its Tenants? *Journal of Policy Analysis and Management* 20 (3): 485–504.

Rosenbaum, James, and Stefanie DeLuca. 2000. *Is Housing Mobility the Key to Welfare Reform? Lessons from the Gautreaux Program.* Washington, DC: The Brookings Institution, 1–8.
——, Stefanie DeLuca, and Tammy Tuck. 2005. "New Capabilities in New Places: Low-Income Black Families in Suburbia." In *The Geography of Opportunity*, ed. Xavier de Souza Briggs. Washington, D.C., 2005, 150–75.
Rosin, Hanna. 2008. "American Murder Mystery," *The Atlantic.* http://www.theatlantic.com/doc/200807/memphis-crime
Sampson, Robert J. 2008. "Moving to Inequality: Neighborhood Effects and Experiments Meet Social Structure." *American Journal of Sociology* 114 (1): 189–231.
Smith, Janet. L. 2006. "Mixed-Income Communities: Designing Out Poverty or Pushing Out the Poor?" In *Where Are Poor People to Live?* ed. Larry Bennett, Janet L. Smith, and Patricia A. Wright. Armonk, NY: M.E. Sharpe, 259–81.
Smith, Neil. 1996. *The New Urban Frontier: Gentrification and the Revanchist City.* New York: Routledge.
Springston, Jonathan. 2007. "Activists Mobilize to Save Atlanta Public Housing, Seek Legal Options," *Atlanta Progressive News.* http://www.atlantaprogressivenews.com/news/0141.html
Stack, Carol. 1974. *All Our Kin.* New York: Harper & Row.
Steinberg, Stephen. 2007. "Social Capital: The Science of Obfuscation," *New Politics* 11 (4): http://www.wpunj.edu/newpol/issue44/Steinberg44.htm
Susser, Ida. 1982. *Norman Street: Poverty and Politics in an Urban Neighborhood.* New York: Oxford University Press.
Thompson, J. Phillip. 1998. "Universalism and Deconstruction: Why Race Still Matters in Poverty and Economic Development," *Politics and Society* 26 (2): 181–219.
Tienda, Marta. 1991. "Poor People and Poor Places: Deciphering Neighborhood Effects on Poverty Outcomes." In *Macro-Micro Linkages in Sociology*," ed. Joan Huber. Newbury Park, CA: Sage, 227.
Williams, Terry M., and William Kornblum. 1985. *Growing Up Poor.* Lexington, MA: Lexington Books.
——. 1994. *The Uptown Kids: Struggle and Hope in the Projects.* New York: Putnam.
Wilen, William P., and Rajesh D. Nayak. 2006. "Relocated Public Housing Residents Have Little Hope of Returning." In *Where Are Poor People to Live? Transforming Public Housing Communities*, ed. Larry Bennett, Janet L. Smith, and Patricia A. Wright. Armonk, NY: M.E. Sharpe, 216–36.
——. Wendy L. Stasell. 2006. "*Gautreaux* and Chicago's Public Housing Crisis: The Conflict between Achieving Integration and Providing Decent Housing for Very Low-Income African Americans." In *Where Are Poor People to Live? Transforming Public Housing Communities*, ed. Larry Bennett, Janet L. Smith, and Patricia A. Wright. Armonk, NY: M.E. Sharpe, 239–58.
Wilson, William Julius. 1987. *The Truly Disadvantaged: The Inner City, the Underclass, and Public Policy.* Chicago: University of Chicago Press.
——, and Bruce Katz. 2005. *The News Hour.* http://www.pbs.org/newshour/bb/weather/july-dec05/rebuild_9-16.html
——, with Richard M. Wheelock and Carol Steele. 2006. "The Case of Cabrini-Green." In *Where Are Poor People to Live? Transforming Public Housing Communities*, ed. Larry Bennett, Janet L. Smith, and Patricia A. Wright. Armonk, NY: M.E. Sharpe, 168–84.
Wright, Patricia. 2006. "Community Resistance to CHA Transformation." In *Where Are Poor People to Live? Transforming Public Housing Communities*, ed. Larry Bennett, Janet L. Smith, and Patricia A. Wright. Armonk, NY: M.E. Sharpe,125–67.
Wyly, Elvin, and Daniel Hammel. 1999. "Islands of Decay in Seas of Renewal: Urban Policy and the Resurgence of Gentrification." *Housing Policy Debate* 10 (4): 711–71.

CHAPTER 16

Integration

Solving the Wrong Problem

JANET L. SMITH

A great emphasis should be put in revisiting the legislation and the linkage between racism and poverty. As long as those marginalized economically and socially are minorities, domestic policies remain inadequate. (Doudou Diene, Senegal, United Nations Special Rapporteur on Racism, 2008)

If we want to use housing assistance to significantly expand opportunity, we should directly target communities with high-performing schools, not rely on poverty rate, let alone a point-in-time rate, as a proxy measure. Since high-performing school districts or school communities are often primarily white, this targeting strategy means directly confronting exclusion and discrimination in the siting of affordable housing and the placement of families that use rental housing vouchers or other assistance. (Ferryman et al. 2008)

Passage of the 1968 Fair Housing Act came swiftly following the assassination of Dr. Martin Luther King, Jr. Most agree that at the time it was the right thing to do, but also that the Act passed without first reaching firm consensus on the goal it was to achieve. While the law clearly aimed to end overt discrimination against blacks and other "minority" groups in the purchase and rental of housing, it did not specify the broader goal of ending segregation or even promoting integration. Moreover, as this chapter discusses, it was not intended to address poverty, but rather to create open housing. However, over the years, and more recently, integration strategies have been employed to improve the education and economic status of poor people primarily of color, on the premise that it will also move people out of poverty. This includes strategies to end housing discrimination and to proactively open up white and usually middle-class communities to people of color via mobility programs. While research supports this approach to helping poor people, it also reveals how these strategies have not reduced the institutional racism that plagued our country four decades ago continues now to produce and sustain poverty ghettos.

Today, these conditions, while improved overall, seem no less insurmountable, especially poverty, as unemployment is on the rise again. But even when employment was higher and it appeared poverty was declining in our cities (Jargowsky 2003), we began to see a new trend as the number of people below poverty living in suburbs caught up with and recently surpassed the number living in poverty in cities (Berube and Kneebone 2006). At the same time, we saw an increase in nonwhites living in suburbs. Furthermore, while we have seen the proportion of blacks living in concentrated poverty decline, the rate of poverty among blacks continues to be three times that of whites, which is not that different from four decades ago (24.3% for blacks, compared to 8.2% for whites in 2006; 34.7% for blacks, compared to 10.0% for whites in 1968; U.S. Census Bureau 2008). Moreover, we have not seen much improvement in the quality of education, especially in cities and older inner-ring suburbs where we now have higher proportions of nonwhites living (Orfield 2008). The Moving to Opportunity three-city study report (Ferryman et al. 2008), for example, found that even when a low-income black family is able to move to a low-poverty "opportunity" neighborhood, this does not assure educational levels will improve, because the family may still be living in a poor school district. While some—including the report's authors—may argue that this outcome should not dissuade us from continuing to promote integration in order "improve the life chances of low-income, mostly minority adults and, in particular, their children" (Ferryman et al. 2008, 1), the findings do raise an important question: *Are we trying to solve the wrong problem?*

Promoting Integration/Preventing Resegregation

Prointegration strategies within the framework of fair housing traditionally have been based on the premise that we need to: (1) open up the market so that those who have been excluded through discriminatory practices can enter and participate fully and equally, and at the same time (2) encourage those who are not discriminated against to consider moving to areas that because of the composition (usually race/ethnicity but also income) they might not otherwise move to. A second related premise is that once "created," these new diverse communities need to be preserved and nurtured in order to prevent resegregation.

Traditional Approach

Prointegration strategies target all participants/stakeholders in the sale and rental of housing: home-seekers (renters and owners), home sellers, rental property owners and managers, real estate agents, and lending institutions. Most strategies to promote and preserve integration are based on the premise that neighborhoods will resegregate and require intervention on the part of local government and other actors to mollify this tendency. Lauber (1991) outlines a wide collection of tools that can be used at the local level to both achieve and preserve racial diversity:[1]

1. Passage of a fair housing ordinance that reproduces the federal act but also gives local jurisdictions the ability to act fast on discrimination complaints. The ordinance can and should deal with specific things like homeowner solicitation, sign bans, intent to sell notification requirements, occupancy permits, and diversity effect statements.[2]
2. Equity assurance programs that can "guarantee" that if the value of the home is not maintained over a fixed period of time, the program will make up some level of difference based on an agreed upon formula.
3. Racial diversity statements providing a pro-integration basis for policy and practice. Note that these policies and subsequent actions must comply with any state and local ordinances regarding fair housing as well as the Fair Housing Act.

In addition, Lauber and others (e.g., Saltman 1990) have firmly pointed out the need to keep schools integrated and prevent them from resegregating, and strongly recommend keeping a careful eye on the racial mix and proactively engaging school officials in finding ways to integrate and maintain the mix of students in all schools in the district—and better yet, the region.

The logic behind many of these strategies is to offset fear and misinformation of racial mixing that contribute to whites moving out of areas when blacks move in, which is reflected in empirical evidence of rapid racial change beginning in the 1950s. Referred to as "tipping" by academic researchers, the tipping point hypothesis assumes that when a certain proportion of blacks move into a neighborhood, whites will move out, often at an accelerated rate, leading the neighborhood to eventually become all-black (Grodzins 1958; Wolfe 1963). However, research by Molotch (1972) and Schelling (1972) suggests that tipping is independent of white residents' decisions to move out. Instead, the tipping point represents a threshold (percentage of nonwhite residents) at which whites no longer are comfortable moving into a racially mixed neighborhood.

Either way, tipping helped to explain the rapid change of neighborhood conditions in many cities that were beginning to experience population loss and to see increasing levels and proportions of minority (primarily black) residents. Tipping research also linked race to declining housing values, reinforcing a negative image of the outcome of racial invasion-succession. For example, Downs (1981) attributes changes in housing values to "ghetto expansion." As blacks moved out of the ghetto into adjacent neighborhoods, housing values initially inflated with the entry of blacks due to competition, and then decreased as the neighborhood became predominantly nonwhite.

Tipping also presumes that mixed-race/ethnicity neighborhoods are inherently unstable (Ottensmann 1995). However, more recent evidence of sustained, racially mixed neighborhoods (see Denton and Massey 1991; Ellen 1998; Farley and Frey 1994; Nyden, Maly, and Lukehart 1997; Wood and Lee 1991) suggests that tipping may have been a temporary phenomenon produced by specific conditions such as the mass migration of blacks from the South to older cities. Still, there remain clearly lingering effects of this phenomenon in contemporary thinking about policy aimed at promoting stable "mixed" (integrated, diverse) neighborhoods. A key problem is defining the terms *stable* and *mixed*. Is it based on a relative measure in space and time (Ellen 1998; R. Smith 1998)?

Another challenge is how to account for stability—should it be based on some relative measure or range of racial mixing that is maintained over time? Static measures alone do little to capture the dynamics that cause a neighborhood to change its racial mix over time. Galster (1998) proposed an alternative view of stable integration, which involves both static *and* dynamic elements. His "stock/flow" model is based on the assumption that a neighborhood is integrated if "1) its stock of households may be classified in the 'mixed' range, and 2) the flow of households into and out of this stock is such that it will be so classified for a minimum period of time in the future" (Galster 1998, 45). Galster assumes that mixed means that no single group makes up more than 75% of the population, and that a minimum time period is a decade. The idea here is to derive "integration stability boundaries" for net migration of white and nonwhite households in a neighborhood.

While fixed proportions (e.g., no more than 75% of any group) and ten-year increments aligned with the decennial Census make it relatively easy to operationalize and measure racial integration, these traditional methods also restrict interpretation of the findings to these arbitrary time and space parameters (J. Smith 1998). More importantly, none of these measures explains why a community is integrated or segregated, or reveals whether or not there is any sort of social integration occurring.

Emerging Approach

Nyden, Maly, and Lukehart (1997) offer a more informative way to look at stable diverse communities in their study of 14 neighborhoods in nine cities around the country. Based on the factors presumed to sustain diversity over time, the researchers classified each case as being one of two types. *Self-consciously* diverse neighborhoods are the result of residents and others actively promoting diversity through programs, organizations, and social networks. *Laissez-faire* neighborhoods are presumed to be diverse due to various circumstances not attributed to intervention by a formal organization or group. Unlike previous research on tipping and even on integration, this study offers some explanation for why some diverse neighborhoods do *not* change that is based in decisions and actions of residents and not based solely on reading the socioeconomic and demographic characteristics of a space.

Maly (2005) extends this research further to provide rich qualitative data that demonstrate how different "hyper diverse" communities (i.e., mixed on numerous demographic dimensions) remain integrated despite change. While the circumstances vary by community, some common factors include: (1) not being biracial; (2) exogenous globalization factors, especially immigration affecting urban areas; and (3) active and responsive community reaction to racial change. On this last point, Maly specifically describes how:

> Local organizations were not, however, recruiting white residents or developing anti-discriminatory lending or real estate programs to preserve integration. These strategies were not necessary given that many incumbent white residents stayed in the community and more importantly, no organization articulated the explicit goal of maintaining or promoting integration. In fact, the organization structure in each community sprouted up to serve the low-income residents and newly arrived immigrants, more general organizations surfaced to stave off residential and commercial decline through image maintenance and physical improvement. Advocates for the poor toiled to provide low-income residents with affordable housing and to ease overcrowding, while other groups formed to strengthen economic development in stagnant commercial districts. (217–18)

This lengthy quote illustrates a more complex response to change but also a different approach to preserving integration in racially, ethnically, or economically changing communities that is important to understand, especially given the changing global landscape of our cities. First, no strategy is employed to convince whites to stay in or move into a changing neighborhood as a means to stabilize it. Second, attention is shifted from the change in racial composition as the potential source of decline to the role played by actors that can either contribute to or prevent neighborhood decline—namely, community organizations, business owners, and affordable housing producers. Finally, instead of employing traditional antidiscrimination strategies to offset "the influence of institutionally structured patterns of inequality (e.g., discrimination) on the racial composition of the community" (Maly 2005, 218), the focus is on strategies that address the effects of past inequality. This includes producing assets to improve the quality of life, which in turn may positively redefine the community's integration identity.

Maly's research makes it evident too that strategies to preserve diversity in lower-income communities may also help offset gentrification, which involves the in-movement of higher-income and usually but not always white households into a lower-income but changing community.[3] This includes deliberate efforts to preserve and even produce more affordable housing but also to sustain local businesses that are likely to cater to the current racial/ethnic populations that can become threatened by rising rents and shifting demand as incumbents are replaced with new consumers. Still, in one of Maly's study communities, Uptown (Chicago), market-rate housing development in the 1990s consistently brought in higher-income white buyers (75% of annual transactions 1992–1998). While still diverse, whites are now the largest percentage in the mix and, with the rapid shift from being a predominantly renter to an owner community, also the majority in terms of ownership and higher income.

In this sense, we might benefit from reconceiving tipping to include the effects of the rapid in-movement of whites in a neighborhood. Instead of ghetto expansion, we have gentrification, and the tipping point is the threshold at which people of color—unless they also have money—no longer seek out or can attain housing in the gentrifying community. This is evident, for example, in gentrifying communities in Chicago, where between 1990 and 2000 white population increased 3% (about 7,000 households) at the same time black households decreased 7% (about 4,500 households) (Zelalem et al. 2006). Currently, according to the standards used by most integration researchers, these neighborhoods are no longer stable integrated because they are less than 10% black (and only about 7% Latino), and in Galster's framework a single group—whites—makes up about 75% of the population.

The point of this example is simple: Integration, segregation, and resegregation are not interpreted and analyzed in the same way for all racial categories. A neighborhood that resegregates and becomes majority black is expected to decline, while a racially mixed neighborhood that resegregates and becomes predominantly white is expected to improve. The question then is why do policymakers and researchers often look past the racial change in gentrifying neighborhoods?

Technically, gentrification and economic displacement cannot easily be fought on fair housing grounds, because income is not a protected class.[4] While this is problematic, more troubling is the fact that this limitation in the Fair Housing Act makes it possible for policymakers to freely use quotas to restrict the number of public housing units in redeveloped "mixed-income" public housing communities, even though many of the affected families are black (*False Hope* 2002). While some have challenged the logic of a policy that on its face appears discriminatory based on race (see *False Hope* 2002; J. Smith 1999), little can be done legally from a fair housing standpoint. Perhaps most troubling—and more important to consider—is the fact that justification for the mixed-income policy in public housing redevelopment was built upon research on the Gautreaux program, which presumed moving blacks into predominantly white suburbs was the best way to improve their lives (Rubinowitz and Rosenbaum 2000), and more recently on the Moving to Opportunity (MTO) demonstration program (e.g., see Turner and Briggs 2008). The next section examines this research to consider how it has constrained contemporary antipoverty policy by focusing on integration.

Moving to Opportunity?

While dispersal is clearly an easy way to quickly get poor minorities out of poor living conditions, it does little to help reduce poverty overall. As Jargowsky demonstrated in *Poverty and Place* (1997), that although relocation strategies can dilute the concentration of poverty, they alone cannot reduce poverty among nonwhites. A recent research report on the MTO demonstration recognizes this fact:

> A change of address alone will never compensate for the major structural barriers low-skilled people face in our economy: the absence of crucial supports for work, such as universal health care and high-quality child care, or persistent inequalities in public education. And initiatives that promote housing mobility should not substitute for investing in the revitalization of distressed communities; both place-based and people-based strategies should be vigorously pursued. (Turner and Briggs 2008, 1)

Although this statement is reassuring, there is still good reason to be cautious in reading this as a harbinger of change in the policy research arena. A great deal has been based on the assumption that moving black people out of poor and usually majority-black communities will improve their lives and life chances. More importantly, many of these same researchers assume that this is what the "minority poor" want, as evidenced by this statement in the same MTO report:

Contrary to the skepticism that the minority poor prefer to live among "their own," many low-income families—including blacks, Hispanics, Asians, and whites—will volunteer for the opportunity to move from high-poverty areas, typically in inner cities, to better neighborhoods in the same cities or in the surrounding suburbs. (Turner and Briggs 2008, 2)

Clearly, demand was high for the Gautreaux program, based on the extraordinary volume of calls to get on the waiting list for relocation vouchers.[5] Similarly, the MTO study had thousands apply, representing about 25% of those eligible in the five cities studied. While impressive, this level of interest should be read with caution. Just as we would not assume that people living in poor-quality homes is evidence of "demand" for substandard housing, it does not necessarily indicate that families were signing up for Gautreaux or MTO because they wanted to move to an integrated neighborhood; rather it could just as easily indicate that many of these families believed moving out of their community was the only way to get access to resources that can produce opportunity. However, without evidence to confirm or deny this, we can only speculate on whether or not the participants were truly demonstrating a preference to live in an integrated community, or the suburbs for that matter.[6] What we do know, for example, is that in Los Angeles: "Experimental families reported that supportive services were critical to relocating to non-poor areas, but many also reported that they would not have moved to their current neighborhood had they not been constrained by the low-poverty requirement" (Hanratty, MacLanahan, and Pettit 1998). This result can be interpreted as a successful outcome for MTO because it opened up communities to people who otherwise would have moved to a higher-poverty area. However, it also bluntly reveals that while MTO may aim to open up communities, the means to the end requires constraining the choices that can be made by poor people and nonwhites.

What we do not know from MTO research is how, prior to moving, these families viewed moving to racially integrated or higher-income communities, and then how their viewpoints compare to other movers in general. Research by Farley, Fielding, and Krysan (1997) suggests that blacks more than whites prefer to live in an integrated community, though they are more comfortable with higher rather than lower percentages of blacks when stating their preferred mix. In comparison, the research found that the likelihood of whites moving into a neighborhood is "inversely related to the density of blacks living there" (Farley, Fielding, and Krysan 1997, 763). The theoretical foundation for this investigation, as the researchers describe, is the neighborhood preferences hypothesis, which assumes that "segregation results not so much from discriminatory practices as from the different preferences of blacks and whites" (766), and that each prefer to live in neighborhoods in which they are numerically the majority. While findings are more nuanced across the four cities in the study, a common thread is evidence that preferences of blacks and whites overlap enough so that there is "potential hope for decline in segregation, provided that the influence of other forces, particularly discrimination, also declines" (Farley, Fielding, and Krysan 1997, 763).

The survey, which was initiated in Detroit in 1976 and then repeated 20 years later, first in Detroit and then Atlanta, Los Angeles, and Boston, is interesting, since it also reveals how blacks and whites are not treated equally when studying racial preferences. By design, the study uses different questions and methods for eliciting responses from blacks and whites. Specifically, the researchers concluded, based on Detroit data, that it would be "a waste of interview time" to use identical preference cards and ask the same questions, since "black respondents had no objection to whites moving into their neighborhood," and that "asking whites about neighborhoods with more than 11 families out of 14 provided no new information because few whites were comfortable with this density of blacks or willing to consider moving into such an area" (Farley, Fielding, and Krysan 1997, 769). While technically appropriate in terms of reducing data collection time, this approach starts from the assumption that blacks and whites have different rather than similar preferences when thinking about the racial mix of their community.

More important is what the study does not tell us about *why* people would move other than because of racial mix or that they found an attractive home in the community. There is no mention of good schools, proximity to work or family and friends, or any other myriad reasons people move, including being displaced. Further, it does not provide any insight as to what knowledge people have about integrated or segregated communities. This is important, since a recent study by Krysan (2008) of the Chicago area suggests that whites, blacks, and Latinos have different "blind spots" when it comes to knowledge about different types of communities, and that there is limited but little overlap between the pool of communities blacks and whites have knowledge about.

American Housing Survey data do provide some insight about motivations to move and neighborhood selection. Table 16.1 below suggests that, with a few exceptions, black movers are not that different from all movers when it comes to reasons for selecting their present neighborhood, though there are some differences between people in poverty when it comes to moving for a new job or being convenient to work. Along similar lines, blacks are less likely to move for a new job or job transfer. Also, while the house itself was an important reason for selecting a neighborhood, it was not as highly ranked for people in poverty as being convenient to friends and family (17–19%), which was more important than being close to work (8–10%). Finally, the

Table 16.1 Primary Reasons People in US Moved in 2005

Main Reason for Leaving Previous Unit	All Households		Blacks Only	
	All	Poverty	All	Poverty
New job or job transfer	10%	4%	5%	1%
Needed larger house or apartment	10%	8%	11%	12%
To be closer to work/school/other	9%	9%	7%	6%
Private displacement	1%	1%	1%	1%
Government displacement	0%	1%	1%	1%
Choice of Present Neighborhood				
Convenient to job	19%	10%	18%	8%
Convenient to friends/relatives	15%	17%	16%	19%
Good schools	7%	8%	6%	5%
Wanted lower rent or maintenance cost	4%	5%	5%	6%
Comparison to Previous Neighborhood				
Move was to better neighborhood	43%	38%	39%	35%

Source: American Housing Survey 2005

data suggest that blacks are not as likely as all households to move to a better-quality neighborhood.

What these data suggest is that there are likely some differences between why blacks move and why poor people move when compared to nonblack and nonpoor movers.[7] This is based on all those surveyed being asked the same questions and in the same way. Farley, Fielding, and Krysan's (1997) research suggests that, just as interpretations of neighborhood racial change have generally been "one-way," so too are interpretations of neighborhood racial preferences. While perhaps not intentional, the effect of both is to discriminate—in the sense that there is differential treatment of blacks and whites, but also because both privilege the white position.

Critical Race Theory (CRT) provides a useful framework to consider why this one-way approach is sustained in contemporary policy research. Generally speaking, CRT assumes that racism is "normal" in American society. As a result, strategies vis-à-vis laws and rules aimed at treating blacks and whites "alike" only get at extreme cases of injustice. Further, little is done about "business-as-usual" forms of racism confronting people daily (Delgado and Stefancic 2001). This includes overt acts such as racial profiling, but also policy and programs that privilege the "white position." The white position—or, as some critical race theorists refer to it, "white supremacy"—reproduces past forms of white domination, though in less overt ways than in the past when racial discrimination was legal. A key argument is that "the merely formal rejection of white supremacist principles will not suffice to transform the United States into a genuinely racially egalitarian society, since the actual social values and enduring political economic structures will continue to reflect the history of white domination" (Mills 2003).

From this perspective, efforts aimed at promoting racial integration that restrict the number of blacks to be the minority in order to assuage white fears of "too many" blacks moving into the neighborhood (Judd 1999) are white supremacist. This includes the proposal by Galster et al. (2003) to impose impaction standards (e.g., no more than 20% assisted housing in a community) in order to assure that efforts to deconcentrate poverty in public housing do not end up resegregating people. While this "facially neutral policy" proposal does not refer to the race of relocatees or communities they move to, most are likely to be black and moving into mixed or even majority white neighborhoods. The justification for this standard is that the rights of assisted tenants and housing providers should not take precedence over valid neighborhood concerns. The solution, then, sustains a belief that responding to poverty means accounting for (and counting) race rather than racism, and using quotas to restrict access an imperative.

Moving Opportunity

When HUD launched the MTO program, it was part of a larger agenda intended to examine three possible ways to respond to the problem of concentrated poverty. This included: (1) moving people to low-poverty neighborhoods; (2) helping families link to jobs in economic opportunity areas; and (3) helping "promote the revitalization of distressed inner-city neighborhoods" (Schroder 2001, 57). MTO clearly aimed to understand the "value" of the first strategy, and to date has received the most attention, at least in terms of the investment of time and resources into a systematic, quasi-experimental longitudinal study. Smaller-scale research on welfare-to-work has been conducted by HUD in relation to housing via its Welfare to Work Voucher Program (Mills et al. 2004).

Noticeably absent from HUD's research agenda is the study of efforts to revitalize neighborhoods. In part, this is a much more complicated endeavor to undertake in any controlled way when compared to the other two. However, it may also reflect the broader view held by many that place-based strategies "have never been set up to succeed *as mechanisms to help people escape poverty or dramatically improve conditions in the most distressed neighborhoods*" (Briggs 2008, 134, emphasis in original). As Briggs describes it, "There is very suggestive research evidence, on both neighborhoods and schools, that there are threshold levels of concentrated distress beyond which even well-funded interventions will struggle mightily to achieve meaningful results" (2008,

134). Moreover, and more important perhaps, some researchers believe that we need to fight "extreme" segregation at the same time we focus on improving communities (Briggs 2008). From this perspective, segregation is intricately linked with poverty, and as long as it persists, we will be hard-pressed to effectively improve places.

Rather than debate this point, I want to consider how this position differs from one that starts with the assumption that society is racist (not just segregated), but also that people have rights wherever they live that include "the right to a standard of living adequate for the health and well-being of himself and his family, including…housing."[8] The first assumption requires us not only to deal with discrimination, whether by intention or effect, based on the behavior of housing actors, but also in the way we fundamentally approach the problem of poverty via current policy and programs. This means looking honestly at the policies we have created that require poor people of color to move out of one community into "opportunity areas," rather than dealing with the messy problem of trying to make over their current community into one that promotes opportunity. The racist litmus test: Would we require lower-income whites to do the same if the higher-income community were majority black?

The other question to ask is: If we are trying to offset the fears of whites who are likely to move out when their majority position declines, then why don't we find compelling positive ways to persuade them to become immobile in a changing neighborhood? Instead of relying on negative tactics such as equity assurance programs, which reify fear that home values may not appreciate in changing neighborhoods, we could focus on ways to positively persuade whites to stay, while at that same time assuring that nonwhites can stay, too. Why not do the same for poor communities in which people may actually want to stay and "live among their own" if they had the same amenities that are offered in white communities where people there have already chosen to live among their own? The point here is not to reinforce or support racial segregation, which is truly based on racism, but rather to put a sharp spotlight on the racially one-sided and biased nature of current policies aimed (and not ironically) at trying to reduce poverty and discrimination among people of color.

The second assumption—the right to an adequate standard of living—is not quite the same as a right to housing (see Bratt, Stone, and Hartman 2006; Hartman 1998), which sets minimum requirements, including legal security of tenure, habitability, service availability, affordability, access, location, and cultural adequacy. The right to housing framework also tends to position adequate housing as the foundation to gaining and maintaining economic security. While this framework brings attention to the need for all societies to provide some basic level of shelter to all people, it also can oversimplify policy solutions by placing too much primacy on housing to produce economic security, or the current extension of that logic: to assume mixed-income housing developments will improve the economic status of poor people (see Joseph 2006). Of course, public housing naysayers might refute this claim on the grounds that housing security has contributed to rather than reduced poverty because it makes poor families too comfortable and complacent, which then leads to generational poverty (e.g., Murray 1984).[9]

The point here is not to dismiss what is clearly growing momentum in support of housing as a human right, which has really expanded in the world and more recently in the United States. Instead, the intent is to reframe housing as a necessary but not sufficient cause of economic security. A standard of living that is adequate must include housing, but also health care, transportation, education, economic opportunity/employment, etc. Of course, this position has its naysayers, too—from the practical concern that such a proposal is impossible to fund and implement, to the politically or economically conservative position that fundamentally the market, and not government intervention in the market, is the proper mechanism to produce these results. Aware of both positions, an emerging angle on the human rights agenda is the "right to the city" movement, which comes directly from poor people and people of color as well as a range of academics, activists, and even some foundations (see Miami Workers Center and Tides Foundation 2008). The right to the city focuses on a wide-ranging justice agenda that includes:

Land for people, not for speculation	Economic justice
Permanent public ownership of land for public use	Indigenous justice
Freedom from state/police harassment	Environmental justice
Services and community institutions	Immigrant justice
Democracy and participation	Rural justice
Reparations	Internationalism

The justice framework takes an approach to rights that is different from a right to housing. Instead of seeking a positive right in the form of a right to have or get something (e.g., housing or shelter), it focuses a great deal on negative rights. Simply stated, a negative right means a right to be free from coercion (King 2000). In the right to the city framework, this means the right to have the government and others *not* do things to poor people that take advantage of their lack of private resources and, more importantly, property, which comes with many rights formally granted and socially accepted (King 2000). This would include the right not to be displaced from public housing in order to sell land to private developers to produce market-rate housing that a developer could produce elsewhere. This can still maintain the positive right to access and use public housing, but also recognizes the rights currently denied propertyless people in the United States (see Sen 1985).

This example is purposeful because it also reveals the puzzle some scholars on rights have trouble solving. As Waldron (1993a) points out, our most basic human rights—sleeping, urinating, washing—are not exercisable without first having a place to exercise them. Therefore, in societies where property rights are strong—particularly, private ownership and control of land—this right may not be exercised easily or freely without first having some agreement in society that people without property (e.g., literally homeless) should have some space to exercise these basic human rights.[10] In this sense, then, besides being "situated," some rights also must be institutionalized because unlike liberties, some rights like housing benefits are not givens. Instead, such claims on society must be agreed upon as worthy of being given because they produce some benefit or serve some social goal.

The right to the city movement is a broad-based organizing framework aimed at rebuilding a movement in cities. Clearly it has limits—practical and political—but its call for radical and inclusive democracy has real implications for any discussion of integration and fair housing. At a minimum, the framework challenges us to look beyond simply trying to integrate communities—something that has proven to be no small undertaking but also with limited effect based on the fact that after four decades we have seen only limited progress based on empirical evidence (Logan 2008). More importantly, a human rights approach, but particularly the right to the city movement approach, reminds us, as Waldron does that: "rights have got to be linked to a theory of social justice that takes seriously the distributive issues they raise" (1993b, 580). The goal here is to get researchers and policymakers to see how critical it is to look beyond trying to attain some end (integration), to also account within a social justice framework for what effects the means to attaining that end (e.g., mixed-income communities) have on the people that policy intends to help. If the end goal of integration strategies is to reduce racism, then as the analysis presented here suggests, we have not made much progress and will not until we deal head-on with structural racism and policies that privilege the white position.

Notes

1. I recognize that the terms *diversity* and *integration* are not the same, but that they do get used interchangeably and often without reflection. While an important point, this is the subject for another treatment, and therefore will not be addressed here. Both words will be used to describe places that are racially, ethnically, or economically mixed.
2. A diversity effect statement aims to identify potential impact on the current diversity of a community, should there be significant change in population, often the result of development, which can produce a negative effect (i.e., less diversity) or positive effect (i.e., more diversity).
3. See J. Smith and Stovall (2008) for an example of black gentrification in a black low-income neighborhood.
4. The exception is in local and state ordinances that bar discrimination based on source of income.

5. The first day for taking names for the lottery literally shut down the telephone system.
6. In reviewing the baseline surveys available (not all were), I found no questions about why people chose to participate in the program, though they are asked neighborhood preferences.
7. Differences are statistically significant.
8. Article 25(1) of The Universal Declaration of Human Rights, of which the United States was a principal drafter and has adopted.
9. The counterargument is that our goal should not be poor-quality housing in bad neighborhoods, but rather quality housing that is relatively indistinguishable from nonpublic housing— whether mixed-income or not.
10. Of course, the next big question that comes up is how much space and where?

References

Berube, Alan, and Elizabeth Kneebone. 2006. *Two Steps Back: City and Suburban Poverty Trends 1999–2005.* Washington, DC: Brookings Institution Metropolitan Policy Program.
Bratt, Rachel, Michael Stone, and Chester Hartman. 2006. *A Right to Housing Foundation for a New Social Agenda.* Philadelphia: Temple University Press.
Briggs, Xavier de Souza. 2008. "Maximum Feasible Misdirection: A Reply to Imbroscio." *Journal of Urban Affairs* 30 (2): 131–37.
Delgado, Richard, and Jean Stefancic. 2001. *Critical Race Theory: An Introduction.* New York: New York University Press.
Denton, Nancy, and Douglas Massey. 1991. "Patterns of Neighborhood Transition in a Multi-Ethnic World: U.S. Metropolitan Areas, 1970–1980." *Demography* 26 (1): 41–63.
Diene, Doudou. 2008. Speech at UN hearings on racism, Chicago. May 23. (UN Special Rapporteur on Racism)
Downs, Anthony. 1981. *Neighborhoods and Urban Development.* Washington, DC: Brookings Institution.
Ellen, Ingrid Gould. 1998. "Stable Racial Integration in the Contemporary United States: An Empirical Overview." *Journal of Urban Affairs* 20 (1): 27–43.
False HOPE. 2002. National Housing Law Project, Poverty & Race Research Action Council, Sherwood Research Associates, Everywhere and Now Public Housing Residents Organizing Nationally Together (ENPHRONT).
Farley, Reynolds, and William H. Frey. 1994 "Changes in Segregation of Whites from Blacks During the 1980s: Small Steps Toward a More Integrated Society." *American Sociological Review* 59 (1): 23–45.
———, Elaine L. Fielding, and Maria Krysan. 1997. "The Residential Preference of Blacks and Whites: Four Metropolis Analysis." *Housing Policy Debate* 8 (4): 763–800.
Ferryman, Kadija S., Xavier de Souza Briggs, Susan J. Popkin, and María Rendón. 2008. *Do Better Neighborhoods for MTO Families Mean Better Schools?* Washington, DC: The Urban Institute.
Galster, George. 1998. "A Stock/Flow Model of Defining Racially Integrated Neighborhoods." *Journal of Urban Affairs* 20 (1): 43–52.
———, Peter Tatian, Anna Santiago, and Kathryn Pettit. 2003. *Why Not in My Backyard? Neighborhood Impacts of Deconcentrating Assisted Housing.* New Brunswick, NJ: Center for Urban Policy Research, Rutgers University.
Grodzins, Morton. 1958. *The Metropolitan Area as a Racial Problem.* Pittsburgh, PA: University of Pittsburgh Press.
Hanratty, Maria H., Sara A. McLanahan, and Becky Pettit. 1998. "The Impact of the Los Angeles Moving to Opportunity Program on Residential Mobility, Neighborhood Characteristics, and Early Child and Parent Outcomes." Working Paper Number 98-18, Bendheim-Thoman Center for Research on Child Wellbeing. Princeton University.
Hartman, Chester. 1998. "The Case for a Right to Housing." *Housing Policy Debate* (9) 2: 223–46.
Jargowsky, Paul. 1997. *Poverty and Place.* New York: Russell Sage Foundation.
———. 2003. *Stunning Progress, Hidden Problems.* Washington, DC: Brookings Institution Metropolitan Policy Program.
Joseph, Mark. 2006. "Is Mixed-Income Development an Antidote to Urban Poverty?" *Housing Policy Debate* 17 (2): 209–34.

Judd, Dennis. 1999. "Why African Americans Got So Little From the Democrats." In *Without Justice for All: The New Liberalism and Our Retreat from Racial Equality,* ed. Adolph Reed. Boulder, CO: Westview Press, 123–50
King, Peter. 2000. "Can We Use Rights to Justify Housing Provision?" *Housing, Theory and Society* 17 (1): 27–34.
Krysan, Maria. 2008. *Racial Blind Spots: A Barrier to Integrated Communities in Chicago.* Chicago: Institute of Government and Public Affairs, University of Illinois at Chicago.
Lauber, Daniel. 1991. "Racial Diverse Communities: A National Necessity." In *Challenging Uneven Development: An Urban Agenda for the 1990s,* ed. Philip Nyden and Wim Wiewel. New Brunswick, NJ: Rutgers University Press, 49–84.
Logan, John. 2008. Data presented at the National Commission on Fair Housing and Equal Opportunity Hearing in Chicago. July 15.
Maly, Michael. 2005. *Beyond Segregation: Multiracial and Multiethnic Neighborhoods in the United States.* Philadelphia: Temple University Press.
Miami Workers Center and Tides Foundation. 2008. "The Right to the City: Reclaiming Our Urban Centers, Reframing Human Rights and Redefining Citizenship." http://www.tides.org/fileadmin/tf_pdfs/TheRightToTheCity.pdf (accessed August 9, 2008).
Mills, Charles. 2003. "White supremacy." In *A Companion to African-American Philosophy,* ed. Tommy L. Lott and John P. Pittman. London: Blackwell, 269–84.
Mills, Gregory, Rhiannon Patterson, Michelle Wood, Ken Lam, and Satyendra Patrabansh. 2004. *Evaluation of the Welfare to Work Voucher Program.* Prepared for U.S. Department of Housing and Urban Development, Report to Congress Contract No. C-OPC-21663. Cambridge, MA: Abt Associates. March.
Molotch, Harvey. 1972. *Managed Integration: Dilemmas of Doing Good in the City.* Berkeley, CA: University of California Press.
Murray, Charles. 1984. *Losing Ground: American Social Policy, 1950–1980.* New York: Basic Books.
Nyden, Philip, Michael Maly, and John Lukehart. 1997. "The Emergence of Stable Racially and Ethnically Diverse Urban Communities: A Case Study of Neighborhoods in Nine U.S. Cities." *Housing Policy Debate* 8 (2): 491–534.
Orfield, Myron. 2008. Data and maps presented at the National Commission on Fair Housing and Equal Opportunity Hearing in Chicago, July 15.
Ottensmann, John. 1995. "Requiem for the Tipping-Point Hypothesis." *Journal of Planning Literature* 11 (2): 132–41.
Rubinowitz, Leonard, and James Rosenbaum. 2000. *Crossing the Class and Color Lines.* Chicago: University of Chicago Press.
Saltman, Juliet. 1990. *A Fragile Movement.* New York: Greenwood Press.
Schelling, Thomas. 1972. "A Process of Residential Segregation: Neighborhood Tipping." In *Racial Discrimination in Economic Life,* ed. Anthony Pascal. New Britain, CT: Lexington Books, 157–84.
Schroder, Mark. 2001. "Moving to Opportunity: An Experiment in Social and Geographic Mobility." *Cityscape* 5 (2): 57–67.
Sen, Amartya. 1985. "The Moral Standing of the Market." In *Ethics and Economics,* ed. Ellen Frankel Paul, Fred D. Miller, and Jeffrey Paul. Oxford: Blackwell, 1–19.
Smith, Janet L. 1998. *Interpreting Neighborhood Change.* Ph.D. diss. Cleveland State University.
———. 1999. "Cleaning Up Public Housing by Sweeping Out the Poor." *Habitat International* 23 (1): 49–62.
———, and David Stovall. 2008. "'Coming Home' to New Homes and New Schools: Critical Race Theory and the New Politics of Containment." *Journal of Education Policy,* 23 (2): 135–52.
Smith, Richard. 1998. "Discovering Stable Racial Integration." *Journal of Urban Affairs* 20 (1): 1–26.
Turner, Margery Austin, and Xavier de Souza Briggs. 2008. *Assisted Housing Mobility and the Success of Low-Income Minority Families: Lessons for Policy, Practice, and Future Research.* Washington, DC: The Urban Institute.
U.S. Census Bureau. 2008. Annual Poverty Levels. Washington, DC: Government Printing Office. http://www.census.gov/hhes/www/poverty/histpov/hstpov2.html (accesed July 26, 2008).
Waldron, Jeremy. 1993a. "Homelessness and the Issue of Freedom." In *Liberal Rights: Collected Papers, 1981–1991,* by Jeremy Waldron. Cambridge, England: Cambridge University Press, 309–38.

Integration • 245

——. 1993b. "Rights." In *A Companion to Contemporary Political Philosophy,* ed. Robert E. Goodin and Philip Pettit. Oxford: Blackwell, 575–85.
Wolfe, Eleanor. 1963. "The Tipping Point in Racially Changing Neighborhoods." *Journal of the American Institute of Planners* 29 (3): 217–22.
Wood, Peter, and Barrett Lee. 1991. "Is Neighborhood Racial Succession Inevitable? Forty Years of Evidence." *Urban Affairs Quarterly* 26 (4): 610–20.
Zelalem, Yittayih, Janet Smith, Martha Glas, and Nancy Hudspeth. 2006. *Affordable Housing Conditions and Outlook in Chicago: An Early Warning for Intervention.* Chicago: Nathalie P. Voorhees Center for Neighborhood and Community Improvement, University of Illinois at Chicago.

CHAPTER 17

The Legacy of Segregation

Smashing Through the Generations

ROGER WILKINS

A little more than a quarter of a century ago, my wife, then just past 40, and I, just past 50, were expecting a baby. We lived in a middle-class development in Washington, DC, right across the street from a public housing project that was home to a substantial number of poor black people—and poor black people only. One of those people was Brenda (a pseudonym), a teenaged girl who was just about as pregnant as my wife was. It was a cultural encounter that intrigued both Brenda and us. Brenda was stunned and somewhat amused that a woman of my wife's age would be having her first baby. We, on the other hand, wondered how a teenager with no husband and a cramped, poor, and disorganized living arrangement was going to be a successful mother. And we wondered about her child's life in a tough segregated public housing project and later in one of our city's poorest elementary schools.

My wife Patricia and I were both university professors, and Brenda was, well, waiting for her baby. There were lots of books in our house—some of which we bought early in the pregnancy for our child-to-come. There was no man in the apartment across the street, nor were there many books either. Our baby, still in Patricia's womb, had excellent prenatal medical care and the best nutrition possible. As we considered the pregnancy across the street, I said to Patricia: "It will be uneven at the moment the children are born—we've been able to take much better care of our child up to now, and the differences in care and nurturing will just keep piling up. At 3, they won't belong in the same nursery school, at 5 not the same kindergarten, and at 21 not the same economy."

And so it came to be. Though we moved a few blocks away when our daughter was still a baby, we tried to keep up with Brenda and Keisha (a pseudonym). At 21, our daughter graduated from Yale and Keisha had apparently left home and gone to places that no one we knew could find.

The past is never dead; in fact, it's not even past. (William Faulkner)

Keisha and her family had been segregated from the rest of society by both class and race. The apartment blocks built for them were far away from the neat and cared-for neighborhoods where the bulk of the middle class of both black and white people live. Many of the wealthy—both black and white—had streamed out of the city into affluent Maryland suburbs. Close to home, their project was bounded on three sides by normal urban desolation. On the west was the middle-class development in which we lived, and our condo had constructed a gated iron fence designed to keep them out. Their segregation of both class and race seemed compounded by their proximity to middle-class people—both black and white—whose basic strategy of dealing with them was to keep a distance and to treat them as invisible. The city of Washington and their neighbors had created for them a segregated and almost sealed compound of want and neglect.

The experience of seeing the two babies and thinking about the disparities in their life prospects drove my mind back to the hopes many of us had harbored in the late 60s when Martin Luther King was planning his Poor People's Campaign and Lyndon Johnson was in the White House. Skeptics muttered about a "culture of poverty" into which poor black people would inevitably collapse, with lives shaped by indolence and violence. The usual conclusion from that observation was that such people should simply pull their socks up, work hard, and succeed like Americans.

That line of thought led me to the rumination that there could hardly be a more American story than that of poor blacks being punished and shunned and used when convenient, but forgotten and ignored as long as they stayed in the darkest and most dangerous places in our civilization "where they belonged." I know that this is a profoundly American story because I have lived little parts of it and have observed much more. When my family moved into a white working-class neighborhood in Grand Rapids, Michigan in 1944, some white kids would throw apple cores and stones at me as I rode by on my bike and they would yell, "Go back where you belong," and worse.

So, I intend here to use some of the incidents of my own life and the impact they had on me to help increase understanding of Brenda, her daughter, and other poor blacks like them—living real American lives, shunned by the wide world, and consigned to segregated lives with "their own kind," where it is believed she belongs: down there at the bottom.

The Long Legacy of Segregation

In the first 60 years after blacks were first brought to Virginia in 1619, relationships between blacks and poor whites were relatively fluid. By 1650, some blacks had achieved a degree of affluence. One such person was Anthony Johnson, who had accumulated so much land that he needed hands to help him farm it, so he purchased several black slaves. Records show that a few other blacks were able to accumulate land, but there is no clear record that they also owned slaves.

There were relationships of various kinds between poor free blacks and poor whites in Virginia who had served out their indentures and who had to scrounge together in order to survive. There appear to have been few, if any, joint interracial economic or political efforts to protest their poverty and their powerlessness until 1676, when a white man named Nathaniel Bacon led an incoherent revolt against the colonial government of the most populous and richest of the new English colonies of North America. Bacon's was a rag-tag army largely composed of free blacks and poor whites who had worked through their indentures. Bacon's group had originally come together to fight Indians, but was stymied by unwelcome orders from the governor, so it turned away from the Indians and attacked the colonial government instead.

The revolutionaries were at a loss when the government fled Williamsburg on British naval vessels, because Bacon died suddenly and had left no overarching vision, not even a simple bill of grievances. Lacking leadership, the rebels were easily sent packing when the governor and his soldiers returned to Williamsburg. Once Bacon's warriors had slipped away into the woods, there was only one enduring legacy of their revolt. The grandees who governed Virginia had learned a powerful lesson: Cross-racial alliances of the poor could pose very serious threats to the dominance of the ruling class.

As a result, Governor William Berkeley and his government chose to divide and conquer in order to guard against any other such dangerous threats to their power and wealth. They diluted white class distinctions by welcoming whites of all levels into the polity and by giving them a bit more access to the grandees themselves. The purpose was to create a sense that the poor whites were now members of a white club which, because of the superiority of all whites, excluded blacks. The shunning of blacks was an essential part of the humiliation and the degradation of blacks, which helped to inflate the self-esteem and cement the loyalty of the poor whites. The grandees finished the social architecture by making the manumission of blacks much more difficult.

A quarter of a century later, about 1700, Robert "King" Carter, the wealthiest Virginian and owner of more slaves than anyone else in the colony, introduced a program designed to defend and enhance his power and to destroy any aspirations that might arise in the breasts of his black slaves. The practice was called "seasoning." It was put into operation each time a visiting cargo ship would deliver a new shipment of slaves to Carter's plantation. Carter and his subordinates would examine the newcomers carefully and would cull out those whose manner and carriage suggested pride, leadership potential, and self-confidence. These people would be "seasoned" by having a finger, a toe, or an ear lopped off. This process served as a powerful message to all in his community that Carter held all the power and that he was not reluctant to use cruel measures to preserve it. Carter's basic purpose in this was to convince his slaves that they were to have no will of their own: Their function was to serve entirely as an extension of his will and to accept the idea of total white supremacy, which by that time was a linchpin of the order and growth of Virginia as it entered the eighteenth century.

Thus, the Virginia gentry added direct physical harm—especially aimed at black leaders or potential leaders—to the shunning that had been developing for the previous quarter of a century. Such behavior requires an explanation, and in this instance, it was that though slavery was anathema even to many of the slave owners, it was profitable and central to the economy of Virginia and the other Southern colonies. One of the ways around this psychic dilemma was to define blacks as both inferior and dangerous, and therefore requiring stern discipline and shunning—being cordoned off, shunned—to the degree possible on plantations and at the spear points of the ever-moving frontier. Binding this all together was the wealth slavery brought to some whites and the lift to the white psyche that this assumption of human superiority provided in a raw and fluid new nation that was ripping into a broad, largely unknown, and dangerous continent. Thus, the shunning was to serve the same purpose that seasoning had in an earlier time: to convince blacks that they were entitled to no will of their own and were to serve at the will or the whim of whites in general.

The power of the ideas of Berkeley and Carter in shaping the culture of America's slave states is demonstrated by a description of blacks which Thomas Jefferson wrote in his book, *Notes on the State of Virginia* ([1787] 1998), published a little more than 100 years after Bacon's rebellion had flickered out. Jefferson, clearly possessor of one of the great minds of early America, asserted essentially that blacks were dumber, smellier, and uglier than whites, in addition to having weaker control over their sexual impulses than white people (he actually drew a comparison between the sexuality of blacks and that of orangutans).

Jefferson also expressed puzzlement that blacks would play music and dance late at night, when sensible whites would have long been in their beds. He used this as an example of the childishness of the black mind. It evidently didn't occur to him that these people, many of whom lived in spare cabins less than 50 yards from his door, chose this time for relaxation, pleasure, and self-expression because that was the only time they were free from the presence of their white minders and from the imposition of the wills of their white masters. I don't mean to single Jefferson out. I use his words because they demonstrate so clearly how deeply the social formula developed by Governor Berkeley in 1676 had grown down into the souls and culture of Southern white Americans by the time of the birth of the nation. Racism had become a core cultural foundation stone on which the new nation was built. And beyond enslaving them and denying them the access to effective education, racism was supported by shunning—separating blacks from whites to the greatest degree possible in order to stoke the white fantasy of white superiority and to use it as a tool to make blacks accept the "fact" that they were indeed inferior.

A century after Jefferson described black people in *Notes on the State of Virginia* ([1787]1998), the South was busy undoing the results of the Civil War. The Supreme Court and two of the leading lights of the white Southern community outlined the contours of seasoning and shunning, updated just in time for the beginning of the twentieth century.

The Supreme Court, in the 1896 case, *Plessy v. Ferguson*, decided that the practice of segregating (shunning) blacks was constitutional despite the fact that the Fourteenth Amendment to the Constitution, adopted just after the Civil War, required that all citizens be accorded equal treatment under the law. The question in the case was whether the Constitution now required that railroad patrons be seated without restrictions based on race.

In rejecting Homer Plessy's assertion that the plain words of the Amendment and the circumstances of its adoption required equal treatment of all customers, regardless of race, Justice Henry Billings Brown wrote: "The object of the Amendment was undoubtedly to enforce the absolute equality of the races before the law, *but in the nature of things* [ital. added], it could not have been intended to abolish distinctions based upon color, or to enforce social, as distinguished from political, equality to a commingling of the two races upon the terms unsatisfactory to either." "In the nature of things," is a sloppy, nonlegal phrase that Justice Brown used to eviscerate the clear intent of a formally adopted amendment to the Constitution. Though the phrase was clearly not a term of art in American constitutional jurisprudence, it was a powerful demonstration of how the racism, developed in a slave colony in the last quarter of the seventeenth century, had become embedded in the psyches of Americans all over the country. The idea of the inferiority of blacks had been driven down into the white American psyche so deeply that it was just as natural as the change of the colors of the leaves in Justice Brown's native Massachusetts. The tool of shunning blacks and disrespecting them had grown to be a deep emotional aspect of what it meant to be a white American.

The Justice's reasoning brings to mind a line that George Bernard Shaw wrote in his play, *Man and Superman*: "The haughty American Nation makes the negro clean its boots and then proves the moral and physical inferiority of the negro by the fact that he is a bootblack."

Early in the twentieth century, the theme was picked up by a United States Senator from South Carolina and one of the most esteemed of Southern educators. The educator, Paul B. Berringer, president of the faculty at the University of Virginia, lectured to Southern educators in 1905 that blacks should be offered nothing more than a Sunday school education, because they were incapable of absorbing anything more and were useful only for manual labor in warm climates. That combination of pushing blacks off to learn by themselves from a severely crimped education was an early twentieth century combination of shunning and seasoning wrapped up in one lethal and evil cocktail.

At about the same time, Senator Benjamin Tillman exploded when he learned that President Theodore Roosevelt had invited Booker T. Washington (the leading Negro in America at the time) to the White House and conversed with him over a meal. In a rage at the President for breaking the code of shunning, Tillman opined in a public speech that whites "would have to kill a thousand niggers" to put blacks back in their place. And that "place" was down below the lowliest white people. Contemporaneously, a lynch mob chased the people who would become my paternal grandparents out of Mississippi because, in the view of the white gentry of Holly Springs, my grandfather had been uppity and hadn't accepted the "place" that white people like Senator Tillman had prepared for him.

The seasoning of blacks, carried out vigorously by whites in the South to drive a sense of inferiority into their souls, had its impact on whites as well. The sense of white mastery and superiority spread broadly and deeply into the psyches of a very large portion of white people of the South as a fundamental element of their culture. It also served an economic purpose by keeping blacks pent up in compounded human misery that provided cheap labor and the psychic and creature comfort provided by cheap household servants. That virus made it into the North as well, but rarely with the violence with which white supremacy was defended in the South.

The Springfield, Illinois riot in 1908 was one of those Northern exceptions. Sparked by a false charge of rape, leveled by a white woman against a black man, the riot resulted in the lynching of at least two blacks, the destruction of a substantial part of the property owned by blacks, and the expulsion of great majority of the black population from Springfield. The sheer ugliness of the Springfield explosion drew national attention which ultimately resulted in the creation of the NAACP in 1909.

Going to Kansas City

Shunning and the provision of indifferent education were standard forms of psychic brutality that were embedded in the white culture into which I was born in a segregated hospital in segregated Kansas City, Missouri in the early Spring of 1932. Much to the dismay of my mother and my grandmother (my father became a patient in the segregated Missouri tuberculosis sanitarium for Negroes before my first birthday), I became aware of the seasoning culture when I was very young. We lived in a tiny black enclave some miles away from the principal Kansas City black community and from downtown. In order to go anywhere, we had to take the streetcar, and in order to reach the streetcar line, we had to walk out of our community and through at least two white blocks to the streetcar stop. According to my mother and grandmother, I asked them one day after an excursion: "Why does everybody up to the big corner smile and say hello to Roger and then across the street and everybody looks mean at Roger?"

My mother and grandmother told me years later about how pained they were when I gave them that early intimation that I was learning the message that segregation was designed to deliver. Another lesson occurred when I was still very young and my grandmother took me with her as she shopped downtown. While we were on the top floor of a department store, I told her that I had to go to the bathroom, so she asked a sales clerk to direct her to the ladies room. She was told that the bathroom for colored was in the basement. According to the story, I was by then doing a little-boy urgency dance and my grandmother said to the clerk: "Can't you see that this child can't wait?" The clerk still insisted that we go all the way to the basement, so my grandmother bent down and began to unbutton my fly and said, "Well, he'll just have to do it here." The clerk immediately relented, and I integrated the ladies room on the top floor of that department store. We prevailed, but I'm sure that the emotional cost of that public ugliness for my grandmother was substantial.

My first educational experience was in a segregated one-room schoolhouse, which was great for nature studies because it was a big old drafty shack that was falling apart and the weather came in. I do not remember it as a place that incubated self-confidence or a love of learning.

The little school was closed after my first year, and the children from my neighborhood were bused past newer and prettier schools for white children to a measurably older and roughly used school in the Negro commercial area of town. The message was clear when we saw our new school: We didn't deserve a school as good as the white kids had.

My main memory of the two years I spent at Crispus Attucks [sic] School is of my father being home, finally, and working just around the corner from the school. His office was in the smallish building where *The Kansas City Call*, the city's Negro paper, was published. His office seemed tiny to me. I knew that he had applied for jobs at white papers and radio stations and had been shown the door.

I also remember my Negro teachers being nice to me, but of the school being very worn and crowded and of the bathrooms being smelly. Since we had to ride past the nicer white schools every day, I imagined the interior of those schools to have newly painted hallways, new books and furniture, and lily white, clean-smelling bathrooms. Despite the fact that my family tried to convince me that Crispus Attucks was a good school, I remained convinced that the white schools were better and that the white kids were better too. I also felt vaguely that I was being punished, but for what, I did not know.

My parents and my grandmother tried hard to counter the brutal sur-round-sound "seasoning" messages of the culture. Blacks were used as comic relief on radio programs. Buffoons, happy darkies, mammies, and fools were the only roles blacks could get. My father wouldn't let me listen to Amos 'n Andy, and my grandmother insisted that white people's hair was not "good" hair as most blacks seemed to say, and she would tell me that good hair was any hair that covers your head. Now, at 76, I accept her point, but by the age of 6 the culture had gripped a substantial chunk of my soul. White was right, as the saying went.

The most vivid memory of segregation that I retain from my nine years in Kansas City was from hearing my parents and their friends "let their hair down" on the front porch after dinner—especially when we had guests. I often listened surreptitiously to their stories of irrational unfairness and sometimes of small victories cunningly achieved (my grandmother with me in the store, for example), but the overall message was always the same: The strongest adults I knew were crammed down into little boxes that were far smaller than their talents and their hopes. I could sense how much my parents and their friends chafed under—and were injured by—the irrational system to which they were subjected.

My parents, both graduates of the University of Minnesota, had segregated jobs—my mother as a social worker at the colored YWCA and my father as a writer and the business manager of the Negro paper. My mother had earned high honors at the university, and my father had been an editor of the student paper. Despite the fact that I had exceptional parents who made it clear that I would go to college some day, I got a strong sense of the atmosphere in our little community and in school: that I was born in a little box and that my parents' trap would someday also get me.

As I listened to grown-ups talk about life in Kansas City, I heard a lot of mordant humor which I later understood to be therapeutic psychic discharges which helped highly intelligent people, who were being held back and often humiliated by the irrational color-coded society they lived in. Their stories were funny, but grew out of a great deal of pain. That pain convinced me that, despite loving parents and a doting grandmother, my future was bleak. In the brief time we had together, my father tried to steel me against a future that he thought he might never see.

I must have been 6 or 7 when I told him idly that I wanted to drive a streamlined train when I grew up. Looking back, I realize that he thought it was his duty as a Negro father to begin instructing me about the American way. He looked sadder than I'd ever seen him when he told me that that would be impossible, because only white people were permitted to drive trains.

I told him that I thought that was unfair, and he agreed with me, but told me that white people made the rules and that I should fight rules like that all my life. I remember having a feeling of helplessness because the rules were made by the most powerful people in the country and they must be wise and good, and therefore there must be something wrong with me. I never told him about that feeling of inferiority, and I have always hoped that I would have had enough faith in myself to tell him of my intimations of inferiority, but soon his time ran out. He died just before my ninth birthday.

On to New York City

My mother, my grandmother, and I moved to New York after his death and I was enrolled in my neighborhood Harlem school, which was de facto semisegregated. When I first got there, all the pupils were black and all the administrators and teachers were white. The building was quite ragged, but not quite as ragged as Crispus Attucks in Kansas City.

At PS 46, we were joined by a thin trickle of kids whose families had fled Hitler and his armies and had moved into upper Manhattan, whereas we blacks lived on the eastern side, which was part of Harlem, but was sometimes called Sugar Hill. My segregation problem in New York was not the school, but the streets. The streets themselves were not segregated by law, but the atmosphere created on the streets by tiny horizons for kids, economic uncertainty, stressed adults, and angry youth, and the knowledge that virtually all of the good things in America were forbidden to us in our carefully circumscribed neighborhoods made life seem as segregated as anything that Kansas City had to offer.

A number of my new black friends (we and the "refugees" did not fraternize outside school) lived split lives, as I did. Upstairs in the apartment, the values, if not the incomes, were middle-class, but downstairs, outside, it was the Harlem streets. The leg men for organized gambling were flashy as they moved ostentatiously through the neighborhood, sending the message that criminal enterprise was one way out of the box we were in. The older boys taught us young ones gambling games where empty match books served as money. They sometimes told stories of grown-up gambling and even, sometimes, wild stories of legendary Harlem criminals. And they educated us about sex, substituting street-knowledge and early-teen braggadocio for anything close to some real understanding of sex and sexuality. There was certainly no discussion of gentleness or respect for women.

I loved most of my friends on my block, but we were all afraid of the street gang based three blocks away. We knew we were poor on our block on 160th Street and that the Harlem Valley only about fifteen blocks south was even poorer than we were and thus the gangs were fiercer than ours on the Hill—even fiercer than the Puerto Rican Rainbows, who, because we didn't know them, were "known" to carry long switchblade knives and to be highly skillful when using them.

We lived near the Polo Grounds, the stadium where the New York Giants played baseball. When big events were held at the Polo Grounds, white people came to 160th Street—to park their cars. We would become extortionists— "Park your car, Mister?" Well, of course we couldn't park the cars, because we couldn't drive. The offer was to "protect" their cars from harm (and of course, not to harm them ourselves).

One day when I was "parking," a white man gave me a dime and said, "Here, Sam, take care of my car." "My name isn't Sam," I said. "OK Sambo," he said, as he moved on down toward the stadium laughing with his friends.

On my block, we thought almost all white people were rich and that they lived in grand apartments, probably near Central Park. My pals and I would go on the subway down to Central Park—the subway only cost a nickel in those days and the AA train took us right down to the Central Park West stops that faced the long impressive phalanx of tall buildings overlooking the park.

The people from those buildings who were strolling in the park weren't happy to see us. It was in the middle of World War II, and we black boys would play "war," with the outcroppings of huge rocks serving as our forts. We would collect stones from the ground and throw at each others' fortifi-cations as hard as we could. The white people didn't like us much, but they were rich and we were poor and it was a public park, and so we kind of liked it that they were a little scared of us.

I guess they should have been, since stones were flying, but as far as I can remember, we never hit any of them, although sometime we'd wing each other pretty good. Then we'd go back uptown on the subway, hooting and laughing about how scared some of those rich white folks seemed to be when we were around. It was a sort of payback for penning us up in Harlem and for their living lives we could never achieve in splendor that we could barely imagine—a little like the insides of the white schools in Kansas City.

And when I was 10 or 11, we started sneaking cigarettes and also stealing stuff from stores. We didn't take big stuff—maybe a candy bar or package of doughnuts. A couple of the older guys in our group did favors from time to time for the flashy guys. As I grew older and taller, the street dangers grew as well. There were gang skirmishes, where demands were made on us neutral boys to join their group or take the consequences.

I didn't join a gang, but I did find a way at school to buy some protection. A boy from the 163rd Street gang shared a double-seat double desk with me. I would let him copy my work, and he would insure that his gang would not only leave me alone in the streets, they would provide protection if I ever needed it. I liked the arrangement and began to dress and bop along the street as they did. And I started importing a lot of street into my vocabulary, but left the rawest part downstairs in the street. My mother noticed some of the changes and was troubled, so she talked to my uncles and one day I heard my Uncle Cecil, a city-savvy man, say, something like—we've got to pay attention and stay close to him.

One of the ways my mother stayed close to me was to arrange once a week or so for me to come down to meet her at her midtown office at the end of the day. Her office was in the mid-fifties on Lexington Avenue, and we would walk over to Fifth Avenue and take the #2 bus uptown (Fifth Avenue had not yet been turned into a one-way street, and the city still deployed double-decker buses). Mom would always insist on sitting on the upper deck because she liked to look into the windows of the swanky apartments we passed. I was mortified by the obvious way she would stare at the little snippets of New York high life she could snatch from those windows as we passed. But even though I hated for her to do this, I was overwhelmed by the yawning gap between what we could glimpse as the bus rolled on toward Harlem and the reality of our lives. We weren't impoverished, but Sugar Hill wasn't Fifth Avenue by a long shot—a fact that was driven ruthlessly into our souls as the bus turned west on 110th Street and then north on Seventh Avenue. There was no glitter to be seen; the streets were dirty, and many of the buildings were shabby. Life on the street was not yet vibrant in the early evenings, and there was a heaviness to the scene as people slowly made their way home at the end of a wearying day of work. And it was a dark scene, because most of the buildings were old and badly lit, unlike those on Fifth Avenue. None of the buildings were bright and new, as was the case in the neighborhood we had just left.

For the most part, people were poorly dressed and though the street would come alive in a few hours, in the early evening it was populated by people who looked like they possessed very heavy souls. I remember that part of the ride as depressing, particularly because I expected that I would spend the rest of my life in Harlem since everything better than what I was seeing

258 • Roger Wilkins

was forbidden to me. I knew that when I was 10. It was many years before I
came to understand that my mother's insistence on sitting on the top deck
was her way of breaking out—even if only a little bit—from the constricted
and largely segregated lives forced upon us by our country. Just as I had
imagined that life just out of reach, like the Kansas City white schools, Mom
was seeing the lives lived by people no smarter than she and no better trained
than she—just out of reach.

Back to the Midwest

Two years later, my mother, a widow for three years, married a physician who
had been courting her for a while, and we moved to Grand Rapids, Michigan,
where he lived and practiced. I rejoiced and was enormously relieved to be
far away from the Harlem streets. One of the guys I left back on the street
did OK. He grew up, finished high school, got a job, got married, and had
children. Most of the rest didn't fare so well. I know that two of them died of
drug overdoses before they were 20. Others went to prison—one for drug-
dealing and another for murder (or so I heard).

My life in Grand Rapids took an entirely different turn. My new stepfather
bought a house in a white working-class neighborhood—the only suitable
house he could find for a new wife, new stepson, and a new mother-in-law.
The school I went to was a combined junior and senior high with 1,200
students. For most of the time I was there, the racial count was 1,199 whites
and 1 black. The first adjustment was brutal—I was an object to be observed,
not a lonely kid to be befriended. But after a little while, things changed. A
wonderful fellow named Don de Young became my companion on walks to
and from school, and he remained a good friend for the next 60 or so years
until he died of heart problems a few years ago. I started off at Creston High
being shunned and isolated and I graduated with honors, having played
basketball, run track, and presided over the Student Council.

The Integration Imperative

I learned two great lessons at that school. The first and most important:
There is no master race. And the second was that, although a lot of white
people had absorbed large chunks of the racist culture of the country, there
were others who were completely unaffected and were generous and loving
people. There were some smart, sensitive, and nurturing teachers. Some of
my closest friends would later say that meeting my family and me was the
most important thing that had happened to them in high school. There is
no question in my mind that the experience made it much easier for me to
navigate the adult world that I encountered in the early 60s when America

was moving slowly toward an integrated workforce. There was never again a question in my mind about whether integration in America was an essential element of a good education.

But even today, as much of our country struggles to transcend old racist lines our cultural history still has a powerful and destructive hold on us. Two years ago, I visited with Geoff Canada, the heralded director of the project to rebuild the social and economic infrastructure of Harlem. Though there are pockets of gentrification in that storied community, and some excellent community and youth development programs are up and running, there is still a great deal of poverty, of unemployment, and of households headed by women and all the dangers that grow out of those traditional problems.

"We can have good programs for the kids, but when they get to their teens is where the problem is: The street gets them," Canada said. "It even occurs in strong families. We've had the problem with some of the kids whose parents work for us."

Few cities with concentrations of poor blacks escape the problem. On August 9, 2008, *The Washington Post* ran a page one story about Washington kids who are growing up today in virtual segregation. Here is how the *Post* story begins.

Monica Watts, two months out of high school, buried another brother this week. She barely remembers her older brother Donald, who was killed during a robbery more than a decade ago. Her baby brother, John, 18, was shot to death July 25 in Forestville as he tried to rob an off-duty officer, Prince George's County police said.

He was a year her junior but felt like her twin. She called him "Streets," and he belonged to the cohort most likely to be killed: young, black, male, involved with the criminal justice system. By her count, Watts, at 19, has lost more than a dozen relatives and friends to violence since 2003. "One was stabbed; the others were shot," she said. These were her people. They ran through the same alleys, attended the same schools and playfully fought with one another as kids. Her adolescence, like many of theirs, has been spent scrounging for enough to eat, a safe place to sleep, something to belong to. That's why they used their fists—and sometimes more—to fight for their small slice of the world in Woodland Terrace, a public housing complex east of the Anacostia River in Southeast Washington.

The isolation of poor blacks in the inner cities today is more lethal in some ways than Springfield, IL was a century ago. The damage done over centuries to families by the blows of shunning and of "seasoning," by economic strangulation, and the withholding of effective education is immeasurable. Policies and practices that force some of the most miserable people in the country into concentrations of poverty, political and administrative failure, and social and family pathology frighten some would-be helpers and cause revulsion in others. During the heated economic debates in the late Summer and early Fall of 2008, I was amazed to see on television a white female member of Congress standing on the floor of the House of Representatives blaming poor blacks for the mortgage, banking, and credit catastrophe. Her screed included no mention whatsoever of the former masters of greed and the universe.

As twentieth century economic conditions evolved, so did the poorest black precincts. During slavery and even during deep segregation, unskilled black labor had economic utility in America. During World War II, when America called itself the "Arsenal of Democracy," there were many jobs for black workers. The need continued during the economic burst after the war, as the country satisfied its enormous appetite for peacetime consumer goods. But over time change occurred: computerized workplaces and vulnerable immigrant workers became staples of the American economy. The need for poor black workers decreased significantly, and crime, poverty, and misery flowed into the poorest black communities in lieu of the incomes previously earned.

These conditions were exacerbated by the housing opportunities made possible by the Civil Rights Movement that enabled affluent blacks to find homes and communities far away from the urban core. For those left in the stew of decay, poverty, and family disintegration, as Monica Watts and her family and presumably "baby" Keisha were, life was like segregation on steroids. The iconic symbols of this new period are largely illiterate black men wandering aimlessly through their days being excess commodities in a fluid, wired world. Bad schools, unemployment, family instability, crime, violence, and decay are the hallmarks of the new segregation.

But the most potent problem of all is the inability of most Americans to understand that the devastation that is Monica Watts' life has been rumbling down through the centuries, smashing into the unluckiest or weakest families, and maiming and destroying human lives from generation to generation, because most of us are unwilling or unable to recognize and to understand that what we see today is a reflection of who we have been as a nation and how much work—like that being done by Geoff Canada—has still to be done.

Some white acquaintances have expressed puzzlement over the years about why more black families couldn't be like mine. There is an implication that poor black families could be just like mine: If they would just pull their socks up and act nice, everything would be just fine. In my case, at least, it wasn't virtue; it was luck. My luck was in the lives of my grandfathers (and of my sainted maternal grandmother—she of the department store showdown). As I wrote above, one grandfather was chased out of Mississippi by a lynch mob sometime around the turn of the last century. Had that not occurred, I might have been born in Holly Springs, MS rather than Kansas City, MO. My other grandfather had a solid job as a sleeping car porter. He spent his adult life as a servant to itinerant white people, who sometimes called him Sam or Sambo, but he was a good, reliable, and determined fellow and father who used that steady job to send all three of his daughters to college. He had a good, sturdy American name, Madison—Madison Jackson. Grandpa Jackson's good luck was that an older black man took him under his wing and got him started on his career as a railroad man.

Both of my grandfathers got out of the South at the beginning of the twentieth century, and all of their children were raised in Minnesota and all of their children went to the university there, and to my great, good fortune, two of those children—Helen Jackson and Earl Wilkins—met there, married, and had me.

Other families, trapped by economic circumstances, or illness, or ignorance about the North, stayed in the rural South too long and missed that period in the North where unskilled blacks could find jobs that enabled them to keep their families together. The longer unskilled blacks waited in the South, the harder it was for them to get a foothold in the North. So the deepest part of the inner city became crowded by the newly arrived poor, and they got neatly cordoned off with red lines, piled on top of one another in the most toxic neighborhoods in America. The lack of available decent jobs dried up, as did the few amenities that were left in the second- or third-hand leftover communities to which the latecomers were consigned. As they became more crowded, these communities began to decay, economically, physically, socially, and morally—human misery inside the red lines of shunning.

Our best chance to mount an effort of a size and complexity to deal with these problems was still alive in the Summer of 1967 when, as an official in the Department of Justice, I talked to Martin Luther King in his Chicago ghetto apartment in the poor black community of Lawndale. He had learned first-hand about urban desperation during his Chicago crusades and about the impenetrability of thick urban bureaucracies and the imperviousness of a bigoted mayor. The experience had stimulated King to concentrate intently on issues of families and poverty. Listening to him, I thought that the poor really had a chance if King and Lyndon Johnson, whom I believed to be dedicated to fighting poverty in America, could cooperate (whether overtly or covertly) in an antipoverty crusade.

Forty years later, I was looking out of my living room window at a wonderful Washington view that includes a park on a peninsula, a golf course, the Washington National Airport, and a conjunction of rivers. I can also look down at a beautiful little park where some people bring their children to play in one area while dog walkers and their dogs use another corner of the green. Our apartment is in an area of Washington that has mixed-income development. Poor people, moderately well-off families, and well-to-do families are fairly close by each other. As I looked, I saw a group of black teens from one of the nearby housing projects whose roughhousing with each other had morphed into throwing stones at whites riding their bikes on the riverside promenade. Pretty soon, I saw the black kids chasing the bike riders to get better shots at them and maybe to steal their bikes. Soon, a couple of police cars arrived and the kids scattered, but some of them were high on their exploits, and I could hear their laughter and their excited voices as they raced away to the shelter of their own subcommunity a few blocks away. Those kids sounded very much like my memories of the sounds that my friends from 160th Street and I made as we used to race out of Central Park those many years ago.

The kids I was watching that day didn't have a mother who had the education and the means to pull them out of the way of the juggernaut rumbling straight at them from the generations of racist destruction, as my mother was able to do for me, or as my grandparents did for their children. It occurred to me that Keisha could easily have been the mother of one or more of those boys.

In lieu of great luck with grandparents, there is no great mystery about what is needed: The most important clearly is stable families with at least one employed parent who is earning a decent wage. There is an urgent need for much better schools with good and dedicated teachers; high-quality social services for children and families in need; employment programs to put parents and able-bodied youth to work; community policing; decent affordable housing; early childhood education; long school days; and volunteers of all ages whose main credentials should be a reasonable level of literacy, reliability, and deep love for children. The real goal is to begin RIGHT NOW to create young people who will be equipped to grow up to be responsible and diligent parents who will forge paths for their own children and who will age well and become strong and inspirational grandparents themselves.

Back in 1968, I was the Justice Department official designated by Attorney General Ramsey Clark to work with Martin Luther King as he planned bringing a Poor People's Movement to Washington that would enable the whole human rainbow of poor Americans—Native Americans, blacks, whites, Asians, Latinos—to present the needs of the American poor to the government and the people of the United States. The goals he had were very close to what I have described above, so there was hope that the lasting brutal aspects of the underside of American history could be confronted once and for all and accepted for what it was: injuries intentionally inflicted by a lusting nation on generation after generation along America's road to power and greatness.

But those hopes evaporated as King's casket was lowered into the ground and Johnson's Administration, mortally wounded by Vietnam, began packing up to leave. That past is neither dead nor past. It remains as an interlocutor testing our capacity to be honest about ourselves and brave enough to shape a future that is decent and full of opportunity for every American.

References

Jefferson, Thomas. [1787] 1998. *Notes on the State of Virginia,* ed. Frank Shuffelton. New York: Penguin.

Pierre, Robert E. and Clarence Williams. 2008. "'Trying to Hold On' Amid Despair of D.C.'s Streets: Teen looks to Dreams of Educaton, Peace." *Washington Post,* August 9: A1.

Plessy v. Ferguson, 163 U.S. 537 (1896)

Shaw, George Bernard 1903. "Man and superman," in *Bernard Shaw: Complete Plays with Prefaces Volume III.* 1962. New York: Dodd, Mead & Company: 497.

Contributors

Dolores Acevedo-Garcia (dacevedo@hsph.harvard.edu) is Associate Professor in the Department of Society, Human Development and Health at the Harvard School of Public Health. Her research focuses on the effect of social determinants (e.g., residential segregation, immigrant adaptation) on health disparities along racial and ethnic lines; the role of nonhealth policies (e.g., housing policies, immigrant policies) in reducing those disparities; and the health and well-being of children with special needs and their families. She is a member of the Social Science Advisory Board of the Poverty & Race Research Action Council, Co-Chair of the Board of Directors of the Fair Housing Center of Greater Boston, and a member of the Board of Directors of Planned Parenthood League of Massachusetts. She is Project Director for DiversityData http://diversitydata.sph.harvard.edu, an interactive website on demographic, socioeconomic, and health indicators in U.S. metropolitan areas. DiversityData is an ongoing project of the Harvard School of Public Health and The Center for the Advancement of Health, supported by the W.K. Kellogg Foundation. Currently, she is on two national expert panels convened by the Centers for Disease Control and Prevention, one on housing and health, the other on social determinants of health. She also serves on the expert panel for the PBS documentary series "Unnatural Causes: Is Inequality Making Us Sick."

F. Willis Caruso (6caruso@jmls.edu) is Co-Executive Director of The John Marshall Law School Fair Housing Legal Support Center, Clinical Director of school's Fair Housing Legal Clinic, and Adjunct Professor of Law at John Marshall. He is a graduate of Northwestern Univ. and the Northwestern Law School. He formerly practiced law with Sidley & Austin; Caruso & Caruso; Isham Lincoln & Beale; and Keck, Mahin & Cate. He served as General Counsel for the Chicago Housing Authority from 1991 to 1994 and General Counsel of the Leadership Council for Metropolitan Open Communities. He has litigated over 1,000 fair housing cases, including the *Village of Arlington Heights v. Metropolitan Housing Development Corporation,* and *Gladstone Realtors v. Village of Bellwood.* He has lectured at a large number legal seminars and authored many outlines, pamphlets, and articles, and a textbook, *Cases and Materials on Fair Housing and Fair Lending Laws, Sixth Edition* (Law Bulletin Publishing Company, 2009).

Cathy Cloud (ccloud@nationalfairhousing.org) is Senior Vice President of the National Fair Housing Alliance in Washington, DC, where she is responsible for supervising NFHA programs in the areas of compliance, membership services, education and outreach, consulting, finances, and administration. She is responsible as well for the development and implementation of Fair Housing School©, NFHA's comprehensive training and education program for fair housing personnel. She has provided training and consulting services to public and private fair housing organizations, the housing industry, federal financial regulatory agencies, mortgage lending institutions, homeowners' insurance providers, and national retail chains. She has served as a member of the Consumer Advisory Council of the Board of Governors of the Federal Reserve System and on the National Advisory Board of the Federal Reserve Banks' Mortgage Credit Partnership Project. She has also published several articles and book chapters on mortgage lending and insurance discrimination.

William A. Darity, Jr. (wd2@duke.edu) is Arts & Sciences Professor of Public Policy Studies and Professor of African and African American Studies and Economics at Duke Univ. Previously, he directed the Institute of African American Research at the Univ. of North Carolina. He was a fellow at the National Humanities Center and a visiting scholar at the Federal Reserve System. He has served as President of the National Economic Association and the Southern Economic Association. Recently, he served as Editor-in-Chief of Thomson Macmillan's second edition of the *International Encyclopedia of the Social Sciences* (Macmillan Reference USA, 2008). He has published more than 200 articles in academic journals over the course of his career.

Stefanie DeLuca (sdeluca@jhu.edu) is an Associate Professor in the Department of Sociology at Johns Hopkins Univ. She is currently engaged in several areas of research involving sociological considerations of education and housing policy issues. In March 2006, she testified in federal court on behalf of the plaintiffs in Baltimore's *Thompson v. HUD* housing desegregation case, using her research on housing programs as the basis for her testimony. She contributes regularly to national press sources, such as the *Baltimore Sun,*

Washington Post, Education Week, and National Public Radio. Her work has been published in academic journals such as *Social Forces, Social Science Research, Housing Policy Debate,* and *Demography* and has been funded by the Annie E. Casey Foundation, the Spencer Foundation, the William T. Grant Foundation, and the U.S. Department of Education.

Nancy A. Denton (n.denton@albany.edu) is Professor of Sociology and Associate Director of the Center for Social and Demographic Analysis at the State Univ. of New York at Albany. Her major research interests are race and residential segregation, and with Douglas S. Massey, she is the author of *American Apartheid: Segregation and the Making of the Underclass* (Harvard Univ. Press, 1993), winner of the 1995 American Sociological Association Distinguished Publication Award and the 1994 Otis Dudley Duncan Award from the Sociology of Population section of the American Sociological Association. Her current research projects include the neighborhood contexts of children by race/ethnicity/immigrant generation.

Mindy Thompson Fullilove (mf29@columbia.edu) is a Research Psychiatrist at New York State Psychiatric Institute and a Professor of Clinical Psychiatry and Public Health at Columbia University's Mailman School of Public Health. She is a board-certified psychiatrist, having received her training at New York Hospital-Westchester Division (1978–81) and Montefiore Hospital (1981-82). She has conducted research on AIDS and other epidemics of poor communities, with a special interest in the relationship between the collapse of communities and decline in health. From her research, she has published *Root Shock: How Tearing Up City Neighborhoods Hurts America and What We Can Do About It* (One World/Ballantine Books, 2004) and *The House of Joshua: Meditations on Family and Place* (Univ. of Nebraska Press, 1999). She has also published numerous articles, book chapters, and monographs. She has received many awards, including inclusion on "Best Doctors" lists and two honorary doctorates (Chatham College, 1999; Bank Street College of Education, 2002). Her work on AIDS is featured in Jacob Levenson's *The Secret Epidemic: The Story of AIDS in Black America.* Her current work focuses on the connection between urban function and mental health.

Robert E. Fullilove (ref5@columbia.edu) is Associate Dean for Community and Minority Affairs and Professor of Clinical Sociomedical Sciences at Columbia University's Mailman School of Public Health. He currently co-directs the Community Research Group at the New York State Psychiatric Institute and Columbia Univ. along with his wife, Mindy Thompson Fullilove. They are also Co-Directors of the degree program in Urbanism and the Built Environment in the Department of Sociomedical Sciences at the Mailman School of Public Health. In 1998, he was appointed to the Advisory Committee on HIV and STD Prevention at the Centers for Disease Control, and in July 2000, he became the committee's chair, serving in that capacity until Fall 2004. He serves on the editorial boards of the journals *Sexually Transmitted Diseases* and *The Journal of Public Health Policy.* He has twice been awarded the Distinguished Teaching Award from the graduating class at the Mailman School of Public Health, and in May 2002, he was awarded an honorary doctorate from Bank Street College of Education.

Shalini Goel (shaluram@gmail.com) is a former Fellow at the Relman & Dane lawfirm. She is a graduate of the Univ. of California Law School, Boalt Hall, and clerked for the Honorable David S. Tatel of the U.S. Court of Appeals for the D.C. Circuit. She is interested in civil rights, fair housing and immigration law.

Chester Hartman (Chartman2@aol.com) is Director of Research for the Washington, DC-based Poverty & Race Research Action Council, for which he was founding Executive Director from 1990-2004 and Associate Fellow at the Institute for Policy Studies. He is founder and former Chair of The Planners Network, a national organization of progressive urban planners. His most recent books are *City for Sale: The Transformation of San Francisco* (Univ. of California Press, 2002); *Between Eminence and Notoriety: Four Decades of Radical Urban Planning* (Rutgers Center for Urban Policy Research, 2002); *A Right to Housing: Foundation for a New Social Agenda* (Temple Univ. Press, 2006); *Poverty & Race in America: The Emerging Agendas* (Lexington Books, 2006); *There Is No Such Thing As a Natural Disaster: Race, Class and Hurricane Katrina* (Routledge, 2006); and *Mandate for Change: Policies and Leadership for 2009 and Beyond* (Lexington Books, 2009).

Lourdes Hernández-Cordero (ljh19@columbia.edu) is Assistant Professor of Clinical Sociomedical Sciences and Co-Director of the Urbanism and the Built Environment track in the Masters in Public Health program at Columbia University's Mailman School of Public Health. As part of the Community Research Group at Columbia, she has been able to combine her interest in community mobilization and the application of research. The relationships built with local organizations as an awardee of the Community Scholar scholarship and Program Coordinator for the Northern Manhattan Community Voices Collaborative have served as the foundation for her work. Currently, she directs the City Life Is Moving Bodies (CLIMB) project, a multilevel intervention to promote physical activity, stewardship, and social capital.

Alicia Jolla (Alicia.jolla@gmail.com) is currently working in the private sector as a supplier diversity manager. In her previous role as Small Business Development Director for the City of Charlotte, she focused on economic development in distressed areas, business recruitment and retention, and building economic capacity with local small businesses. She completed her graduate studies at the Univ. of North Carolina at Chapel Hill, where her research focused on educational disparities between white students and students of color.

Elizabeth K. Julian (ekjulian@inclusivecommunities.net) is President of the Inclusive Communities Project, a nonprofit organization in Dallas that works for the creation and maintenance of racially and economically inclusive communities through advocacy and education. From 1994-99, she served in the Clinton Administration at the Department of Housing and Urban Development as Assistant Secretary for Fair Housing and Equal Opportunity, Deputy General Counsel for Civil Rights, and., in the second term, as Secretary Andrew Cuomo's Representative for the Southwest. Prior to joining the Administration, she engaged for 20 years in the practice of poverty and civil rights law in Texas, where she represented primarily low-income clients in cases involving housing discrimination, voting rights, municipal services discrimination, and indigent health care. She was co-counsel in the landmark housing desegregation cases against HUD in Dallas (*Walker v. HUD*) and East Texas (*Young v. Pierce*), and the Dallas City Council redistricting case (*William et al. v. City of Dallas*), which significantly expanded minority representation on the Dallas City Council. She was Executive Director of Legal Services of North Texas from 1988-90. She received the 2001 Mexican American Bar Association's President's Award, the 2004 Martin Luther King, Jr. Justice Award by the Dallas Bar Association, and the 2005 Outstanding Service Award by the William Wayne Justice Center for Public Interest Law, Univ. of Texas School of Law.

George Lipsitz (glipsitz@blackstudies.ucsb.edu) is Professor of Black Studies and Sociology at the Univ. of California, Santa Barbara. He studies social movements, urban culture, and inequality. His books include *The Possessive Investment in Whiteness: How White People Profit from Identity Politics* (Temple Univ. Press, 2006); *A Life in the Struggle: Ivory Perry and the Culture of Opposition* (Temple Univ. Press, 1988); *Dangerous Crossroads: Popular Music, Postmodernism, and the Poetics of Place* (Verso, 1994); and *Time Passages: Collective Memory and American Popular Culture* (Univ. of Minnesota Press, 1990). He has long been active in struggles for fair housing and educational equity.

Kris Marsh (kmarsh@socy.umd.edu) is Assistant Professor of Sociology at the Univ. of Maryland. Her research interests are in the areas of family sociology, urban demography, race and ethnicity, and spatial analysis. Her most recent publications are "The Love Jones Cohort: A New Face of the Black Middle Class?" in *Black Women, Gender & Families* (co-authored with Lynda Dickson) and "The Emerging Black Middle Class: Single and Living Alone" in *Social Forces* (co-authored with William A. Darity, Jr., Philip N. Cohen, Lynne M. Casper, and Danielle Salters).

Marc Mauer (mauer@sentencingproject.org) is Executive Director of The Sentencing Project, a national nonprofit organization in Washington, DC engaged in research and advocacy on criminal justice policy. He has written extensively and testified before Congress and other legislative bodies. His critically acclaimed book, *Race to Incarcerate* (New Press, 2006) was named a semifinalist for the Robert F. Kennedy Book Award, and he is co-editor of *Invisible Punishment* (New Press, 2002), a collection of essays that examine the social costs of incarceration. He frequently lectures before a broad range of national and international audiences, appears regularly on television and radio networks, and is an adjunct faculty member at George Washington Univ. He is the recipient of the Donald Cressey Award for contributions to criminal justice research and the Alfred Lindesmith Award for drug policy scholarship.

Nancy McArdle (nancymcardle@comcast.net) is a Research Analyst in the Department of Society, Human Development, and Health at the Harvard School of Public Health, where she is co-developer of the DiversityData website, a user-friendly source of information on measures of social well-being across U.S. metropolitan areas. Formerly, as Project Director of the Metro Boston Equity Initiative at the Harvard Civil Rights Project, she performed and managed research on the changing opportunity structure for people of color in the areas of housing, education, and employment. She has served as an expert witness in major school and housing segregation legal cases and is a board member of the Fair Housing Center of Greater Boston. She is a contributing author to *Twenty-First Century Color Lines: Multiracial Change in Contemporary America* (Temple Univ. Press, 2008).

Demetria L. McCain (dmccain@inclusivecommunities.net) serves as the Director of Advocacy & Education for the Inclusive Communities Project (ICP), a Dallas-based affordable fair housing organization, and is responsible for the training of ICP's staff on various fair housing, civil rights, and general housing laws and issues, while overseeing ICP's fair housing counseling services. She monitors the operations of "The Walker Projects," ICP-supported subsidized housing located in three Dallas suburbs, and serves as liaison to the Dallas Housing Authority regarding housing mobility matters on behalf of ICP's Mobility Assistance Program. Additionally, she coordinates research and public education campaigns while responding to local, regional, and state housing and land use decisions and policies that have the potential to serve as opportunities for or impediments to fair housing. On a national level, she pushes for fair housing and civil rights interests in the federal housing context, including the current reauthorization of the HOPE VI program. She also serves on the board of the Poverty & Race Research Action Council.

Samuel L. Myers, Jr. (myers006@umn.edu) is the Roy Wilkins Professor of Human Relations and Social Justice at the Hubert H. Humphrey Institute of Public Affairs, Univ. of Minnesota. He is a member and past chair of the National Science Foundation's Committee on Equal Opportunities in Science and Engineering, an elected Fellow of the National Academy of Public Administration, and past president of the National Economic Association and of the Association for Public Policy Analysis and Management. His most recent books are *Racial and Ethnic Economic Inequality: An International Perspective* (Peter Lang Publishing, Inc., 2006) with Bruce P. Corrie; *Faculty of Color in Academe* (Pearson Education, 2000) with Caroline Turner; and *Persistent Disparity* (Edward Elgar, 1998) with William A. Darity, Jr.

Melvin L. Oliver (moliver@ltsc.ucsb.edu) is the SAGE Sara Miller McCune Dean of the Division of Social Sciences, and Professor of Sociology at the Univ. of California, Santa Barbara. Previously, he was Vice President of the Asset Building and Community Development Program at the Ford Foundation. He is co-author of *Black Wealth/White Wealth: A New Perspective on Racial Inequality* (Routledge, 2006), which received both the C. Wright Mills Award from the Society for the Study of Social Problems and the Distinguished Scholarly Publication Award from the American Sociological Association. He is also the coauthor of *Prismatic Metropolis: Inequality in Los Angeles* (Russell Sage, 2000) and numerous articles on urban and racial inequality.

Theresa L. Osypuk (t.osypuk@neu.edu) is Assistant Professor at Northeastern Univ. in the Bouvé College of Health Sciences. She is a social epidemiologist, researching how place and residential segregation matter for racial/ethnic and socioeconomic health disparities, particularly in relation to housing markets and neighborhoods. She also studies how social policies may mitigate racial/ethnic health inequality, and she is a co-developer of the DiversityData website, which presents metropolitan patterns of racial/ethnic inequality across a range of social domains. Her research has been published recently in *American Journal of Epidemiology, Health Affairs,* and *Urban Affairs Review.*

John P. Relman (jrelman@relmanlaw.com) is the founder and director of the Relman & Dane lawfirm. Since 1986, he has represented scores of plaintiffs and public interest organizations in individual and class action discrimination cases in federal court. From 1989 to 1999, he served as Project Director of the Fair Housing Project at the Washington Lawyers' Committee for Civil Rights and Urban Affairs. His better-known cases include *Timus v. William J. Davis, Inc.* ($2.4 million jury verdict for housing discrimination against families with children); *Dyson v. Denny's Restaurants* ($17.7 million class settlement for racial discrimination against customers); *Pugh v. Avis Rent-A-Car* ($5.4 million class settlement for racial discrimination in the rental of cars); *Kennedy v. City of Zanesville* ($10.8 million jury verdict for discrimination in provision of public water to an African-American community); and *Gilliam v. Adam's Mark Hotels* ($2.1 million class settlement for racial discrimination against guests). He has written and lectured extensively in the areas of fair housing and fair lending law and practice, and has provided numerous training classes and seminars for plaintiffs' lawyers, fair housing organizations, the real estate industry, and lending institutions. He is the author of *Housing Discrimination Practice Manual* (West Group, 2008). He teaches public interest law at Georgetown Univ. Law Center, where he serves as Adjunct Professor.

Florence Wagman Roisman (froisman@iupui.edu) is the William F. Harvey Professor of Law at the Indiana University School of Law-Indianapolis. Her career—litigation and other advocacy, teaching, and scholarship—has focused on low-income housing, homelessness, and racial discrimination and segregation. She was the first recipient (1989) of the Kutak-Dodds Memorial Prize, the first recipient (2004) of the national Equal Justice Works Outstanding Faculty/Staff Award, and the first recipient (1994) of the Georgetown Univ. Law Center Equal Justice Foundation Award for Outstanding Faculty Commitment to Public Interest Law. She received the D.C. Bar's Thurgood Marshall Award in 2000 and was honored by the Alliance for Justice in 1991. She was a co-founder and until 2008 served on the board of the Poverty & Race Research Action Council, and currently serves on the boards of the national American Civil Liberties Union, the ACLU of Indiana, and the Inclusive Communities Project of Dallas. She served two three-year terms (until 2008) on the board of the Society of American Law Teachers.

James E. Rosenbaum (j-rosenbaum@northwestern.edu) is Professor of Sociology, Education, and Social Policy at Northwestern Univ. His books include *Crossing the Class and Color Lines,* (Univ. of Chicago Press, 2000), and *Beyond College for All* (Russell Sage Foundation., 2001), which was awarded the Waller Prize in Sociology. His book *After Admission: From College Access* *to College Success* (Russell Sage Foundation) was published in 2006. He has studied the Gautreaux housing mobility program and examined the changes in low-income black youth whose families were assigned under the program to middle-class suburbs or to inner-city areas. His research has been published in sociology and policy journals, and has been reported in the *New York Times*, the *Washington Post*, the *Wall Street Journal*, *Fortune Magazine*, *Chronicle of Higher Education*, and *Sixty Minutes*.

Glenn Schlactus (gschlactus@relmanlaw.com) is Counsel at the civil rights lawfirm Relman & Dane, PLLC. He represents individuals and organizational clients as plaintiffs in housing, fair lending, public accommodations, and other civil rights cases. As assistant to the president at Public Citizen, he lobbied Congress and federal agencies on issues of automobile safety and tort law. A 1998 graduate of Georgetown Univ. Law Center, he was a law clerk to the Hon. Patricia M. Wald of the United States Court of Appeals for the District of Columbia Circuit.

Michael P. Seng (7seng@jmls.edu) is a Professor of Law at The John Marshall Law School. He teaches, among other courses, Constitutional Law, Federal Jurisdiction, Fair Housing Law, and Predatory Home Lending Law. He is the Co-Executive Director of The John Marshall Law School Fair Housing Legal Support Center and Executive Director of The John Marshall Law School Fair Housing Legal Clinic. He has authored many articles on civil rights and fair housing law. He is chairman of the Illinois Residential Mortgage Board, an appointed body to advise the State of Illinois Office of Banks and Real Estate. In 2003, he was awarded a Pioneer of Fair Housing Award by the U.S. Department of Housing and Urban Development, Office of Fair Housing and Equal Opportunity. In 2006, he was awarded the Elmer Gertz Award for Civil Rights by the Illinois State Bar Association and the Blind Services Association of Illinois.

Janet L. Smith (janets@uic.edu) is Associate Professor of Urban Planning and Co-Director of the Nathalie P. Voorhees Center for Neighborhood and Community Improvement, Univ. of Illinois at Chicago. Her teaching, research, and community service focuses on equity issues in local housing planning and policy implementation. Recent research includes the transformation of public housing in Chicago and the U.S.; housing and health outcomes; expanding housing opportunities for people with disabilities; housing voucher usage in Illinois; immigrant housing issues in suburban Cook County; and implementing community-driven strategies to preserve affordable housing. She is co-editor of, and contributor to, *Where Are Poor People to Live? Transforming Public Housing Communities* (M.E. Sharpe, 2006) with Larry Bennett and Patricia Wright, She is also an advisor to Movesmart. org, a new organization that will use Internet technology to encourage racial and economic integration by empowering housing-seekers, governmental agencies, and community-based organizations with contextualized, comprehensive, relevant, and accessible information about communities and their opportunities.

Shanna L. Smith (Shanna1016@aol.com) is the President/CEO of the National Fair Housing Alliance in Washington, DC, which works to eliminate all forms of housing discrimination and ensure equal housing opportunity for all people through leadership, education, outreach, membership services, public policy initiatives, advocacy, and enforcement. She supervises NFHA's national enforcement programs and multimedia campaigns. She has pioneered testing and investigations of interstate real estate sales practices, mortgage-lending, private mortgage insurance, appraisal practices, homeowners' insurance, and sexual harassment in housing, She has testified frequently before committees of the U.S. Senate and House on issues involving the use of credit and credit scores in housing, mortgage-lending practices, private mortgage insurance, and homeowners' insurance practices, as well as before oversight committees evaluating the work of HUD's Office of Fair Housing and the Department of Justice's fair housing program. She serves on the board of directors of the Leadership Conference on Civil Rights and co-chairs its Fair Housing Task Force. She is also a board member of the Center for Responsible Lending and was appointed to the Federal Reserve Board's Consumer Advisory Council in January 2008.

Gregory D. Squires (squires@gwu.edu) is a Professor of Sociology, and Public Policy and Public Administration at George Washington Univ. He is on the board of the Woodstock Institute, the Advisory Board of the John Marshall Law School Fair Housing Legal Support Center, and the Social Science Advisory Board of the Poverty & Race Research Action Council. He has served as a consultant for civil rights organizations around the country and as a member of the Federal Reserve Board's Consumer Advisory Council. He has written for several academic journals and general interest publications, including *Housing Policy Debate, Urban Studies, Social Science Quarterly, Urban Affairs Review, Journal of Urban Affairs, New York Times*, and *Washington Post*. His recent books include *Privileged Places: Race, Residence and the Structure of Opportunity* (Lynne Rienner, 2006) with Charis E. Kubrin, and *There is No Such Thing as a Natural Disaster: Race, Class, and Hurricane Katrina* (Routledge, 2006) with Chester Hartman.

Stephen Steinberg (ssteinberg1@gc.cuny.edu) is Professor of Sociology in the Department of Urban Studies at Queens College and the PhD Program in Sociology at the Graduate Center of the City Univ. of New York. His most recent book is *Race Relations: A Critique* (Stanford University Press, 2007). Other books include *The Ethnic Myth: Race, Ethnicity, and Class in America* (3rd ed., Beacon Press, 2001) and *Turning Back: The Retreat from Racial Justice in American Thought and Policy* (2nd ed., Beacon Press, 2001), which received the Oliver Cromwell Cox Award for Distinguished Anti-Racist Scholarship. In addition to his academic publications, he has published articles in *The Nation, New Politics, Journal of Blacks in Higher Education, Reconstruction,* and *The UNESCO Courier.*

Roger Wilkins (rwilkins@gmu.edu) is Clarence J. Robinson Professor Emeritus, George Mason Univ. He served as an Assistant Attorney General in the Johnson Administration and as a member of the team that was cited in the *Washington Post's* award of the Pulitzer Gold Medal for Public Service in 1972 for the paper's Watergate coverage. The team included Bob Woodward and Carl Bernstein for news reporting, Herbert Block (Herblock) for editorial cartoons, and himself for editorials. He serves on many boards, including the Education Trust. Among his several books is *Quiet Riots* (Pantheon, 1988), co-edited with Fred Harris.

Index

A

Acevedo-Garcia, Dolores, 6, 131
Achievement gap, *see* Education
Advanced Placement programs, 102, 106–110
Advancement Via Individual Determination
  (AVID), 113, 114
Aetna, 21n10
Affirmative action, 67–84
Affirmative marketing, 47–49, 51
Affluent Society, The (Galbraith), 99
Agriculture, U.S. Department of, 155
Alabama, 16, 180; *see also* Montgomery
Albuquerque, New Mexico, 34
Alito, Samuel, 69
Allah, Mohandas Salaam, 204
Allstate, 21n9, 21n10
Arlington Heights, Illinois, 57
As Long As They Don't Move Next Door
  (Meyer), 7
Asia, immigration from, 25–26, 29
Asians, 3, 15, 23
  and Gifted and Talented programs, 107,
    108
  and neighborhood diversity, 31, 32, 33, 34
  and school attendance, 164
Atlanta, Georgia, 2, 123
  and fair housing centers, 20n5
  and felony disenfranchisement, 181
  as immigrant destination, 30
  and media campaign, 19
  and neighborhood choice, 30
  and population concentration, 237
  and public housing, 222

B

Bacon, Nathaniel, 249

Baker v. Carr, 55
Baldwin, James, 214
Baltimore Housing Authority, 196
Baltimore Regional Housing Coalition
  (BRHC), 196
Baltimore, Maryland, 57, 164, 195
Bell, Derrick, 216
Bergen-Passaic, New Jersey, 123
Berkeley, William, 249, 250, 251
Berringer, Paul B., 252
Bethel, Evelyn, 204
Bishop, Mary, 207
Black Jack, Missouri, 57
Bolden, Frank, 206
Bond, Horace Mann, 103
Boston Federal Reserve, 120
Boston Housing Authority, 41, 42
Boston Redevelopment Authority, 42
Boston, Massachusetts, 15, 16, 41–42, 123
  and neighborhood choice, 30
  and Operation Ceasefire, 174–175
  and population concentration, 237
  and public housing, 43
Boulder, Colorado, 34
Breyer, Stephen, 76
Briggs, Xavier de Souza, 30, 221, 222, 239
Brooke, Edward, 10, 40
Brooklyn, New York, 17–18, 179
Brown, Henry Billings, 251
Buffalo, New York, 20n5
Burnham, James, 99, 100
Bush, George H.W., 69, 95
Bush, George W., 11, 69

C

Cairo, Illinois, 56

California, 20n5, 28, 29, 176; *see also* Fresno; Los Angeles; Oakland; Orange County; Riverside; Sacramento; San Diego; San Francisco; San Jose; Santa Barbara
Camden, New Jersey, 163
Canada, 170
Canada, Geoff, 259, 260
Cantal-Dupart, Michel, 208, 209–210
Carter, Robert "King", 249–250
Carter, William, 79
Caruso, F. Willis, 6, 53
Cashin, Sheryll, 2, 59
Castells, Manuel, 219
Center for Educational Performance and Information, 107
Charlotte, North Carolina, 201
Cherokee Nation, 216
Chicago Housing Authority, 57
Chicago, Illinois, 13, 33, 123, 127
    employment rates in, 172
    fair housing efforts of, 20n5, 61
    and housing programs, 67, 185–196, 213–215
    and immigrant concentration, 29, 30
    and racial concentrations, 3, 69, 171
Chicago, University of, 214
Cincinnati, Ohio, 21n10, 102, 123
Cincinnatus Association (CA), 18, 19
Cisneros, Henry, 213, 215
Citizens' Commission on Civil Rights, 20n6
Civil Rights Act of 1866, 10, 11, 70–71
Civil Rights Act of 1964, 57, 165
Civil Rights Act of 1968, 9, 53, 73
Civil Rights Movement, 1, 2, 3, 162
    and housing opportunities, 260
    and incarceration rates, 171
    progress of, 169
Clark, Ramsey, 262
Claytor, Walter, 204
Clearing the Way (Goetz), 217
Cleveland, Ohio, 13, 20n3, 123
Clinton, William J., 70, 81, 95
Cloud, Cathy, 5, 9
Columbus, Ohio, 123
Commission on Civil Rights, U.S., 156
Communities, 19, 185–186
    and social capital, 5, 6, 141, 178, 179
    accumulation of, 120
    and displacement, 200–201, 203, 205
    impact of mass incarceration, 177–180
Community Development Corporations, 220

Community Research Group, 199
Comptroller of the Currency, Office of, 162
Congress, U.S., 53, 54
    1949 Housing Act, 96
    affirmative duty of, 62, 63, 78
    Civil Rights Act of 1968, 9
    Fair Housing Act, 39, 40
    and Native Americans, 216
    and promotion of integration, 44
    and sentencing laws, 172
    and subprime lending crisis, 260
Constitution, U.S., 67–84
    Fifteenth Amendment, 71
    Fifth Amendment, 68, 69, 79
    Fourteenth Amendment, 62, 71, 161, 163, 251
        Equal Protection Clause, 41, 43, 46, 49, 51n9, 68, 69, 79
    Thirteenth Amendment, 6, 62, 68, 70–73, 77–80n5
Crack cocaine, *see* Criminal justice system and drug markets
Crime, *see* Criminal justice system
Criminal justice system, 4, 259
    crime rates, 134, 135, 136, 206
    and drug markets, 172–173, 175, 190
    felony disenfranchisement, 180–181
    and incarceration rates, 4, 128, 169–176
    litigation against, 56
    minority leadership in, 174
    prisons, and Census enumeration, 181
    and race-identified gangs, 175–176
    War on Drugs, 176–177, 180, 206–207
Critical Race Theory, 238
Crutchfield, Robert, 178
Curry, Constance, 101

D
D'Souza, Dinesh, 217
Dallas Housing Authority, 91
Dallas, Texas, 6, 70, 89–94, 123
Darity, William A. Jr., 6, 99, 119
Davis, Thulani, 101, 102
Dayton, Ohio, 20n3
Deluca, Stefanie, 6
Denton, Nancy A., 6, 23
Detroit, Michigan, 123, 127
    and employment rates, 172
    and neighborhood choice, 30
    population concentration in, 3, 171, 237
    and racial steering, 18
Diary of Anne Frank (Frank), 100

Diette, Timothy, 109
Dirksen, Everett, 10
Disabilities, 15, 142
Displacement, *see* Housing, forced
   displacement
Dissimilarity Index, 30–31, 35, 36n2, 120–125,
   128n1
District of Columbia, *see* Washington, DC
Douglas, William, 53
DuBois, W.E.B., 101, 102
Durham, North Carolina, 110, 111, 114

E

Earnings, *see* Employment, earnings
East Orange, New Jersey, 206
Edsall, Mary, 3
Edsall, Thomas, 3
Education, 3, 13; *see also* Schools; Advanced
   Placement programs
   and achievement gap, 103, 110–112, 114
   and community diversity, 19, 20
   and race-conscious action, 67
   segregated, 99–114
Education, U.S. Department of, 106, 112
El Paso, Texas, 34
Elderly, 26, 64n30, 35
   and subprime mortgage crisis, 160
   and tax credit developments, 94
Elizabeth, New Jersey, 206
Employment, access to, 29–31, 176, 186–187,
   189, 193
   and concentrated disadvantage, 141
   decline in, 172
   and earnings inequality, 119–128
   and spatial mismatch thesis, 126–127
Environmental hazards, 4, 134, 165
Equal Protection Clause, *see* Constitution,
   U.S., Fourteenth Amendment
Erie Insurance Company, 21n9
Eugene, Oregon, 34
Europe, and rates of incarceration, 170

F

Failures of Integration, The (Cashin), 2
Fair Housing Act of 1968, 1, 9, 161, 229,
   231; *see also* Housing and Urban
   Development, U.S. Department of
   (HUD); New York City Housing
   Authority
   and affirmative duty, 62–63, 67–68, 73,
   75–77, 86–87, 94
   dual purpose of, 19

enforcement of, 10, 20n6
   and individual actions, 59–61
   limitations of, 235
   and private litigation, 53–66
   prointegration programs under, 39–51
   and punitive damages, 11
   and structural lawsuits, 55–58
Fair Housing Amendments Act of 1988
   (FHAA), 11
Fair Housing Legal Support Center, John
   Marshall Law School, 6
Feagin, Joe, 2
Federal Bureau of Investigation (FBI), 206
Federal Housing Administration (FHA), and
   exclusionary policies, 154–155, 163
Federal Reserve Board, 162
Ferguson, Ronald, 102
Financial services industry, 10
   and lending disparities, 15, 20n3, 120–127
   mortgage lenders, 12, 156
   and predatory lending, 4, 13, 159–161, 163,
   164
   and redlining, 11, 57, 160, 201–202
Florida, 16, 28; *see also* Miami; Tallahassee
Food, 134, 147–148, 181
Foreclosures, *see* Financial services industry,
   predatory lending
Forsyth County, North Carolina, 114
Fort Worth, Texas, 123
Fresno, California, 15
Friedman, Paul, 155
Fullilove, Mindy Thompson, 6, 155, 199
Fullilove, Robert E., 6, 199
Fund for the Future of Shaker Heights, 49

G

Galbraith, John Kenneth, 99–100, 109, 110,
   115n1
Gale, Dennis, 202, 203
Galster, George, 232, 234
Garbis, Martin, 77
Gary, Indiana, 20n5
Gautreaux program, 4, 5, 6, 185–196, 220
   demand for, 235, 236
Gender, 14, 21n15, 178
Gentrification, *see* Housing, gentrification
Georgia, 16
Gifted and Talented (G&T), programs,
   107–110, 111, 112–114
Giuliani, Rudolph, 175
Goel, Shalini, 6, 39
Goetz, Edward, 217, 219, 220

Great Depression, 170
Greenbaum, Susan, 221, 223
Greensboro, North Carolina, 123
Gulfport, Mississippi, 15, 16

H
Harlem, New York, 200
Hartman, Chester, 1, 220
Health and Retirement Study (HRS), 158, 159
Health care, 3, 4, 133, 134, 142, 162
  universal, 235, 241
Health, 196; *see also* Environmental hazards
  child, 131–148
  and effects of displacement, 200–201
  and effects of incarceration, 179
  mental, and treatment programs, 176
Heifetz, Alan, 59, 60
Heinz, Thomas, 59, 60
Hernandez, Jesus, 160
Hernández-Cordero, Lourdes, 6, 199
Hispanics, 15; *see also* Latinos
  and homeownership rates, 157–159
  and neighborhood diversity, 31, 32, 33, 34
  and subprime mortgage crisis, 160–161
Hispanics/Latinos, and residential segregation,
  3, 23, 134, 142, 143
Home Mortgage Disclosure Act (HMDA),
  122, 162
Home Owners' Loan Corporation (HOLC),
  201–202
Homeowners' insurance, *see* Insurance
  industry
Homeownership, 134
  and lending disparities, 119
  rate of, 153–165, 172
Homestead Act (1862), 154, 163
HOPE VI, 4, 5, 193, 204–206
  and demolitions, 185
  and forced displacement, 203, 206, 213–217,
  220, 222
  and transportation, 208–209
Housing, 4–5, 29
  forced displacement, 200–210, 214–215, 220
  gentrification, 5, 12, 205–206, 223, 259
  as human right, 240–241
  low-income, 39, 41, 43, 85, 87, 203
    new construction, 44, 86, 215
  mixed-income, 42
  mobility, 85–96, 186–196
  multifamily, 57–58, 93–94
  neighborhood choice, 30–31, 32, 33
  public, 42–43, 87, 221, 222

and deconcentrating poverty, 239
and litigation, 54, 56
and race-conscious remedy, 67
eligibility for, 41
high-rise, 203, 213, 214, 219
imbalance in, 46
low-rise, 214, 221
quotas, 50, 235
siting of, 93, 94
and racial tipping point, 40, 44–45
rental, 10, 15–16, 40, 89, 191, 229
Section 8, 89, 186–190, 221
and urban renewal programs, 5, 6, 155, 156,
  199, 200–210
Housing Act of 1934, 154
Housing Act of 1949, 96, 199, 207
Housing and Urban Development Act of 1968,
  156
Housing and Urban Development, U.S.
  Department of (HUD), 5, 14, 164
  and administration law judge (ALJ) process,
  11
  affirmative duty of, 42, 43, 76–77
  and Affirmative Fair Housing Marketing,
  47–47
  complaints to, 61
  creation of, 10
  and effect of programs, 44
  enforcement mechanisms of, 53, 54, 55
  and fair housing organizations, 15
  and Fair Market Rents, 91
  and homeowners' insurance, 13
  and Moving to Opportunity, 205, 230
  and prompt judicial action, 59
  redlining by, 156
  strengthening of, 62–63
  and Welfare to Work Voucher Program, 239
Housing Discrimination Study (HDS 2000),
  14, 15, 16, 17, 21n13
Houston, Texas, 15, 16, 123

I
Illinois, 28, 29; *see also* Arlington Heights;
  Cairo; Chicago, Chicago Housing
  Authority; Chicago, University of; Park
  Forest; Springfield
Imbroscio, David, 220
Immigrants, 30, 233, 260
  gateways for, 28–29, 30
  and health issues, 133, 140
  and population projections, 36n1
  segregation of, 23, 24–25

Inclusive Communities Project (ICP), 6, 89–94
Index of Dissimiliarity, *see* Dissimilarity Index
Indian Removal Act (1830), 216
Indianapolis, Indiana, 123
Insurance industry, 162
  Homeowners' insurance, 10, 12, 20n3,
    21n9-10, 13
  redlining by, 11, 13, 57, 202
Irvington, New Jersey, 206

J
Jackson, Andrew, 216
Jackson, Helen, 261
Jackson, Madison, 261
Jefferson, Thomas, 250, 251
Jim Crow system, 56, 88, 103, 170
  and shunning, 252, 253, 259, 261
Jobs, *see* Employment
Johnson, Anthony, 249
Johnson, Lyndon, 9, 248, 261, 262
Jolla, Alicia, 6, 99
Journal of Negro Education, The, 101
Julian, Elizabeth K., 6, 85
Justice, U.S. Department of, 10, 11, 53, 54, 57,
    64n23

K
Kansas City Call, 254
Katrina, 222
Katz, Bruce, 222
Katzenbach, Nicholas, 81n11
Kennedy, Edward, 54, 55
Kerner Commission (National Advisory
    Commission on Civil Disorders), 55,
    64n21
King, Martin Luther Jr., 131–132, 135, 165, 261
  assassination of, 10, 229, 263
  Open Housing marches, 161
  and Poor People's Campaign, 248, 262

L
Las Vegas, Nevada, 123
Latin America, immigration from, 25–26, 29
Latinos, 13, 107, 112, 169; *see also* Hispanics
  and health issues, 139, 140
  and racial steering, 12, 21
  and rates of incarceration, 170
  and school attendance, 164
Lauber, Daniel, 231
Lee, Harper, 100
Lending disparities, *see* Financial services
  industry, lending disparities

Liberty Mutual, 13, 21n10
Lipsitz, George, 6, 153
Loans, *see* Financial services industry, lending
Los Angeles, California, 29, 30, 237
Louisville, Kentucky, 69
Low Income Housing Tax Credit (LIHTC), 92,
    93, 97n8
Lucas Metropolitan Housing Authority, 42
Lucas, Mrs. Wendell, 105
Lukehart, John, 233

M
Malcolm X, 199, 214
Maly, Michael, 233, 234
Man and Superman (Shaw), 252
Managerial Revolution, The (Burnham), 99,
    100
Maplewood, New Jersey, 102
Marcantonio, Vito, 97n9
Marsh, Kris, 6, 119
Marshall, John, 78
Marx, Karl, 218
Massey, Douglas, 171
Massoglia, Michael, 179
Mauer, Marc, 6, 169
Mazique, Edward, 105
McArdle, Nancy, 6, 131
McCain, Demetria L., 6, 85
McFarland, Dennis, 101
Meyer, Stephen Grant, 7
Miami, Florida, 29, 123
Michigan, 107; *see also* Detroit, Michigan
Michigan, University of, 69, 158
Milwaukee, Wisconsin, 3, 20n5, 21n10, 121,
    122, 123
Minneapolis-St. Paul, Minnesota, 123, 127
Mondale, Walter, 1, 7, 10, 39, 74
Montgomery, Alabama, 15
Mortgage lenders, *see* Financial services
Mortgage loans, *see* Financial services
  industry, mortgage lenders; lending
  disparities
Moving to Opportunity (MTO), 4, 5, 6, 97n5,
    185–196, 230, 235
  demand for, 236
  and forced displacement, 220
  and housing mobility, 87
  and Native Americans, 216
Myers, Samuel L. Jr., 119

N
Nashville, Tennessee, 123

Nassau-Suffolk, New York, 123
National Advisory Commission on Civil
    Disorders, 39
National Association for the Advancement of
    Colored People (NAACP), 252
National Center on Minority Health and
    Health Disparities, 147
National Fair Housing Alliance (NFHA), 19
    and enforcement testing, 17–18, 21n10
    and paired testing, 14, 15–16
    and redlining, 13
National Institute of Aging, 158
National Institute of Mental Health, 224n5
National Institutes of Health, 147
National Science Foundation, 224n5
Nationwide, 21n10
Native Americans, 15, 216, 217, 222
Neighborhoods, see Communities
New Jersey, 20n5, 28, 107; see also Bergen-
    Passaic; Camden; East Orange;
    Elizabeth; Irvington; Maplewood;
    Newark; Princeton
New Orleans, Louisiana, 15, 21n10, 123, 185
New York City Housing Authority, 44, 76
    and affirmative duty, 44–45, 76
New York Times, 3
New York, New York, 20n5, 28, 123
    and displacement, 199–200
    and employment rates, 172
    and immigrant concentration, 29
    and style of policing, 175
New Industrial State, The (Galbraith), 99
Newark, New Jersey, 123, 127, 202, 203,
    205–206
Nixon, Richard M., 213
Norfolk, Virginia, 123
North Carolina, 106, 107, 108, 109, 110; see
    also Charlotte; Durham; Forsyth
    County; Greensboro; Oakwood;
    Raleigh-Durham
Northwestern University, 87
Not In My Back Yard (NIMBY), 93, 221
Notes on the State of Virginia (Jefferson), 250,
    251
Nyden, Philip, 233

O
O'Bryant, Constance, 60
O'Connor, Sandra Day, 69
Oakland, California, 123
Oakwood, North Carolina, 113
Obama, Barack, 1

Ochs, Phil, 1, 7
Ohio, 20n5; see also Cincinnati; Cincinnatus
    Association; Cleveland; Columbus;
    Dayton; Lucas Metropolitan Housing
    Authority; Shaker Heights; Toledo;
    Toledo Fair Housing Center
Oliver, Melvin L., 6, 153
Olympia, Washington, 34
Orange County, California, 123
Osypuk, Theresa L., 6, 131

P
Paired testing, see Housing; Real estate
    industry; Financial services; National
    Fair Housing Alliance (NFHA)
Park Forest, Illinois, 47–48
Pease, Robert, 202
Pennsylvania, 20n5; see also Philadelphia;
    Pittsburgh; Pittsburgh, University of;
    Scranton
Peterson, Carlos, 206
Philadelphia, Pennsylvania, 123, 171
Phoenix, Arizona, 30, 123
Pittsburgh, Pennsylvania, 201, 202, 205, 206,
    207
Pittsburgh, University of, Graduate School
    of Public Health Center for Minority
    Health, 208
Plessy, Homer, 251
Polikoff, Alexander, 224n4
Portland, Oregon, 123
Posner, Richard, 58
Poverty, 140–146, 187–188, 191, 230
    concentration of, 3–4, 5, 7, 136, 137
    and myth, 213–223
    as rationale, 217–219
powell, john anthony, 30, 164
Prince Edward (McFarland), 101
Princeton, New Jersey, 163
Project on Human Development in Chicago
    Neighborhoods, 141
Prudential, 21n10
Pruitt-Igoe housing project, 203
Public housing, see Housing, public

R
Race, and "tipping point," 18–19, 231–232, 234
    and population concentrations, 120, 127,
    164, 171
    and quotas, 40, 42, 48–50
    and race-conscious action, 41, 42–49 67–80
Race, Racism, and American Law (Bell), 216

Racial steering, *see* Real estate industry;
    Financial services industry
Raleigh-Durham, North Carolina, 123
Reagan, Ronald, 69, 155
Real estate industry, 9, 10, 11, 13–14, 20, 21n15
    and blockbusting, 154, 156
    and development, 199–210
    and racial steering, 12, 14–15, 17–18, 48, 56,
        154, 156
    and redlining, 201–202
    and restrictive covenants, 120, 154, 160, 201
Redlining, *see* Financial services; Real estate
        industry; Insurance industry
Reich, Robert, 99
Relman, John P., 6, 39
Resnick, Lauren, 108, 112, 114
Restrictive covenants, *see* Real estate industry
Richmond, Virginia, 20n5, 21n10
Right to the city movement, 241–242
Riverside, California, 123
Roanoke, Virginia, 203–204
Roisman, Florence Wagman, 6, 67
Roithmayr, Daria, 154
Roosevelt, Theodore, 252
Rosenbaum, James, 6

S
Sacramento, California, 123, 160
Saint Louis, Missouri, 123
Salt Lake City, Utah, 34, 121, 122, 123
San Antonio, Texas, 15, 16, 123
San Diego, California, 113
San Francisco, California, 201
San Jose, California, 123
Santa Barbara, California, 34
Satcher, David, 132
Schlactus, Glenn, 6, 39
Schools, 4, 24, 99–114, 132, 135; *see also*
        Education
    access to, 30, 31, 185, 186, 187, 191–194
    information about, 91, 92
    quality of, 29, 127, 142, 143, 146
    and resegregation, 231
Schwemm, Robert, 53, 74
Scranton, Pennsylvania, 34
Seattle, Washington, 69, 123, 178
Seng, Michael P., 6, 53
Shaker Heights, Ohio, 48–50, 51, 102
Shaw, George Bernard, 252
Sikes, Melvin, 2
Slavery, 63, 72–73
    and black aspirations, 249–250

legacy of, 251, 260
    and shunning, 249, 250, 251
Smith, Janet L., 229
Smith, Neil, 222
Smith, Shanna L., 5, 9
Snead, David, 110–112
Social capital, *see* Communities
South Carolina, 180
Spatial mismatch thesis, 126
Springfield, Illinois, 252, 259
Squires, Gregory D., 1
St. Anselm's School, 105
Stable Integrated Neighborhoods (Cincinnatus
        Association), 18
State Farm Insurance Company, 19, 21n10
Steinberg, Stephen, 7
Stephen H. Wilder Foundation, 18
Subprime mortgage crisis, *see* Financial
        services industry, predatory lending
Suburbia, 29, 94
    and Drug War, 177, 230
    exclusionary practices in, 93, 217
    and Section 8 vouchers, 186–190
Sunflower County, Mississippi, 101
Supreme Court, Ohio, 58
Supreme Court, U.S., 19
    and Fair Housing Act, 10, 39
    and prison system, 176
    and race-conscious action, 67, 68–69
    and racial steering, 20n4
    and school integration programs, 146
    and segregation, 251
    and structural lawsuits, 56, 58

T
Tallahassee, Florida, 178–179
Taxes, 156, 163
Tegeler, Philip, 70
Tennessee, 16; *see also* Nashville
Texas, 16, 17, 28; *see also* Dallas; Dallas
        Housing Authority; El Paso; Fort
        Worth; Houston; San Antonio
Tienda, Marta, 224n6
Tillman, Benjamin, 252
To Kill a Mockingbird (Lee), 100, 101
Toledo Fair Housing Center, 20n9–20n10
Toledo, Ohio, 13, 20n3, 21n10, 42
Transportation, 4, 92, 126, 142, 208–209
    assistance, 186, 190, 194, 195
Travelers, lawsuit against, 21n10
Truly Disadvantaged, The (Wilson), 218
Tulsa, Oklahoma, 155

U
Udin, Sala, 202–203
United for a Fair Economy, 161

V
Virginia, 249; *see also* Norfolk; Richmond;
 Roanoke
Voting Rights Act of 1965, 165
Voting, 180–181

W
Wacquant, Loic, 170–171
Waldron, Jeremy, 242
Walton, Reggie, 175
Washington Post, 2, 259
Washington, Booker T., 252
Washington, DC, 247–248
 and crime, 175, 178, 180
 and lending disparities, 123, 127
 and middle class flight, 248

 and public education, 103–105
 and racial concentrations, 30, 164
Watts, Monica, 259, 260
Wealth creation, 119, 132, 133, 135, 153–166
Wells Fargo Banking Corp., 57
Western, Bruce, 171, 176
White flight, *see* Race
Wilkins, Earl, 261
Wilkins, Roger, 7, 247
Wilson, William Julius, 172, 218–219, 222,
 224n3
Wilson, Woodrow, 105
Women, 136–137
World War II, 170, 172, 256, 260

Y
Yonkers, New York, 57

Z
Zoning, 72, 92, 93, 154, 185

Rights and Permissions

Chapter 1

Chapter 10

Chapter 15

University Readers™
Reading Materials Evolved.

Introducing the

SOCIAL ISSUES COLLECTION

A Routledge/University Readers Custom Library for Teaching

Customizing course material for innovative and excellent teaching in sociology has never been easier or more effective!

Choose from a collection of more than 300 readings from Routledge, Taylor & Francis, and other publishers to make a custom anthology that suits the needs of your social problems/ social inequality, and social issues courses.

All readings have been aptly chosen by academic editors and our authors and organized by topic and author.

Online tool makes it easy for busy instructors:

1. Simply select your favorite Routledge and Taylor & Francis readings, and add any other required course material, including your own.

2. Choose the order of the readings, pick a binding, and customize a cover.

3. One click will post your materials for students to buy. They can purchase print or digital packs, and we ship direct to their door within two weeks of ordering!

More information at www.socialissuescollection.com

Contact information: Call your Routledge sales rep, or
Becky Smith at University Readers, 800-200-3908 ext. 18, bsmith@universityreaders.com
Steve Rutter at Routledge, 207-434-2102, Steve.Rutter@taylorandfrancis.com.

Routledge
Taylor & Francis Group
an **informa** business